Surveys in Social Research

This book is due for return

SOCIAL RESEARCH TODAY

Series editor
Martin Bulmer

Surveys in Social Research

Fourth edition

D. A. de Vaus

Australian Institute of Family Studies, Melbourne

PRESS

First published in 1985
Fourth edition 1996
Second impression 1996

Published in Australia by:

Allen & Unwin Pty Ltd
9 Aitchison Street, PO Box 8500
St Leonards, NSW 2065, Australia

Published elsewhere (excluding North America
UCL Press Limited
University College London
Gower Street
London WC1E 6BT

The name of University College London (UCL) is a registered
trade mark used by UCL Press with the consent of the owner.

British Library Cataloguing in Publication Data
A catalogue record for this book is available from the British Library.

ISBN: 1-85728-542-5 PB

Printed and bound by Biddles Ltd,
Guildford and Kings Lynn, England.

Contents

Tables and figures

Tables

Figures

Preface

This book is intended as a textbook for university and college students and for people doing their own surveys. For the last 15 years I have been conducting or teaching survey research but have yet to find a suitable textbook. Many research methods books are available but their treatment of survey research is inadequate. In one class of books survey research is treated superficially together with a range of other methods. Because of their breadth these books provide little help on the practicalities and process of survey research and are weak on how to analyse data. Another type of book is the social statistics book which explains the technicalities of statistics used in survey research. For most social science students these books are too specialised and intimidating and divorce statistical analysis from the whole research process. As such, students normally fail to apply what they learn to actual research. A third type of book provides specialised and practical help about many technical aspects of conducting surveys, but little help with analysis, and mainly fails to show the links between theory and research. As such these books do not adequately place surveys in context and while helping people become good survey technicians, they are less successful in teaching the art of survey research.

I have tried to avoid these problems by concentrating on one method and providing a sound working knowledge of how to do good surveys. This has enabled a detailed treatment of both the methods of conducting surveys and the statistical analysis of the results in the one book. This makes this book a different type of textbook on survey research to those currently available.

The book has a number of specific aims. As well as showing how to *do* good surveys, it provides the tools to enable readers to be critical consumers of research. A sound knowledge of the tricks of the trade is the best way of being able to evaluate other peoples' research intelligently. While the book is primarily practical, common criticisms of surveys also are evaluated.

It also demonstrates how the logic of surveys and statistical analysis is simply a more systematic extension of the logic we use in everyday life. In this respect the book aims to demystify research.

It also aims to demystify statistics. Statistics are widely used to analyse survey results but they intimidate many people. The focus of this book is on the logic and purpose of statistical procedures. It concentrates, in some detail, on when to use particular techniques and how to make sense of the answers and only deals with formulae and computation when they help clarify the logic and purpose of the statistics. It is a 'modern' book in that it recognises that most of the computational work is done by computer packages.

The computational content has been minimised also because a computational focus often causes students to lose sight of the point of statistics. They become competent at the arithmetic but lack a broader understanding of what it is all for.

I show throughout that research is a process in which there is an ongoing interplay between theory and data, initial analysis and further analysis. The role of theory is emphasised. Survey research is no simple step by step procedure but a process which requires creativity, imagination, skill, compromises, improvisation and so forth: it is an acquired art and the book provides practical hints to acquire the art.

Textbooks which deal with quantitative research are often derogatorily labelled 'cookbooks'. I have never been clear what this means. If it means that the books portray research as a simple step by step procedure which only requires following set rules without creative thinking, then this book certainly is not a cookbook. If, however, a cookbook is a practical book which helps people do research rather than argue about method, then it is a cookbook and I have no apologies for it.

Acknowledgements

I am grateful to many friends and colleagues who have over the years helped me learn about research or who have helped with this book directly. Gerry Rose introduced me to the logic of research and Gordon Ternowetsky and Bob Powell have provided many handy hints about data analysis. David Hickman has always encouraged me to look at data in new and creative ways and has generously read and commented on parts of this book. Ken Dempsey has helped me to be more aware of the problems of surveys and stimulated me to try to avoid these problems. Ron Wild provided valuable encouragement to write this book and together with Yoshio Sugimoto and Alf Clark made useful comments on various chapters.

I am also grateful to Roselyn Giddings, Bronwyn Bardsley and Elaine Young for typing the manuscript and to Jill Gooch for organising it.

Finally, I want to acknowledge my special debt to my wife June who read every word in various drafts. Her comments and encouragement were invaluable and her willingness to take on extra work herself is deeply appreciated.

Note: Labor has been spelt 'Labour' throughout, as it refers to both the Australian Labor Party and the English Labour Party.

Part I THE SCOPE OF SURVEY RESEARCH

1 The nature of surveys

Surveys are a method of social research which, like any other method, has its advocates and critics. The primary aim of this book is to provide guidance on how to do good surveys rather than to provide a detailed defence of surveys. However, it is important to realise that many criticisms of surveys are based on misunderstandings of what surveys can be.

The outline of how to do good surveys takes into account some of these criticisms and shows that there are ways of dealing with them. The solution to criticisms of a method need not be to abandon the method but first to see if it can be improved. The focus of this book then is to show what can be achieved with surveys and how to do it.

In this chapter I shall clarify what survey research is and then briefly outline some of the common criticisms. In my definition of survey research and the following discussion I rely partly on an excellent book by Catherine Marsh (1982) titled *The Survey Method: the contribution of surveys to sociological explanation*.

What is a survey?

Marsh insists that a survey is not synonymous with a particular technique of collecting information: questionnaires are widely used but other techniques such as structured and in-depth interviews, observation, content analysis and so forth are also appropriate. The distinguishing features of surveys are the form of data collection and the method of analysis.

Form of data collection

Surveys are characterised by a structured or systematic set of data which I will call a variable by case data matrix. All it means is that we collect information about the same variables or characteristics from at least two (normally far more) cases and end up with a data matrix (see Table 1.1).

Table 1.1 A variable by case matrix

Cases

	Person 1	Person 2	Person 3	Person 4	Person 5
Sex	male	male	female	male	female
Age	36 yrs	19 yrs	30 yrs	55 yrs	42 yrs
Political orientation	progressive	moderate	progressive	traditionalist	traditionalist
Class	working	lower middle	upper working	upper middle	middle

Variables

In other words, for each case we obtain its attribute on each variable. Put together we end up with a structured or 'rectangular' set of data. However, the technique by which we generate the data need not be highly structured so long as we obtain each case's attribute on each variable. Because questionnaires are the easiest way of ensuring this structured data matrix they are the most common technique used in survey research. But there is no *necessary* connection.

In the example in Table 1.1 each case was a person but this need not be so. A case (called a unit of analysis) could be a country, a year or virtually anything so long as we collect attributes of that case (see section on units of analysis in Chapter 3). If countries were the cases, a list of countries would be across the top of the table instead of people, and attributes of countries (e.g. population size, area, density, unemployment rate) would be listed down the side. If years were the cases, years (e.g. 1950, 1960, 1970, 1980) would be listed across the top with attributes relevant to years down the side (e.g. inflation rate, divorce rate).

The variable by case matrix is fundamental for survey analysis which is based on comparison of cases. It is this method of analysing data which is the second distinguishing feature of surveys.

Methods of analysis

One function of survey analysis is to describe the characteristics of a set of cases. Thus if we want to describe how a group of people will vote, we need to know how each person in that group intends to vote. A variable by case matrix provides this information.

But survey researchers are also interested in causes of phenomena. The survey analyst tries to locate causes by comparing cases. By looking at how cases vary on some characteristic (e.g. some cases will be progressives and others will be traditionalists), the survey analyst will see if the progressives are systematically different from the traditionalists in some additional way. For example, in Table 1.1 there is variation across cases in how they vote. This is systematically linked to variations in class: the progressives are working class and the traditionalists are middle class. In other words, survey research seeks an understanding of what causes some phenomenon (e.g. vote) by looking at variation in that variable across cases, and looking for other characteristics which are systematically linked with it. As such it aims to draw causal inferences (e.g. class affects vote) by a careful comparison of the various characteristics of cases. It does not end there. The next step is to ask why class affects vote. Survey researchers need to be very careful, however, to avoid mistaken attribution of causal links (simply to demonstrate that two things go together does not prove a causal link).

This style of research and analysis can be contrasted with other methods. For example, the case study method involves data collection about one case. Since there are no other cases for comparison quite different strategies for understanding the behaviour and attitudes of that case have to be employed. The experimental method is similar to the survey method in that data are collected in the variable by case matrix form, but is fundamentally different in that the variation between the attributes of people is created by intervention from an experimenter. Some medical research serves as an example. An experimenter wanting to see if a drug cures a disease would take a group of sufferers and divide them into two similar groups. The drug would be administered to only one group and then the recovery rates of the drug and non-drug groups would be compared. Here the variation between the two groups (i.e. drug/non-drug) has been created by the experimenter. A survey approach would not create the variation but would find 'naturally occurring' variation—that is, find a group of sufferers who did have the drug and compare them with a group of sufferers who did not have the drug. The problem for survey researchers is that they cannot be sure

Figure 1.1   A range of methods of research and techniques of data collection

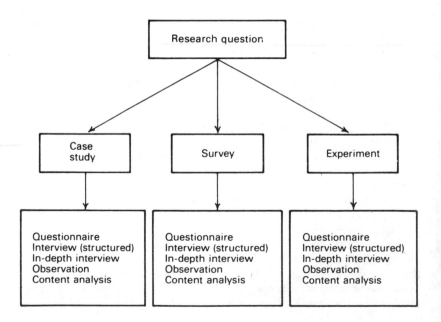

that the two groups are similar in other respects, whereas the experimenter begins with two similar groups and the only difference (in theory) is that only one group receives the treatment. Therefore any difference in recovery rates must be due to the drug. Apart from the potential ethical problems of experimental research, these different approaches to obtaining variation between groups lead to quite different methods of analysis.

In any particular study a range of methods can be used. For example, a study of causes of strikes could involve a survey of attitudes of management and workers, a case study of a particular strike or a particular factory and an experiment where groups of workers work under different conditions to see if this affects their strike frequency.

The techniques by which data are collected using any of these methods can vary considerably. In a survey we could observe each case, interview them, give them a questionnaire and so on.

In summary, survey research is one method of collecting, organising and analysing data. The relevant data can be collected by a variety of techniques and in many studies it may be appropriate to use a variety of research methods (see Figure 1.1).

Criticisms of surveys

The most common criticisms of surveys can be classified into three categories: philosophical, technique based and political. These will simply be mentioned here, but will be taken up again in the final chapter.

Philosophically based criticisms

1   Surveys cannot adequately establish causal connections between variables. For example, even though older people are more conservative than younger people we cannot be certain that growing older causes conservatism. We shall see to what extent survey analysis can overcome this type of objection.
2   Surveys are incapable of getting at the meaningful aspects of social action. Because actions are the actions of conscious people who make choices, have memories, wills, goals and values which motivate behaviour, research must take these into account when developing and evaluating why people behave and think as they do. We shall see that survey research can go a long way towards arriving at such 'meaningful' explanations.
3   Surveys just look at particular aspects of people's beliefs and

actions without looking at the context in which they occur. Taken out of context it is easy to misunderstand the meaning of behaviour. For example, if a person goes to church regularly it may mean they are highly religious, but it *could* mean they are searching for a religious faith, or they cannot avoid going because of social pressure, or they go because of important contacts at church and so on. We shall see that with care survey research need not lead to contextless pieces of information and the consequent misunderstanding of that information. (The problem will always remain of how much and which information is needed about context to avoid misunderstanding.)

4   Surveys seem to assume that human action is determined by external forces and neglect the role of human consciousness, goals, intentions and values as important sources of action. We shall see to what extent this accusation of determinism is a necessary part of surveys or whether it is simply because surveys have been used more by positivist sociologists than by others. (It is worth noting that Marx attempted a survey involving 25 000 posted questionnaires and that Weber also used a survey in his study of factories.)

5   Survey research is equated with a sterile, ritualistic and rigid model of science centred around hypothesis testing and significance tests, which involves no imagination or creative thinking. By showing how to do survey research we shall see just how wrong this view is.

6   Survey research is basically empiricist (C.W. Mills). That is, it merely collects a mass of facts and statistics and provides nothing of theoretical value. We shall see throughout this book that theory and interpretation is fundamental to well-conceived survey research and analysis.

7   Some things are not measurable—especially by surveys. For example, a survey researcher would probably have great difficulty in actually measuring the extent to which Rupert Murdoch has power. No claim is made in this book that surveys are *the* method of social research. Surveys should only be used where they are appropriate and other methods should be used when they are more appropriate.

Technique-based criticisms

8   Surveys are too restricted because they rely on highly structured questionnaires which are necessarily limited. This criticism is based on too narrow an understanding of what techniques can be used in surveys.

9 Surveys are too statistical and reduce interesting questions to totally incomprehensible numbers. While many studies are unnecessarily statistical and sterile, the logic involved in these statistical analyses is important and the same logic is widely used in both statistical analyses and much more qualitative analyses. It is this logic and the role of creative thinking that will be emphasised in this book. Statistics should be the servant rather than the master of the survey analyst.

'Political' criticisms

10 Survey research is intrinsically manipulative and is described by the Frankfurt Marxists as 'scientistic' and 'technistic'. It is seen to be manipulative in two ways. First, the knowledge it provides about the social world gives power to those in control and this can lead to an abuse of power. Second, survey research leads to ideological manipulation. It does not produce knowledge about reality but is an ideological reflection whose acceptance by 'the public' furthers particular interests. (See Marsh 1982 for a full discussion of this criticism of surveys.)

Practice vs ideal types

A basic difficulty when trying to describe how to do research is the gap between textbook accounts of how research *should* be done and how it actually *is* done. A number of valuable books have now been published in which some researchers 'come clean' and provide accounts of how they did their research (Hammond, 1964; Bell and Newby, 1977; Bell and Encel, 1978). Like my own experience, theirs does not conform to the textbook models.

What ought to be done in a book like this? To describe an 'ideal-typical' model of survey research, in which each step of research is outlined, is not to describe what researchers do. As such it can mislead. When you actually do some research you will find that you are not doing what you 'should'. So should the book describe the reality? Perhaps. But which one? The course that a piece of research actually takes will be peculiar to that piece of research: it is affected by the research topic, the technique of data collection, the experience and personality of the researcher, the 'politics of the research', the types of people or situation being studied, funding and so on. I could describe my experiences but like an ideal-typical model they would not reflect other people's.

I have decided to do a bit of both. I will outline the key steps which a survey researcher must take at some stage and describe the reasoning behind the order in which it is normally suggested they be taken. But I will also point out that in practice some steps are omitted, things are done out of order and we move backwards and forwards between steps. Guidelines that are provided are not meant to be prescriptive. The guidelines I describe are like signposts or a map to provide some direction and give us clues as to where to go when we get lost. As you become more familiar with the territory you can manage more easily without the map and learn short cuts. What I describe will not always reflect your research experience but will provide guidance. You should not try to follow each step slavishly. The prime goal of research should be to gain accurate understanding and as a researcher use methods and techniques which enhance understanding. Use the method: do not let it use you.

Further reading

Catherine Marsh's book *The Survey Method* (1982) is the best description of the survey method available. Her outline and evaluation of the most substantial criticisms of surveys is direct, clear and stimulating. Denzin's *The Research Art* (1978) provides a critique of survey research from a symbolic interactionist perspective as does Blumer's paper 'Sociological analysis and the variable' (1956). Chapter 3 of the *Sociological Imagination* (1959) by C.W. Mills on abstracted empiricism is a well known attack on certain forms of survey research.

2 Theory and social research

We can conduct research and show that in the last 100 years social mobility has increased, religion declined, the structure of the family changed and values have been transformed. These are important changes to describe but why have they occurred? We might show which types of people are most mobile or are least religious, and we can document the character of modern families and describe who holds what values. But why are some mobile while others are not, why are some less religious than others? We know that a large number of people live on or below the poverty line. But why?

Social researchers can try to answer two fundamental questions about society. *What* is going on (descriptive research) and *why* is it going on (explanatory research). I believe that the central role of social research is to try to answer both the 'why' and the 'what' questions. The aim is both to describe and understand society.

Sociological theories are attempts to answer these sorts of 'why' questions. They are attempts to explain, and as such the role of sociology is to theorise: it is not just social arithmetic.

The interaction of theory and research

Observations require explanation but equally explanations need to be tested against the facts. It is not enough simply to collect facts. Nor is it sufficient simply to develop explanations without testing them against facts. Fundamentally sociological research involves a constant interplay between observation and explanation, collection of further facts to test the explanation, a refinement of the explanation and so on.

The development of good explanations involves two related processes: theory construction and theory testing. These two processes are not alternative ways of arriving at good theories but represent two stages with different starting points (see Figure 2.1).

11

Figure 2.1 Theory construction and testing

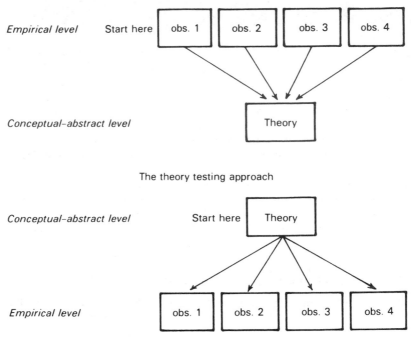

The theory construction approach

Empirical level   Start here | obs. 1 | obs. 2 | obs. 3 | obs. 4

Conceptual–abstract level   Theory

The theory testing approach

Conceptual–abstract level   Start here | Theory

Empirical level   obs. 1 | obs. 2 | obs. 3 | obs. 4

Note: obs. = observation

Theory construction is a process which begins with a set of observations (i.e. description) and moves on to develop theories of these observations. It is also called grounded theory because it is based on observations—not simply armchair speculation. Others call it *post factum* theory (Merton, 1968) or *ex post facto* theory since the theory comes after the observation rather than before.

Theory testing differs in that it starts with a theory. Using the theory we predict how things will be in the 'real' world. If our predictions are correct this lends support to our theory. If they are wrong either the theory is wrong or our prediction was illogically derived from the theory.

Theory building is, in my view, the first stage of developing good explanations, and theory testing follows as an attempt to test rigorously the tentative theory we have arrived at in the theory construction phase. In practice there is a constant interplay between constructing theories and testing them (Baldamus, 1976). Rarely are we purely constructing a theory or purely testing a theory.

The process of theory construction

Having made particular observations, the basic question to ask is: *is this observation a particular case of some more general factor?* If it is then we can gain a better understanding of the significance and meaning of the particular observation. For example, Durkheim observed that the suicide rate was higher among Protestants than among Catholics. But is religious affiliation a particular case of something more general? Of what more general phenomenon might it be an indicator? Similarly, women seem to be more religious than men. Is gender simply a particular case, or an indicator, of some more general concept? Gender might reflect position in the social structure: that women are socially less valued than men and are in this sense deprived. Thus the observation that women are more religious than men might simply indicate a more general pattern that social deprivation leads to increased religiousness.

Establishing the meaning of observations

There is a fundamental difficulty however. How do we know of what more general phenomenon a particular observation might be an indicator? How do we even get ideas of what it might be indicating? It is no simple task to know what particular observations might be indicating at a more general level. There is a real role for creative imagination, a craft which some people seem to be able to master more easily than others. Although there is no ideal solution there are a number of helpful approaches.

1 *Locating the common factor:* If several different factors have a similar outcome we can ask: *what do each of them have in common?* This principle is used in IQ tests where a number of items are listed and you have to pick the odd one out. For example, given the list of pelican, eagle, duck and seagull we work out the odd item by seeing which three items share something in common which the fourth does not. The technique of locating the commonality between particular factors with the same outcome helps us work out the more general concept that the individual observations might represent.

This is what Durkheim did in his study of suicide (Durkheim,

1970). As well as seeing that the suicide rate was higher among Protestants than Catholics, he also noted it was higher among the old than young, urban dwellers than rural dwellers, unmarried than married, childless than parents, men than women, wealthy than poor. When trying to work out why this was so, he asked what do Protestants, old people, urban dwellers, unmarried people, men, childless and wealthy people have in common? Of what more general factor might all these be indicators? To cut a long story short he argued that all these types of people were likely to be relatively poorly integrated into society and that it was for this reason that each of these particular types had higher suicide rates. In other words all his particular observations were simply particular cases of the general principle that the less well integrated people are, the more likely they are to commit suicide. The likelihood that this induction is correct is increased because he had looked at a number of factors which have the same outcome (higher suicide rate) and it seemed that each factor had something in common.

2   *Existing theories and concepts as a source of ideas:* Making a set of observations will not always or even normally lead to the development of new concepts or a new theory. Any attempt to make sense of a set of observations will often use existing concepts and theories. If concepts and theories developed by others seem like reasonable summaries or accounts of what we have observed then we will make use of them. There is little point in continually reinventing the wheel. Where our observations are new or different or are not adequately summarised by existing concepts and theories we may need to adapt or modify the existing ideas.

A major problem in using existing theories and concepts is that we may not be open to equally plausible interpretations of the observations. This is especially a problem if we are committed to a perspective. The problem is not so much in using existing concepts but in the level of commitment to them and in failing to examine whether they are the most appropriate ones. When we are committed to a model, whether it be Freudian, Marxist, Weberian, Skinnerian or Meadian, we might ignore equally plausible alternative explanations and see everything as yet further evidence for our model. This is very much against the spirit of the theory construction approach where the aim is to let the concepts and ideas emerge from observations. Of course it is never as simple, since when we try to make sense of what we see, we bring our commitments, biases and values with us as we interpret. The important thing is to realise this and to accept that our interpretations are likely to be clouded by our commitments.

Thus we must accept that our interpretations, although plausible or even convincing to ourselves, need to be rigorously tested.

3 *Context:* An important way of working out the meaning of an observation is to look at it in context. This is particularly so for the characteristics, behaviour and attitudes of people. For example, take a person who earns $30 000 a year. Do we take this as indicating that they have a reasonable income? Do we classify two people earning $30 000 as being equally well off? The meaning of a $30 000 income depends on many other factors, such as whether it is the only income in the family, the number of dependants, the age of the income earner, other expenses and so on. We have to see this apparently simple observation in the context of other factors to interpret what it indicates. Attitudes to the Australian Prime Minister, Bob Hawke, need to be understood within a context. Since he tends to be a moderate with a progressive party does disapproval of Hawke indicate conservatism or radicalism? People on the left wing of the Australian Labor Party (a progressive party) disapprove of Hawke as do many supporters of the more conservative Liberal Party. To work out what disapproval of Hawke indicates for a particular person we need to look at other attitudes people hold to give us clues.

4 *Ask respondents:* In many cases it is wise to ask people why they act or think as they do. This can provide clues about motivations behind actions and assist in interpreting what a particular action or attitude indicates for that person. This is not to say that we accept the stated reasons uncritically, but it can help provide insight into the meaning of behaviour.

5 *Introspection:* When we are familiar with a particular type of situation it is worth trying to put ourselves in the role of other people and try to understand their behaviour from their point of view. For example, we might observe that in families where the father or husband loses his job there is more violence than in families where the male is employed. To understand what that violence indicates and why it occurs it is helpful to try to imagine ourselves in the same situation. Our ability to do so varies according to our familiarity with a situation and also with the ability of particular researchers to put themselves in the position of someone else.

Levels of generality

Regardless of the means by which we move from the particular observations to working out what it might indicate at the more general level we can then go further to even more general levels. For example, using Durkheim's suicide example we developed the generalisation that

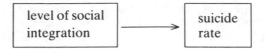

Using the same approach as outlined we can ask: *is this simply a particular example of an even more general pattern?* It could be that it is a particular case of the more general pattern that

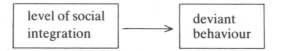

Plausibility and the need for theory testing

The general approach I have been describing is called the inductive approach. It is the process by which we develop explanations by moving from the particular to the general: from observations to theory. The basic principle is to try to see to what more inclusive set of phenomena our observation might belong. I have outlined five techniques by which this is done and suggested that the same approach can be used to move from one level of generality to higher levels.

Theories or explanations arrived at in this way are not the end of the explanation process. These explanations need to be tested rigorously. This is because such *ex post facto* explanations, although consistent with the observed facts, are not necessarily compelling and because a number of quite different explanations might be equally consistent with the facts—we need to have some way of working out which one is best (Merton, 1968:93).

One simple example can illustrate this notion of plausibility and the need for rigorous testing of *ex post facto* theories. Studies in many countries have consistently found that on all sorts of measures women are more religious than men. A number of 'explanations' have been developed, all of which are consistent with the facts.

1 *Guilt theory:* Women are more religious because religion relieves guilt feelings. Since women have more guilt feelings they are therefore more religious.
2 *Freudian theory:* God is portrayed as a male—a father figure.

According to Freud people identify with the opposite sex parent. Therefore women are attracted to a religion with a male god. This also fits with the additional observation that among Catholics men and women are about equally religious. That is because men identify with the Virgin Mary!

3 *Deprivation theory:* In our society women are more deprived than men and since religion fulfils a comforting role it will be the deprived who are most attracted to religion.

4 *Social learning theory:* The socialisation of girls teaches them to be nurturant, obedient, emotional, passive and submissive. Since religion encourages these attributes women find religion more attractive than do men.

5 *Role theory:* Women tend to have primary responsibility for childrearing. Because of the church's emphasis on the family, children's activities associated with the church and the church's role in moral training, mothers get drawn into the church via their children.

No doubt I could think up other explanations. The point is, on the basis of the facts they are all plausible but given the facts we cannot choose between them. We would need to select further crucial facts to test any explanation.

The process of theory testing

To test a theory we use the theory to guide our observations: we move from the general to the particular. The observations should provide a crucial test of the theory. Thus if we were testing the guilt explanation for the greater religiousness of women, we would at least expect that the greater a woman's feelings of guilt the more religious she would be. Further, we would expect that the preponderance of women over men would be more marked in religions emphasising forgiveness than in religions where forgiveness was not an important theme.

The basic idea then is to derive from the general theory more limited statements which follow logically from the theory. The key is to derive these statements in such a way that if the theory is true so will be the derived statement. Having derived these more limited statements we collect data relevant to them and then look at the implications of these data for the initial theory. This is the process of theory testing and is probably best explained with an example. I will outline six ideal-typical stages in this process.

Six stages in theory testing

1 *Specify the theory to be tested:* As an example we will use the theory that industrialisation, because of the need for a mobile and skilled workforce, is a principal cause of the decline of the extended family and the rise of the nuclear family. The need to move because of jobs and training breaks down family ties (Parsons, 1949). That is

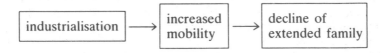

2 *Derive a set of conceptual propositions:* A proposition is a statement which specifies the nature of a relationship between two factors. The previous statements—the greater the guilt the more religious, or the more a church emphasises forgiveness the greater the proportion of women—are both examples of propositions. They are conceptual propositions in that the key terms (guilt, religious, forgiveness) are abstract terms: they are not directly observable.

Stinchcombe (1968:18–20) argues that the more propositions tested the stronger the test of a theory. Given the theory above, the following propositions seem to follow logically:

a *Industrialised countries* will be characterised by *nuclear families* more than will *relatively non-industrialised countries*.

b Within any country, *rural areas* will be characterised by *extended family structures* more than will *industrialised urban areas*.

c People who *move for work or education* will have *weaker ties with their extended family* than will people who *do not move*.

d In industrialised countries there will be little evidence of *nuclear families before industrialisation*.

No doubt other conceptual propositions could be derived. You will notice that they are all still fairly abstract: the key terms which are italicised are still abstract concepts. Although these conceptual propositions provide us with a better idea of what observations to make they still do not provide enough clues. What, for example, is an industrialised country? What is an extended family or a nuclear family? The next stage in the process then is to develop testable propositions.

3 *Restatement of conceptual propositions as testable propositions:* This stage of theory testing involves a whole set of tasks called

operationalisation, the process of deciding how to translate abstract concepts (e.g. industrialisation) into something more concrete and directly observable (see Chapter 4). Having made these decisions we can simply restate each conceptual proposition in testable terms.

The form of the testable proposition is very similar to that of the conceptual proposition. One proposition can serve as an example:

Rural areas will be characterised by extended family structures more than will industrialised urban areas.

To test this we need an 'operational definition' of the key concepts: rural, urban, extended family. Suppose we define urban areas as areas with a population density of over 60 people per square kilometre and choose a particular city as an example. Rural areas might be defined as areas with a population density of less than eighteen per square kilometre and we may choose a particular area as an example. Our indicator of the extent to which people live in an extended family might be the proportion of a specified set of extended kin (e.g. siblings, parents, cousins, aunts, grandparents) with whom they have face-to-face contact at least weekly. These indicators of the concepts are operational definitions.

We can now restate the conceptual proposition in its testable form:

People in [selected rural area] will have weekly face-to-face contact with a greater proportion of their extended kin (i.e. aunts, uncles, cousins, etc.) than will people living in [selected city].

The testable proposition then has the same form as the conceptual proposition. It is, however, more specific, since the concepts have been replaced with indicators of the concepts. We now have a very clear idea of precisely what observations to make.

4   *Collect relevant data:* Having decided what data are relevant to test our theory, we would then collect it (see Chapters 5 and 7).

5   *Analyse data:* Data are then analysed to see:

a   how much support there is for the testable propositions;

b   in turn how much support there is for the conceptual propositions;

c   in turn how much support there is for the initial theory.

This process of analysis is not as mechanical as is often portrayed in textbooks. It typically involves experimentation, puzzlement and creativity (see Chapter 17).

6   *Assessing the theory:* Rarely is the initial theory completely supported by the research: results are typically ambiguous and

conflicting. The theory is supported in some respects but not in others: some results will be unanticipated and confusing. This is good since it makes us think and modify or develop the initial theory and is what leads to progress. When we try to make sense of them we are really starting on the theory construction phase yet again. That is, we will modify the initial theory to take account of the observations we have made. As such the modified theory will need to be tested rigorously.

Theory construction and testing: an ongoing process

Wallace (1971) has described the process of theory development as an ongoing interaction between theory and observation and between theory construction and testing. This logic of the research process involving the shuttling back and forth between theory and observation is summarised in Figure 2.2.

Even though the terms I have used are not always applied and the steps not formalised (often not even recognised), the logic of what I have described is common in research. People do not always say 'I'm theory testing now' or 'I'll do a bit of inductive theorising now' or 'what's my conceptual proposition', but if you boil it down this is effectively what a lot of researchers do. Furthermore, the practice of research does not by any means always fit neatly into these systematic approaches. I have outlined them because they provide a helpful structure to help organise research and give it some direction. In practice we will often have to improvise, and compromise. The models help us organise.

The need for theory and observation

The emphasis on basing theories on observations and evaluating them against further observations may seem to be common sense. However, it is not universally practised in sociology. The practice of some sociologists involves the formulation of 'explanations' which are never systematically tested empirically. At best they use examples as proof. Examples, however, are a weak form of evidence, for regardless of the explanation we can find some examples to illustrate the argument. The key to empirical testing is to look for evidence which will *disprove* the theory, not simply to find supporting illustrations.

Other people, not necessarily sociologists, have accepted theories on other non-empirical criteria. The authority criterion is common: people will accept a theory because of *who* proposed it not because of

Figure 2.2 The logic of the research process

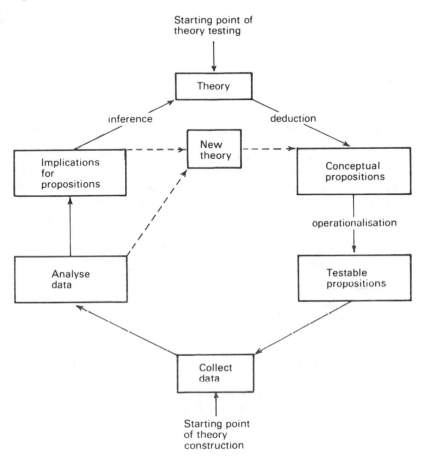

the evidence for it. Kuhn (1964) has argued how important this is in many academic disciplines.

Intuition or 'gut feelings' are another common but non-empirical way of assessing the validity of explanations. Values and basic assumptions are also crucial in affecting how convincing and appealing (and thus how popular) a theory is.

Another non-empirical way of assessing or developing a theory is to use the rules of logic rather than of evidence as the main criterion. This rationalist approach is illustrated by the classic example of a group of philosophers who, wishing to know how many teeth there were in a horse's mouth, consulted Aristotle (for rules of logic) rather than looking in the horse's mouth. A contemporary version of a rationalist approach is illustrated in the Willers' book *Systematic Empiricism* (1974).

One reaction to these non-empirical ways of deriving and evaluating explanations has been the empiricist position which is equally at odds with the approach I have outlined. Advocates of this approach encourage us simply to collect all the facts and let the facts speak for themselves rather than contaminating the 'true facts' with theory. This approach is untenable: it is neither possible to collect all the facts nor to let them speak for themselves.

In 1984 Ronald Reagan was re-elected as U.S. president by the greatest majority ever. To explain this by collecting all the facts we would have to do precisely that—collect *all* the facts. This is not only extremely inefficient, it is impossible. So we might decide to collect only the *relevant* facts. But how do we know which facts are relevant and which are irrelevant? The only way is if we have ideas about why Reagan was so popular. These theories which we hold either implicitly or explicitly dictate which observations we make. Theories then are crucial in guiding the observations we make: they provide the foundation for focused observation.

The empiricist position also is unrealistic in that the facts do not speak for themselves. Observations take on significance and meaning within a context. Durkheim's observation that suicide rates were higher among Protestants than Catholics took on much more significance and meaning within the context of his theory about social integration and suicide. Febvre (in Burke, 1973) put it this way: 'when one does not know what one is looking for, one does not realise what one finds'. Theories help interpret the meaning of observations and patterns, and highlight their significance. They help us 'realise what one finds'.

Further, simply to collect a number of facts gives no idea about how they relate to one another. Only theories can provide a way of ordering observations and producing plausible accounts of how they interrelate.

Sources of theories

The ideas we use when developing theories and making sense of our data often come from a variety of sources.

Sociological perspectives

Within sociology there are a number of distinct perspectives through which the world is interpreted and researched: symbolic interactionism, structural functionalism, Marxism, Weberianism, conflict theory and exchange theory are but a few examples. Different perspectives draw attention to different factors when trying to arrive at explanations.

Imagine we wanted to know why some people vote for progressive parties while others prefer more traditional parties. An interactionist perspective emphasises the way in which social life is influenced by interactions among individuals and the extent to which people can affect their own behaviour rather than being controlled by external forces. In explaining voting choice it draws attention to the ways in which interactions with certain people influence voting preferences. A person using a social learning perspective will focus on the way in which a person's socialisation and role modelling behaviour affects voting preferences. More psychological approaches would focus on personality characteristics such as authoritarianism and paranoia. A Freudian approach might draw attention to unresolved childhood conflicts leading to identification with certain sorts of leaders. A Marxist perspective might focus on a person's position in the class structure or use the notion of false consciousness or class consciousness. A structural functionalist who sees society as a system of interdependent parts would explain voting as a result of what is happening in other parts of society. Thus conservative voting patterns may be seen as a response to rapid social change and an attempt to restore some sort of equilibrium. An exchange perspective emphasises that behaviour is basically motivated by the desire to maximise rewards and minimise punishment. Thus it would focus on how people see a particular party as benefiting themselves. Other perspectives would lead us to focus on different factors when trying to understand voting.

My aim is not to explain these perspectives but simply to highlight their fundamental importance in affecting the types of observations we make. They affect which facts we see as relevant and important and how we interpret them. Depending on our perspective(s) we ask different questions and will be sensitised to different observations.

These perspectives provide clues about what to look for: they are a source of theories about particular aspects of society. All are relevant to a wide range of social phenomena and while no perspective is explicitly about voting, they have implications for voting. They are models of society rather than theories of particular phenomena. They provide ideas about possible explanations and give clues about how to make sense of what we see. As such they provide a set of glasses through which to view the world.

I do not intend to explore the sources of the various perspectives: that is a task for the history of ideas. However, a good many of them are illustrated in the classic works of a discipline. Thus the works of Marx, Durkheim, Weber, Freud, Skinner, Mead and Parsons are important sources of these perspectives and provide a rich source of ideas when trying to develop theories.

Other sources

Previous research on the topic which you are exploring can be invaluable in providing leads, helping articulate theories to test and alerting you to possible interpretations of what you observe. Our own imagination and experience can be a useful source of theories. Reflecting on why we behave as we do can provide ideas. Wide reading in sociology, related disciplines, novels, plays and so on can stimulate the imagination. Earlier, the contribution of inductive reasoning and a number of ways of working out what a particular observation might mean were discussed. These same processes can be valuable sources of theories.

The role of descriptive research

The emphasis on explanation so far does not mean that descriptive research is unimportant. Descriptive research deals with questions of *what* things are like, not *why* they are that way. It includes a wide range of areas such as market research, public opinion polling, media research (ratings surveys), voter intention studies and the like. Governments sponsor a lot of descriptive research: the census, unemployment rate surveys and the Household Expenditure Survey are examples. Sociological studies which describe the social structure of a community, social changes over the last 50 years, or the workings of an organisation are further examples of descriptive research. Descriptive research can be very concrete or more abstract: it depends on what we wish to describe. At the fairly concrete level we might describe the income levels of different types of people or their ethnic background, or we can address more abstract questions such as 'is the modern family isolated?', 'are working class people charac- terised by class consciousness?' and 'is society becoming secularised?'

Good description is important. It is the basis for sound theory. Unless we have described something accurately and thoroughly, attempts to explain it will be misplaced. As a descriptive statement we might say that families are getting smaller since the industrial revolution and then try to explain this. But if they are not getting smaller (as is being shown to be the case—see Laslett, 1972) our explanations will be both wrong and pointless. Furthermore good description can provide a stimulus for explanation and research. Descriptions can highlight puzzles which need to be resolved and as such provide the basis for theory construction.

In addition, descriptive research plays a key role in highlighting the existence and extent of social problems and can stimulate social action. Survey research has demonstrated the extent of poverty in many countries (this was the focus of early survey research—see Marsh, 1982:9–36) and the unemployment surveys can affect public attitudes and government policies. Competent description makes it more difficult to deny the existence of problems. Of course there is poor descriptive research just as there is poor explanatory research but this is not inherent in description itself. Some descriptive research seems to be based on empiricist assumptions and ends up as an exercise in mindless fact gathering. But this lack of direction and focus need not characterise good description. Some descriptions seem trivial—no doubt many are—but equally many are important or potentially so.

Summary: the centrality of theory

The theme of this chapter has been that as soon as we try to answer 'why' questions about society we necessarily start to theorise. I have argued that theories should be empirically based (theory construction) and evaluated against empirical reality (theory testing). I have emphasised that:

1 theory development is an important goal of social research;
2 theories which we are testing either implicitly or explicitly guide us to which observations might be relevant to a problem. Theory testing therefore is central to efficient data collection;
3 theories can help us make sense of a set of observations by helping us see what broader concepts our observations might reflect and by providing a plausible account of how various observations relate to one another;
4 theories provide guides for analysis: propositions emerge from theories and propositions form a key focus around which data are analysed.
5 theories provide a context in which to place particular observations which helps us see the possible significance and meaning of

observations. As such it sensitises us to observations we might otherwise ignore;

6   theories can help us pose challenging questions and to be aware of certain problems. Hopefully they help avoid asking trivial questions and reducing research to social arithmetic.

While theory is central to the research enterprise there is nothing sacred about any theory. Theories are always tentative attempts to find some plausible explanation for a set of facts. They ought to be rigorously tested and be subject to modification and revision. In fact the principle of trying to disprove a theory should guide the design of research. Our aim should not simply be to design research to enable us to obtain results favourable to our theory.

Further reading

Merton's *Social Theory and Social Structure* (1968) provides good and well known introductory discussions of the relation between theory and empirical research in Chapters 2, 3 and 4. Mills provides stinging criticisms of non-empirical theory and non-theoretical enquiry in Chapters 2 and 3 of *The Sociological Imagination* (1959). The whole book is worth reading because of its insistence that sociology is a craft. Chavetz in *A Primer on the Construction and Testing of Theories in Sociology* (1978) provides a useful and readable book on the nature of theory construction and testing as does Dubin in *Theory Building* (1969). Walter Wallace expands on the circular model of research discussed in this chapter in *The Logic of Science in Sociology* (1971). But the best analysis of the logic of social research is Rose's *Deciphering Sociological Research* (1982). Glaser and Strauss provide a classic discussion of the nature of theory and the process of theory construction in *The Discovery of Grounding Theory* (1967). Denzin also provides an excellent account of one type of theory construction approach in *The Research Act* (1978) pp. 191–6. Homans provides a brief and readable discussion of the importance of deduced propositions for the development of sociological explanations in his famous, if controversial, book *The Nature of Social Science* (1967). To see how some of the famous sociological theorists applied their theories to research look at Freidheim's *Sociological Thoery in Research Practice* (1976).

3 Formulating and clarifying research questions

Research questions need to be focused. For example, it is not enough to say 'I'm interested in getting some answers about inequality'. What answers to what questions? Do you want to know the extent of inequality, its distribution, its causes, its effects or what? What sort of inequality are you interested in? Over what period?

It is tempting but inefficient to collect data before the research topic is clearly defined. This is highly inefficient since you normally end up collecting the wrong data. This chapter provides some guidelines on how to clarify research questions. However, this does not mean that the initial research question is the final one. While it is important to know what we are looking for, it is a mistake to let this initial focus blind us from other unanticipated questions which are perhaps more interesting, important or manageable than the initial one. Questions can be refined and new issues emerge while reviewing literature or collecting and analysing data.

Types of research questions

There is no simple way of refining research questions but I will outline a number of different types of questions and provide some guidelines to help focus research. First, however, it is helpful to define a few terms.

A *variable* is a characteristic which has more than one category (or value). Thus sex is a variable with the categories male and female. Age is a variable with many different categories (one year old, two years old, etc.). Any person, however, will only be in one category. A variable then is a characteristic on which people can differ from one another. In cause and effect terms we can distinguish between *dependent*, *independent* and *intervening* variables. The *effect* is called a *dependent* variable (symbolised Y): it is the variable which is dependent on something else. The assumed *cause* is called the *independent* variable (symbolised X). For example, if we want to see whether level of education affects income, then income would be the dependent variable and education would be the independent variable. An *intervening* variable (symbolised Z) is the *means* by which the independent variable affects the dependent variable. In this example we could say that education affects the type of job people get which in turn affects income level. Here job is the intervening variable, that is

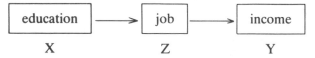

$$X \qquad\qquad Z \qquad\qquad Y$$

Once we have selected a broad topic ask 'what do I want to know about this topic?' Broadly, interests will be descriptive, explanatory or both.

Descriptive research

We might start with a broad topic such as divorce. The following questions can help focus the topic.

1   What is the *time frame* of our interest? Do we want to know about divorce now or in the past, or do we want to look at the trends over say the last 50 years?
2   What is the *geographical location* of our interest? Do we want to know about divorce in a part of the country, for the whole nation or for other countries? Or is our interest *comparative*: do we want to compare one country with other countries? If so, which countries?
3   Is our interest in broad description or in *comparing* and *specifying* patterns for subgroups? For example do we simply want to know the national divorce rate or do we want to see if it differs according to age of marriage, occupation, length of marriage, educational level and so on?
4   What *aspect* of the topic are we interested in? Is it the divorce rate, divorce laws, problems with property and custody, attitudes to divorce, ways in which people adjust to divorce or something else?
5   How *abstract* is our interest? Are we interested in the raw facts or in what they might indicate at the more abstract level? For example, is our interest in the divorce rate as such or in what it might reveal about, say, level of social conflict? If it is the latter, we will collect other data relevant to measuring conflict (e.g. level of

industrial disputes, crime rates, legal actions). If it is in divorce *per se*, we will collect only information on this topic.

Explanation: searching for causes or consequences

The next three types of research question all involve explanatory research. They vary in terms of their focus and complexity.

Over the last 50 years the divorce rate in most western countries has increased markedly. We may want to know why but have no idea. Diagrammatically then the problem is

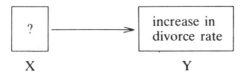

Alternatively our interest might be in discovering the consequences of the increased divorce rate. Diagrammatically this is

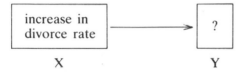

The first step then is to decide whether we are looking for causes or consequences. Second, we must clarify what it is we are seeking the causes or consequences of (e.g. increased divorce rate from 1935 to 1985). The next step is to list possible causes or consequences and then collect relevant data. There are a number of ways of coming up with such a list.

1 *Previous research:* Using a library, look to see what other researchers have found on the topic. We will often notice gaps in the research, lack of evidence and unresolved debates. These can help focus the research.

2 *The 'facts':* Detailed description of a phenomenon can stimulate ideas about possible causes. For example, if the pattern of divorce over the last 50 years showed a big increase in 1945–47, a decline in the mid-1950s and a dramatic increase in say 1976, we could ask what other changes have also occurred at these times and over the 50 year period. These might have something to do with the divorce rate and provide clues about possible causes (e.g. decline of religion except in the mid-1950s, changes in the law such as 1976 in Australia, changed beliefs about personal fulfilment, increased

workforce participation for women, changes in welfare provisions).

3 *Our own hunches:* Our own ideas, impressions, beliefs and experiences are valuable sources of ideas so long as we test them against the evidence and are not limited only to them.

4 *Talk to informants:* Often there are people who are particularly well placed to provide ideas and can provide good jumping off points for research. In this case marriage counsellors, solicitors and social workers may all provide helpful insights.

Once ideas about possible causes have been collected in this exploratory way we might stop there, collect information to test all the ideas or focus on just one or two possible causes.

Explanation: exploring a simple idea

This approach to formulating explanatory research questions is more focused than the previous approach. Instead of asking what has caused the increased divorce rate, we would be more specific and ask: 'has X (e.g. decline in religion) led to the increased divorce rate?' The research then concentrates on this specific question. Diagrammatically we could represent this as

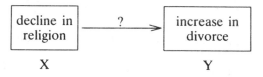

Given this idea we would evaluate it by using the theory testing approach.

Explanation: exploring more complex ideas

The above idea is relatively simple because it deals with only two concepts. We might find that it is true that the decline of religion has been accompanied by an increase in divorce but what are the mechanisms? Why should religious decline lead to divorce? Can we fill in the links? If we can, we should have a better understanding of why divorce has increased. From a variety of sources (see the earlier section on searching for causes and consequences) we might develop the model in Figure 3.1.

In summary there is a variety of types of research questions varying from descriptive to more complex explanatory problems. For descriptive research we must try to be clear and specific about what we want to describe. For explanatory research ask

Figure 3.1 A model for the increased divorce rate

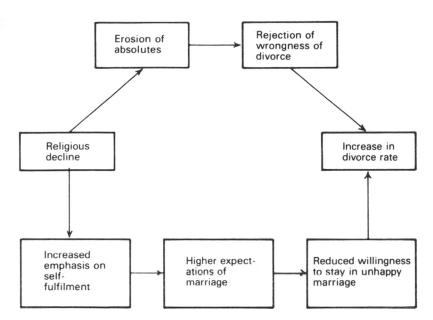

1 What am I trying to explain?
2 What are the possible causes?
3 Which causes will I explore?
4 What are the possible mechanisms?

It can be helpful to draw diagrams like those earlier in this section: they can help clarify our thinking. Often these different types of research questions can represent different stages within the one study. Initially we might be interested simply in describing a phenomenon, but then the 'why' questions about causes develop. As we proceed we might focus on one particular cause and then start asking more complex questions about that particular factor. This illustrates that the task of clarifying research questions is a process rather than a once-and-for-all task which is completed at the beginning of a study.

Scope of the research

As well as specifying what is to be explained and in what terms it is to be explained, it is helpful to resolve three issues related to the scope of the research before collecting data.

Particular but exhaustive or general but partial?

Will the research focus on a particular case and try to find as many causes as possible or will it seek partial explanations of a class of events? For example, a study of strikes could focus on a particular strike and try to discover all the factors behind that strike (including those peculiar to it alone). Alternatively, it could look at strikes in general and try to locate some factors that tend to be of importance for strikes in general. The first approach of focusing on thorough accounts of particular cases is called idiographic explanation (like idiosyncratic). Finding a partial explanation of a class of cases (e.g. strikes) is called nomothetic explanation. If we are committed to doing a survey then we will need to formulate the research question in these terms. If the question is really more suited to an idiographic approach we would be best advised to try another research method.

Units of analysis

A unit of analysis is the unit from which we obtain information: it is the unit whose characteristics we describe. In survey research the unit of analysis often is an individual. In a survey we might ask 2000 people whether they have ever been on strike or what might cause them to go on strike. But other units of analysis are possible. Any region (e.g. country, county, state) could be used so that we look at the strike rate of various regions for example. Time periods can be used. We might compare different years in terms of the strike levels. Events can be used too. Thus a study could be designed around collecting data about various strikes. A group or organisation (e.g. particular unions) could be the unit of analysis. Many other units of analysis can be used depending on the issue at hand. Poems, paintings, buildings, jokes, newspapers, families and so on could be used.

Working out the unit of analysis is important in two respects. Firstly, being aware of the range of possible units of analysis can help formulate more useful and interesting research questions and highlight a range of types of relevant data. Only to think of collecting data from and about individuals can lead to asking only rather restricted research questions. Secondly, if data cannot be collected using a particular unit of analysis, the general thrust of the question may be retained simply by changing to a unit of analysis about which data are available. For example, we may want to know whether prosperous economic conditions encourage or discourage industrial disputes. Initially we might try to collect data from a country for the last 50 years but if this was unavailable for a particular country we could try another approach by comparing disputation levels in different countries with varying economic conditions. By changing the units of analysis from years to countries we have a different handle on the problem.

Where a number of units of analysis can be used in the one study we can be more confident in the general thrust of the results. It provides a tougher test of a theory. In a study on the effect of economic conditions on strikes it would be best to use both years and countries as units of analysis since this enables us to approach the same question from a variety of angles.

Research design

With either descriptive or explanatory research it is necessary to have a frame of reference within which to interpret the results — a frame of reference that enables one to do more than simply report the results.

Descriptive research

When dealing with descriptive questions the need for a frame of reference is fairly obvious. For example, the inflation rate of a country might be 9 per cent. But is this high or low, good or bad, improving or deteriorating? To obtain an appreciation of this figure we need to know how it compares with the inflation rate of other countries or of other years: we need a context to make sense of most data. When collecting data it is necessary therefore to design strategies to ensure that the data needed to provide this context are collected.

Two particularly useful types of information are data about other groups and about the same group of people over time. These can provide a context in which to view a single piece of data and help avoid drawing faulty conclusions from it. Suppose we have collected information about the levels of self-esteem of women with young children who are out of the workforce, and that we have found that many of these women exhibit low levels of self-esteem. What does this mean? On its own it means very little. It would be much more helpful to be able to compare the findings for these women with those for some other groups. How do they compare with the results for comparable women who are in the workforce? How do they compare with those for men with young children who are out of the workforce? Without making such comparisons it is difficult to draw many conclusions from the simple finding. We might be tempted to conclude that being out of the workforce has a detrimental effect on women's self-esteem, but on its own the finding does not justify this conclusion. We need to know whether the self-esteem of women out of the workforce is different to that of other comparable groups.

As well as comparing these women with other comparable groups it would be desirable to examine their levels of self-esteem over a period of time and see what their self-esteem was like before they left the workforce, what it was like when they were out of the workforce and what it was like when they returned. Looking at the same group of people over time helps provide a context in which to understand the low self-esteem of mothers out of the workforce.

Explanatory research

When asking research questions that deal with *causal processes* an appropriate research design is absolutely essential. Where the goal is to develop an explanation of the patterns in the data we need to eliminate as many alternative explanations of the patterns as possible. If we develop a causal model that proposes that X produces Y we need to be as sure as we can that it is in fact X and not A, B or C that produces Y. Paying careful attention to research design is an important way of ensuring that possible alternative explanations of the data are eliminated and of giving us more confidence in the conclusions we draw about the causal processes operating.

People use the term 'research design' in different ways. Some use it broadly to include the issues of problem formulation, operationalisation (see next chapter), sampling and the selection of data collection techniques. Like Stouffer (1950) I use the term much more narrowly to refer to the *structure of the data* rather than the particular data. The central point of a good research design is that it provides suitable frames of reference so that an appropriate context is provided in which relatively unambiguous statements can be drawn. The aim is to move our conclusions about causal processes from the realm of the plausible and possible to the convincing and compelling.

In the sections that follow I outline a number of research designs following Stouffer's (1950) discussion. I begin with a description of the *experimental design* and then deal with a number of common variations. Although the experimental design is impractical for most social science research problems, it nevertheless provides a useful benchmark against which to compare other designs and highlight their weaknesses. In so doing it can help us both design and consume research more intelligently and critically. The experimental design also highlights the logic behind many of the statistical techniques covered later in this book.

Figure 3.2 Classic experimental design

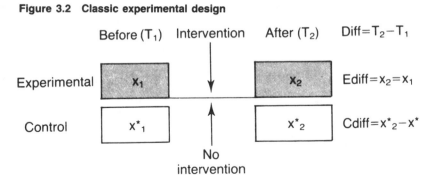

Effect of intervention is the difference between Ediff and Cdiff.

The classic experimental design

In its simplest form the experimental design has two groups: an experimental group and a control group. It also extends over time so that data are collected at at least two points in time (before and after). Between time one (before) and time two (after) the experimental group is exposed to an experimental intervention. The control group is left alone. At both time one and time two the experimental and control groups are measured in relation to the key dependent variable that is of interest in the study. In Figure 3.2 the measure of the dependent variable is indicated by x_1 and x_2, indicating the measure for the group at times one and two respectively. The measures for the control group on the same variable are indicated by x^*_1 and x^*_2.

Since the experimental group has been exposed to the experimental intervention, we might suppose that differences in the experimental group between time one and time two might be due to the influence of the intervention. So we measure the difference between x_1 and x_2 and obtain the difference between time one and time two (Ediff) for the experimental group.

However, the observed difference for the group between time one and time two might be due to factors other than the experimental intervention. A change could occur due to the passing of time, be a result of being measured at time one, or be caused by a whole set of other possibilities. For this reason a control, or comparison, group is needed. Ideally this group should be identical to the experimental group at time one. However, unlike the experimental group, they are not exposed to any experimental intervention. We can measure them on our dependent variable at both time one and time two and

Figure 3.3 An experimental design to measure the effect of newspapers on party preference

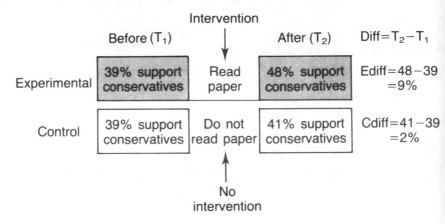

Effect of intervention is the difference between Ediff and Cdiff.

obtain a measure of change or difference over that time (Cdiff). Since this group was not exposed to the experimental intervention, any change in this group will not be due to this factor.

The crucial thing to look at is whether the experimental group changed more than the control group. If it changed significantly more, we normally would conclude that this is because of the experimental intervention.

Of course, this conclusion is warranted only if both groups were the same to start with and had identical experiences between time one and time two. In order to ensure that they are the same to start with, people will be assigned randomly to the experimental and control groups. So long as the groups are large enough, this should ensure that they are very similar in most respects. Ensuring that they have the same experiences between time one and time two is more difficult and is one reason why experiments are often held in laboratories where this can be controlled to some extent.

An example of an experimental design is illustrated in Figure 3.3. Here the research is designed to test the proposition that a particular newspaper produces support for conservative rather than reformist political parties. We might be tempted to see whether people who read the paper are more conservative than those who do not read it. But even if we found this, we could not conclude that the paper produced the conservatism. A quite plausible explanation is that, rather than the newspaper producing conservatism, conservative people are more likely to read papers that support their views.

An experimental design helps resolve this. If we were to undertake this research we would randomly allocate people into the experimental and control groups. This should ensure, among other things, that the two groups would initially display similar levels of support for the conservatives. We would measure the degree of support for the conservatives in each group and ensure that over a specified time only the experimental group read the paper. At the end of the experimental period we would remeasure the level of support for the conservatives in each group. In this example, support for the conservatives increased by 9 per cent from 39 per cent to 48 per cent in the experimental group. In the control group, which did not read the paper, support for the conservatives increased by 2 per cent.

We might conclude that some (2 per cent) of the increased support for the conservatives among the experimental group is due to factors other than reading the paper. But the level of conservative support in the experimental group increased by 7 per cent more than in the control group. On the assumption that the two groups were similar to start with and that, with the exception of reading the newspaper, they were exposed to similar influences in the experimental period, we could conclude that reading the newspaper produced 7 per cent more support for the conservatives.

By designing the research with the before and after dimension and the experimental and control groups, we are in a position to draw much more unequivocal conclusions than we could without that design. We are much more able to draw conclusions about causal processes.

There are a number of problems which make it extremely difficult to use an experimental design for social research. In many situations it is not possible to obtain repeated measures for the same group, thus making it impossible to get measures at both times one and two. Often it is difficult to obtain a control group. Practical and ethical considerations often make it impossible to introduce experimental interventions. For example, we might be interested in the effect of marital breakdown on the social adjustment of young children. Obviously we cannot allocate people randomly to two groups and somehow cause marital breakdowns in one group and leave the other group alone.

Panel design

This design (see Figure 3.4) uses only the top two cells of the experimental design. It looks at the same group of people over a

Figure 3.4 Panel design

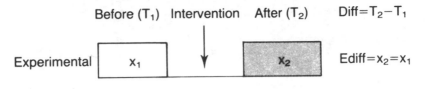

period of time: measurements of some variable are made at both points and an 'intervention' of one sort or another is made. The difference between time one and time two enables us to measure change over the period.

An example of this design might be a study that examines the religious orientation of students when they first enrol at university and then measures the views of the same students three years later. The 'intervention' in this case has been their time at university. Research that has done this has often assumed that the change that has occurred is due to their experience at university. The secularising effect of their university studies has been taken to be responsible for the change in religious views of students.

But it is impossible to draw this conclusion using this design. We would need to know the extent to which comparable people who did not attend university changed their religious views over the same period. Unless we have such a group (effectively a control group) we are in no position to draw conclusions about the causal influence of the university experience on their religious change.

Quasi-panel design

This is similar to the panel design except that *different* groups of people are studied at the two points of time (see Figure 3.5). This design might be used to avoid the difficulties of keeping track of the same people over time. Using the above example, this design would involve obtaining measures of the religious orientation of a sample of first year students at the beginning of their first year and then three years later obtaining the views of a sample of students at the end of their third year. In obtaining the third year sample we would endeavour to match it as closely as possible with the initial sample in terms of factors such as course taken, gender, religious background, class and so forth.

This design has the problems of the panel design for drawing causal inferences and has the further problem of being unable to fully match the samples at time one and time two. Differences

Figure 3.5 Quasi-panel design

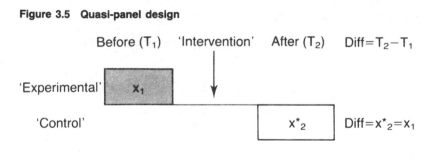

Figure 3.6 Retrospective panel design

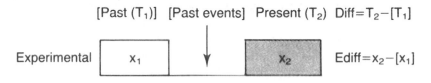

observed between time one and two might be due to the influence of university, but they might also be due to difficulties in matching the samples. We cannot even be sure that we have measured change — something that the panel design is at least good at.

Retrospective panel design

The panel design has the disadvantage of having to keep track of people over time and of having to wait for a long time on occasions before the results can be collected. Often it is simply not feasible to follow a group of people over time and the drop out rate in the study can create serious difficulties with comparing time one and time two results.

An alternative approach that can be used to provide a time dimension to the study is to obtain information at one time only but to ask about two or more time points and to find out about events in between these two times (see Figure 3.6). Thus we might ask students at the end of their university course about their religious orientation and then ask them to recall their position on the same issues at the beginning of their course.

Apart from the other shortcomings of the panel design, this design has the difficulty of selective memory and is open to the possibility that people will reinterpret the past in the light of the

Figure 3.7   Retrospective experimental design

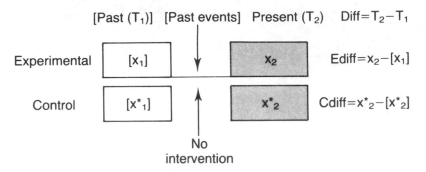

Effect of intervention is the difference between Ediff and Cdiff.

present. Even if such a study detects 'changes' we cannot be sure whether the changes are real or perceived.

Retrospective experimental design

The retrospective panel design suffers from the dual problem of the shortcomings of retrospectivity and from having no control group. The first problem means that we cannot be certain about the extent of real change while the absence of a control group means that it is difficult to draw conclusions about causal processes. The retrospective experimental design (see Figure 3.7) is an attempt to deal with the control group problem.

Using this approach we would interview two groups of people. The first would be a group of third year university students (i.e. after their university training) and a matched group of people who had not attended university. By obtaining their current religious views and asking them to recall what their position was three years ago we would have the design in Figure 3.7. We could then calculate the change in each of the two groups between time one and time two and ascertain whether it had been greater in the experimental group.

Cross-sectional or correlational design

The most common design used in survey research is the cross-sectional design (see Figure 3.8). Using this approach we collect measures from at least two groups of people at the one point of time and compare the extent to which the two groups differ on the dependent variable (e.g. religious orientation).

Figure 3.8   Cross-sectional design

[Past (T$_1$)]   [Past events]   Present (T$_2$)

'Experimental'

$$X_2$$

'Control'

$$X^*_2$$

$$\text{Diff}=X_2-X^*_2$$

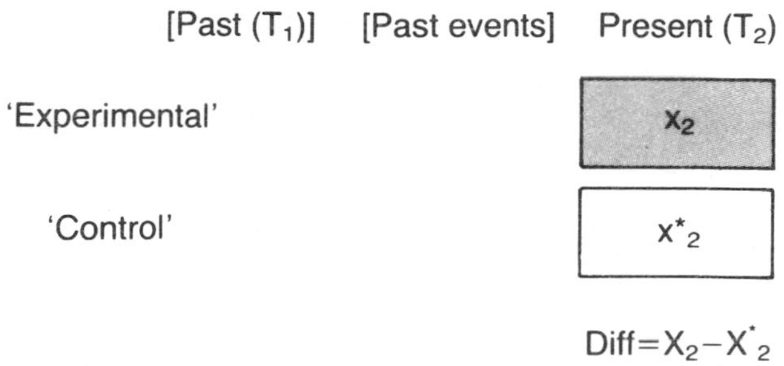

For our example we would examine a group of third year university students and a group of people who had not been to university and measure their religious orientation. We might want to attribute any difference between the students and non-students to the fact that one group had been to university. But clearly we cannot do this. Students and non-students will be different in many other respects. They may differ in terms of age, gender, class and other characteristics that are well known to be related to religious orientation. We would need to remove these as possible explanations before we could even begin to draw conclusions about any possible effect of university. In other words we would need to *match* the two groups as closely as possible. This can be done by a variety of statistical techniques that will be discussed later in the book (Chapters 12 and 13).

The cross-sectional design does not have a time dimension and thus we cannot use this to help look at causal influences. Instead it attempts to simulate this by the statistical elimination of differences between the two groups at time two. The assumption is that if we can match the two groups in all ways except on the experimental variable (going to university) then any differences in the dependent variable (religious orientation) must be due to the effect of the experimental variable.

In the end we cannot be sure that we have completely matched the two groups or controlled for all the factors that might possibly lead to the observed differences between the groups. We can only do our best and control for factors about which we have information and which, on the basis of previous research, have been shown to be relevant. The problem of not being able to control for all variables is not very different to the problem encountered with the non-laboratory experimental design where we can rarely be sure that the

Figure 3.9 One-shot case study design

[Past (T$_1$)]   [Past events]   Present (T$_2$)

'Experimental'   Diff=X$_2$−?

'Control'

two groups have been exposed to identical influences (except for the experimental intervention) between time one and time two.

Although the discussion so far has been limited to two groups this is not a requirement. Any number of groups can be built into a design. In cross-sectional designs this is particularly common. If we were interested in the effect of age on religiosity we could have two groups — young and old — and see whether the young were different to the old group. But we could have, say, six age groups and compare the different levels of religiosity across all six groups. To the extent that the religiosity of the groups differs, we might conclude, other things being equal, that age is related to religiosity.

One-shot case study

The most primitive design — of little use when trying to analyse causal processes — is one which has only one cell of the experimental design (see Figure 3.9). This involves collecting information from one group at one point in time. For our study of religious orientation it would involve asking a group of final year students about their religious orientation. We might observe that not many appear to be very religious or even interested in religion. This might be of interest for descriptive purposes, but is of no use if we are to understand anything about causal processes.

To use this design for causal analysis requires that we rely on plausible conjecture and our preconceptions and assumptions about the data that might be in the other cells of the design. It requires that we fill in the cells from our imagination rather than from systematic observation. Thus, having observed low levels of religiousness among final year students, we might assume or believe that first year students would be more religious and therefore infer change. Further we might assume that other people outside the university would be more religious and thus manufacture an imaginary control group. Clearly this type of analysis is unsatisfactory: it relies on the creation of data rather than collection of data — a process which promotes conclusions based on prejudice and ignorance rather than research and analysis.

Conclusion

The aim of this outline of research design has been fourfold. Firstly, rather than suggesting that the experimental design is the only way to proceed, the intention has been to create an awareness of the limitations of designs where cells are missing and to suggest ways of filling in at least some of the cells. The more cells that are filled in with data the better the design will be. In many situations in social research the experimental design either will be impracticable or impossible. Secondly, the aim has also been to highlight the logic behind the experimental design, for it is in this logic that the rationale of multivariate analysis lies. The use of multivariate analysis with a cross-sectional design is the most common way in which survey researchers attempt to approximate the logic of the classical experiment. An understanding of design principles therefore lies at the heart of an understanding of the more sophisticated methods of statistical analysis. Thirdly, an understanding of the principles of research design should help us be more critical consumers of social research. Finally, an appreciation of design issues highlights the importance of what data to collect (e.g. do we need to ask retrospective questions?) and of thinking through the issues of whom we should collect it from. It is therefore important in questionnaire design and in developing sampling strategies.

Summary

In this chapter I have emphasised the importance of having clearly defined research questions to focus data collection and have outlined a number of guidelines which may help. I have also emphasised that the formulation of a research problem is a process involving interaction between the problem and data. The final research problem will evolve in this process as we reflect on and try to make sense of the data, but we still need to work out where we intend to go at the beginning.

Surveys are often seen to inhibit this process of problem formulation because they frequently use structured questionnaires and collect data at one time, thus limiting the extent to which the problem can be redefined and refocused. This view is based on too narrow a conception of surveys. Data need not be collected by structured questionnaires nor at one point of time. Even though it may be difficult to go back and reinterview people in a mass survey, not all survey research involves this sort of approach. When other units of analysis are used, and with individuals as well, it is often possible to collect more data as a research problem changes. Even when it is not possible to collect additional data, there is still a great deal of flexibility at the analysis stage to reorient a study's emphasis. Even a limited amount of data can be analysed in many different ways to address many different questions.

Nevertheless, in practice there are limits to which a research question can be reformulated once data have been collected. Most researchers work within severe constraints of time and money and there is a natural reluctance to keep on modifying a topic—especially if this means starting all over again. These problems are by no means restricted to survey researchers and they highlight the importance of thinking carefully about the research topic before collecting data extensively.

Further reading

Remarkably few books seriously address how to clarify research problems. The books by Bell and Newby, *Doing Sociological Research* (1971), Bell and Encel, *Inside the Whale* (1978) and Hammond, *Sociologists at Work* (1964) are all valuable because they show that in actual practice the formulation of research problems is a process. Clark in Part I of *Social Science: Introduction to theory and method* (1983) provides a very concise and helpful approach to assist in refining research questions. Babbie in *The Practice of Social Research* (1983) provides a useful account of options and decisions when designing a research project. Cooper's (1989) book, *Integrating Research: A Guide for Literature Reviews*, provides some useful hints on reviewing the literature as a way of clarifying research questions. An advanced book outlining a variety of research designs that is well worth the effort of reading is Campbell and Stanley's *Experimental and Quasi-Experimental Designs for Research* (1963). However it is worth reading Stouffer's paper on 'Some observations on study design' (1950) first. Hakim's *Research Design* (1987) is a thorough, accessible and slightly differently oriented approach to research design. It is highly recommended.

Part II COLLECTING DATA

4 Developing indicators for concepts

To be useful, concepts must have empirical indicators: if we cannot say what behaviours, attitudes or characteristics reflect conservatism, authoritarianism or social status, for example, then for the purposes of research the concept is useless. The difficulty is in developing good indicators for concepts. This chapter examines how to translate concepts into indicators by looking at three steps:

1   clarifying the concepts;
2   developing initial indicators;
3   evaluating the indicators.

Before looking at these steps it is helpful to look at an example which illustrates the process of developing indicators and highlights the difficulties. Suppose we are interested in the theory which argues that religiousness is a response to deprivation: that religious faith serves to compensate people for their frustrations and disappointments. We might propose that the more deprived people are, the more religious they will be. To test this we must work out who is deprived and who is not, who is religious and who is not. We might use income to distinguish between the deprived and non-deprived: those earning $10 000 or less a year being classified as deprived and those earning $20 000 a year as being non-deprived. We could use church attendance to indicate religiousness: monthly and more regular attenders could be defined as religious with less regular attenders being classified as non-religious. Suppose, contrary to expectations, we find only 15 per cent of those with low incomes attend church regularly, while 50 per cent of those with higher incomes do so. Can we then reject the theory that deprivation leads to religiousness? There would be two fundamental problems with this 'research'.

1   We have not clarified the meaning of 'deprivation' and 'religious-ness'. Unless we are clear about the meaning of the concepts we cannot develop measures of them.

2   We do not know whether the indicators we have used are adequate. Does church attendance adequately measure religiousness? Does income indicate deprivation? Before answering these questions we need to know what the concepts mean.

Clarifying concepts

Concepts are simply tools which fulfil a useful shorthand function: they are abstract summaries of a whole set of behaviours, attitudes and characteristics which we see as having something in common. Concepts do not have some sort of independent existence 'out there': they do not have any fixed meaning. Concepts are terms which people create for the purpose of communication and efficiency. When developing indicators for concepts, the task is not to find indicators which match some concept which has a set definition. It is up to us to first define what we mean by the concept and then develop indicators for the concept *as it has been defined*. By their very nature definitions are neither true nor false: they are only more useful or less useful.

There is a problem here. If concepts have no set meaning then anyone can define a concept any way they wish. The result would be that the concept would become useless; unless people mean the same thing by a word, communication is impossible. In sociology lack of agreement about how words are defined leads to confusion and pointless debates. For example, debates about the extent to which a country is secularised, equal or democratic depend substantially on definitions of religion, equality and democracy respectively.

The view that concepts do not have real or set meanings can lead to conceptual anarchy, a problem with no entirely satisfactory solution. The most practical action is to make it very clear how we have defined a concept and to keep this definition clearly in mind when drawing conclusions and comparing the findings with those of other researchers. Although we can define a word any way we wish, there seems to be little value in developing entirely idiosyncratic definitions. Since concepts are used to communicate, it makes most sense to use the word in its most commonly understood sense. If the definition of the concept is idiosyncratic this should be made very clear. Where a concept takes on a number of widely held but different meanings, we will need either to decide on (and justify) one, or to design the research so that we have indicators of each of the different meanings.

How to clarify concepts

Since concepts have no set meanings yet it is crucial that the concepts used in research be defined, how do we go about clarifying them? In practice people use different approaches. I will describe three steps which help in the process.

1 *Obtain a range of definitions of the concept:* Before adopting one definition of a concept look for the ways in which sociologists use the concept then look at lay definitions. People do not always provide formal definitions so we may need to work out what they mean by the way they have used the term (i.e. their definition may be implicit rather than explicit).

   Once we have an idea of the range of ways in which the term is used, we may find that we can classify definitions into a number of categories. Developing a definition of religion can serve as an example. There are many sociological and lay definitions but they can be grouped into two main categories:

   a Inclusive or functional definitions: this approach, which derives from Durkheimian and functionalist theorising, defines beliefs and behaviour as religious, not by their content, but by their function for either individuals or society. Thus any set of beliefs which provides people with meaning in life may be defined as religious. There are a large number of diverse definitions which fit into this category.

   b Exclusive or substantive definitions: these definitions are based on the content of belief and typically specify that the beliefs must include some notion of a supernatural being.

   An alternative approach is to look at common elements of definitions and develop a definition based on these. Hillery (1955) listed 94 definitions of 'community' and Bell and Newby (1971) note that the majority of definitions include three elements: area, common ties and social interaction. This approach could then form the basis of a definition which incorporates the generally understood meaning of the concept.

2 *Decide on a definition:* Having listed types of definitions or delineated the most common elements of definitions, we need to decide on which definition to use. We might opt for an existing one, create a new one, choose a classic definition or use a more contemporary one. Regardless of which we do, we need to justify the decision.

   In practice, the process of conceptual clarification continues as data are analysed. Clarification is not a once-and-for-all process which precedes research. It is an ongoing process: there is an interaction between analysing data and clarifying concepts. As a result of analysing data we are often in a better position to say what we mean by a concept than before we began. Nevertheless, this process must begin before data collection.

To assign a definition to a concept is to give it a nominal definition: it is a working definition which is used in the research. It provides a focus for research and guidance about the type of information to collect, but does not tell us precisely which information to collect. For example, we might define religious beliefs as those with a supernatural element. This helps focus on the range of beliefs to examine but does not specify which beliefs to examine. This is the task of an operational definition which will be dealt with shortly.

3 *Delineate the dimensions of the concept:* Many concepts have a number of different aspects or dimensions. When clarifying concepts it is often helpful to distinguish between those dimensions. This may result in using only one of the dimensions in the study or it may lead to a more systematic development of indicators for each dimension. Distinguishing between dimensions can lead to more sophisticated theorising and more useful analysis.

Deprivation is an example of a multidimensional concept: social, economic, political, psychic or physical deprivation can be delineated. Distinguishing between these dimensions can force us to clarify what our theory is about and in so doing ensure that we develop measures relevant to that theory. Earlier we noted the model which says deprivation causes religiousness. By delineating dimensions we are forced to ask, do we mean any sort of deprivation will lead to any sort of religiousness? Perhaps we might become more specific and state that social deprivation leads to religious beliefs (one of the dimensions of religiousness). If we decided this was the theory we were testing, we would need to include questions relating only to one type of deprivation and one aspect of religiousness.

We might want to develop measures of each type of deprivation and each aspect of religiousness. If so, delineating the separate dimensions helps in choosing indicators systematically.

Developing indicators

The process of moving from abstract concepts to the point where we can develop questionnaire items to tap the concept is called 'descending the ladder of abstraction'. It involves moving from the broad to the specific, from the abstract to the concrete. In clarifying concepts we begin to descend this ladder. A further step is taken when dimensions are specified. Sometimes these dimensions themselves can be further subdivided into some more specific categories. For example, there may be different types or aspects of social deprivation: it may involve social isolation or it may mean the absence of socially valued roles or social skills. These dimensions of social deprivation are more specific and give more clues about which questions to ask in a questionnaire (Figure 4.1).

When delineating dimensions and dimensions of dimensions it is helpful to define the terms on the way. If one aspect of social deprivation is social isolation, what do we mean by this? Does it mean lack of friends, not seeing your family, not belonging to organisations and so on? Before concepts can be measured we must descend from the lofty and often vague heights of some theories and deal with these more mundane issues. The process of descending the ladder of abstraction is summarised in Figure 4.1.

When we get to the point where we can develop indicators there are three broad problems to deal with:

1 how many indicators to use;
2 how to develop the indicators;
3 how to form items into a questionnaire (this will be dealt with in Chapter 6).

How many indicators to use

There is no simple answer to this problem but the following guidelines are useful.

1 When there is no agreed way of measuring a concept it may be helpful to develop indicators for a range of definitions and see what difference this makes to the results and interpretations.
2 If the concept is multidimensional, consider whether you are really interested in all dimensions. Are they all relevant to the theory?
3 Ensure that the key concepts are thoroughly measured. The behaviour and attitudes that we are trying to explain and the theorised causes must be carefully measured using several indicators.
4 Typically attitudes and opinions are complex and are best measured with a number of questions to capture the scope of the concept (see Chapter 15).
5 Pilot testing indicators is a way of eliminating unnecessary

Figure 4.1 Clarifying concepts: descending the ladder of abstraction

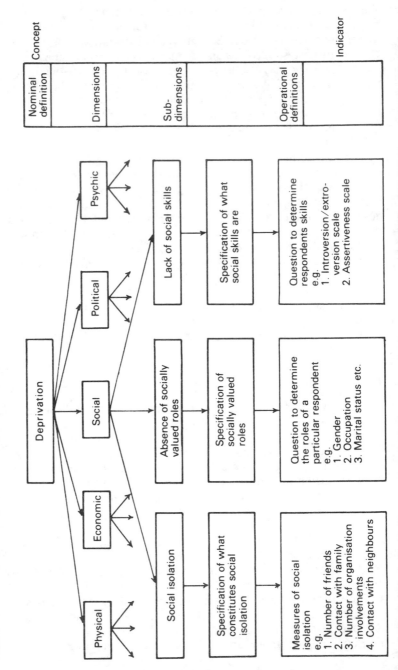

questions. Initially we might have 50 questions to measure authoritarianism but find that we need only 10 of these items: the additional 40 items might not add anything to our index (see Chapter 15).

6 The number of items is affected by practical considerations such as overall length of the questionnaire and method of administration (see Chapter 7).

How to develop indicators

For many concepts, developing an indicator is simple and the indicators are well established (e.g. marital status, education level), but for others, particularly the more abstract concepts, it is more difficult. There seem to be three main approaches to developing initial indicators in questionnaire research. In each case these initial indicators will be refined during the evaluation stage.

First, measures developed in previous research can be used. There are many well-established and tested scales which we ignore at our peril. Ideally we should try to evaluate these measures: they may need updating or rewording to fit a particular context or a particular sample. Using well-established indicators has the enormous advantage of enabling comparison of results with those of other researchers. This can be helpful in building up a cumulative body of knowledge rather than each person carrying out their own idiosyncratic research with idiosyncratic measures (see references at the end of this chapter).

Secondly, for some research topics, especially those where we are surveying a special group (e.g. migrants, Aborigines, young people, childless couples) it is very helpful to use a less structured approach to data collection first (e.g. observation, unstructured interview). This can help us understand things through the eyes of these people, learn of their concerns and ways of thinking, and this can be extremely helpful in developing relevant and appropriately worded questions for that group.

A third alternative is to use 'informants' from the group to be surveyed. Such people can provide useful clues about meaningful questions. For example, if surveying a union it would be helpful to talk to key types of people in the union to get their ideas and comments on questions.

In the end we have to decide which indicators to use and how to word them. In doing so we need to be as informed as possible about the study population, to be clear about what we want to measure, to look at other people's efforts and to evaluate our own indicators.

Evaluating indicators

Having developed indicators we have to make sure that they measure the concept we think they are measuring (validity) and ensure that we can rely on the answers people give to our questions. A question is of little use if people answer it one way one day and another the next (this is a question of reliability).

It is wise to assess the reliability and validity of indicators before carrying out the actual study. This is called pilot testing and is done by administering the questions to a similar but smaller sample to that to be used in the actual study. Sometimes people avoid pilot testing by including a large number of indicators in the study and only using those which prove to be valid and reliable. This seems to be the wrong way of doing things since we will end up by defining the concept in terms of the indicators which 'worked'. If this is done then the indicators may not represent the concepts or the theory we set out to test and as such the research can end up having little relevance to the original research question. Do not take the risk. Pilot test first.

Reliability

A reliable measurement is one where we obtain the same result on repeated occasions. If people answer a question the same way on repeated occasions then it is reliable. I will consider three aspects of reliability.

1   *Sources of unreliability:* A question may be unreliable due to bad wording: a person may understand the question differently on different occasions. Different interviewers can elicit different answers from the respondent: the sex, ethnic background and dress of the interviewer can influence responses. Another source of error can occur at the coding stage: different coders might code the same response (e.g. occupation) differently. Asking questions on issues about which people have no opinion or have insufficient information can lead to very rough-and-ready answers.

      Even well developed questions will be subject to unreliability problems. For example, studies of the same respondents over time show that they give different answers to questions on different occasions, even though there should have been no change in fact. One study (Schreiber, 1976) shows that for questions about gender, the state where the respondent was born and where they grew up, between 1 per cent and 14 per cent replied differently on the two occasions on which they answered the question (two years apart). Questions asking about the size of the place where they grew up, the respondent's education level and their father's occupation had even higher levels of unreliability, ranging from 22 per cent to 34 per cent error.

2   *Testing reliability*: There are a number of well-established methods of testing the reliability of indicators. The best methods, however, only apply to measuring the reliability of scales where we have a set of questions to measure the one concept rather than single-item indicators (see pages 255–6).

Where we have a single question to measure a concept or characteristic it is particularly important to make sure it is reliable. Basically the *test-retest method* is the only way to check on the reliability of single questions: ask the same people the same questions at intervals of two to four weeks and calculate the correlation co-efficient between the answers on both occasions. If the correlation is high (a rule of thumb is 0.8 or above) then we assume that the question is reliable. Unfortunately the test-retest method is a poor one. It is often very difficult to give the same test to the same sample twice. A way to alleviate this problem is to try out the question on a smaller but similar practice sample to that to be used in the study—here it may be possible to test-retest. Another problem is memory: people may remember their answers on the first occasion and answer the same way the second time to be consistent. This can artificially inflate the apparent reliability of the question.

3   *Increasing reliability:* The best way to create reliable indicators is to use multiple-item indicators: they are more reliable and we have easier methods of assessing their reliability (see Chapter 15). But for many issues it is appropriate only to ask a single question. There is little point in asking how old someone is, or asking their sex in six different ways. The best course is to use well-tested questions from reputable questionnaires.

Other methods of improving reliability involve careful question wording, interviewer training and working out methods of coding. It is wise to avoid questions about which people are unlikely to have an opinion or knowledge, or at least to provide 'do not know' or 'cannot decide' responses.

Validity

A valid measure is one which measures what it is intended to measure. In fact, it is not the measure that is valid or invalid but the use to which the measure is put. We might use educational level to measure social status. The issue is not whether we have measured education properly but whether this is a suitable measure of social status. The validity of a measure then depends on how we have defined the concept it is designed to measure. There are three basic ways in which to assess validity. Ultimately none of them is entirely satisfactory but they are the best we have.

1   *Criterion validity:* Using this approach we would compare how people answered our new questions to measure a concept, with existing, well-accepted measures of the concept. If people's answers on both the new and the established measure are highly correlated this is taken to mean the new measure is valid.

   There are two problems with this approach. Firstly we must assume the validity of the established measure. A low correlation between the new and existing measure is interpreted as meaning the new measure is invalid. But it could be the old one that is invalid. Often we will be developing a new measure because we are unhapppy with the existing measure. So to validate the new test by using the old one seems self-defeating. Secondly, for many concepts in social sciences there will not be existing well-established measures against which to check our new measure.

   A related approach is to give our measure to criterion groups. Thus a new measure of political conservatism might be given to members of conservative and radical political groups. If the members of the conservative group come out as conservative on the measure and the radical group members come out as radical, this provides good evidence for the measure's validity. Unfortunately, for many concepts criterion groups are not available.

2   *Content validity:* This approach to evaluating validity emphasises the extent to which the indicators measure the different aspects of the concept. A test of arithmetic skills which deals only with subtraction and does not measure ability at multiplication, addition or division lacks content validity. The test may be a fine test of abilities at subtraction and would be a valid measure of this but would not be a valid test of arithmetical skills. The validity of a test depends on the use to which it is put and not on the test *per se*. Whether we agree that a measure has content validity depends ultimately on how we define the concept it is designed to test. Given the disagreement about the 'content' of many social science concepts it is difficult to develop measures which have agreed on validity. Ultimately the content validity of a measure must be tied to the nominal definition of the concept we are using.

3   *Construct validity:* This approach evaluates a measure by how well the measure conforms with theoretical expectations. Suppose we

have developed a new measure of alienation and we wish to evaluate it. First we might say on the basis of theory that class will be related to alienation: the lower the class the higher the alienation. We administer the alienation questions to people and also determine their class. If our evidence shows that using this test the lower the class the higher the alienation we might say the new measure has construct validity. This approach may be all right if the theory we use is well established but it is open to two dangers. First, if using the new measure, the theoretical proposition is not supported, how do we know whether it is our new measure that is invalid: the theory may be wrong or the measure of the other concept (class) may be invalid. Second, we must avoid developing a test so that it supports the theory. If we use a theory to validate our measure and then use the (valid!) measure to test the theory we have established nothing.

In the end there is no ideal way of determining the validity of a measure. The method chosen will depend on the situation. If a good criterion exists use it; if the definition of the concept is well defined or well accepted use this approach; if there are well-established theories which use the concept which we wish to validate, use this approach. If all else fails we have to say this is how the concept is defined and these measures, on the face of it, seem to cover the concept, and to give the measure to other people (referred to as a panel of judges) to see what they think.

The problem of meaning

One of the problems in developing valid indicators is interpreting the meaning of people's responses. The same behaviour may mean different things or indicate different things for different people (see pages 13–16). Whilst it is difficult to eliminate this problem with any research technique, there are steps that can be taken to help alleviate it. For an excellent discussion of this issue see Marsh (1982).

One approach is to use a variety of methods of data collection. In particular, observation and in-depth interviewing can give the researcher insight into the meaning of behaviour and attitudes expressed in questionnaires. This can help in more intelligent interpretations of the patterns discovered in the analysis of questionnaire data.

The pattern of people's responses also can help us understand the meaning of particular responses. For example, we will interpret the meaning of regular church attendance differently for the person who also prays regularly and expresses agreement with religious doctrines than for the regular attender who does neither of these things. In other words we can use other information to help put the response to a particular question in context.

We also can be more direct and ask people why they behave in a particular way or why they express a particular attitude. While people are not always aware of the reasons, answers to these why questions can provide valuable insights (see Marsh, 1982:104–11).

None of these approaches resolves the problem of accurately finding the meaning particular behaviours and attitudes have for particular people. It is important to be aware of the problem and to take what steps are available to minimise it. An awareness of the problem should encourage survey researchers to be more thorough in the way data are analysed and be more sensitive in the way results are interpreted. It also should cause survey researchers to supplement their questionnaire studies with more in-depth data collection techniques.

Summary

This outline of developing indicators for concepts is not meant to make the process sound fixed and formal. While it is crucial to define concepts and develop indicators before collecting data, in practice it does not end there. During analysis we will often find that we need to refine the concepts more, or that the several dimensions we have measured are no longer useful. Despite pilot testing there may still be reliability and validity problems with some indicators and they may have to be dropped. A carefully developed scale may not 'work' with the sample and may have to be modified. We may have had multiple indicators of the one concept and the process of analysis may help us decide which ones are the most meaningful (this is not defined as simply finding the ones which support the theory). We may have developed indicators for different definitions of a concept and during the analysis we will need to work out which definition and which set of indicators are of most help in making sense of the data.

The crucial point is that although we must develop indicators before collecting data there is still flexibility in which ones are used and in how the concepts are finally defined. The development and use of both concepts and indicators is a process: it begins before data collection and continues during analysis. It is often not till we write up the research and try to make sense of the results that we find out how we should have done it.

Further reading

Often the problems of developing indicators for concepts are reduced to discussions of reliability and validity. For a thorough and clear discussion of issues involved in assessing reliability and validity see Carmines and Zeller's paper 'Reliability and Validity Assessment' (1979). They provide a more advanced and statistical treatment of these measurement issues in Zeller and Carmines, *Measurement in the Social Sciences* (1980). For a less statistical approach to issues of measurement Bateson's *Data Construction in Social Surveys* (1984) provides an excellent and sophisticated discussion of data construction and develops a theory of this process. Classic papers on the translation of concepts into indicators are in the edited collection by Lazarsfeld and Rosenberg, *The Language of Social Research* (1955) and their *Continuities in the Language of Social Research* (1972). Some useful examples are provided by Hirschi and Selvin in *Delinquency Research: an appraisal of analytic methods* (1967) Chapter 11 and in Glock and Stark's, *Religion and Society in Tension* (1965) Chapter 2. Berger provides a useful discussion on the nature of definitions in his paper 'Some second thoughts on substantive definitions of religion' (1974) and Babbie's discussion on the nature of concepts in *The Practice of Social Research* (1983) Chapter 5 is of interest.

5 Finding a sample

One way of finding out about a group of people is to collect information from everyone in the group. For large groups of people this is prohibitively expensive and impractical. The alternative is to collect information from only some people in the group in such a way that their responses and characteristics reflect those of the group from which they are drawn. This procedure is much cheaper, faster and easier than surveying all members of a group. This is the principle of sampling.

Before outlining techniques of sampling it is worth introducing a few technical terms. A *census* is obtained by collecting information about each member of a group. All the members of a group are called a *population*. A *sample* is obtained by collecting information about only some members of the population. Samples can reflect the populations from which they are drawn with varying degrees of accuracy. A sample which accurately reflects its population is called a *representative* sample.

To ensure that a sample is representative of the population it is crucial that certain types of people in the population are not systematically excluded from the sample. If we tried to obtain a sample of a suburb by going around during the day and knocking on every twentieth door we would be systematically under-representing those types of people who are not at home during the day (e.g. men, dual career families, single parent families). Such a sample is *biased* and without making suitable statistical adjustments during analysis it cannot be used to generalise to the population.

There are two broad types of samples: *probability* and *non-probability*. A probability sample is one in which each person in the population has an equal, or at least a known, chance (probability) of being selected while in a non-probability sample some people have a greater, but unknown, chance than others of selection. The surest way of providing equal probability of selection is to use the principle of random selection. This involves listing all members of the population (this list is called a *sampling frame*) and then, in effect, 'pulling their names out of a hat'.

It is unlikely, however, that the sample will be perfectly representative. By chance alone there will be differences between the sample and the population. These differences are due partly to *sampling error*. The important thing is that the characteristics of most randomly selected samples will be close to those of the population. For example, if just before the next national election 53 per cent intend to vote for the Labor Party then most samples will come up with estimates close to this figure. Since most random samples produce estimates close to the true population figure we can use probability theory to help estimate how close the true population figure is likely to be to the figure obtained in the sample (called a sample estimate). A statistic called *standard error* is used for this purpose (see the discussion on sample size in this chapter and the last section of Chapter 9).

Probability samples are preferable because they are the more likely to produce representative samples and enable estimates of the sample's accuracy. Most of this chapter will deal with probability sampling: types, required size, minimising cost and dealing with non-response. The final section considers the role of non-probability sampling.

Types of probability sample

There are four main types of probability sample. The choice between these depends on the nature of the research problem, the availability of good sampling frames, money, the desired level of accuracy in the sample and the method by which data are to be collected.

Simple random sampling (SRS)

There are five steps in selecting an SRS.

1 Obtain a complete sampling frame.
2 Give each case a unique number starting at one.
3 Decide on the required sample size.
4 Select that many numbers from a table of random numbers (see Table 5.1).
5 Select the cases which correspond to the randomly chosen numbers.

The process can be illustrated with a detailed example. Figure 5.1 provides a complete sampling frame for a population of 50 people

Figure 5.1   A sampling frame illustrating samples drawn with SRS and systematic sampling

SRS	Systematic sample	Name	SRS	Systematic sample	Name
1	1	Adams, H.	26	26	Mand, R.
2	2	Anderson, J.	㉗	27	McIlraith, W.
3	③	Baker, E.	28	㉘	Natoli, P.
4	4	Bradsley, W.	29	29	Newman, L.
5	5	Bradley, P.	30	30	Ooi, W.L.
6	6	Carra, A.	31	31	Oppenheim, F.
7	7	Cidoni, G.	㉜	32	Peters, P.
8	⑧	Daperis, D.	33	㉝	Palmer, T.
9	9	Devlin, B.	㉞	34	Quick, B.
10	10	Eastside, R.	35	35	Quinn, J.
11	11	Einhorn, B.	36	36	Reddan, R.
12	12	Falconer, T.	㊲	37	Risteski, B.
13	⑬	Felton, B.	㊳	㊳	Sawers, R.
14	14	Garratt, S.	39	39	Saunders, M.
15	15	Gelder, H.	40	40	Tarrant, A.
16	16	Hamilton, I.D.	41	41	Thomas, G.
17	17	Hartnell, W.	42	42	Uttay, E.
18	⑱	Iulianetti, G.	43	㊸	Usher, V.
19	19	Ivono, V.	44	44	Varley, E.
⑳	20	Jabornik, T.	45	45	Van Hoffman, P.
㉑	21	Jacobs, B.	㊻	46	Walters, J.
22	22	Kennedy, G.	47	47	West, W.
23	㉓	Kassem, S.	48	㊽	Yates, R.
24	24	Ladd, F.	49	49	Wyatt, R.
㉕	25	Lamb, A.	㊿	50	Zappulla, T.

and each person has been given a number between 1 and 50. To draw a sample of ten people we select ten numbers from the table of random numbers. Since the highest identifying number on the sampling frame is a two-digit number (50) we select 10 two-digit numbers from the random number table. In Table 5.1 all numbers are five digits. To select only two-digit numbers simply decide on any two digits (e.g. first two or last two) and stick to this for the rest of the procedure. Then decide where in the table to start from by randomly designating a column and row—e.g. column 1 row 2. This gives us 20749. Assume we have decided to use the first two digits to create

Table 5.1 A table of random numbers

74605	60866	92941	77422	78308	08274	62099
20749	78470	94157	83266	37570	64827	94067
88790	79927	48135	46293	05045	70393	80915
64819	73967	78907	50940	98146	80637	50917
55938	78790	04999	32561	92128	83403	79930
66853	39017	82843	26227	25992	69154	38341
46795	21210	43252	51451	47196	27978	49499
95601	36457	34237	98554	46178	44991	43672
98721	44506	37586	67256	88094	51860	43008
61307	12947	43383	34450	62108	05047	15614
37788	01097	15010	97811	27372	81994	60457
36186	66118	90122	45603	94045	66611	69202
96730	13663	14383	51162	50110	16597	62122
98831	31066	21529	01102	28209	07621	56004
35450	24410	88935	84471	46076	60416	10007
92031	42334	27224	09790	59181	66958	91967
02863	16678	45335	72783	50096	52581	15214
80360	89628	47863	21217	62797	11285	42938
58193	16045	72021	93498	99120	36542	41087
66048	95648	94960	58294	07984	87321	23919
64013	08546	27779	23500	95216	02657	00507
16954	81754	99033	52841	70010	36264	00456
54678	59531	48092	54160	11913	16121	90023
42645	98295	26669	82199	81890	63100	62017
66160	44633	73068	55216	61896	83069	05327
20647	01061	18227	20195	38221	05767	63331
30807	93837	42210	81908	41729	86416	04579
51949	41361	35632	06696	57875	97196	73625
82283	46591	43057	01390	60051	13297	11149
49497	00053	78513	54381	88898	03418	06810
78519	88085	94119	19122	86546	47939	14878
13027	42777	93563	91253	81867	70344	44417
04734	27419	72065	23390	13789	85943	00374
78999	63470	24174	50695	53931	85452	02490
51891	19873	53220	27585	38457	46553	76585
64929	13632	66676	99334	75326	69810	43893
30319	67589	00013	23301	37314	22905	13887
13761	05561	10013	89946	57017	45797	50868
79180	44011	38067	99802	53490	18590	18818
85304	85681	87825	46262	84748	94568	56604

the two-digit number. This means we will select person 20 (T. Jabornik) for our sample.

We then need to select the other numbers by deciding on a pattern of movement through the table and sticking to it. We might decide to move across the table selecting numbers from every second column and every row. In the first selected row, our method of movement means that we end up in the last column of that row. Because we are selecting from every second column, this means that on the next row we would look at the second column for an eligible number (i.e. we have skipped a column from the last selection). We would then look at the fourth and sixth columns. Using the same principle of skipping every second column, we would select from the first, third, fifth and seventh columns of the third selected row. If a number comes up twice, or a number is selected which is larger than our population number, we simply ignore it and keep moving through the table according to the fixed pattern. In this case we would select the following numbers: 20, 37, 46, 50, 32, 25, 38, 21, 27, 34. The sample would then consist of people who corresponded to those numbers.

One of the problems of SRS is that it requires a good sampling frame. While these may be available for some populations (e.g. organisations such as schools, churches, unions), adequate lists are often not available for larger population surveys of a city, state or country. In addition, where a population comes from a large area as in national surveys and where data are to be collected by personal interviews the cost of SRS is prohibitive. It would probably involve interviewers travelling long distances just for one interview. To survey a large area it is best to use either another sampling strategy (see the outline of multistage cluster sampling), or another method of collecting the data such as mail questionnaires or telephone surveys. In other words SRS is most appropriate when a good sampling frame exists and when the population is geographically concentrated or the data collection technique does not involve travelling.

Systematic sampling

Systematic sampling is similar to SRS and has the same limitations except that it is simpler. To obtain a systematic sample work out a sampling fraction by dividing the population size by the required sample size. For a population of 50 and a sample of 10 the sampling fraction is ⅕: we will select one person for every five in the population.

Given a sampling fraction of ⅕ we simply select every fifth person from the sampling frame. The only problem is working out where to start. Since the sampling fraction is ⅕ the starting point must be somewhere within the first five people on the list. To decide where precisely, select a number from a table of random numbers as described previously. If the starting point was person three we would then select every fifth person after this (see Figure 5.1). This is called a random start.

Figure 5.2   The effect of periodicity

1	2	3	4	5	6	7	8	9	10	11	12	13	14
(H)	W	H	W	(H)	W	H	W	(H)	W	H	W	(H)	W

Notes:	Random start at 1		H = husband
	Sampling fraction ¼		W = wife
	Circled cases selected		

Apart from the problems systematic samples share with SRS they can encounter an additional one: periodicity of sampling frames. That is, a certain type of person may reoccur at regular intervals within the sampling frame. If the sampling fraction is such that it matches this interval, the sample will include only certain types of people and systematically exclude others. We might have a list of married couples arranged so that every husband's name is followed by his wife's name. If a sampling fraction of four was used (or any even number in this case) the sample would be all of the same sex (Figure 5.2).

If there is periodicity in the sampling frame then either mix up the cases or use SRS.

Stratified sampling

Stratified sampling is a modification of SRS and systematic sampling designed to produce more representative and thus more accurate samples, but this comes at the cost of a more complicated procedure. On the whole it has similar limitations to these methods. To be representative the proportions of various groups in a sample should be the same as in the population. Because of chance (sampling error) this will not always occur. For example, we might get too many middle-class people, or too many young people. Sometimes this may not matter, but if the characteristic on which the sample is unrepresentative is related to the focus of the study then we will get distortions. For example, in a study on voting behaviour a sample in which young people are under-represented would produce misleading overall figures about voting intention because young people tend to vote differently to older people.

Stratified sampling helps avoid this problem. To use this method we need to select the relevant stratifying variable(s) first. A stratifying variable is the characteristic on which we want to ensure correct representation in the sample. Having selected this variable we will order the sampling frame into groups according to the category (or strata) of the stratifying variable and then use systematic sampling to select the appropriate proportion of people within each strata. For example, we may wish to survey the student population of a college or university to determine attitudes towards a national student union. We might stratify by faculty of enrolment to ensure proper proportions from each faculty. To do this we need to know the faculty of each student and then order the sampling frame so that students from the same faculty are grouped together. Then draw a systematic sample. We might use a sampling fraction of $\frac{1}{20}$ and select every twentieth person after a random start. Since people from the same faculty are grouped this means we will select every twentieth person within each group, thus ensuring the correct proportions from each faculty in the final sample. This is illustrated in Table 5.2. Imagine a sampling frame in which the names of the 500 agriculture students come first, then the 3000 arts students and so forth. By using the $\frac{1}{20}$ sampling fraction we would obtain the numbers from each faculty as indicated in the second last column of the table. Notice that the sample and population proportions from each faculty are identical.

More complex stratification could be employed by stratifying for several characteristics such as faculty, year of course and courseload simultaneously. To do this we would first group the sampling frame into faculties, then within each faculty group people into year levels (1st, 2nd, 3rd, 4th) and within each year level group people separately according to whether they are part-time or full-time students. Once the sampling frame has been so grouped simply use normal systematic sampling. The secret of stratified sampling is the way people are organised in the sampling frame.

Some sampling frames automatically stratify at least roughly. An alphabetically arranged list will guarantee that people whose names begin with X and Z are sampled in their correct proportion. Membership lists in which people are ordered according to length of

Table 5.2   An illustration of stratified sampling

Faculty	Population N	%		Sample fraction = $\frac{1}{20}$		Sample N	%
Agriculture	500	5	→	Pop N ÷ sample fraction	→	25	5
Arts	3000	30				150	30
Science	2000	20				100	20
Medicine	500	5				25	5
Engineering	700	7				35	7
Commerce	1600	16				80	16
Law	700	7				35	7
Education	1000	10				50	10
N	10 000					500	

membership would automatically stratify for this. Staff lists of organisations may be ordered in terms of seniority or employment category. Unless this ordering produces a periodicity problem do *not* mix up the list unless you want to stratify for something else. Ordered lists will normally produce better samples than unordered ones. The main difficulty of stratifying samples, apart from those shared with SRS and systematic sampling, is that information on the stratifying variable is often unavailable.

The problem with all the sampling techniques considered so far is that they are of limited use on their own when sampling a geographically dispersed population with whom we want to conduct face-to-face interviews. They are also of no direct help when drawing a sample in which no sampling frame is available. When conducting large area surveys (e.g. national or even city wide) both these problems exist. Multistage cluster sampling is an attempt to overcome these difficulties.

Multistage cluster sampling

This technique of obtaining a final sample really involves drawing several different samples (hence its name) and does so in such a way that the cost of final interviewing is minimised.

The basic procedure is first to draw a sample of *areas*. Initially, large areas are selected and then progressively smaller areas within the larger ones are sampled. Eventually we end up with a sample of households and use a method of selecting individuals from the selected households.

It is possible to divide a large city into a number of districts (e.g. electorates, census districts). This list of districts is a sampling frame of districts and a sample of districts is selected using SRS (see Figure 5.3). Since everyone lives in a district, everyone has an equal chance of being selected in the final sample. Next divide each of the selected districts into blocks, using an up-to-date street directory or census maps, and then select a sample of blocks within each chosen district. Having selected blocks we need to draw up a list of all the households on each block (enumerate) and then draw a random sample of households within each block. To select people to interview within households we can use the grid method described below. The result of this method of sampling is that interviews will be geographically clustered thus minimising travelling costs (see Figure 5.3).

How are individuals selected from the chosen households? One widely used method designed to avoid bias is to use a procedure developed by Kish (1949). Once households have been selected they are numbered systematically from 1 to 12. When interviewers arrive

Figure 5.3   Steps in multistage cluster sampling

Stage one

1	2	3	4	5	6	7	8	9	10
11	12	13	14	15	16	17	18	19	20
21	22	23	24	25	26	27	28	29	30
31	32	33	34	35	36	37	38	39	40

41	42	43
44	45	46

Divide city up into districts and select a sample (shaded areas selected)

Stage two

1	2	3	4	5	6
7	8	9	10	11	12
13	14	15	16	17	18
19	20	21	22	23	24

High Street

North Road

Deep Street

New Road

Old Street

Ruda Street — Penlyne Avenue — Trinian Street — Bachus Road — Moss Avenue — Sainsbury Avenue — Box Road

Divide district into blocks and select a sample within each selected district (shaded blocks selected)

Stage three

1.	1 Box Road	13.	67 Sainsbury Avenue
2.	3 Box Road	14.	65 Sainsbury Avenue
3.	5 Box Road	15.	63 Sainsbury Avenue
4.	7 Box Road	16.	61 Sainsbury Avenue
5.	9 Box Road	17.	59 Sainsbury Avenue
6.	11 Box Road	18.	57 Sainsbury Avenue
7.	52 Old Street	19.	12 New Road
8.	50 Old Street	20.	10 New Road
9.	48 Old Street	21.	8 New Road
10.	46 Old Street	22.	6 New Road
11.	44 Old Street	23.	4 New Road
12.	42 Old Street	24.	2 New Road

In each selected block list each household and randomly select households (circled)

Stage four
List names in each selected household and use selection grid to select a person

Table 5.3 **Grid for selecting individuals in multistage sampling**

Assigned number of address	Total number of eligible persons					
	1	2	3	4	5	6 or more
1 or 2	1	1	2	2	3	3
3	1	2	3	3	3	5
4 or 5	1	2	3	4	5	6
6	1	1	1	1	2	2
7 or 8	1	1	1	1	1	1
9	1	2	3	4	5	5
10 or 11	1	2	2	3	4	4
12	1	1	1	2	2	2

Source: Hoinville et al., 1977:82

at a particular house they make a list of all people in the household who fit the requirements of the sample. The list is arranged so that all males are listed first from eldest to youngest, then females in the same way. Then using the grid (Table 5.3) they select a particular person based on the number assigned to that household (between 1 and 12) and the number of eligible people in the household. Thus in a household assigned number nine in which there were four eligible people the fourth person would be interviewed.

An important issue in multistage sampling is how many clusters (whether they be districts, blocks or households) to sample at each stage. Given a set final sample size there will be a direct tradeoff between the number of clusters selected and the number of units subsequently chosen within it. Thus if only one district is selected we could sample virtually every block in it, or if only a few blocks were chosen in total we could sample almost everyone in them. On the other hand, if we have a lot of clusters we can finally select only relatively few individuals within each cluster. Otherwise the final sample size will be too large and thus too expensive.

The general principle is to maximise the number of initial clusters chosen and consequently only select relatively few individuals or units within each cluster. The reason for this is that it is important that different districts are included. If only one or two were selected (e.g. two upper-middle-class suburbs) we could end up with a very unrepresentative sample. By maximising the chance for variety initially, we increase the chance of maintaining representativeness at later stages. The problem is that as the number of clusters chosen initally increases so do the travelling costs later on. In the end a compromise between cost and sampling error has to be made.

One way of minimising the effect of reducing clusters on representativeness is to use stratification techniques. Thus, when selecting districts, put them into various strata (e.g. status, prices, density, age composition, etc.) and then randomly select districts within the strata. The same principle can apply when selecting blocks.

Another problem with sampling areas is that the number of households in various districts or blocks will differ. This could easily lead to missing blocks in which there is a large number of a particular type of household. For example, we might survey a city and miss out on all the blocks with high-rise government housing. This would clearly lead to an unrepresentative sample. This danger is reduced by maximising the number of districts sampled and by using stratifying procedures. Another approach is to use a modified version of multistage cluster sampling known as probability proportionate to size (PPS) sampling (Kish, 1965:217–246). It is unnecessary to go into this in detail here but it operates so that the probability of a block being chosen depends on how many households are in it. Thus a block with four times as many households as another has four times the chance of being selected. To avoid biasing the final sample the same number of people are chosen from each block. Thus the block with 100 households has four times the chance of being chosen than a block with only 25 households. But since, say, only five households are chosen in each block, regardless of size, the higher probability of a large block being chosen is compensated for by the lower probability of a particular household on that block being chosen. The point of PPS sampling is simply to ensure proper representation of densely populated blocks.

The principles of multistage cluster sampling can be applied to other contexts where there are no easily available sampling frames. For example, a survey of members of a national organisation such as a church or union might start by sampling areas of the country, then districts within each area. Within each district a list of branches (comparable to blocks) could be compiled and sampled. For each selected branch, membership lists could be obtained and a sample drawn from these.

Sample size

The required sample size depends on two key factors: the degree of accuracy we require for the sample and the extent to which there is variation in the population in regard to the key characteristics of the study.

We need to decide how much error we are prepared to tolerate. In

Table 5.4   Sample sizes required for various sampling errors at 95% confidence level (simple random sampling)

Sampling error[a] %	Sample size[b]	Sampling error	Sample size
1.0	10 000	5.5	330
1.5	4 500	6.0	277
2.0	2 500	6.5	237
2.5	1 600	7.0	204
3.0	1 100	7.5	178
3.5	816	8.0	156
4.0	625	8.5	138
4.5	494	9.0	123
5.0	400	9.5	110
		10	100

Notes: a   This is in fact two standard errors (see page 117).
         b   This assumes a 50/50 split on the variable. These sample sizes would be smaller for more homogeneous samples (see Table 5.6).

Table 5.4 the sample sizes required to obtain samples of varying degrees of accuracy are listed. The figures in this table are calculated so that we can be 95 per cent confident that the results in the population will be the same as in the sample plus or minus the sampling error. Thus if in a sample of 2500 cases we found that 53 per cent intended to vote for the Labour Party, we can be 95 per cent confident that 53 per cent plus or minus 2 per cent (i.e. between 51 and 55 per cent) of the population intends to vote Labour.

There are several things to note about the relationship between sample size and accuracy. First, when dealing with small samples a small increase in sample size can lead to a substantial increase in accuracy. Thus increasing the sample from 100 to 156 reduces sampling error from 10 per cent to 8 per cent. With larger samples, increasing the sample does not have the same payoff. To reduce sampling error from 2.5 per cent to 2 per cent we need to increase the sample by 900 cases. The rule is that to halve the sampling error we have to quadruple the sample size. Beyond a certain point the cost of increasing the sample size is not worth it in terms of the extra precision. Many survey companies limit their samples to 2000 since beyond this point the extra cost has insufficient payoff in terms of accuracy.

Second, the size of the population from which we draw the sample is largely irrelevant for the accuracy of the sample. It is the absolute size of the sample that is important. The only exception to this is when the sample size represents a sizable proportion of the popu-

Table 5.5   Required sample sizes depending on population homogeneity and desired accuracy

Acceptable sampling error[a]	Per cent of population expected to give particular answer					
	5 or 95	10 or 90	20 or 80	30 or 70	40 or 60	50/50
1%	1 900	3 600	6 400	8 400	9 600	10 000
2%	479	900	1 600	2 100	2 400	2 500
3%	211	400	711	933	1 066	1 100
4%	119	225	400	525	600	625
5%	76	144	256	336	370	400
6%	—[b]	100	178	233	267	277
7%	—	73	131	171	192	204
8%	—	—	100	131	150	156
9%	—	—	79	104	117	123
10%	—	—	—	84	96	100

Notes: a   At the 95 per cent level of confidence
b   Samples smaller than this would normally be too small to allow meaningful analysis

lation (e.g. 10 per cent). In such cases a slightly smaller sample is equally accurate (see Moser and Kalton, 1971:147 for the formula to make the adjustments).

The third point is that the figures in Table 5.5 assume a heterogeneous population. For a population in which most people will answer a question in a particular way or very few answer in a particular way, a smaller sample will do. Thus for a study on voting, a population where 50 per cent intend voting Labour and 50 per cent for other parties (a 50/50 split) would require a larger sample than one where 80 per cent (or only 20 per cent) intended to vote Labour. Table 5.5 lists the required sample sizes depending on the degree of accuracy required and the estimated population variation for the key study variables.

There are difficulties in applying these techniques to determine sample size. Apart from requiring that we can specify the degree of precision needed, we must also have a rough idea how people are going to answer the question (i.e. we must have an idea of the split). The problems with this are twofold—we often do *not* have this information, and surveys often have more than one purpose. On one key variable of interest there may be an anticipated split of 80/20 but on another it may be closer to 50/50. For such multipurpose surveys it seems best to play safe and determine size on the basis of the variables on which there is likely to be greatest diversity within the sample.

The other problem is that often we wish to analyse subgroups separately, to look, for example, at the voting intentions of different age groups. We might have an overall sample of 2000 (sampling error is 2.2 per cent at 95 per cent confidence) but for those 18 to 30 years old there might be only 400 people. This means that the figures for this subgroup are subject to a sampling error of +5 per cent.

This brings us to a final point. Despite all the figures in the tables we should think ahead to how we intend to analyse the results. In practice a key determinant of sample size is the need to look separately at different subgroups. Make sure that the sample is sufficiently large so that when it is broken down into separate subgroups (e.g. age, class, sex) there will be sufficient numbers in each. As a rule of thumb try to ensure that the smallest subgroup has at least 50 to 100 cases (Hoinville et al., 1977:61).

Of course desired accuracy is not the only factor in working out the sample size: cost and time are also key factors. The final sample size will be a compromise between cost, accuracy and ensuring sufficient numbers for meaningful subgroup analysis.

Non-response

For a variety of reasons people selected in a sample may not finally be included. Some will refuse, others will be uncontactable and others will be uninterviewable. Non-response can create two main problems: unacceptable reduction of sample size and bias. The problem of sample size can be tackled in two ways. First, employ techniques designed to reduce non-response. These include paying attention to methods of collecting data, careful training of interviewers (Hoinville et al., 1977), use of interpreters, calling back at several different times of the day and week. Second, we can draw an initial sample that is larger than needed. Assuming good techniques we will still get about 20 per cent non-response, so we might draw an initial sample that is 20 per cent larger than we expect to end up with.

This, however, does nothing to avoid the problem of bias. Often non-responders are different in crucial respects to responders (e.g. older, lower education, migrant background) and increasing the sample size does nothing to produce the correct proportions of various groups if some types systematically do not respond. The difficulty is not so much the bias itself, since there are statistical techniques for minimising its influence in the analysis (see page 299), but in working out what the bias is and to what extent it occurs. Once this is known, suitable allowances can be made (Smith, 1989). There are three main ways of obtaining information to enable adjustments for bias.

First, use what observable information can be picked up about non-responders. Where contact is made but people refuse to participate, information about sex, age, ethnic background can be gleaned. A person's house, car and suburb can provide additional clues.

Second, some sampling frames can provide useful information. For example, if official records provided the sampling frame for members of an organisation, we could identify characteristics of the non-responders by using information in the records such as sex and age; depending on the organisation we might learn about income, education and so forth.

Third, if characteristics of the population from which the sample is drawn are known we can simply compare the characteristics obtained in the sample with those of the population. Any differences indicate the areas of bias and the extent of the differences indicates the degree of bias. With this information adjustments can be made during analysis to neutralise the effect of non-response bias.

Secondary analysis

For many of us it is extremely difficult to obtain samples that are sufficiently large and representative to allow adequate analysis: we do not have the time, money or expertise to obtain a really good sample. This problem is compounded when we need data for a whole nation rather than a local area, when we need to collect data over a period of time for a longitudinal study or when data are required from different countries to allow comparative analysis. All too often the 'solution' is either to abandon the project or to collect a very inadequate sample (too small and unrepresentative) and retreat to the position that the study is only exploratory.

But in many cases there is an alternative: data collected by other people or agencies can often be appropriately used to address the research question at hand. This is called *secondary analysis*. Major research is conducted by government agencies (e.g. census offices), large research organisations and well established research teams which have excellent samples and often include data about a wide range of attitudes, behaviours and personal attributes which make them suitable for research projects well beyond the purposes envisaged in the initial survey. It is becoming conventional (and is often a requirement of publicly funded projects) that, with appropriate safeguards to guarantee anonymity, data are deposited in a publicly accessible data archive once the primary researchers have completed their analyses. The resultant data sets are available for purchase at extremely low prices.

There are a number of well established, general-purpose data sets. The obvious example is data collected in the regular census. In some countries, such as Australia, a 1 per cent sample of the census data is made available to researchers, thus providing a large data set and an excellent probability sample that can be used to examine a wide range of important questions. Not only does this provide data about the general population, but it yields a sufficient number of people from minority groups well beyond that available from the typical national survey to allow analysis of groups that would otherwise be neglected. Of course, such analysis is limited to information provided by the questions asked in the census, but these data nevertheless are highly relevant to a wide range of social research questions. Government departments also regularly conduct other surveys on topics such as household expenditure, employment, health, family structure and the like. These surveys typically have at least 2000 respondents and employ probability sampling techniques and provide national data.

In Australia, Britain, Europe and the United States there are well established, regularly conducted, general-purpose national surveys that use probability samples designed to cover a wide range of topics. Surveys are regularly conducted around election times to obtain views about candidates, but a great deal of other information about attitudes, behaviour and attributes is also collected. Similar questions are asked from one election to another, thus providing data about *changes over time*. The Eurobarometer survey which provides data for a large number of European countries is conducted regularly and provides excellent data on a wide range of issues, thus allowing for both comparative and longitudinal analyses. In most years since 1972 the General Social Science Survey has been conducted in the United States providing very good longitudinal and nationally representative data on many topics over a period of time. In Australia the National Social Science Survey provides a similar function. In the mid 1980s the Values Studies Survey Group co-ordinated a worldwide series of nationally representative surveys to provide a unique set of data from over 25 countries on the same attitudes to enable productive comparative analyses. Other more specialised surveys are regularly conducted and the data for these are deposited in data archives. Typically the data are made available to secondary users on magnetic computer tape together with a copy of the original questionnaire and details about how questions were coded.

By purchasing these data the whole questionnaire construction, administration and sampling phase is bypassed. Because of the greater speed, minimal cost and superior samples, the analysis of secondary data opens up the field of survey research to a much wider range of people than would otherwise be the case. These data sets provide an ideal opportunity for graduate students and academic social scientists who rarely have access to either the time or funds to obtain adequate samples and also mean that the data collected by others are more thoroughly analysed than they might otherwise be. Without access to these types of data sets, both comparative and longitudinal analysis would be virtually impossible.

Even where data sets are not available from data archives they can sometimes be constructed by the researcher from published data. Government Year Books and other publications provide an ideal source of longitudinal and possibly comparative data. Each year statistics are published on a wide range of matters including social welfare, crime, income, education, migration and the like. The data are provided in aggregate form for a state or country for that year and are not appropriate for analyses in which the individual is the unit of analysis. But where a country, year or region can appropriately be used as the unit of analysis (page 32) data sets can be constructed where the aggregate figures provided become the value for the variable for that unit. For example, crime statistics, social welfare expenditure, unemployment levels and so on are published each year. Using year as the unit of analysis, a number of variables can be created from these figures. Variables for a number of different types of crime could be created and the values for those variables would be the rate or number of those crimes for that year. Similarly, variables for the level and type of welfare expenditure could be created. A number of unemployment variables such as rate of youth unemployment, rate of unemployment amongst 20–year-olds and the like could be created. The data for these variables would form a variable by case matrix (page 3) which would then provide a data set to enable systematic analysis (Figure 5.4).

Of course, there are disadvantages to secondary analysis. The data sets that we need for our particular research problem may not be available. Often the questions that have been asked in the survey are not quite what we would have asked ourselves. Or in surveys conducted in different countries or in different years the question wording or the response categories may vary. There will undoubtedly be many situations in which secondary analysis does not provide a solution for the researcher. But with a little imagination, creativity, ingenuity and compromise it is often possible to obtain satisfactory measures for the concepts required in one's own research. At first sight certain variables might not be provided in the data set but often the building blocks of these variables are available which enable the researcher to create the required variables. (Dale et al., 1988). Typically there is the need to trade off between having less than ideal measures of the concepts on the one hand and having an unsuitable sample or not conducting the study at all on the other.

Figure 5.4 A data matrix

Variables	Years (Unit of analysis)								
	1950	1951	1952	1953	1954	...	1988	1989	1990 ...
N of homicides									
N of robberies									
N of assaults									
N of frauds									
N of rapes									
...									
...									
...									
$ spent on welfare									
Gross domestic product									
N unemployed									
% unemployed									
Population size									

Non-probability sampling

There are often situations where probability sampling techniques are either impractical or unnecessary. In such situations the much cheaper non-probability techniques are used. These techniques are appropriate when sampling frames are unavailable or the population so widely dispersed that cluster sampling would be too inefficient. For example, it would be very difficult to obtain a random sample of homosexuals or marijuana users. Any attempt to do so would either be so expensive that we would end up with a sample too small for meaningful analysis or the rate of dishonesty and refusal would produce such a bias that the sample would not be representative despite probability sampling methods.

In the preliminary stages of research, such as testing questionnaires, non-random samples are satisfactory. On occasions researchers are not concerned with generalising from a sample to the population and in such cases representativeness of the sample is less important. Instead they may be interested in developing scales (see Chapter 15) or in a tentative, hypothesis-generating, exploratory look at patterns. Some research is not all that interested in working out what proportion of the population gives a particular response but rather in obtaining an idea of the range of responses or ideas that people have. In such cases we would simply try to get a wide variety of people in the sample without being too concerned about whether each type was represented in its correct proportion.

Purposive sampling is a form of non-probability sampling where cases are judged as typical of some category of cases of interest to the researcher. They are not selected randomly. Thus a study of leaders of the conservation movement might, in the absence of a clearly defined sampling frame or population, select some typical leaders from a number of typical conservation groups. While not ensuring representativeness, such a method of selection can provide useful information.

Political polling often uses purposive sampling. Here districts within an electorate are chosen because their pattern has in the past provided a good idea of the outcome for the whole electorate. Or key electorates which generally reflect the national pattern (i.e. they are typical) are paid special attention. While not using probability sampling techniques, such a method can provide cheap and surprisingly efficient predictions.

Quota sampling is another common non-probability technique aimed at producing representative samples without random selection of cases. Interviewers are required to find cases with particular characteristics: they are given quotas of particular types of people to fill. The quotas are organised so that in terms of the quota characteristics the final sample will be representative. To develop quotas we decide on which characteristic we want to ensure that the final sample is representative of (e.g. age), find out the distribution of this variable in the population and set quotas accordingly. Thus if 20 per cent of the population is between 20 and 30 years old and the sample is to be 1000, then 200 of the sample (20 per cent) will be in this age group. If 20 people were doing the interviewing and each had identical quotas of 50, each interviewer would find ten people in this age group (20 per cent of 50). Quite complex quotas can be developed so that several characteristics (e.g. sex, age, marital status) are quotaed simultaneously. Thus an interviewer would be assigned a quota for unmarried females between 20 and 30 years, married females between 20 and 30 years and for each other combination of the three quota variables (see Moser and Kalton, 1971:129).

Quota techniques are non-random because interviewers can select any cases which fit certain criteria. This can lead to bias as interviewers will tend to select those who are easiest to interview and with whom they feel most comfortable (e.g. friends). Another difficulty is that accurate population proportions may be unavailable. Finally, since random sampling is not used, it is impossible to estimate the accuracy of any particular quota sample.

Availability samples are also common but must be used with caution and only for specific purposes, and are the least likely of any technique to produce representative samples. Using this approach anyone who will respond will do. Surveys where newspapers ask readers to complete and return questionnaires printed in the paper or TV stations conduct 'phone-in' polls are examples of such samples. While these techniques can produce quite large samples cheaply their size does not compensate for their unrepresentativeness. This type of sample can be useful for pilot testing questionnaries or exploratory research to obtain the range of views and develop typologies, but must not be used to make any claim to representing anything but the sample itself.

Summary

Sampling can provide an efficient and accurate way of obtaining information about large numbers of cases. Just how efficient and accurate depends on the type of sample used, the size of the sample and the method of collecting data from the sample. In the end the decisions about samples will be a compromise between cost, accuracy, the nature of the research problem and the art of the possible.

Further reading

Moser and Kalton provide a first rate introduction to the main issues of sampling in Chapters 4–7 of *Survey Methods in Social Investigation* (1971) and in Kalton (1983). A particularly good illustration of multi-stage sampling is given in Chapter 5 by Warwick and Lininger in *The Sample Survey: Theory and Practice* (1975). Lavrakas (1987) provides a clear discussion of the special issues involved in obtaining samples for telephone surveys. The definitive reference is Kish's *Survey Sampling* (1965). This provides a comprehensive discussion which ranges from the simple to complex mathematical issues. For a book that is a little more accessible read Sudman's *Applied Sampling* (1976) which deals with many practical problems, provides examples and is realistic. Hyman's book *Secondary Analysis of Sample Surveys* (1972) remains an excellent introduction to secondary analysis. Hakim's *Secondary Analysis in Social Research* (1982) provides an overview of the range of types of secondary data available in Britain together with the addresses of many data archives from which data are available. Information about American Data Sets and Archives as well as some of the technical issues involved in using secondary data is provided in Kiecolt and Nathan's *Secondary Analysis of Survey Data* (1985). Dale, Arber and Proctor offer a thorough discussion of the benefits and costs of secondary data and provide many practical pointers about how to evaluate and effectively use secondary data in *Doing Secondary Analysis* (1988).

6 Constructing questionnaires

In Chapter 1 it was argued that a number of techniques can be used to collect survey data: the important thing is to end up with a variable by case matrix (see Table 1.1). The data can be collected by observation, in-depth interviews, content analysis, questionnaire or by a range of other techniques (see Sommer and Sommer, 1980). The most widely used technique is the questionnaire. Questionnaires can be filled out by the respondent and returned to the researcher or administered by interviewers. The questionnaire is a highly structured data collection technique whereby each respondent is asked much the same set of questions. Because of this, questionnaires provide a very efficient way of creating a variable by case matrix for large samples but they are not the only method.

Since questionnaires are the most widely used survey data collection technique this chapter focuses on questionnaire design. Four aspects of questionnaire development are considered: selection of areas about which to question, construction of actual questions, evaluation of questions and the layout of a good questionnaire.

Selecting areas

Typically, when using questionnaires, it is difficult to go back to people to collect additional information we might later discover we need. Therefore it is crucial to think ahead and anticipate what information will be needed to ensure that the relevant questions are asked.

There are a number of ways of working out which questions to ask. First, the research problem will affect which concepts need to be measured (Chapter 3). Second, the indicators we devise for these concepts are crucial in determining which questions to ask (Chapter 4). Third, our hunches about the mechanisms by which variables are linked or about factors which might explain relationships will require that certain questions be included (Chapter 12). Fourth, the way data are to be analysed affects what information is needed: it is pointless collecting information which cannot be analysed and frustrating to discover that you do not have the necessary data for certain analysis. It is not possible to develop a questionnaire which can be analysed properly unless you first understand methods of analysis (see Chapters 9 to 13). Finally, the method by which the questionnaire is to be administered affects what type of questions can be asked. If it is administered by a trained interviewer more complex questions can be used since there is opportunity for clarification. Also, follow-up questions which draw on answers to earlier questions can be used. With self-administered questionnaires such as those sent out by post you need to concentrate on clarity and simplicity.

For explanatory research it is useful to think of four aspects of the questionnaire:

1 *Measures of the dependent variable(s):* Clarify what it is you are trying to explain (Chapters 2 and 3) and develop questions to measure this.
2 *Measures of the independent variable(s):* Make sure you have questions to tap each of the 'causal' variables.
3 *Measures of test variables:* These are variables which help clarify the nature of the links between independent and dependent variables (read Chapter 12 carefully).
4 *Background measures:* Questions about characteristics such as age, sex, religion, education, occupation, marital status, stage in the life cycle, ethnic group and so on are fairly routinely asked. This information helps us see whether patterns differ for various subgroups (see Chapters 12 and 16).

For descriptive research, questions will concentrate on the phenomenon we are trying to describe and on background characteristics.

In summary, the art of questionnaire design involves thinking ahead about the research problem, what the concepts mean and how we will analyse the data. The questionnaire should reflect both theoretical thinking and an understanding of data analysis.

Question content

It is helpful to distinguish between four distinct types of question content: behaviour, beliefs, attitudes and attributes (Dillman, 1978: 80). Imagine we were conducting a study on the topic of workforce participation of mothers of pre-school age children and we had a sample of mothers — some with young children, others with older children. Before we could formulate any questionnaire items we would need to be very clear about precisely what it is that we are interested in.

If we were interested in *behaviour* we would formulate questions to establish what people *do*. For example, we could ask whether the respondent is working or did work with a pre-school age child. Depending on the precise research question this can provide useful information. It can provide a map of which types of mothers work and which types do not and may help locate factors which facilitate or hinder workforce participation. But too often researchers try to use behavioural measures to extrapolate to beliefs and attitudes. This is open to real dangers of misinterpretation. Since people are neither very consistent nor rational and may not have the luxury of behaving as they might like, any conclusions we can draw about beliefs or attitudes from behaviour are very limited.

If we are interested in *beliefs* — in what people believe is *true or false* — we need to ask quite different types of question. For example, we might ask people for their estimate of the percentage of mothers with pre-school aged children who are in the paid labour force or ask about what they believe to be the effects of day care centres on the emotional development of pre-school age children. The focus of belief questions is on establishing what people think is true rather than on the accuracy of their beliefs.

Belief questions can be distinguished from those that aim to establish the respondent's *attitudes*. Whereas belief questions ascertain what the respondent thinks is true, attitude questions try to establish what they think is *desirable*. An attitudinal focus might ask about attitudes regarding whether or not mothers with pre-school age children ought to participate in the workforce.

Finally, *attribute* questions are designed to obtain information about the respondent's characteristics. Such questions would normally include information about their age, education, occupation, gender, ethnicity, marital status and so forth. For the study of workforce participation of mothers with pre-school age children we would be particularly interested in attributes such as the number of children, the age of the child, income, type of job, whether the job was full time or part time and other related information.

It is important to be clear about the precise type of information required for a number of reasons. First, the failure to adequately distinguish between these four types of information, which arises from a lack of clarity about the research question and inadequate conceptualisation, can lead to the collection of quite the wrong type of information. If we are interested in exploring people's actual behaviour, a set of questions that in fact taps beliefs or attitudes will be of little use. Second, we might be interested in all four types of information. An awareness of the four types of information that can be collected should lead to the systematic development of questions for each type rather than a haphazard set of questions on the broad topic which may or may not tap all types of data. Third, when it comes to analysis and the development of scales (Chapter 15), it is important to develop composite measures; however, these normally need to be composite measures of the same type of information. Attitude questions can be combined with other attitude questions to form an index of some sort or another but it would normally be quite inappropriate to combine the four types of information into a single measure: they tap quite different things.

Wording questions

Considerable attention must be given to developing clear, unambiguous and useful questions. To do this the wording of the questions is fundamental. The following checklist of fourteen questions will help in avoiding the most obvious problems with question wording.

1   *Is the language simple?* Avoid jargon and technical terms. Look for simple words without making questions sound condescending. Use simple writing guides or a thesaurus to help (see Gowers, 1962; Strunk and White, 1972). A question such as 'Is your household run on matriarchal or patriarchal lines?' will not do!

2   *Can the question be shortened?* The shorter the question the less confusing and ambiguous it will be. Avoid questions such as: 'Has it happened to you that over a long period of time, when you neither practised abstinence nor used birth control, you did not conceive?'.

3   *Is the question double-barrelled?* Double-barrelled questions are those which ask more than one question at once. The question 'how often do you visit your parents?', is double-barrelled. Separate questions about a person's mother and father should be asked.

4   *Is the question leading?* Try to ensure that respondents can give any answer without feeling that they are giving a wrong answer or a disapproved of response. Questions such as 'Do you oppose or favour cutting defence spending even if cuts turn the country over to communists?' are obviously leading. Questions can also be leading by using phrases such as 'Do you agree that ...', by attaching the names of prestigious people with one view, by providing only a limited range of alternative answers and by using loaded words in certain contexts.

5   *Is the question negative?* Questions which use 'not' can be difficult to understand—especially when asking someone to indicate whether they agree or disagree. The following question could be confusing:

Marijuana should not be decriminalised

[ ] Agree   [ ] Disagree

Rewording the question to 'Marijuana use should remain illegal' avoids the confusion caused by using 'not'.

6   *Is the respondent likely to have the necessary knowledge?* When asking about certain issues it is important that respondents are likely to have knowledge about the issue. A question which asks 'Do you agree or disagree with the government's policy on foreign aid' would be unsatisfactory. For issues where there is doubt, first ask a filter question to see if people are aware of the government's policy on foreign aid and then ask the substantive question only if people answered 'yes' to the filter question.

7   *Will the words have the same meaning for everyone?* Depending on factors such as age group, subcultural group and region, the meaning of some words will vary, so care must be taken either to avoid such words or to make your meaning clear. People also vary in how they define certain terms. For example, the answers people give to a question that asks them if they have been a victim of a crime in the last five years will depend on what they include in their definition of crime. For example, despite its illegality, some people may exclude domestic violence from their definition of crime, thus leading to its under-reporting.

8   *Is there a prestige bias?* When an opinion is attached to the name of a prestigious person and the respondent is then asked to express their own view on the same matter, the question can suffer from prestige bias. That is, the prestige of the person who holds the view may influence the way respondents answer the question. For example, 'What is your view about the Pope's policy on birth control?' could suffer from prestige bias. Effectively the question is double-barrelled: the answer may reflect an attitude about the Pope or about birth control—we cannot be sure which.

9   *Is the question ambiguous?* Ambiguity can arise from poor sentence structure, using words with several different meanings, use of negatives and double negatives, and using double-barrelled questions. The best way to avoid ambiguity is to use short, crisp, simple questions.

10 *Do you need a direct or indirect question?* When questioning in a particularly sensitive area it is often better to avoid blunt direct

questions such as 'Have you murdered your wife?' There are several indirect approaches (see Barton, 1958).

a The casual approach: 'Do you happen to have murdered your wife?'
b The numbered card approach: 'Will you please read off the number of this card which corresponds with what became of your wife?'
c The everybody approach: 'As you know, many people have been killing their wives these days. Do you happen to have killed yours?'
d The other people approach: 'Do you know any people who have murdered their wives?' Pause for reply and then ask 'How about yourself?'

The point is serious! If a question cannot be asked directly these approaches can help.

11 *Is the frame of reference for the question sufficiently clear?* If you ask 'How often do you see your mother?', establish within what time frame—within the last year? the last month? If you mean the frequency within the last year, ask 'Within the last year how often would you have seen your mother on average?' and then provide alternatives such as 'daily' through to 'never' to help further specify the meaning of the question.

12 *Does the question artificially create opinions?* On certain issues people will have no opinion. You should therefore offer people the option of responding 'don't know', or 'no opinion'. This can lead to some people giving these responses to most questions which can create its own problems, but not including them will produce highly unreliable and therefore useless responses.

13 *Is personal or impersonal wording preferable?* Personal wording asks respondents to indicate how 'they' feel about something, whereas the impersonal approach asks respondents to indicate how 'people' feel about something. The approach you use depends on what you want to do with the answers. The impersonal approach does not provide you with a measure of someone's attitudes but rather the respondent's perception of other people's attitudes.

14 *Is the question wording unnecessarily detailed or objectionable?* Questions about precise age or income can create problems. Since we normally do not need precise data on these issues we can diffuse this problem by asking people to put themselves in categories such as age or income groups.

15 *Does the question have dangling alternatives?* A question such as 'Would you say that it is frequently, sometimes, rarely or

never that . . .' is an awkward construction. The alternative answers are provided before the respondent has any subject matter to which to anchor them. The subject matter must come *before* alternative answers are listed.

16 *Is the question likely to produce a response set?* Where respondents are asked to agree or disagree with a statement there is the danger that some people will simply agree regardless of their true opinion. A set of such questions can create an *acquiescent response set*. Questions on some topics can produce a *social desirability response set* where people provide answers that make themselves look good. People may exaggerate their income, glamorise their type of job, under-report the amount of alcohol they consume and overestimate the frequency with which they attend church or the amount they give to charity. When asking questions where this may be a problem take care to help people feel comfortable regardless of the answer they might give. Avoid making certain answers appear normal or unusual.

Selecting question type

The other aspect of question construction is to decide on the response format. Should it be open or closed? If a closed format is used then a number of alternative types are available.

Open and closed formats

A closed or forced-choice question is one in which a number of alternative answers are provided from which respondents are to select one or more. An open-ended question is one for which respondents formulate their own answers.

There is disagreement about which style is preferable. A major problem of forced-choice questions is that on some issues they can create false opinions either by giving an insufficient range of alternatives from which to choose or by prompting people with 'acceptable' answers. Further, the forced-choice approach is not very good at taking into account people's qualifiers to the answers they tick.

There are, however, a number of advantages to *well-developed-* forced-choice questions. Where the questionnaire is long or people's motivation to answer is not high, forced-choice questions are useful since they are quick to answer. This is particularly so if the questionnaire is self-administered rather than administered by a skilled interviewer who can establish rapport and increase motivation.

From a researcher's point of view, forced-choice questions are easier to code (see Chapter 14). Answers to both closed and open questions need to be grouped into categories at some stage. The difficulties of doing this with open-ended questions often mean that they never get used. Even if they are grouped, researchers normally interpret answers and put them in categories. Researchers can misinterpret the answers and thus misclassify responses. Forced-choice questions allow respondents to classify themselves, thus avoiding coders misclassifying what people meant.

A further advantage of closed questions is that they do not discriminate against the less talkative and inarticulate respondents. Asking people to formulate their own responses is fine for those who can do it but the danger is that researchers will be overly influenced by these responses and ignore the opinions of the less articulate and less fluent.

A set of alternative responses can serve as useful prompts for respondents. For example, a question asking about what newspapers and magazines a person has read in the last week will detect a higher readership level if the names of newspapers and magazines are listed in a checklist than if the open-ended question is simply asked without the list of responses.

If forced-choice questions are used, it is necessary to put a lot of thought into developing alternative responses. The range must be exhaustive: a thorough range of responses must be listed to avoid biasing responses. This can be done by careful pilot testing using less structured approaches to locate the range of likely responses and by using the category called 'other (please specify)' to allow for unanticipated responses. To avoid forcing people to offer opinions on issues on which they have no opinion, it is useful to have a 'don't know' response.

The choice of open or closed questions depends on many factors such as the question content, respondent motivation, method of administration, type of respondents, access to skilled coders to code open-ended responses and the amount of time available to develop a good set of unbiased responses. There is no right or wrong approach. For key variables it may be worth using a combination of open and closed questions. Gallup (1947) suggested the following combination:

1 a closed question to see if the respondent has thought about or is aware of the issue;
2 an open question to get at general feelings on the matter;
3 a closed question to get at specific aspects of the issues;
4 open or closed questions to find out respondents' reasons for their opinions;
5 closed question to find out how strongly the opinion is held.

Figure 6.1   Examples of rating scales

Verbal
e.g. Nobody ever learned anything really important except through suffering
[   ] Strongly agree   [   ] Disagree
[   ] Agree   [   ] Strongly disagree
[   ] Cannot decide

Diagrammatic

1 ├─────────────────────┼─────────────────────┤
   −   0   +

2 Strongly   Strongly
   disagree   1   2   3   4   5   6   7   8   9   10   agree

Types of forced-choice response formats

Below are some of the most widely used approaches to providing responses for forced-choice questions.

1   *Likert-style formats: rating scales:* This general approach involves providing people with statements and asking them to indicate how strongly they agree or disagree. The format in which this is presented may be verbal or diagrammatic (see Figure 6.1).

2   *Semantic differential formats:* This format consists of choosing adjectives to represent the two extremes of a continuum and asking respondents to put a mark between the two extremes. An example is

How would you describe your mother?
Warm   1   2   3   4   5   6   7   Cold
Lonely   1   2   3   4   5   6   7   Not at all lonely
Dominant   1   2   3   4   5   6   7   Submissive

3   *Checklists:* These consist of a list of items and respondents are asked to circle each relevant item. An example is

What things do you talk to your mother about?
sport   food   relatives
religion   jobs   TV
neighbours   feelings   health
marital problems garden   books or films
children   hobbies
weather   politics

4   *Ranking formats:*   Respondents can be given a list of alternative answers, but rather than selecting between them they are asked to rank their importance. For example, people have often been given a list of thirteen qualities they think are desirable in

children (e.g. good manners, honesty, neat and clean, tries hard, self-control, obedient, responsible, considerate, gets on well with other children, etc.). They can then be asked to rank these qualities from most to least important by placing a 1 next to the most important, a 2 next to the second most important and so forth, down to 13 beside the least important quality. In face-to-face interviews it is highly desirable to give the respondent a written list of all these alternatives to read while the interviewer asks the question. It is too difficult for respondents to keep these long lists in their mind and also supply reliable answers.

Long lists that require exhaustive ranking can be highly unreliable. Normally it is only necessary to ask which items the respondent would rank among the two or three most important and then perhaps follow this up by asking which of these is the most important. We might also look at the other extreme by asking which two items are the least important.

5 *Attitude choices rather than agree–disagree statements:* Although the agree–disagree question format is one of the most widely used, it can suffer from the 'acquiescent response set' problem where some people agree with the statements regardless of their content. One way of avoiding this is to provide a number of alternative views and ask respondents to select the view that is closest to their own. For example, we may be interested in people's views about government assistance for students from poor families. Instead of asking people to agree or disagree with a statement such as 'The government should provide financial grants to help students whose parents have a low income to attend university', we could ask 'Some people think the government should provide financial grants to help students whose parents have a low income attend university. Others think the government should provide grants that would have to be paid back while others believe there should be no government assistance. Which option do you favour?

[ ] Government give grants
[ ] Government make loans
[ ] No government assistance
[ ] Cannot choose'

Direction, extremity and intensity of attitudes

It is important to distinguish the *direction* of a person's attitude from both the *extremity* of their position and the *intensity* with which they hold that position. Each of these three aspects of an attitude requires a different sort of question.

We may wish to know people's views about whether government economic policy ought to be directed more at reducing inflation and the government deficit or at reducing unemployment. We could discover the *direction* of a person's attitude by simply asking them which of the two they think is the most important priority. But we could learn more by asking how *extreme* their view is. There are two ways in which this is commonly done. The first is to provide a statement that expresses a *position* (e.g. the government's first priority ought to be to reduce unemployment even if this leads to increased inflation and problems with the deficit) and asking them to say how strongly they agree or disagree with it. Alternatively, a seven-point scale might be used in which 'reduce inflation' is placed at one end and 'reduce unemployment' at the other. Respondents can be asked to indicate where they would place themselves between these two positions.

This approach does not necessarily detect the *intensity* with which a position is held. Although extremity and intensity of an attitude may often go together, they are not the same thing. A person can hold extreme positions but do so with little passion. People may vote for extreme left- or right-wing political parties without having a fervent commitment to that party. Questions that measure a person's attitude *position* can usefully be followed up with questions to detect the attitude *intensity*.

Vignettes

One problem with attitude measurement in surveys is that the questions are often too abstract and vague. Often, in response to questions, people would like to answer 'It depends'. That is, their answer depends on a context. For example, if we asked people whether they think that grown children should be prepared to share their home with an elderly parent, many people would probably provide different answers depending on things such as the state of the parent's health, nature of relationship with the parent, whether the parent was on their own and so forth. The problem when asking simple, abstract attitude questions is that this sort of context is not provided. Respondents tend to make up their own context and answer in relation to this. But each person makes up a different context, which means that each person is effectively answering a different question.

Vignettes provide one way of minimising this problem. Vignettes are very short stories in which certain circumstances are specified to provide at least some standardisation of the context.

Vignettes are used in two different ways. The first use is mainly aimed at standardising the context and then asking questions given the common context (e.g. Finch, 1987). A second use is in causal analysis (e.g. Alexander and Becker, 1978).

Using this second approach, a set of related vignettes is developed in which there are standard features in each story. But other parts of the story are *systematically* varied between vignettes. We can then focus on the way in which changing parts of the story affect the way people answer questions about it.

This is best understood by using an example. Below is a vignette about a dual-career couple and a decision about one partner wanting to change jobs. In it three elements can be varied in different versions of the story. The parts that will be varied are printed in capitals and indicated by A, B and C. The rest of the vignette will be standard for all vignettes. By varying three pieces of information we are effectively asking three questions: (A) Is the answer dependent on whether it is the husband's or the wife's job that initiates the move? (B) Does the reason for the job change affect the answer? (C) How important is the job outcome for the other partner in the answer? Does this vary according to whether the partner who follows is male or female?

> John and Barbara Dixon are both in their mid-forties and their children now have jobs overseas. Barbara is a research scientist in a medical laboratory and John is an accountant. They own their own home and are comfortably off. [JOHN/BARBARA] (A) is offered a promotion that would mean [A LARGE RISE IN INCOME/ ONLY A SLIGHT INCOME RISE BUT A MUCH MORE ENJOYABLE JOB] (B) but would also mean that they would have to sell up and move several hundred kilometres. [BARBARA/ JOHN] could also get a job in the new location [BUT IT IS NOWHERE NEAR AS GOOD AS THEIR PREVIOUS JOB/WHICH IS VERY SIMILAR TO THEIR CURRENT JOB] (C). [JOHN/ BARBARA] would like to make the move but [JOHN/ BARBARA] does not want to give up his/her current job. [The references to John and Barbara in the last sentence would be varied so that the person who is offered the new job wants to move while their partner does not want to move.]

A question or set of questions would follow the vignette. The style of questions can vary. A simple open-ended question such as 'What should they do?' could be used. This might be followed up by asking people 'Why?' Alternatively, the respondent could be asked to choose between one of a set of alternative solutions provided in a closed question.

By varying the information in the parts marked (A), (B) and (C) we would have eight different vignettes. One vignette would involve moving for John's job, to get a large pay rise but leading to a

Figure 6.2   Different answering formats for closed-choice questions

Square brackets, parentheses or boxes (tick the box)
1	[ ]	Agree		1	( )	Agree		1	□	Agree
2	[ ]	Disagree	OR	2	( )	Disagree	OR	2	□	Disagree
3	[ ]	Can't decide		3	( )	Can't decide		3	□	Can't decide

Precoding (circle the number)
  1   Agree
  2   Disagree
  3   Can't decide

deterioration in Barbara's job. Another would be similar but lead-ing to no deterioration in Barbara's job. A third vignette would be moving for John's job, for greater job satisfaction for John, but leading to a deterioration in Barbara's work. A fourth scenario would be moving for John for the sake of job satisfaction, but where the move does not adversely affect Barbara's job. Another set of four vignettes would be produced by Barbara having the chance to move.

Questionnaire layout

There are six areas to which attention needs to be given when combining questions into a questionnaire.

Answering procedures

With open-ended questions ensure that you leave sufficient space for answers to avoid people cramming responses but do not leave so much as to discourage completing the questionnaire because of the time it will apparently take.

   With closed questions people can be asked to either tick approp-riate boxes or brackets or circle a number next to responses (see Figure 6.2).

   When using any of these procedures, the area for answering can be on the left or right of the response but make sure you justify your typing on the answer side as below.

1	[ ]	Agree		Agree	[ ]	1
2	[ ]	Disagree	OR	Disagree	[ ]	2
3	[ ]	Can't decide		Can't decide	[ ]	3

   When a series of Likert-style questions are to be used it can be efficient to present them in a matrix format (see Figure 6.3).

Figure 6.3   A matrix presentation of Likert-style questions

	Strongly agree	Agree	Disagree	Strongly disagree	Don't know
This country has a rich cultural life in music, art, and literature.	[ ] 1	[ ] 2	[ ] 3	[ ] 4	[ ] 9
Unfortunately this country is a long way from the centre of things.	[ ]	[ ]	[ ]	[ ]	[ ]
Only a small proportion of young people can get a decent education in this country.	[ ]	[ ]	[ ]	[ ]	[ ]
This country is a good place for a person to start a small business.	[ ]	[ ]	[ ]	[ ]	[ ]

Figure 6.4   An illustration of contingency questions

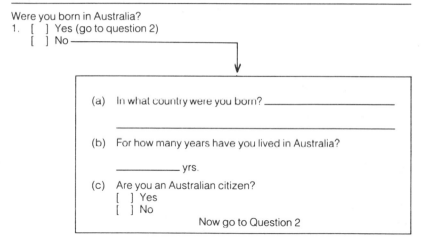

Were you born in Australia?
1.   [   ] Yes (go to question 2)
     [   ] No

(a)   In what country were you born? _____

_____

(b)   For how many years have you lived in Australia?

_____ yrs.

(c)   Are you an Australian citizen?
      [   ] Yes
      [   ] No
                        Now go to Question 2

Contingency questions

Since you do not want respondents to waste time reading questions which are not relevant to them we can use filter or contingency questions as in Figure 6.4.

The use of arrows and inset boxes to highlight follow-up questions is a useful way of avoiding confusion when using contingency questions.

Instructions

To provide flow, use the following types of instructions where appropriate.

1 *General instructions:* These should include an introduction to the purpose of the questionnaire, assurance of confidentiality, how the respondent was chosen, how and when to return the questionnaire (where relevant).
2 *Section introductions:* When the questionnaire can be divided into subsections provide a brief introduction to each section such as 'Finally we would like to know just a little about your background so we can see how different people feel about the topics about which you've answered questions'.
3 *Question instructions:* Indicate how many responses the respondent can tick (e.g. the mȯst appropriate, as many as apply, one only).
4 *'Go to' instructions:* Ensure you make use of these when using contingency questions.

Use of space

To encourage people to complete a questionnaire avoid cluttering it. The following hints many help:

1 Print questions on one side of the page only. It is too easy for people to miss questions printed on the backs of pages. The blank backs of pages also are useful for respondents to write additional comments.
2 Provide a column about 2.5 centimetres wide on the right hand side for computer coding (see Chapter 14).
3 Leave sufficient space for open-ended questions.
4 List alternative responses down rather than across the page.

Order of questions

A good questionnaire is one in which there is a good logical flow to questions. The following points provide some guidelines.

1 Commence with questions the respondent will enjoy answering.
   a These should be easily answered questions.
   b Factual questions should be used initially.
   c Do not start with demographic questions such as age, marital status, etc.

    d Ensure that the initial questions are obviously relevant to the stated purpose of the survey.

2 Go from easy to more difficult questions.

3 Go from concrete to abstract questions.

4 Open-ended questions should be kept to a minimum and where possible placed towards the end of the questionnaire.

5 Group questions into sections. This helps structure the questionnaire and provides a flow.

6 Make use of filter questions to ensure that questions are relevant to respondents.

7 When using a series of positive and negative items to form a scale, mix up the positive and negative items to help avoid an acquiescent response set.

8 Where possible try to introduce a variety of question formats so that the questionnaire remains interesting.

Setting up for coding

If the data are to be analysed by computer it is useful to prepare for this by allocating codes to responses in the questionnaire so that a number is printed in the questionnaire next to responses. This precoding is possible only for forced-choice questions (see Figures 6.2 and 6.3). In addition, computer card column numbers should be allocated to each variable in the right-hand margin (see Chapter 14).

Telephone questionnaires: additional considerations

In general, the principles outlined in this chapter apply to questionnaires administered by mail, face to face and by telephone. But because telephone interviews rely totally on verbal communication, they have some special requirements.

Question wording

The reliance on respondent's retaining all the spoken information in the question places real limits on how much information can be packed into one question. If *too many response categories* are included in the question, there is a danger that the respondent will arbitrarily select one. There are three main approaches to help alleviate this problem.

    First, the number of response categories can be reduced. This is the most obvious approach when questions have a large number of response categories that are ordered on a continuum. Figure 6.5 shows how a question on job satisfaction could be modified by

Figure 6.5   Simplifying response categories for telephone surveys

Initial format:
How satisfied are you with your job?

TERRIBLE 1
VERY UNHAPPY 2
UNHAPPY 3
MOSTLY DISSATISFIED 4
MIXED FEELINGS 5
MOSTLY SATISFIED 6
PLEASED 7
VERY PLEASED 8
DELIGHTED 9

Alternatives:
(a) Fewer categories
How satisfied are you with your job?

VERY DISSATISFIED 1
DISSATISFIED 2
MIXED FEELINGS 3
SATISFIED 4
VERY SATISFIED 5

(b) Numerical scale
Imagine a scale that measured how satisfied you are with your job where 1 means that you think it is terrible, 10 means that you are delighted with it and 5 means you are neutral. Where, between 1 and 10, would you put yourself on this scale?

| 1   2   3   4   5   6   7   8   9   10 |
| Terrible   Neutral   Delighted |

reducing the number of response categories (Figure 6.5(a)). Because this can lead to an undesirable loss of detail, an alternative is to adopt the format in Figure 6.5(b) where the response categories are converted to a numerical scale and people are asked to say where on the scale they would lie. Because of its numerical character, it is more readily retained when described verbally.

A second approach is to use a two-step procedure and divide the question into two parts with the first part designed to find out the respondent's direction of feeling while the second asks about the intensity or specifics of their feelings (Figure 6.6).

A third way of dealing with the retention problem is to repeat the alternatives by building the responses into the question as well as listing them as a set of alternative responses (Figure 6.7).

Layout

Since it is the interviewer rather than the respondent who sees the questionnaire, the primary concern with questionnaire layout for a

Figure 6.6   Two-step method for reducing question complexity

Initial format:
Which of the following is the most important to you in a job:

                    GOOD PAY 1
                   GOOD HOURS 2
          CHANCE TO USE INITIATIVE 3
                      SECURITY 4
                     CHALLENGE 5
         OPPORTUNITY FOR PROMOTION 6
                    CREATIVITY 7
                    FULFILMENT 8

Alternative for telephone interview:
Which sorts of things do you think are most important in a job

            CONDITIONS OF EMPLOYMENT 1
            WHAT YOU ACTUALLY DO IN THE JOB 2

Which of the following four things do you think is the most important in a job?

                    GOOD PAY 1
                   GOOD HOURS 2
                     SECURITY 3
         OPPORTUNITY FOR PROMOTION 4

Which of the following four things do you think is the most important in a job?

          CHANCE TO USE INITIATIVE 1
                     CHALLENGE 2
                    CREATIVITY 3
                    FULFILMENT 4

Figure 6.7   Incorporating responses into the question

Among the things that people look for in a job are good pay, flexible hours, security and opportunities for promotion. Which of these four do you think is the most important?

                    GOOD PAY 1
                   GOOD HOURS 2
                     SECURITY 3
         OPPORTUNITY FOR PROMOTION 4

telephone survey must be to assist the interviewer to administer it accurately and to code the answers as the interview proceeds. The following guidelines should be helpful.

1   Provide detailed guides to interviewers *on the questionnaire* next to the relevant questions rather than on a separate sheet of paper.
2   Make it very clear to the interviewer whether the alternative responses are to be read out. This can be achieved by giving

Figure 6.8   Use of typefaces to distinguish between parts of the question

---

(a) **If a federal election was held tomorrow how likely is it that you would vote?**
... *(READ OUT)*

			GO TO
	WOULD NOT VOTE	1	(c)
(CODE ONE ONLY)	UNLIKELY TO VOTE	2	
	WOULD PROBABLY VOTE	3	
	WOULD DEFINITELY VOTE	4	
	(Undecided)	5	(c)

(b) **What types of issues would be important in deciding the way you voted?**
(PROBE BUT DO NOT *READ OUT PROMPTS)*

(Environmental issues)	1
(Economic)	2
(Unemployment)	3
(Social welfare)	4
(CODE AS MANY AS APPLY) (Defence)	5
(Education)	6
(Nuclear)	7
(Crime/law and order)	8
(Transport)	9
(Corruption)	10
(Interest rates)	11
(Other) *(RECORD DETAILS)*	12

(c) *(ASK ALL)*
Which of the following statements best describes the way you feel about the current government?
...
...

---

specific instructions and by highlighting responses to be read out by using upper-case characters (see Figure 6.8). Precoded responses that are not to be read out should be clearly distinguished from those that are. Using lower-case characters in brackets is helpful in this respect.

3   Clearly distinguish between instructions (use upper-case italics) and the question.

4   State how many responses can be coded.

5   Where filter questions are used, make it as clear as possible where the interviewer is to go next. The format described earlier may be used but the one used in Figure 6.8 may be more effective in telephone interviews where big jumps in the questionnaire are required.

6   Place the codes to the right of the question, as close to the coding column as possible. Right justify the responses (see Figure 6.8).

Pilot testing: evaluating questions and questionnaires

Once a questionnaire has been developed, each question and the questionnaire as a whole must be evaluated rigorously before final administration. Evaluating the questionnaire is called *pilot testing* or *pretesting*. Converse and Presser (1986) provide one of the rare discussions of pilot testing.

Three phases of pilot testing

Phase 1—Question development: Questionnaire items come from many sources. Some will come from previous questionnaires, while others will need to be developed for the particular study. The purpose of testing at this stage is to establish how to phrase each question, to evaluate how respondents interpret the question's meaning and to check whether the range of response alternatives is sufficient. While new questions will need to be intensively pretested, previously used (and tested) questions also should be evaluated. Questions that 'worked' in one context may be inappropriate for the particular sample you are using. Questions that worked in the 1950s for a general population sample in the United States may no longer be appropriate in a study of 18-year-old students in Australia or Britain in the 1990s.

In this testing phase, respondents are told that the questions are being developed and they are being asked to help improve them. It is therefore called a *declared* or participating pretest. The respondent is quizzed intensively about a set of individual questions. They might be asked how they would phrase the question, what they had in mind when they gave a particular answer and whether there were unavailable alternative answers they would have preferred to have given. We might present a respondent with different wordings for the same question and ask them if they would give the same answer now or ask which they found clearest and so forth. Because of its intensive nature, only a limited number of questions can be tested in this phase of pilot testing.

Phase 2—Questionnaire development: By administering a complete questionnaire (usually considerably longer than the final questionnaire), this phase enables the further evaluation of individual items and the questionnaire as a whole. Rather than relying on respondents' comments about the questions, this phase analyses their answers and uses the interviewer's comments to improve the questionnaire.

More often than not, this phase is *undeclared*. That is, in order to simulate the final questionnaire administration, respondents are not told that the questionnaire is still under development.

Phase 3—Polishing pilot test: We use the information gained in Phase 2 to revise questions where necessary, shorten the questionnaire, reorder questions and finalise the skip patterns for filter questions. Attention should also be given to the final *layout* of the questionnaire to ensure that it is clear for interviewers and respondents.

Pilot testing items

The evaluation of individual questionnaire items should examine at least six points.

1   *Variation:* If most people give similar answers to a question, it will be of little use in later analysis. Imagine the following question as a measure of political conservatism: 'In a country such as this, assassination of political leaders is acceptable in order to bring about political change.' Most people will disagree with this, and accordingly most people would emerge as equally conservative. The extreme character of the question would not enable us to distinguish between the levels of conservatism of most people and thus it would not normally be very useful.

　　Questions with low variation also create serious problems at the data analysis stage by producing some categories with a very small number of cases. Equally importantly, questions with low variation make correlational analysis very difficult and produce very low correlations (see page 293).

2   *Meaning:* Check to ensure that respondents understand the intended meaning of the question and that you understand the respondent's answer. In one pilot test I used a question from a major survey to ascertain people's ethnicity. Because I wanted to discover something about their subjective ethnicity, I needed to go beyond simply asking their country of birth. So I asked people: 'With which ethnic group do you most strongly identify?' When examining people's answers, I discovered that a substantial number of people had misunderstood what I meant by 'identify'. A number of people said 'all groups' and had interpreted the question to mean 'Which ethnic groups *do you like or get on with?*' Others mentioned a wide number of ethnic groups and I suspect that they interpreted the question as meaning 'Which ethnic groups *can you identify or recognise?*'

3   *Redundancy:* If two questions measure virtually the same thing, only one is needed in the final questionnaire. If two items are designed to tap the same concept and correlate over, say, 0.8, then you can drop one of the items (see Chapter 15).

4   *Scalability:* If a set of questions is designed to form a scale or index (see Chapter 15), check to ensure that they do. There is no

point including items in the final questionnaire which do not belong to the scale for which they were designed.

5　*Non-response:* The refusal of a large number of people to answer a particular question produces difficulties at the data analysis stage (see pages 273–4, 282–6) and can lead to serious reductions in sample size. Questions which, in Phase 1, produce respondent hesitation, reluctance or refusal to answer are likely to produce a high level of non-response later.

　　Non-response can arise for a variety of reasons. The question might be unclear, too intrusive, provide insufficient responses or appear to be too similar to previously answered questions. Questions that appear to have nothing to do with the stated purpose of the survey can also result in high non-response, as can open-ended questions that appear to require considerable effort to answer. Questionnaire layout, including cramming and confusing skip instructions, can lead to accidental non-response.

6　*Acquiescent response set:* Questions that ask respondents to agree or disagree with a statement can suffer from the tendency of some people to agree with the statement, regardless of the question content. This tendency, called the 'acquiescent response set' problem, is related to education and is thus of particular relevance when the research question involves an examination of the relationship between the set of questions and education. One way of detecting an acquiescent response set is to take questions that seem completely contradictory and see how many people agree with both of them. If there is evidence of a response set, it is best to replace the agree–disagree format with another type of question (see page 89).

Pilot testing questionnaires

As well as testing individual questions, the questionnaire as a whole needs evaluating. At least four things should be carefully checked.

1　*Flow:* Do questions seem to fit together? Are the transitions from one section to another smooth? Does the interviewer find the skips difficult to follow, resulting in awkward pauses? Do the transitions sound long-winded? Does the questionnaire move too quickly or jump from topic to topic too quickly to allow respondents to gather their thoughts? *Listening* to an interviewer rather than reading the questionnaire helps detect problems in its flow.

2　*Question skips:* Where filter questions are used, it is important to ensure that the skip patterns do not lead to skipping more questions than was intended. To help ensure that the skip patterns are correct, draw a flow chart based on the question in-

Figure 6.9 Flow chart for checking skip patterns

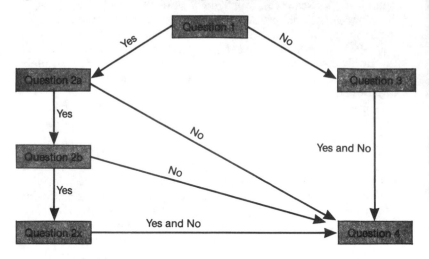

structions. Imagine a set of questions as represented in Figure 6.9, where each question simply has 'yes' and 'no' answers and the questions that a person is required to answer depend on their previous answers. We want everyone to answer question 1 and 4, but whether or not they should answer questions 2a, 2b, 2c and 3 depends on how they have answered the previous question. Drawing such a diagram from the skip instructions on the questionnaire helps detect whether all the instructions are included, whether they are logical and whether they lead to the intended places.

3   *Timing:* The Phase 2 questionnaire will be much longer than the final one, but it is helpful to time each section (or even subsection) so that you can gain some idea of how much needs to be cut for the final phase. The final phase should also be carefully tested to ensure that it takes approximately the estimated time both so that respondents can be told how long the questionnaire will take and so that accurate survey budgeting can be completed. If the questionnaire is too long, then fewer questionnaires can be administered (assuming telephone or face-to-face administration methods). This can lead to an unacceptable reduction of sample size.

4   *Respondent interest and attention:* If respondents seem to be

getting bored, the questionnaire may be too long. A greater variety of types of question (see pages 86–9) may help avoid monotony. Particular sections or questions might lead to a particular loss of attention. These should be noted and either restructured, removed or placed at the end of the questionnaire, where they will do less damage. Bored respondents will provide unconsidered and unreliable answers and produce high non-response to questions.

How to pilot test

1 *Who to pretest?:* As far as possible, pretesting should be conducted on people who will resemble the types of people to whom the questionnaire will finally be given. Depending on the content of the questionnaire, it will be important to match particular characteristics of the pilot and final samples. Age, gender, educational and ethnic characteristics should normally be matched. The importance of other features such as employment status, religion, family life stage and the like may depend on the purpose of the survey. Naturally, the closer the match between the pilot sample and the final sample, the better.

When the survey is of a particular subgroup (e.g. organisation, ethnic group) it is helpful to get responses from key insiders who have a good knowledge of people in the group. They can help avoid questions that will be offensive, highlight questions that could be particularly useful in tapping the desired concepts and highlight problems with language (e.g. too complex, ambiguous meaning, special meaning for the group, etc.), as well as alerting the researcher to misunderstandings about the group. This is particularly valuable in Phase 1.

2 *How many to pretest?:* Because of the intensive nature of Phase 1, it is often not possible to test a large number of people. Since the evaluation of the questionnaire in Phases 2 and 3 involves the quantitative analysis of respondents' answers, it is important to give the questionnaire to as many people as possible. Too few respondents may well mean that problems such as non-response, variation, response sets and the like remain undetected. Somewhere between 75 and 100 respondents provides a useful pilot test.

3 *Who should do the interviews?:* A selection of interviewers that represent the range of experience of those who will finally administer the questionnaire will provide the most realistic simulation of the administration of the survey. There is value in the questionnaire designer also administering, or at least sitting in on,

some pilot interviews to help keep in touch with the realities of
the interview situation.

4 *Code responses:* Try coding responses to the Phase 2 questionnaire—especially the open questions and 'other (please specify)' responses to closed questions. Difficulties in coding these
questions can highlight problems with the question wording (e.g.
frame of reference not clear, ambiguity, etc.), or even indicate
that the investigator is unclear what the question is really about.
It also can be useful to ask interviewers to code some of the
questionnaires, as this can help make them aware of the coding
problems produced by poor interviewing and help them interview more precisely (e.g. it can help sharpen up the precision
with which interviewers obtain occupational data).

5 *Interviewer debriefing*: Since the interviewer has the hands-on
experience with the questionnaire, it is essential to learn from
their experience as well as from the respondents' answers to
questions. It is useful to give the interviewer a brief questionnaire
to complete after each pilot interview. A variety of evaluation
questions are possible, but Converse and Presser (1976: 72)
suggest asking the interviewer at least to indicate:

a   any questions that made the respondent uncomfortable;
b   questions that had to be repeated;
c   questions that appeared to be misinterpreted;
d   questions that were difficult to read or questions the inter-
    viewer came to particularly dislike;
e   sections that dragged;
f   sections where the respondent seemed to want to say more.

In addition interviewers should be encouraged to provide marginal comments on the main questionnaire itself, and the questionnaire designer should talk with the interviewers about the
questionnaire.

The advice to pilot test questionnaires is probably one of the most
ignored suggestions regarding questionnaire design. The pressure to
get things done, over-confidence combined with inexperience and
practical difficulties all too often cause people to take the chance
and skip this whole stage. It is a risk that is not worth taking.

Summary

This chapter has outlined a number of stages and principles of
questionnaire design. A questionnaire will be the product of the
research problem, the theory, method of administration, and methods of data analysis. Although questionnaires have obvious limit-

ations many of these can be minimised by careful thinking ahead and pilot testing. Good questionnaires do not just happen: they involve careful thinking, numerous drafts, thorough evaluation and extensive testing. Despite shortcomings questionnaires have the great advantage of generating a systematic variable by case matrix, of enabling coverage of a large, representative sample and of being relatively efficient. They are, however, only one method of collecting data and will be unsuitable for many research problems and situations.

Further reading

A useful and readable introduction to question wording is *The Art of Asking Questions* (1951) by Payne. Warwick and Lininger provide a useful introduction to questionnaire design in Chapter 6 of *The Sample Survey* (1975) but Oppenheim's *Questionnaire Design and Attitude Measurement* (1968) and Converse and Presser (1986) are more comprehensive treatments of questionnaire construction. In recent years a number of more advanced, specialist books containing research about the best way of wording questions and constructing questionnaires have become available. The best of these are Bradburn and Sudman *Improving Interview Method and Questionnaire Design* (1979), Schuman and Presser, *Questions and Answers in Attitude Surveys* (1981) and Sudman and Bradburn, *Asking Questions: A Practical Guide to Questionnaire Design* (1982). All these are well worth careful reading as they provide evidence about question format and help confront a lot of the folklore about questionnaires. Two books which examine how questionnaire design ought to be affected by the method of administration are Dillman, *Mail and Telephone Surveys: the total design method* (1978) and Groves and Kahn's *Surveys by Telephone: a national comparison with personal interviews* (1979). All these books provide excellent bibliographies on more specialised aspects of questionnaire design. Belson provides detailed guidance on technical matters of wording in *The Design and Understanding of Survey Questions* (1981) and Singer and Presser (1989) and Turner and Martin (1984) contain sets of excellent specialised papers on question construction.

Books which provide sets of questions to tap various concepts and provide useful questions and ideas are worth examining. Some useful ones are Miller, *Handbook of Research Design and Social Measurement* (1970), Robinson et al., *Measures of Political Attitudes* (1968a) and *Measures of Social Psychological Attitudes* (1968b), Shaw and Wright's *Scales for the Measurement of Attitudes* (1967), the *American National Election Studies Data Sourcebook 1951–1978* (Miller et al., 1980), the cumulative codebook for the General Social Survey (National Opinion Research Center, 1990), the *Sourcebook of Harris National Surveys: Repeated Questions 1963–1976* (Martin, et al., 1981). The Gallup Poll Questions (Gallup, 1935–81), the (1980) *American Social Attitudes Data Sourcebook 1947–1978* by Converse et al. (1980) and *National Social Science Survey Codebook* (1987).

7 Administering questionnaires

It is impossible to separate the questions of sampling and question-naire design from the issue of questionnaire administration. The method of administration affects sample quality, the type of questions that can be asked, the design of the questions and the layout of the questionnaire. This chapter focuses on two main issues. First, it compares three main methods of administration (face to face, mail and telephone) in terms of their response rates, sampling quality, the implications for questionnaire structure, the quality of answers and practicalities of administering the questionnaires. It then provides some practical guidelines designed to help in implementing questionnaires.

While face-to-face interviews deservedly have had the best reputation, there are good reasons for considering alternatives. Mail and telephone techniques have improved markedly in recent years, while face-to-face surveys are encountering new problems. One of the big advantages of face-to-face surveys has been their high response rates, but in recent years these have declined by about 15 per cent (Steeh, 1981) due both to increased refusal levels and greater difficulties in locating respondents. This has led to both increased costs and a decline in sample quality. The consequent cost increases have led to sample size reductions or fewer callbacks, both of which produce problems of sample quality, thus making the alternatives more attractive.

Three methods compared: strengths and weaknesses

When implementing any survey, the alternatives to face-to-face interviews need careful consideration. Drawing on the more extensive discussion by Dillman (1978), this section outlines the relative merits of the three approaches by focusing on five broad considerations:

1   response rates;
2   ability to produce representative samples;
3   limitations on questionnaire design;
4   quality of responses and;
5   implementation problems.

Response rates

One of the most common criteria by which a method is judged is the response rate it achieves. Face-to-face interviews have traditionally been seen as the most effective in this respect while telephone and particularly mail surveys have developed the reputation of being plagued by low response rates. But this is misleading. The response rate obtained in a particular study will be due to the combined effect of the topic, the nature of the sample, the length of the questionnaire, the care taken in implementing the particular survey and other related factors. There will be situations where a well administered mail survey will yield response rates at least equal to both personal and telephone interviews and at a much lower cost. The important thing is to identify the situations in which different approaches should and should not be used.

Personal and telephone surveys tend to achieve higher response rates than mail questionnaires in *general population* samples, but even here it partly depends on the topic of the survey. Dillman reports that by using his Total Design Method, telephone surveys of the general public average a response rate of about 85 per cent. With well conducted mail surveys of the general public he reports a typical response rate of between 60 and 75 per cent. In surveys of *specific, more homogeneous groups* (e.g. members of an organisation, teachers, nurses), mail surveys seem to be about as good as other techniques — especially when the topic under investigation is of particular relevance to the group.

One problem in comparing the different methods is that the method of calculating response rates is likely to overestimate the non-response for mail questionnaires. A common way of calculating the response rate is with the formula:

$$\text{Response rate} = \frac{\text{Number returned}}{\text{N in sample} - (\text{Ineligible} + \text{Unreachable})} \times 100$$

In face-to-face interviews and in telephone interviews it is easier to work out how many were ineligible or unreachable. But in a mail survey we have to assume that a non-response is a refusal unless informed otherwise. This relies on ineligible people contacting the researcher or the post office returning questionnaires of unreachable respondents — neither of which can be relied on.

Obtaining representative samples

Since non-responders tend to be different from those who respond (older, less educated, non-English-speaking background), low response rates introduce *bias* into the sample. Since mail surveys require reading and writing rather than listening, they are more prone to this type of bias.

Other factors also introduce bias, or at least make it difficult to estimate and thus correct for any bias. A representative sample must be one where there is an equal or at least known probability of all members of the population being selected. Where a complete list of the members of a population is available then all members have an equal chance of selection regardless of the method by which the questionnaire is administered. In surveys of the general public there are no complete lists and this introduces problems for which face-to-face methods are the most appropriate solution. Samples for face-to-face surveys can be drawn by the cluster sampling techniques described in Chapter 5. But for mail and especially telephone surveys, lists of one sort or another are normally used. Since these lists are often out of date and do not cover the whole population (as in the case of telephones especially), some categories of people will be systematically under-represented.

To obtain a representative sample it is necessary to have some *control over who completes the questionnaire*. With personal and telephone interviews it is possible to obtain a listing of household members and then ask for the person who meets the selection requirements (see Table 5.3). But with mail questionnaires it is much more difficult to control who fills out the questionnaire. Although we can ask the person who receives the mail questionnaire to pass it on to the appropriate person, we cannot be sure that this happens.

Gaining access to the selected person can be a problem with personal interviews. Where respondents are widely scattered, the cost and time involved in locating respondents can be prohibitive. Simply gaining access to some respondents can be difficult — especially where people have dogs or other protection devices. In contrast, mail and telephone methods avoid this problem but encounter a problem in ensuring that the mail is sent to the correct address — a not insignificant problem in samples with high levels of geographical mobility.

Effects on questionnaire design

Because of the varying input of the interviewer, the different methods impose different constraints on the type, format and number of questions that can be asked.

In general, personal interviews provide the greatest flexibility in terms of question design and, other things being equal, is the best method when dealing with complex research topics.

The method of administration is often seen to dictate the *length of the questionnaires* with the common view being that mail questionnaires must be very brief while face-to-face questionnaires can be much longer. But it is not quite as simple as this. The optimal length of a questionnaire will depend on the nature of the sample and the topic under investigation: the more specialised the population and the more relevant the topic, the longer the questionnaire can be. Indeed, for some topics a short questionnaire will produce low response rates because people will consider it too trivial or superficial. Dillman's research with mail questionnaires shows that with general public surveys the optimal length is about twelve pages or 125 items. After this point the response rate drops from about 75 per cent to nearer 60 per cent. In surveys of specialised populations with relevant topics length seems to be less important.

Telephone surveys seem to be relatively unaffected by their length and can feasibly last up to 30 minutes. Once people start an interview on the phone they are very unlikely to hang up.

Because of the personal contact, face-to-face interviews can last longer than the other two methods. However, the ability to extend personal interviews has its disadvantages. In long interviews either tiredness or impatience can affect the quality of answers as the interview progresses.

The method of administration also affects the type of question that can be asked. *Complex questions* are best asked in face-to-face interview situations where trained interviewers can work their way through what might be a confusing set of filter questions. It is easier to use visual aids and clarify misunderstandings. In mail questionnaires respondents may simply give up if they find the questionnaire difficult. Because telephone interviews have no visual or written material, great care must be taken to avoid questions with a large number of possible responses. People simply cannot keep this information in their heads long enough to answer the question reliably (see pages 96–7).

Mail questionnaires also have difficulty in coping with *boring questions*. Because of the personal contact involved, both telephone and particularly face-to-face interviews encounter fewer difficulties with boring questions. Related to this is the problem of *item non-response*. With telephone and personal interviews, trained interviewers can check that questions have not been accidentally missed and even can try to coax answers from respondents.

Open-ended questions are best used in situations where people are able to give their answer verbally rather than in writing: many people experience greater difficulties putting their ideas in writing. Mail questionnaires are therefore not well suited to open-ended questions.

Filter questions are most easily used in telephone and personal interviews where the trained interviewer can work through the questionnaire, thus avoiding the difficulty that some respondents have. Careful design can help reduce this in mail questionnaires but it can nevertheless lead to questionnaires appearing very long.

In some situations the *sequence* in which people read questions can affect answers. Mail questionnaires provide no control over the order in which people answer questions, thus obscuring the extent to which answers might be affected by later questions. For example, in a series of questions about attitudes to tax reductions and attitudes about government programs to assist the unemployed, the order in which people read the questions could easily influence the way they answer them.

Quality of answers

It is one thing to obtain answers but quite another to obtain accurate answers. In this respect, face-to-face interviews perform less well while mail questionnaires are probably the best. Responses to sensitive or controversial questions can be affected by *social desirability* considerations: giving acceptable rather than true opinions. While this danger exists regardless of the administration method, it will increase with increasing personalisation.

Another problem that is especially evident in face-to-face interviews is that the *observable characteristics* (e.g. gender, race, class) of even the best-trained interviewer can affect the way people answer questions. For example, the sex of the interviewer relative to the interviewee is likely to produce quite different responses on questions such as abortion and attitudes to sexual mores.

There are times when interviewers simply do their job poorly and thus contaminate results: some interviewers will place their own interpretation on questions and reveal their opinions. Interviewers may even fabricate results. Telephone interviews conducted and supervised from a central location should avoid this problem while mail surveys are largely free from this type of *subversion*.

The *opinions of other people* can also distort responses. Mail questionnaires are open to this problem; in fact we can never be sure who actually completes the questionnaire. In face-to-face interviews the presence of another person can considerably affect responses while telephone interviews are the least affected by this problem.

All three methods have problems when there is a *need to consult with others*. Information about behaviour (e.g. amount spent each week at the supermarket) or attributes (e.g. partner's membership of a trade union) may not be known by the respondent and they may need to consult someone else in the household to obtain accurate information. Theoretically mail questionnaires should be the best at coping with this problem since they do not have to be completed immediately, thus allowing time and opportunity to consult, but they confront the problem of the respondent being insufficiently motivated to consult.

Implementing the survey

By far the most serious problems of the face-to-face interview are related to its implementation. Despite their other problems, mail and telephone surveys come into their own at this level.

Nowhere is this clearer than in relation to *obtaining suitable staff*. Personal interviewers require careful training, need to be available for night and weekend work, must be willing to face potentially unpleasant situations alone and be able to approach strangers, and need to have the personal skills to conduct an objective interview. Because of difficulties in readily obtaining such interviewers it is often necessary to rely on less than well trained or committed people thus creating the possibility of not following proper sampling procedures, subversion, expressing their own opinions and responding inappropriately to the respondent's answers. This undermines many of the potential advantages of the face-to-face interview.

Telephone surveys are less demanding in this respect. They do not require night and weekend travel and avoid the dangers of working alone with strangers. It is therefore easier to find interviewers. Furthermore, because time is not spent in travelling, fewer interviewers are required to conduct a telephone survey. If conducted from a central location, they allow for closer supervision and on-the-job training and mean that interviewers do not have to be as experienced as the face-to-face interviewer. Mail surveys are the least demanding in terms of staffing requirements. Rather than finding people with interviewing skills, they require a well organised person with good clerical skills. A large mail survey can be conducted readily by one or two staff.

In situations where *speed* is important, telephone surveys have great potential. Callbacks are easy and it is possible to conduct a large survey in a matter of days. In contrast, mail surveys are not quick. The time needed for questionnaires to reach people, to allow time to complete the questionnaire and to allow for two or three follow-up periods requires an administration period of six to eight weeks. Unlike telephone and personal surveys, the implementation time for mail surveys is not affected by the length of the questionnaire or the size of the sample. The time taken for personal interviews also is affected by the geographical spread of the sample and the difficulty of locating respondents. In general it is the least flexible method in terms of speed.

As well as speed, another crucial factor that often determines the choice of method is the *cost* of conducting the survey. The relative advantages of the three methods depend very much on what type of survey is being conducted. For national probability surveys face-to-face interviews would cost on average about five times as much as telephone surveys and up to 20 times more than a mail survey (Dillman, 1978: 71), but for a small local community survey the relative costs of the various methods can be very similar. The cost advantages of any method depend on how geographically dispersed the sample is: the greater the dispersion, the more expensive the face-to-face survey. Mail surveys are barely affected by greater distance while telephone charges can be affected to some extent. The extent to which distance affects the cost of telephone interviews depends on the length of the interview. Face-to-face interviewing is similarly affected while mail interviews remain unaffected. The cost of printing will be greater for mail questionnaires where considerable attention has to be given to presentation but the cost of this per interview declines as the sample size increases. Costs will vary depending on the number of callbacks made — with face-to-face interviews being the most dramatically affected by this.

If any broad conclusions were to be drawn about how to administer questionnaires it would be that face-to-face surveys are normally better at obtaining representative samples and produce the fewest constraints in terms of questionnaire construction and question design, with mail questionnaires being the least satisfactory in these respects. But the reverse is true as far as the quality of answers is concerned: mail questionnaires are likely to be best in this regard while face-to-face interviews encounter more problems than either mail or telephone methods. In general, face-to-face interviews are the least satisfactory when it comes to the practicalities of administration while mail and telephone methods have considerable, though different, advantages. In the end it is impossible to decide which method is best: the relative strengths and weaknesses vary according to the characteristics of the survey. Decisions about sample size and distribution, the number of callbacks, types of questions, nature of the population, survey topic, amount of money available, availability of skilled personnel and time constraints must all be taken into account when selecting a method of administration. See Table 7.1 for a summary of the advantages and disadvantages of the various methods of administering questionnaires.

Table 7.1   Advantages and disadvantages of mail, personal and telephone methods of administering questionnaires

	Face to face	Telephone	Mail
Response rates			
General samples	Good	Good	Good
Specialised samples	Good	Good	Good
Representative samples			
Avoidance of refusal bias	Good	Good	Poor
Control over who completes the questionnaire	Good	Satisfactory	Good
Gaining access to the selected person	Satisfactory	Good	Good
Locating the selected person	Satisfactory	Good	Good
Effects on questionnaire design			
Ability to handle:			
Long questionnaires	Good	Satisfactory	Satisfactory
Complex questions	Good	Poor	Satisfactory
Boring questions	Good	Satisfactory	Poor
Item non-response	Good	Good	Satisfactory
Filter questions	Good	Good	Satisfactory
Question sequence control	Good	Good	Poor
Open-ended questions	Good	Good	Poor
Quality of answers			
Minimise social desirability responses	Poor	Satisfactory	Good
Ability to avoid distortion due to:			
Interviewer characteristics	Poor	Satisfactory	Good
Interviewer's opinions	Satisfactory	Satisfactory	Good
Influence of other people	Satisfactory	Good	Poor
Allows opportunities to consult	Satisfactory	Poor	Good
Avoids subversion	Poor	Satisfactory	Good
Implementing the survey			
Ease of finding suitable staff	Poor	Good	Good
Speed	Poor	Good	Satisfactory
Cost	Poor	Satisfactory	Good

[Adapted from Dillman (1978)]

Maximising response rates in personal interviews

A number of techniques can increase the response rate in face-to-face interviews.

1　If a respondent is not at home, call back up to four times. Call twice on different weekdays, once during the evening and once at the weekend.
2　The timing of the visits should take into account the characteristics of respondents: daytime will be most difficult for locating men and evenings will be less appropriate for those who may feel vulnerable to night visitors.
3　An advance letter may help allay suspicion of visits by interviewers.
4　A confident approach which assumes co-operation but avoids argumentativeness and belligerence will improve co-operation.
5　Avoid looking like a salesperson: use a clipboard rather than a briefcase.
6　Dress in a neat but neutral manner.
7　When introducing yourself give your and the organisation's name, explain the purpose of the survey and emphasise its confidentiality. Be ready to explain how the person came to be selected and to meet possible objections to participating.
8　Provide a written sheet from the survey organiser in which these things are explained and a contact number is provided.
9　Use an identity card with your photograph and the name of the survey organisation attached to your clothing.
10　Do not imply that the respondent is required to participate: the voluntary nature of the survey should be made clear.
11　If the respondent is too busy, try to make a specific time at which to return.
12　Try to avoid people refusing on behalf of others. If the required person is unavailable, try to find out when you might call back and talk with them.
13　Addresses where an interview is refused might be given to another, more experienced interviewer, perhaps with different characteristics (gender, age, class) to the initial interviewer.

Ensuring quality in personal interviews

Some general factors that can improve the frankness and care with which questions are answered are:

Training and supervision

1 To give new interviewers learning experience and confidence they should be accompanied by a supervisor on their first few interviews. The supervisor should largely conduct the initial interview, progressively playing a smaller role.

2 Supervisors should provide immediate feedback on interviews and completed schedules. This provides the opportunity to give positive feedback and identify problems with coding, probing, legibility or completion to avoid problems in subsequent interviews.

3 Selection and training should focus on the interviewer's ability to read fluently, speak clearly and be able to ad lib answers to interviewee's questions.

4 Random checks by supervisors on completed interviews should ensure that the interview has actually been conducted.

Techniques for personal interviewing

A wide range of techniques to improve rapport and assist in the interview process are available, including the following.

1 Promote a relaxed atmosphere in which the respondent can concentrate (avoid doorstep interviews).

2 Try to discourage the presence of third parties.

3 Discourage a third party from offering opinions by politely suggesting that their opinions would be of interest at the end of the interview.

4 Sit opposite the respondent.

5 Use eye contact to establish rapport.

6 Never leave a questionnaire behind for the respondent (or someone else in the household) to complete at their leisure.

7 An interview is not an equal exchange of information. Try to keep the respondent on the track but avoid making the interview sound like a test. Avoid trying to educate or convert the respondent.

8 To discourage respondents giving answers that they think the interviewer might want, it is important to avoid giving the interviewee any idea of your opinions. Avoid showing anger or surprise. If they ask for your views, deflect the question at least until the end of the interview, saying that it is best to wait till then.

9 When a person seems to provide an answer to a later question in response to an earlier question, still ask them the later question. Since question order can affect responses it is important that all

interviewees answer the questions in the same order. In such situations the apparently redundant question might be prefaced by saying 'I'd just like to check...'

10 Open-ended questions often require probing to encourage full answers. This can be accomplished by the use of an expectant glance, or phrases such as 'mmm', 'and?', 'Can you tell me more?' 'I'm not quite clear what you mean by that', 'What other reasons?', 'What else?', 'Exactly why do you think that's important', 'Could you be a little more specific?'

11 Because uniformity is important, questions should be read exactly as they appear on the interview schedule.

12 Rather than relying on memory, answers should be recorded as they are given.

13 The schedule should be checked at the completion of the interview to ensure that no questions have been missed.

Smooth implementation of personal interviews

1 Careful route planning by the interviewer is required to minimise the time and expense of travelling.

2 Notification to the police will help alleviate anxiety about strangers visiting houses in the neighbourhood.

3 A field controller normally will be required to allocate addresses to interviewers, arrange payment, keep time sheets, answer queries from both interviewers and respondents, ensure a supply of questionnaires, check completed questionnaires and ensure that interviews are being completed at a satisfactory rate.

4 A system by which interviewers record details of interviews, travel, callbacks and times of visits needs to be carefully organised before the interviews commence.

Maximising response rates in postal surveys

The cover letter

The cover letter is the main chance to motivate the respondent to complete the questionnaire. It should be simple, businesslike, written on official letterhead and no more than one page in length. It should include the following (Figure 7.1):

1 official letterhead;
2 date on which the questionnaire is mailed;
3 full name and address of the respondent (where available);
4 an explanation of the study's purpose and usefulness;

5 an explanation of how the respondent was selected and the importance of their response;
6 an assurance of confidentiality and a brief explanation of the purpose of the identifying number on the questionnaire;
7 an indication of what will be done with the results and an offer to make the results available;
8 an offer to answer any questions that might arise;
9 a handwritten signature in blue ink that stands out as being personalised;
10 position of researcher.

Figure 7.1 Initial covering letter for a mail survey

Department of Sociology

La Trobe University
Bundoora Victoria
Australia 3083
Telephone (03)479 1111
25 May 1991

Peter Johnstone
15 Queens Road
Southport, Victoria 3095

The government is planning to introduce laws restricting the places in which people are permitted to smoke tobacco products. These laws will have direct effects both on people who smoke and those who do not. However, no one knows exactly what people want and what sort of restrictions they think are reasonable and we believe that it is important that they be heard.

Your household is one of a small number in which people are being asked to give their opinion on this matter. It was drawn in a random sample of the entire country and to be truly representative it is crucial that you and no one else completes the questionnaire and that each questionnaire is returned.

Your answers will be completely confidential. The identification number on the first page is used simply to check whether we have received your questionnaire back. Your name will never be placed on your questionnaire.

The results of the survey will be made available in statistical form to government departments, politicians and the media. If you would like a summary of results for yourself, simply write 'copy of results' and your name and address on the back of the envelope when returning the questionnaire. Please **do not** put this information on the questionnaire itself.

I would be happy to answer any questions you might have. Please write or call. The special, toll-free telephone number is (008) 438 3444.

Thank you for your assistance

Yours sincerely,

William Vines
Project Director

[Adapted from Dillman, 1978, 169]

Preparing the envelopes

Since the first task is to get the respondent to open the envelope, it is important to personalise it and avoid making it look like advertising. To do this, type the respondent's name on the envelope rather than on a sticky label and use stamps rather than bulk postage. Include a stamped, self-addressed envelope to minimise the effort involved in returning the questionnaire. Use stamps rather than a business reply system to produce a greater sense of personalisation.

Using incentives

Small incentives such as a felt pen or postage stamps can be sent with the first mail-out to induce a feeling of obligation in the respondents. As an inducement to return the questionnaire, the respondent might be promised that, on return of the questionnaire, they will be placed in a draw for free lottery tickets.

Material incentives can help increase response rates, but can add considerably to the cost of a study. More important than material incentives is the necessity of maximising non-material rewards (feeling of doing something useful, being treated as important) and minimising costs (time, frustration) (Dillman, 1978: 12–18).

Selecting the mail-out date

Mailing on Tuesday is probably best. This avoids the Monday pile-up in the post office and should ensure that the questionnaire reaches the respondent by Thursday, giving them the chance to complete it by the end of the weekend. Mailings in December or during holiday periods should be avoided both because of delivery delays and absences due to holidays.

Follow-ups

Two or three follow-ups are needed to achieve response rates similar to those obtained with either telephone or personal questionnaires. Each follow-up provides an opportunity to persuade the respondent to complete the questionnaire and will take a slightly different approach.
Pre-survey contact: Contacting respondents by mail or telephone advising them to expect a questionnaire can increase response rates.
The first follow-up: One week after the first mail-out, the first follow-up should be sent to all respondents. This can even be prepared at the same time as the initial questionnaires are sent out. It takes the form of a postcard with the respondent's address typed on one side and a brief reminder on the other. It is designed to

Figure 7.2   First follow-up postcard

> 1 June 1991
>
> Last week a questionnaire asking for your views about the government's plans to restrict smoking was mailed to you.
>
> If you have completed the questionnaire already please accept our sincere thanks. If not, could you please return it today? Because it was sent to a small representative sample it is most important that your views are included in the study if we are to represent people's views adequately.
>
> If by some chance you did not receive the questionnaire or have mislaid it please call me on our tollfree line (008 438 3444) and I will send you another copy today.
>
> Yours sincerely,
>
> William Vines
> Project Director

[Adapted from Dillman, 1978:184]

thank early responders and to remind rather than persuade non-responders. Figure 7.2 provides an example of the contents of this first reminder.

The second follow-up: This follow-up should be sent only to people who have not responded after three weeks and will contain a new letter, a replacement questionnaire and a new stamped return envelope. The cover letter will tie the letter to the previous ones and be similar in content to the first one but more insistent in tone.

The third follow-up: If funds and time allow, or the level of response requires, a third follow-up may be used. The effectiveness of this follow-up will come not from a more strongly worded letter but from the persistence of the researcher: this will be the fourth letter the respondent will have received. To emphasise the importance of the survey, certified mail is sometimes used to induce a sense of urgency and importance. The cover letter will deal with similar areas to the initial letter using slightly different words, but place more emphasis on the importance of completing the survey, provide an explanation of why certified mail is being used (to ensure delivery) and be accompanied by a further copy of the questionnaire. Another return envelope should be included. Rather than using certified mail it may be possible to use telephone calls or even personal visits to encourage respondents to complete the questionnaire.

Undelivered questionnaires

A proportion of questionnaires will be returned either because the address is unknown or the respondent had moved. The addresses should be checked against the original list from which the sample was drawn and corrected where possible. Where the respondent has moved it might be possible to obtain a more recent address by using another list (e.g. check electoral roll, telephone book, employer). If the respondent has died they should be dropped from the sample. It is important to record the reasons why questionnaires were not delivered as this is important when calculating the response rate (see page 107).

Answering respondents' questions

Since some respondents will have questions, it is important that someone is readily available to help. They may need to clarify how the respondent was selected or the importance of the study, or to advise the caller what to do in the case of the respondent being away, too ill or being unable to read.

Smooth implementation of postal questionnaires

It is important to develop a thorough timetable of the steps of the survey indicating on what dates various tasks are to be performed and listing the supplies that will be needed.

Supplies

As far as possible, *all* supplies and printing should be completed before sending out the first questionnaire. The dates printed on the letters should reflect the actual dates on which the questionnaires or letters are sent.

Failure to ensure that all supplies are available when required can lead to major problems with follow-up procedures. The number of supplies required depends on response rates at each stage, decisions about how many follow-ups to use and so forth. Table 7.2 provides an estimate of the supplies needed per 100 initial sample members with three follow-ups and assuming a response rate of 35 per cent to the initial mailing, 60 per cent after the first reminder and 70 per cent after the second reminder.

Identification numbers

To avoid duplicating or missing identity numbers on questionnaires and ensuring that the identity numbers on your records correspond

Table 7.2 Supplies per 100 sample members in a mail survey

	Initial mail out	Follow-up			
		1st	2nd	3rd	Total
Envelopes (mail and return)	200	00	80	60	340
Stamps (mail and return)	200	100	140	60	500
Letters	100	100	40	30	270
Questionnaires	100	00	40	30	170

with those on the questionnaires, it is important to put the identity numbers on questionnaires just prior to mailing and to check that the name on both the envelope and the cover letter match with each other and with the identification number on your files.

Staffing

Someone needs to be available to answer queries from respondents and to maintain records of responders and of ineligible sample members. Although there probably will not be many of these, provision still needs to be made. Careful records need to be kept indicating which questionnaires have been returned so that unnecessary reminders will not be sent and to enable the calculation of the current response rate. Coding can be done for closed questions as the questionnaires are returned.

Maximising response rates in telephone surveys

Obtaining good response rates with telephone interviews depends on two main factors: locating the respondent and getting them to agree to take part in the interview. Once a person begins an interview they nearly always complete it.

Locating the respondent

Once a sample of names or households has been selected (see below) the interviewer first has to make contact with that telephone number and then with the appropriate person within the household. Timing of calls is therefore important. While the most appropriate time to call people will depend on the nature of the sample, it is possible to provide some general guidelines for general population surveys. Dillman (1978) recommends that the initial call commences early in the week. For numbers that do not answer, the next call should be at the weekend, either in the afernoon or evening. For those still not contacted, weekday afternoons are tried next followed by weekday mornings. If time permits, the remaining non-contacts can be put aside for a week or so before trying one last call. Care should be taken to call at socially acceptable times and if contact is made at an inappropriate time apologise and try to arrange a more suitable time.

Once a number is located we need to ensure that it is the type of number that is appropriate to the study (e.g. a household rather than a business) and then select the appropriate member of the household to interview. Methods of selection are outlined in Table 5.3.

Gaining co-operation

The interviewer needs to state concisely the purpose of the call. Respondents will normally listen to this introduction before they decide to co-operate or refuse. But it must be brief: it will cover similar areas to those dealt with by the covering letter in a mail survey. After ascertaining that you have the correct number and that it is a household residence, an introduction similar to the following could be used:

'This is _____ from _____ university. We are doing a statewide research study to find out people's views about government proposals to restrict smoking in public places. Your telephone number was drawn from a random sample of the entire state. The questions I need to ask will take about __ minutes. If you have any queries I'd be happy to answer them. Could I ask you these questions now?'

If specific household members were to be interviewed, a respondent selection procedure would need to be inserted into the introduction.

One way of increasing acceptance rates and providing more information about the study is to send an advance letter three to five days before ringing. The format and content of the letter would be similar to that for the initial mail questionnaire except that it would warn people to expect a call soon.

When contact is made with the respondent they may have questions or raise objections as to why they could not participate in the study. It is important to be prepared for these. Dillman (1978: 260–263) provides a set of likely problems and useful responses.

Ensuring quality in telephone surveys

The quality of a telephone survey will be affected by the quality of the questionnaire, the ability of interviewers to conduct interviews and the sample quality. Questionnaire design has been covered elsewhere and the principles of interviewing are similar to those already covered for face-to-face interviews and need not be covered here. But sample considerations deserve further attention.

There are essentially two methods of obtaining a list of telephone numbers to call: obtaining a systematic sample from telephone directories (directory listing) or obtaining a randomly generated set of telephone numbers for the exchange areas covered by the survey (random digit dialling).

For the *directory listing* method to be effective, up-to-date directories of the whole sample area are needed. To the extent that this is not possible the sample will be biased and this will add to bias caused by people with unlisted numbers. We would then estimate the number of relevant numbers (e.g. residences) in each directory, decide on the sample size, determine an appropriate sampling fraction and thus draw a systematic sample (see pages 64–5).

Random digit dialling involves obtaining a list of exchanges (indicated by the first three or four numbers in a telephone number) and using a table of random numbers to generate the remaining four or so numbers that will be attached to the exchange number to make up a telephone number. This method avoids the need to obtain directories, together with the tedious work of obtaining numbers from a telephone directory, and should enable contact with unlisted numbers. Unfortunately it does not enable one to select between business and residential addresses and can thus produce a lot of unnecessary calls. Further, not all possible telephone numbers in an exchange are allocated, thus leading to a lot of time spent trying to contact nonexistent numbers. These problems make it difficult to determine the reasons for unanswered calls, thus creating complications when calculating response rates.

Smooth implementation of telephone surveys

A central telephone interviewing facility will greatly assist the conduct of a telephone survey. Not only does it assist with interview quality and integrity by enabling good supervision, but it also assists in ensuring that calls are made in the most systematic and efficient manner.

Once a sample of telephone numbers is generated, a number, address and name (if appropriate) needs to be attached to each interview schedule — a task that can be accomplished as each call is made. Each interview schedule should have a cover page to which this information is attached and which allows the interviewer to easily make a record of calls to that number. The cover sheet should make provision to record which call it is, the date and time, the interviewer, the outcome of the call and space to note down specific times at which a callback has been arranged. Space should be provided to record the final outcome of the number — was an interview refused, contact never made, number disconnected and so forth.

A system for making callbacks needs to be implemented. Interview schedules should be sorted according to their status: weekday callback, evening callback, weekend callback, specific time callback, refusal, completed interview, wrong number and so forth. This enables the supervisor to systematically organise callbacks.

Since a telephone call cannot tolerate long silences it is important that all supplies are readily available and that the interview schedule is constructed in such a way that it is easy for interviewers to find their way around it. Some more elaborate systems involve computer programs where the questions are on the computer and, depending on what answers are given (the interview is coded as the interview progresses), the next appropriate question automatically appears on the screen.

Care needs to be given to employing sufficient interviewers for the various stages of the interview program. Telephone interviewing can be exhausting and breaks are required. It is helpful initially to have up to 50 per cent more interviewers on duty than are actually interviewing at any one time. As the interviewing program proceeds and mainly callbacks are required, fewer interviewers will be needed to deal with the number of calls that can be made in a particular session.

Summary

Although three methods have been outlined, various combinations of these methods can be developed. For example, interviews can be supplemented by a leave-behind questionnaire that the respondent mails back latter. Mail surveys can be supplemented by a follow-up telephone interview. Longitudinal surveys might commence with interviews at the first stage but once personal contact has been established in this way, mail or telephone methods might be used for further stages.

The decision about the method by which a questionnaire will be administered must take into account the content matter of the survey, the nature of the survey population, the importance of sample quality and size and the amount of time and money available. There is no correct method, only methods that are more or less appropriate to particular situations. Once the decision about method is made, attention has to be given to motivating the respondent to participate, ensuring that the information provided is complete and accurate and to ways of successfully completing the administration phase.

Further reading

Dillman's *Mail and Telephone Surveys* (1978) provides an excellent and detailed description of these techniques and has a comprehensive bibliography relating to various aspects of these techniques. The journal *Public Opinion Quarterly* contains many articles on all three methods. Hoinville, Jowell and associates provide good introductions and a good bibliography to personal and postal surveys in *Survey Research Practice* (1978). Beed and Stimson (1986) provide useful discussions of telephone surveying, while Lavrakas (1987) provides a very thorough practical guide for the conduct of telephone surveys. Instruction manuals given to interviewers by market research companies or research centres such as the University of Michigan's Survey Research Center's *Interviewer's Manual* provide very useful advice to interviewers. A splendid set of papers on modes of administration and interviewer effects is provided in Singer and Presser (1989).

Part III   ANALYSING DATA

8 Overview of analysis

Once data have been collected they have to be analysed. This chapter outlines three broad factors which affect how they are analysed. Subsequent chapters examine the particular methods of analysis and related statistics in more detail. Three factors which affect how the data are analysed are:

1 the number of variables being examined;
2 the level of measurement of the variables;
3 whether we want to use our data for descriptive or inferential purposes.

The number of variables

How we analyse data depends on what we want to know. If we simply wish to describe one characteristic of the sample at a time (e.g. sex, vote, income level) we will use a univariate (one variable) method of analysis. If we are interested in two variables simultaneously we will use a bivariate (two variable) method. For example, if we wanted to see if sex and voting preference were related (i.e. do women vote differently from men?) we would use a bivariate method. If our research question makes use of three or more variables we would use a multivariate technique. We might be interested in income: why do some people earn more than others? We might say it is due to two factors: education level and sex. Since we are using three variables here, we would use a multivariate technique.

Before analysing data we must be clear about the question we are trying to answer. This will dictate the broad type of analysis we choose. Once we have decided, for example, that we need to use a bivariate technique, we will then need to choose between a range of such techniques. In practice we develop and refine our research questions in the process of analysis so we move between univariate, bivariate and multivariate techniques. Initially, for example, we might formulate a question: do people's incomes vary because of different levels of education? Initial bivariate analysis might show that they do to an extent but that we need to look at other variables together with education. Thus we reformulate the question. This question might then require the use of a multivariate technique.

Levels of measurement

Having decided to use univariate, bivariate or multivariate techniques we have to decide which particular technique to use within these broad categories. A key factor in this choice is the level of measurement of the variables being used.

Any variable is composed of two or more categories or attributes. Thus sex is a variable with the categories male and female, country of birth is a variable with the categories being particular countries. Level of measurement of variables refers to how the categories of the variable relate to one another. There are three main levels of measurement: nominal, ordinal and interval/ratio. These can be explained best with three examples.

Religious affiliation is an example of a nominal variable. A nominal variable is one where we can distinguish between categories of a variable but cannot rank the categories in any order. We know that people in different categories differ from one another but it is not meaningful to quantify how much difference there is. Country of birth, sex and marital status are all examples of nominal level variables.

An ordinal variable is one where it is meaningful to rank the categories: there is some justifiable order between the categories. However, it is not possible to quantify precisely how much difference there is between the categories. We might ask people how strongly they agree or disagree with a particular statement. The categories can be rank ordered in terms of the strength of agreement they reflect toward a statement or attitude. If people were asked to what extent they are in paid work with the responses of 'not at all', 'part-time only' and 'full time', this would be an ordinal variable. The categories can be ordered in terms of the amount of paid work. Any variable in which categories can be ranked but where the difference between the categories cannot be quantified in precise numerical terms is an ordinal variable.

An interval/ratio variable is one in which the categories have a natural ranking and it is possible to quantify precisely the differences between the categories. Age, if it is measured in years, is an interval variable because as well as ranking people according to their age, the

Table 8.1 **Working out levels of measurement**

	Level of measurement		
	Nominal	Ordinal	Interval
Are there difference categories?	yes	yes	yes
Can I rank the categories?	no	yes	yes
Can I specify the differences between categories numerically?	no	no	yes

precise difference between the ages can be quantified. If age was simply measured as young, middle aged and old it would only be an ordinal variable. If we ask people how many hours of paid work they have weekly, it is an interval variable. In general, variables in which the categories are naturally numeric (e.g. income in dollars, age, height, number of children, years of education) are interval level variables. The intervals between categories can be specified precisely.

When trying to work out the level of measurement of variables (something that must be done before analysing data) the questions in Table 8.1 should help.

Influencing the level of measurement

The level of measurement of some variables can be determined by the researcher by how the question is asked in the first place, how it is coded and by the purpose for which it is to be used.

1 *The format of the question and response categories:* In many cases the way a question is worded and the way the response categories are organised can affect the level of measurement of a variable. If we ask people how much paid work they have and provide 'none', 'part-time' and 'full-time' as response categories, the variable will be ordinal. If we ask them how many hours per week they work it will be interval. If we ask how many hours per week and provide the responses of 'none', '1–10', '11–20', '21–30', '31–40' and '40 plus', it is an ordinal variable. This is because the difference between people in the various grouped categories cannot be specified precisely. One person may be in the 11–20 category and another in the 21–30 category. Since we do not know the precise number of hours they each work we cannot tell how much difference there is in the hours each works. It could be between one and nineteen hours.

2 *The application:* In some situations it is legitimate to rank the categories of a variable, thus treating it as ordinal, and for other

applications it is not meaningful to rank them. For example, a list of religious affiliations would not be ranked if we simply wished to classify the group to which a person belonged (e.g. Methodist, Presbyterian, Baptist, Catholic, Anglican, Jehovah's Witness, Jewish, Moslem, etc.), but if we wanted to use religious affiliation to reflect something about level of integration into mainstream groups in society it could be meaningful to rank religious groups for this purpose.

Which level of measurement to aim for

Since the level of measurement of a variable can be affected by a researcher's decisions, which is the best level to aim for? There are at least seven things to consider.

1   A wider range of methods of analysis is appropriate as·the level of measurement of variables increases.
2   More powerful and sophisticated techniques of analysis are appropriate for interval level variables.
3   Higher levels of measurement provide more information — but is this really necessary?
4   Questions which require a lot of precision and detail can be unreliable since people often do not have accurate, detailed information.
5   People may be reluctant to provide precise information but may provide it in more general terms (e.g. income bracket, age cohort).
6   Numerical data collected in grouped form (e.g. age, income categories) can be converted to interval data if we make particular assumptions.
7   If variables are measured at an interval level it is simple to reduce it to ordinal or nominal level. With the exception already noted, data collected at low levels of measurement cannot be converted to higher levels.

In summary, it is generally advisable to measure variables at the highest level appropriate to that variable, but considerations of reliability, response rate and need will mean that measurement at lower levels often makes most sense.

Methods of analysis

The method of analysis adopted depends on the complexity of the research question. If it involves only one variable, select a method of

Figure 8.1 Flow chart for selecting analysis and statistical techniques

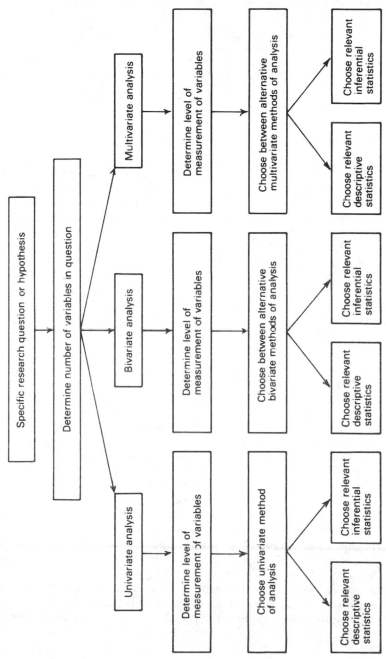

Table 8.2 List of some methods of analysis for survey analysis

Univariate methods	Bivariate methods	Multivariate methods
1 Frequency distributions	1 Crosstabulations 2 Scattergrams 3 Regression 4 Rank order correlation 5 Comparison of means	1 Conditional tables 2 Partial rank order correlation 3 Multiple and partial correlation 4 Multiple and partial regression 5 Path analysis

analysis appropriate for univariate analysis. If the question involves two variables we will use a method designed for bivariate analysis and so on (see Figure 8.1). Within each level of analysis (univariate, bivariate, multivariate) there is a range of methods of analysis (Table 8.2). The choice between methods is determined in part by the level of measurement of the variables involved: some methods of analysis are appropriate only for variables measured at certain levels (e.g. interval). Having chosen an appropriate method of analysis, the choice of statistics to be used with that particular method is affected both by the metho ' of analysis itself and the level of measurement of the particular v?   s. These points are discussed in detail in Chapters 9 to 13.

Descriptive and inferential statistics

Only two points need to be made about statistics at the moment. The choice of statistics is determined by many previous decisions such as the method of analysis, level of measurement of the variables and complexity of the research question (univariate, bivariate or mult-ivariate). The analyst's task is to work out, given these decisions, which statistics to use. Statistics are only a tool for analysis: we need to choose the appropriate tool for the job in hand.

There are two basic types of statistics: descriptive and inferential. Descriptive statistics are those which summarise patterns in the responses of people in a sample. They provide information about, say, the 'average' income of respondents or tell us whether education level affects the voting patterns of people in the sample. Typically, however, we are not interested primarily in the attitudes and char-acteristics of the 2000 people in the sample, but in generalising from the results in the sample to the population. The function of inferential statistics is to provide an idea about whether the patterns described in the sample are likely to apply in the population from which the sample is drawn. For example, before any election, samples of about 2000 people are asked who they will vote for. Let us say 52 per cent say Labour and 48 per cent say other parties. People do not want to know how these 2000 people would vote but how the whole electorate is likely to vote. Inferential statistics help estimate how close to the sample's voting preferences the population's vote will be: inferential statistics enable us to infer from the sample to the population.

Following chapters focus mainly on descriptive statistics. The use of these statistics requires the most imagination and skill and is the most productive in terms of understanding any phenomenon. Once we have analysed data using these techniques we may wish to use inferential statistics (tests of significance) to see whether the patterns and processes we have detected in the sample hold in the population. But the first and key task is to discover these patterns and processes. This is the task of descriptive statistics.

Summary

The aim of this chapter has been to provide a map of steps in deciding how to analyse data. It has outlined some factors which affect such analysis and steps to take when trying to work out how to analyse data and in choosing summary statistics. Figure 8.1 summarises these steps.

Having clarified the particular question we must see how many variables we are working with and work out whether we need a univariate, bivariate or multivariate technique. Then we ascertain the level of measurement of the variables and this affects which univariate, bivariate or multivariate technique we use (Table 8.2). Having chosen the analysis technique we will use descriptive statistics appropriate to that technique (and to the level of measurement) to summarise the results. If we have a random sample, we will then use inferential statistics to see if the patterns we have found for the sample are likely to apply to the population.

The next five chapters are organised around the distinctions made in this chapter. Chapter 9 examines univariate methods of analysis and Chapters 10 and 11 deal with a range of bivariate methods. Chapter 12 provides an introduction to the logic of simple multivariate techniques while Chapter 13 outlines some more complex multivariate models. Within each chapter it is made clear whether the method is used for nominal, ordinal or interval variables.

Further reading

Useful discussions of the distinctions made in this chapter are made in most introductory statistics books. Brief outlines are available in section A of Freeman's *Elementary Applied Statistics* (1965) and Johnson's *Social Statistics Without Tears* (1977). Very thorough discussions are available in Loether and McTavish, *Descriptive Statistics for Sociologists* (1974), Chapters 1 and 2 and in their *Inferential Statistics for Sociologists* (1974), Chapters 1 and 10.

9 Univariate analysis

This chapter is divided into two main sections. The first deals with descriptive statistics and will separately examine statistics used for nominal, ordinal and interval variables. The second section deals with inferential statistics, particularly those called interval estimation statistics.

Descriptive statistics

Frequency distributions

Each variable will have at least two answers—many will have far more answers. The first thing to do when all the data are collected is to count how many people gave particular answers to each question: we look at how the sample is spread or distributed in the various categories of each variable. This counting exercise results in *frequency distributions*.

The simplest way of obtaining a frequency distribution is to draw up a table in which each possible answer to the question is placed in the left-hand column. Separate columns will also be provided for the number of people who provided each answer (the *frequency column*—labelled N) and for the percentage of people who gave that particular response (the *percentage column*) (see Table 9.1).

When calculating percentages, you will have to decide what to do with people who did not answer the question. Normally it is best to exclude them from the calculation of percentages so that the number (N) on which you base the percentages is the number of people who answered the question. The frequency column is not always provided in tables—the percentage figures can provide a very good picture of the distribution on the variable. If you omit the frequency column, make sure that you indicate the total number of cases on which percentages are based so that it is possible to reconstruct the actual number of people in each category.

137

Table 9.1   Three frequency distributions

What is your favourite subject?			'Examinations are the best way of assessing ability'			How old are you?		
Answer	N	%	Answer	N	%	Age	N	%
Literature	41	5.5	Strongly agree	254	34	7	10	1.3
Geography	102	13.7	Agree	201	27	8	22	2.9
History	75	10.0	Can't decide	119	16	9	30	4.0
Mathematics	125	16.8	Disagree	97	13	10	66	8.8
Writing	60	8.0	Strongly disagree	75	10	11	145	19.4
Languages	92	12.3				12	200	26.8
Chemistry	190	25.5	Total	746	100	13	143	19.1
Other	61	8.2				14	68	9.1
						15	32	4.3
Total	746	100				16	20	2.7
						17	10	1.3
						Total	746	99.7

Source: Hypothetical
Note: Four people did not answer each question.

When presenting a frequency table, you should include the following information:

1   table number and title;
2   labels for the categories of the variable;
3   column headings to indicate what the numbers in the column represent;
4   the total number on which the percentages are based;
5   the number of missing cases;
6   the source of the data. This is particularly important if the data are from a source other than the survey described in the report. The source is normally noted beneath the table, as in Table 9.1.
7   It may be necessary to provide footnotes to the table in which the actual question or working definition on which the table is based is provided.

The information in frequency tables can be displayed as a graph rather than in a table. A variety of ways of presenting graphs are available, and these are outlined in detail in Loether and McTavish (1974a). One common method is to use a *histogram*. To do this we draw a graph like that in Figure 9.1 which has two axes: a horizontal axis (called the *X* axis) and a vertical axis (called the *Y* axis). We

Figure 9.1 Histograms of data in table 9.1

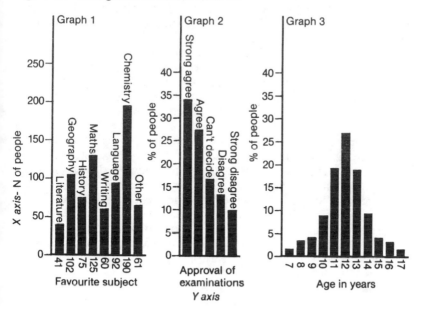

divide the horizontal axis into sections to reflect the categories of the variable. The vertical axis is also divided into sections to reflect the frequency with which a particular response is given. The vertical axis can be divided to represent *numbers* in each category (Graph 1) or the *percentages* in each category (Graphs 2 and 3 in Figure 9.1). Thus for the variables in Table 9.1, the graphs would look like those in Figure 9.1. For example, in the second graph that indicates approval of examinations, the first bar shows that almost 35 per cent of people (see the *Y* axis) strongly agree with examinations.

As well as displaying distributions with either a table or a graph, we can describe them in terms of their *shape*. When examining a distribution, it is useful to ask at least three questions regarding its shape.

1 Is it *skewed*? If so, in what direction?
2 How widely *spread* are cases. Are they mainly concentrated in a few categories or widely dispersed across many categories?
3 What are the most *typical* responses? In which categories are cases most commonly found?

The categories of ordinal and interval variables have a natural order ranging from low to high (e.g. Graphs 2 and 3 in Figure 9.1). In these cases we can look at the distribution to see if the bulk of people are clustered towards the low end, the high end or whether they are evenly balanced on both sides of the middle of the variable. In Graph 2, indicating approval of examinations, people are clustered towards the 'low' end of the variable. The variable is said to be positively *skewed*. If people were clustered towards the 'high' end, the distribution would be negatively skewed. In the graph of age, we have a peak at the age of 12, indicating that 12-year-olds were the most common age group in our sample. Looking at each side of the distribution, we see that the shape of the distribution on each side of this peak is almost identical. Where a distribution has this balanced appearance, it is said to be *symmetrical*.

We can also look at how widely and how evenly spread cases are in the distribution. If, for ordinal and interval variables, cases are clustered together in a small number of adjacent categories, the distribution is said to have a low level of variability. For nominal variables the concentration of cases in any small number of categories constitutes low variability.

It is also useful to examine in which categories people are most heavily concentrated. Which responses are most frequently chosen? When examining a graph or a frequency table, look for the peaks in the distribution, as these will often give an idea of typical responses. Sometimes there might be several peaks or several 'typical' responses. The discussion below outlines different ways of determining what responses are typical in distributions.

As well as displaying distributions we can summarise them. Most commonly they are summarised by statistics broadly called measures of central tendency and of dispersion. Central tendency measures try to pinpoint the average or typical response to a question. For example, a group may be characterised by a wide range of ages but what is the most typical age? Overall is the group made up of young people, middle-aged or old people? Measures of central tendency describe a group in terms of what is typical. Since not everyone in a group is typical we need to know how much people in the group differ from what is typical. Measures of dispersion provide this information and thus tell us how well the measure of central tendency sums up the distribution.

There is a variety of ways of arranging frequency tables and graphs and there are different measures of central tendency and dispersion. Which ones are used depends largely on whether the variables we are dealing with are nominal, ordinal or interval.

Nominal variables

Since a nominal variable is one for which there is no necessary ranking of categories, it does not matter in what order the categories are arranged in a frequency table. However, there may be a logical order. Thus a list of countries could be arranged according to their region (e.g. Australasia, Western Europe, Africa), by size or a number of other criteria depending on the use of the data.

Often it is helpful to combine different categories. This avoids having very large and unreadable tables with many categories which are very similar or have very few people in them. In these situations we can combine categories which are similar for the purpose of analysis and put categories with very few people in them together with another appropriate category. This makes the table more readable by making it easier to get an overview of it. Be careful to avoid distorting the results by combining different responses: we should be able to provide a justification for how the data has been reorganised.

Central tendency: the mode

With nominal variables the only way to pick out the typical response is to pick out the single most common response. This is called the mode. In Table 9.2 the single most common response is 'now married', thus 'now married' is the mode.

There are problems with using the mode to measure typicality. First, picking out the most common response does not tell us how typical it is. For example, in a group of ten people, three might have been born in Australia and this might be the mode for the group but it is not typical of the group as a whole. We need to know how typical the mode is (see Dispersion: the variation ratio). Second, some distributions have more than one mode so it is not possible to use one figure to summarise these bimodal or multimodal distributions.

Table 9.2   Frequency table for marital status (population over 20 years old)

	per cent
Never married	18
Now married	67
Separated	3
Divorced	4
Widowed	8
Total	100

Third, the mode is very vulnerable to how the categories of a variable have been collapsed. If we combine some categories, we can get a lot of people in some categories and thus this combined category could become the mode. Had we not combined them or combined them differently we could have obtained a different mode. In this sense the mode is unstable and open to manipulation. Nevertheless, with nominal data it is the best we have.

Dispersion: the variation ratio

The variation ratio (symbolised as v) is most easily calculated by seeing what percentage of people are *not* in the modal category. The higher this percentage the more poorly the mode reflects the overall distribution. The variation ratio is normally expressed as a proportion. This is simply done by moving the decimal place on the percentage figure two places to the left. Thus if 70 per cent of people are not in the modal category, then v is 0.70.

Ordinal variables

Since the categories of ordinal variables can be ranked it is crucial that they be put in their correct rank order in a frequency table. Failure to do so will distort both patterns in the data and statistics used to summarise them. Frequency tables also can have an additional column to that already described—the cumulative percentage column illustrated in Table 9.3.

The cumulative percentage is a rolling addition of each of the percentages in the earlier categories of the variable. Thus the cumulative percentage of 52.4 per cent means that 52.4 per cent saw their mother weekly or more often. The cumulative percentage is helpful for working out the median.

Table 9.3   Frequency of adults seeing their mother

	N	per cent	cumulative per cent
Daily	35	7.5	7.5
Several times a week	79	17.0	24.5
Weekly	130	27.9	52.4
2–3 weeks	89	19.1	71.5
Monthly	33	7.1	78.6
2–3 months	34	7.3	85.9
2–3 times a year	31	6.6	92.5
Less often	35	7.5	100.0
Total N = 466		100%	

Central tendency: the median

While the mode can be used for ordinal data the median is preferred because it takes account of the fact that people can be ranked on ordinal variables. The median is worked out by ranking each case in a distribution from low to high on the variable and finding the middle person. Whatever category the middle person belongs to is the median category (see Figure 9.2).

Whenever there is an even number of people in a group there is no actual middle person. The median will be the point between the two cases each side of the imaginary middle person (Figure 9.3).

When dealing with large numbers of people as is normally the case in survey research, it is quite easy to work out the median category (i.e. the category to which the middle person belongs) by using the cumulative percentage column in a frequency table. Simply look down this column until you see the cumulative percentage nudge over 50 per cent and then look at the category of the variable that corresponds to this. The middle person is this 50th per cent person in the cumulative percentage column (see Table 9.4).

For continuous data where there is a continuum of categories (e.g. height, weight, age, $ income) rather than discrete categories, there are formulae to give a precise numerical value to the median but

Figure 9.2   Working out the median with an odd number of cases

Case						middle case					
	1	2	3	4	5	6	7	8	9	10	11
Social class	LWC	LWC	UW	UW	LM	MM	MM	MM	UM	UM	UC

median = MM

Notes: LWC = lower working class; UW = upper working;
LM = lower middle; MM = Middle middle;
UM = upper middle; UC = upper class

Figure 9.3   Working out the median with an even number of cases

Case					middle case					
	1	2	3	4	5	6	7	8	9	10
Social class	LWC	UW	UW	MM	MM	MM	MM	UM	UM	UC

median = MM

Table 9.4   Frequency table of beliefs about the effect of conservative governments on the level of industrial disputes

	N	per cent	cumulative per cent
Certainly decrease	31	6.3	6.3
Probably decrease	79	15.9	22.2
Wouldn't change	175	35.3	57.5
Probably increase	162	32.6	90.1
Certainly increase	49	9.9	100.0

Total N = 496

these need not concern us here (see Loether and McTavish, 1974a:127).

Dispersion: the decile range

If most cases in a distribution are in ranked categories close to the median category, the median is a good summary of the group. If many cases are a long way from the median category it is not so good. One way to assess the summarising value of the median has been to look at the entire range of scores in a distribution. The wider the range the less adequate the median is. The problem with using the range is that its size can be exaggerated by a few extreme cases, thus underestimating the summarising value of the median (see Figure 9.4).

To avoid this distorting effect of extreme cases we can drop the bottom 10 per cent of cases (called the first decile) and the top 10 per cent. This gives us the decile range: we look at the range of the middle 80 per cent of the cases. This enables us to look at the variability of most of the sample without being unduly influenced by a few extreme cases.

Interval variables

Interval level variables are those in which categories can be ranked and the differences between categories can be quantified in precise numerical amounts. Frequency tables for interval variables will be similar to those for ordinal variables. Since many interval variables can have an enormous number of values (e.g. age, $ income), it is often desirable to group values. Thus age is often grouped into broad

Figure 9.4 Attributes of the range

Case	1 2 3 4 5 6 7 8 9 10

a N. of children   0 1 2 2 2 2 2 2 3 10

↑
Median

Median = 2   Because of extreme score, high range underestimates the
Range = 10   usefulness of the median
Decile range = 2

b N. of children   0 1 1 2 2 2 2 2 2 3

↑
Median

Median = 2   Low range reflects adequacy of median
Range = 3
Decile range = 1

c N. of children   0 1 2 2 2 2 5 6 9 11

↑
Median

Median = 2   High range accurately shows inadequacy of median
Range = 11
Decile range = 8

ten-year categories (e.g. 20–29, 30–39 etc.). When grouping in this way it is often desirable to make all categories of similar width. Thus with age we should avoid having some categories employing a ten-year span while others have only a five-year span. However, for the top category it is often necessary to have an open-ended category. Thus for income the top income category might be $45 000 plus. This is done so that we do not have endless categories with very few people in them.

Central tendency: the mean

The mean (expressed as $\bar{X}$) is the most common measure of central tendency for interval variables. It is calculated simply by adding up the scores for each case in the sample and dividing this by the number of cases in the sample (see Table 9.5).

The main problem with using the mean is that it can be distorted by extreme cases. Thus if a person who earned $1 million was added to Table 9.5 the mean would be $108 091. In this case the mean does not adequately reflect the bulk of the group. Another problem is that it is possible to obtain the same mean for two quite different distributions (see Table 9.6). For these reasons it is necessary to have some way of knowing how well the mean summarises the distri-

Table 9.5   Calculating the mean

	$ income			$ income
Case 1	12 000	Case	6	20 000
2	13 000		7	21 000
3	15 000		8	22 000
4	16 000		9	25 000
5	18 000		10	27 000

Total income = $189 000
Total cases = 10
X̄ = $18 900

Table 9.6   The same mean for two different distributions

Group A		Group B	
Age	N	Age	N
30	0	30	40
35	10	35	10
40	20	40	0
45	40	45	0
50	20	50	0
55	10	55	10
60	0	60	40

Total N = 100   Total N = 100
    X̄ = 45 years   X̄ = 45 years

Note: In these tables the X̄ has been obtained by
multiplying the relevant age categories by the
number of people (N) in that category

bution. To do this the appropriate measure of dispersion is used; either variance or the standard deviation can be employed.

Dispersion: variance and standard deviation

The logic and interpretation of these two closely related statistics is best illustrated by an example. Suppose we have two groups of people as in Table 9.6.

Despite the same mean the distribution of the ages in the two groups is vastly different, the mean being a more adequate summary in group A than B. The standard deviation would tell us this without us having to look at the frequency table.

The logic of calculating this statistic is to see how 'far' each case is from the mean, then add up all these 'deviations' and obtain an overall average of these deviations to use as the measure of dispersion. The actual procedure is a little more complex but is worth going through as it illustrates the logic. We will do this for group A. The formula for variance (s^2) is

$$s^2 = \frac{\Sigma(X_i - \bar{X})^2}{N}$$

and the standard deviation (s) is simply the square root of s^2,

$$s = \sqrt{s^2}.$$

Here X_i = an individual's score on the variable (e.g. age),
$\bar{X}$ = the mean (e.g. 45 years old),
Σ = the sum of,
N = total number of people in the sample.

To calculate the variance

1 Subtract the mean from each individual's score to see how much each person differs from it, i.e. $(X_i - \bar{X})$.
2 Square each of these numbers. We have to do this because the amount of variation of cases below the mean will be the same as that above the mean. Since all these differences have to be added later the negative and positive differences would add to zero we square each number: $(X_i - \bar{X})^2$.
3 Add up all these 'squared deviations': $\Sigma (X_i - \bar{X})^2$.
4 Divide this answer by the number of cases in the sample to get the 'average of the squared deviations' or variance. That is

$$s^2 = \frac{\Sigma(X_i - \bar{X})^2}{N}$$

For our example this would work out as in Table 9.7.

Since variance is not easily interpretable we can calculate the standard deviation (symbolised s) which is the square root of the variance. In Table 9.7 the standard deviation is about 5.5.

The lower s is, the better the mean is as a summary measure. This can be seen in relative terms. In group B where the mean is obviously a less satisfactory measure, s is 14. In other words s shows that the mean is a more accurate summary for group A than for group B.

The standard deviation also has a very precise interpretation. It is known from probability theory that in a normal distribution it is always true that 68 per cent of cases will lie within one standard deviation above or below the mean. In this case the size of a standard deviation is 5.5, that is 5.5 years, and the mean is 45 years. We know therefore that 68 per cent of cases will be within the range of

Table 9.7   Working out the standard deviation

1 Age	2 N	3[a] $(X_i - \bar{X})$	4 $(X_i - \bar{X})^2$	5[b] col. 2 × col. 4 $(X_i - \bar{X})$
30	0	—	—	—
35	10	−10	100	1000
40	20	−5	25	500
45	40	0	0	0
50	20	5	25	500
55	10	10	100	1000
60	0	0	—	—

Total N = 100
$\bar{X} = 45$ Total 3000

Given the variance formula this means that

$$s^2 = \frac{3000}{100} = 30.$$

Notes: a   This would be the deviation for each person in this age category.
           b   Since there are a number of people in this category we can get the total squared variation for all those in that category by multiplying column 4 by column 2.

45 years (the mean) plus or minus 5.5 years (one standard deviation), that is within the range 39.5 to 50.5 years. Probability theory also tells us that 95 per cent of cases will always lie within plus or minus two standard deviations of the mean. In this case that means eleven years of the mean, or between 34–56 years.

When a distribution is not normal, the percentage of cases which lie within various numbers of standard deviations of the mean cannot be predicted with as much precision. This is summarised in Table 9.8.

In summary, the standard deviation provides a measure of the summarising value of a mean and tells us within what range of the mean a given percentage of cases lies.

The standard deviation has another use. Any person's 'score' on a variable can be converted into a standard score (often called a z-score). This is simply a particular score expressed as standard deviation units. Thus for a distribution in which the mean age is 50 years and the standard deviation is five years, we can express the age of a 60-year-old with a z-score of 2, that is the mean (50) plus two standard deviations (10). An age of 45 could be expressed with a z-score of −1 (the mean minus one standard deviation). An age of 53 would be expressed with a z-score of 0.6 (the mean plus 6/10 of a

Table 9.8 **Per cent within various standard deviations for various types of distribution**

Number of standard deviations from $\bar{X}$	Minimum for any distribution	Minimum for any unimodal and symmetrical distribution	Value for a normal distribution
1.00	0	56	68
2.00	75	89	95
3.00	89	95	99.7

standard deviation). To convert any score into a z-score use the formula

$$z = \frac{(X_i - \bar{X})}{s}$$

Thus to convert 53 into a z-score

$$z = \frac{(53 - 50)}{5}$$

$$= \frac{3}{5}$$

$$= 0.6$$

Converting raw scores into standard scores enables us to work out the exact standing of a particular score in a distribution. We can work out the proportion of cases falling above and below the score. To do this we would consult a table like that in Appendix A. We simply look down the z column until we come to the relevant z-score and then look across. Thus for our 53-year-old we go down to 0.6 in the z column and then go across to the third column where we find 0.7257. This means that 72.57 per cent of cases are below the z-score of 0.6, that is 72.57 per cent are younger than 53 in that distribution. The next column tells us what proportion is older than 53. In this case the figure is 0.2743 or 27.43 per cent. If the z-score was a negative number the meaning of these figures would be reversed. The figure of 0.7257 would therefore mean 72.57 per cent were above (older than) the 47-year-old.

The other reason for discussing z-scores is that they are used in some of the more complex analysis techniques (e.g. multiple regression) and an understanding of them is helpful when dealing with these procedures.

Inferential statistics

Inferential statistics are used to help extrapolate from the patterns in a sample to likely patterns in the population from which the sample was drawn. Interval estimates are the most common inferential technique for univariate analysis.

Interval estimates for interval variables

If in a sample the mean income is $18000, we might want to know what the mean for the population is. Since samples are unlikely to be perfect reflections of the population (sampling error), we cannot simply use the sample mean (called the sample estimate) to work out the actual mean income for the population (called the population parameter).

What we need is a way of estimating how accurate our sample estimate is likely to be. If our sample is a random sample then probability theory again provides the answer. If we take a large number of random samples most will be close to the mark: they will come up with means close to that which actually exists in the population. In only a few samples will the sample estimates be way off the mark. In fact the sample estimates would approximate a 'normal' distribution (Figure 9.5).

The problem is that if we have just one sample how do we know how close *our* sample mean is to the true population mean? Our sample could be one of those which is way out but it is *more probable* that it will be one of those close to the true population mean (since most samples will be close). But even so, *how close* is it likely to be?

Figure 9.5   A distribution of random sample means

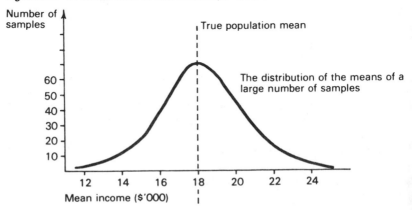

To estimate this we can calculate a statistic called the *standard error* of the mean using the formula

$$S_m = \frac{s}{\sqrt{N}}$$

where
S_m = standard error of the mean
s = standard deviation
N = total number in the sample.

Having calculated the standard error, probability theory tells us within what range of the sample mean the population mean is likely to be. Probability theory tells us that for 95 per cent of samples the population mean will be within ∓2 standard error units of the sample mean. Put differently, it means that in our sample there is a 95 per cent chance that the population mean will be within ∓2 standard errors of the population mean. We can therefore estimate within a range where the population mean is likely to be. This range is called the confidence interval and our degree of certainty that the population mean will fall within that range (95 per cent) is called the confidence level. The figure we get from calculating S_m is always expressed in terms of the units of the variable concerned. If the variable is $ income and S_m is 1000, this means $1000.

What does this all mean in everyday language? Let us say that our sample mean is $18 000 and the standard error is $1000. Therefore there is a 95 per cent chance that the population mean is within the range $16 000–$20 000 (i.e. $18 000 ∓2 standard errors). The size of the standard error is a function of sample size. Thus to be able to estimate the population mean within narrow limits (i.e. within a small confidence interval) we need to reduce the standard error. To do this increase the sample size: quadrupling the sample size halves the standard error.

Inference for non-interval variables

When the mean cannot be calculated (e.g. for nominal or ordinal data) we have to use a slightly different procedure to that already outlined. To use this approach the variable must have only two categories; often we have to combine categories to achieve this. Having done this we would compute the standard error for the binominal distribution using the formula

$$S_B = \sqrt{\frac{PQ}{N}}$$

where
S_B = standard error for the binominal distribution
P = the per cent in one category of the variable
Q = the per cent in the other category of the variable
N = total number in the sample.

We look at the percentage of people answering a question in a particular way and ask how close to it the percentage in the population is likely to be. For example, a Gallup poll of 1000 people might find before an election that 52 per cent intend to vote Labour (therefore 48 per cent will vote other ways). We can estimate from this how the population will vote.

We calculate the standard error using the formula above. In this case it is

$$S_B = \sqrt{\frac{(52)(48)}{1000}}$$
$$= \sqrt{\frac{2495}{1000}}$$
$$= \sqrt{2.5}$$
$$= 1.6$$

We can now use this figure, 1.6 per cent, in the same way as previously. There is a 95 per cent chance that the percentage in the population who favour Labour will be within ∓ 2 standard errors of the sample percentage; that is 52 per cent ∓ 3.2 per cent (two standard errors) or between 48.8 per cent and 55.2 per cent.

In summary, since samples are always liable to some error, it is crucial when trying to generalise from sample estimates to use the relevant inferential statistics. With univariate analysis the most widely used technique in survey research is to use the standard error which enables us to estimate the population patterns within a range. This procedure is called *interval estimation*.

Summary

In this chapter I have outlined a range of descriptive and inferential statistics for univariate analysis. I have emphasised that the statistics chosen depend on the level of measurement of the variables and these are summarised in Table 9.9.

Table 9.9 Selecting statistics for univariate analysis

	Descriptive statistics		Inferential statistics
Level of measurement	Central tendency	Dispersion	
Nominal	Mode	Variation ratio	Interval estimate using standard error of the binomial
Ordinal	Median	Decile range	As above
Interval	Mean	Standard deviation or variance	Interval estimate using the standard error of the mean

Further reading

For a very clear, well organised and simple account of descriptive summary statistics see section B of Freeman's *Elementary Applied Statistics* (1965) or Johnson's *Social Statistics Without Tears* (1977). Both provide gentle introductions and show how to calculate these statistics. Mueller, Schuessler and Costner also do this in *Statistical Reasoning in Sociology* (1977), Chapters 3–7 as well as providing more detail on graphic presentation. A very comprehensive outline is provided by Loether and McTavish in part II of *Descriptive Statistics for Sociologists* (1974). Chapters 3 and 4 of *SPSSX: Introductory Statistical Guide* (1983) by Norusis also provides a very accessible account of these statistics.

Inferential statistics for univariate analysis are discussed fully in Loether and McTavish's *Inferential Statistics for Sociologists* (1974), Chapter 5 and in Mueller et al., Chapter 13.

10 Bivariate analysis: crosstabulations

This· chapter concentrates on one method of bivariate analysis: the use of crosstabulations. The next chapter will consider some alternative approaches. The focus is on the logic of the approach and when to use particular statistics. It concentrates on how to interpret the answers provided by various statistics without becoming preoccupied with the precise details of computation. The aim of this and the next chapter is to provide an overview of the range of methods of bivariate analysis and a framework for selecting the most appropriate method.

The heart of bivariate analysis is to see whether two variables are related (associated). The various methods of analysis and statistics simply differ in the way they assess this factor. Two variables are said to be associated or related when the distribution of values on one variable differs for different values of the other. Thus if the way people vote differs according to their social class then vote and class are associated. If the pattern of voting is much the same despite class differences then the two variables are not associated, but are independent of one another. In other words, when subgroups differ on another variable the variables are associated. When subgroups do not differ they are independent of one another. If we know that two variables are associated this can help us predict on the basis of limited information. If education and income are associated, then if.we know someone's education level we will have an idea about their likely income level. We think in terms of association constantly in everyday life. On the basis of limited information about people or situations, we predict other characteristics that we expect go with those we already know about. We would expect business people to vote conservatively and builder's labourers to support more left-wing parties. We build up these associations from either experience or prejudice. Bivariate analysis provides us with a systematic way of measuring association.

The main purpose of trying to detect a relationship between two variables is to help in the task of explanation. For example, it is one thing to show, using univariate analysis, that people vary in how conservative they are. It is quite another to explain why some people are more conservative than others. Is it because of their sex, their social class, their education, or so forth? If we find that women are more conservative than men we say we have partly explained conservatism (i.e. why some people are more conservative than others): it is because of their sex. We would then go further and ask why are women more conservative than men. Our answer may be speculative or may be based on further analysis (multivariate analysis). Looking for relationships between two variables is only a first step but it is fundamental.

Tables

Crosstabulations are a way of displaying data so that we can fairly readily detect association between two variables. There are a large number of statistics available which provide concise summaries of the association in a crosstabulation. These summarising statistics are all called correlation co-efficients or measures of association. This section will deal with how to construct and read tables to detect the existence of association. I shall then describe the range of summarising statistics available, their characteristics, when to use them and how to interpret them.

The structure of a crosstabulation

A crosstabulation consists of:

1 labels and title;
2 rows and columns;
3 cells and cell contents;
4 marginals;
5 notes.

Table 10.1 provides a simple crosstabulation of two variables: voting intention and occupation. When constructing a crosstabulation, one variable (usually the independent variable) is placed across the top of the table and a *column* is drawn for each category of that variable (white collar, blue collar). The other variable (usually the dependent variable) is placed on the side of the table and a *row* is drawn for each category of that variable (Labour voter, other voter). Tables can be described by their size, which is represented by the number of rows and columns. Table 10.1 is a two-by-two table.

Table 10.1 Vote by occupation (raw figures)

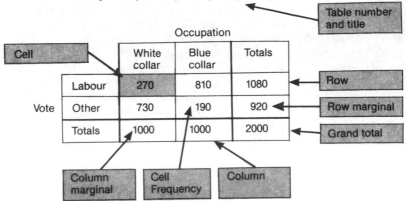

Each column and row should be labelled so that it is clear which category of the variable the column or row represents. The name of the variable that is across the top should be clearly labelled, as should the name of the side variable.

The intersection of a row and column is called a *cell*. The cell is used to represent cases which have the characteristic of *both* that column and that row. Thus the top left-hand cell represents people who have a white-collar occupation (column) and vote Labour (row). In each cell we indicate how many (or the percentage) people are in that cell. In Table 10.1 these are actual numbers of cases and are referred to as the count or cell frequency. As we shall see in Table 10.2, these numbers can be replaced with various sorts of percentages.

Marginals represent totals of one sort or another. The *column marginals* (1000, 1000) indicate the total number of cases in that column. *Row marginals* (1080, 920) indicate the total number of cases in that row. The *grand total* (2000) indicates the total number of people in the sample. The sum of the row totals or the sum of the column totals should be the same as the grand total. In Table 10.1 these marginals are actual numbers of people, but in Table 10.2 these are converted into percentages of the total in the particular row or column.

Percentaging a crosstabulation

It is normally easier to interpret percentages than raw numbers when trying to detect association in a table. Here we confront a difficulty because we can convert each cell frequency into three different percentages each having an entirely different meaning.

A percentage is calculated by seeing what proportion of the total a particular number represents. What percentage is 810 (top right-hand cell) of the total? We calculate this by $\frac{810}{\text{total}} \times \frac{100}{1}$. But which of the three totals do we use—the column total (1000), the row total for the cell (1080) or the grand total (2000)? Depending on which total is used we get a different percentage with a different interpretation.

1 The column total will produce a column percentage. Using this we get $\frac{810}{1000} \times \frac{100}{1} = 81\%$. This means 81 per cent of the 1000 blue-collar workers (i.e. of people in that column) voted Labour. It does not mean that 81 per cent of Labour voters were blue-collar workers.

2 The row total will produce a row percentage. This gives us $\frac{810}{1080} \times \frac{100}{1} = 75\%$. This means that 75 per cent of Labour voters are blue-collar workers.

3 The grand total will produce a total percentage which in this case gives us $\frac{810}{2000} \times \frac{100}{1} = 40.5\%$. This means 40.5 per cent of the whole sample were blue-collar Labour voters.

Table 10.2 includes all three percentages as well as the cell frequency in each cell. Which figures you use and include in the table depends on the purpose for which you are using the table. These issues are discussed more fully below.

An important point should be noted about cell and row percentages. Column percentages should always add to 100 per cent within a column. Row percentages add to 100 per cent within the row. Total percentages should add to 100 per cent over the whole table. If you are not sure which percentages are being used in a table, look to see which way they add to 100 per cent. Often the figure of 100 per cent is placed at the bottom of a column to indicate the direction in which percentages are calculated.

In addition to the cell percentages, I have included some additional marginal figures in Table 10.2. The marginal percentages (54%, 46%, 50%, 50%) reflect the percentage of the total sample that were in that row or column. Thus the figure of 54 per cent in the Labour row means that 54 per cent of the sample were Labour voters.

Table 10.2 Vote by occupation (marginal, row, column and total per cents)

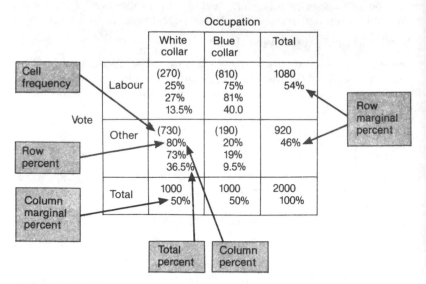

Source: Hypothetical
Notes: a. Only cases currently in the workforce are included in the analysis.
b. Vote was determined by asking 'If an election was held tomorrow for the House of Representatives, for which party would you be most likely to vote?'

Reading a crosstabulation

A table like this becomes very difficult to read: we must decide which percentages to use. The choice depends both on our purpose and the way we have arranged the table in the first place. We will concentrate on which percentages to use when we are trying to detect association in a table. Total percentages are of no value for this. We need, then, to choose between row and column percentages. We make this choice by first determining which variable is to be treated as independent and which will be assumed to be dependent (see page 27). Without this we cannot choose between row and column percentages.

Having seen the elements of a table, how do we read it to see if the two variables in it are associated? What we are doing when trying to detect association between two variables is comparing subgroups in terms of their characteristics on the dependent variable. Since occupation in our example is the independent variable, we have white-collar and blue-collar groups. We will look at the voting preferences of each subgroup.

If these subgroups (or categories) of the independent variable differ in terms of their characteristics on the dependent variable (i.e. if they vote differently), we would say occupation and vote are associated; if there is no difference they are not associated. In this case we compare white-collar and blue-collar workers and see that they do differ, so there is an association.

When trying to detect association in a table the steps are to

1   Determine which variable is to be treated as independent.
2   Choose appropriate percentage: column percentage if the independent variable is across the top; row percentage if it is on the side.
3   Compare percentages for each subgroup of the independent variable *within* one category of the dependent variable at a time. Thus

   a   If the independent variable is across the top, use column percentage and compare these across the table. Any difference between these reflects some association.
   b   If the independent variable is on the side use row percentages and compare these down the table.

The character of relationships

Once we have determined from a table whether or not there is a relationship we can describe its character also. There are three aspects to look at.

1   *Strength:* If there are large differences between subgroups there is a strong relationship. That is, if the subgroup to which people belong makes a big difference to their characteristics on the dependent variable, then the two variables are strongly related (see Table 10.3). If the differences are small, the relationship is weak.
2   *Direction:* When dealing with either ordinal or interval variables we can also describe the direction of the relationship: it can be positive or negative. A positive relationship is one in which people who score high on one variable are more likely than others to score high on the other variable; those who score low on one variable are more likely than others to score low on the other. There is a consistency in their 'position' on the two variables. Table 10.4 illustrates a positive relationship. Treating education as the independent variable we compare column percentages

Table 10.3   Vote by occupation (column percentages only)

	Occupation	
	White collar	Blue collar
Labour	27%	81%
Other	73	19
Total	1000	1000

Table 10.4   Income by education (a positive linear relationship)

		Education		
		Low	Medium	High
Income	Low	75%	50%	20%
	High	25	50	80
	Totals	500	300	450

Table 10.5   Education by age (a negative linear relationship)

		Age		
		Young	Middle	Old
Level of	Low	50%	70%	80%
education	High	50	30	20
	Totals	600	400	250

across the table. Those with low education are the most likely to be low income earners (75 per cent) and those with high education the least likely (only 20 per cent). On the other hand the highly educated are the most likely to be high income earners (80 per cent).

A negative relationship is one in which people who are high on one scale tend to be low on the other and vice versa (see Table 10.5).

3 *Nature:* Association of ordinal or interval variables can be either linear or curvilinear. The statistics to be described later mainly measure linear association so we need to be able to detect curvilinear association by looking at a table. A linear relationship means a 'straight line' relationship. Tables 10.4 and 10.5 reflect

Table 10.6 Achievement motivation by number of sibs (a linear relationship)

		Number of sibs in family							
		0	1	2	3	4	5	6	7
Achievement	High	80%	71%	65%	68%	64%	62%	54%	43%
motivation	Low	20	29	35	32	36	38	46	57
	Totals	170	200	500	350	225	102	41	7

Table 10.7 Income by age (a curvilinear relationship)

		Age		
		Young	Middle	Old
Income	Low	75%	25%	68%
	High	25	75	32
	Totals	196	205	127

linear relationships. We can tell this because as we compare across the subgroups (categories of the independent variable) the percentages change in a consistent direction: as we move across the low income row (i.e. seeing whether the percentages earning a low income vary as level of education gets higher) the percentages steadily decrease. In Table 10.5 they increase. In each case the relationship is linear. Sometimes in tables where there are many categories, there may be small 'bumps' as we move across but if there is a basic trend in one direction the relationship most probably is linear (Table 10.6).

A curvilinear relationship shows a different pattern (see Table 10.7). Comparing across the categories of age we see that the percentages are high, low, and then high again on the low income category. It is a curvilinear relationship because both extremes of the scale are similar, while those in the middle are different.

4 *Tables without a clear pattern:* On occasions tables display no clear pattern in terms or direction or linearity of relationship but there will still be some sort of association. In Table 10.8 there is association since people of different marital status vary in how they vote, but there is no clear pattern. A statistic used to summarise the relationship in this table would show very little

Table 10.8   Vote by marital status (a relationship without a clear pattern)

		Married	Single	Marital status Widowed	Divorced	Separated
Vote	Labour	80%	30%	70%	75%	21%
	Other	20	70	30	25	79
	Totals	360	180	90	120	240

Table 10.9   Skeleton version of Table 10.2

		Occupation White collar	Blue collar
	Labour	27%	81%
Vote	Other	73	19
	Total	1000	1000

Source: Hypothetical
Notes: a Only cases currently in the workforce are included in the analysis.
          b The vote was determined by asking 'If an election was held tomorrow for the House of Representatives, for which party would you be most likely to vote?'

linear relationship. In tables where this pattern occurs, use a statistic that does not measure linear association (any statistic designed purely for nominal level data) but be careful how you interpret it.

Presenting crosstabulations

The basic principle in presenting readable tables is to provide only the information necessary for accurate interpretation: avoid cluttering tables. It is becoming conventional to put the independent variable across the top. When presenting a table we can include a lot of information, but normally a skeleton of basic information is all that is necessary (Table 10.9) since we can reconstruct the full table from the skeleton should the need arise (see Davis, 1968).

We can delete the following information from the full table

1   total and row percentages (as these do not illustrate association when the independent variable is across the top);

2 all marginals except column frequencies;
3 all cell frequencies (these can be reconstructed by dividing column percentages by 100 and multiplying this by the column total frequency);
4 the grand total (these can be reconstructed by adding column frequencies);
5 With samples of more than 200 odd it is often desirable to round off percentages to whole numbers. When you have a number ending in .5 round it to an even number (e.g. round 37.5 to 38 and round 38.5 to 38).

When presenting a table be sure to include

1 a table number and title in which the names of both variables are stated. The title should read: dependent variable by independent variable, for example 'Table 10.1: Vote by occupation';
2 footnotes to the table to elaborate on some variables where necessary and to avoid lengthy titles;
3 percentage signs: place '%' after the first percentage in each column. This avoids confusion since the reader will not think the numbers are raw numbers (see Table 10.3);
4 labels clearly identifying each variable and each category of each variable;
5 if 'don't know' and 'no answer' responses have been excluded from the calculations, a footnote to the table indicating how many were in this 'missing data' category.
6 Assuming the independent variable is across the top of the table, column percentages should be placed in each cell. Normally this will be the only information in each cell.
7 Place the column marginal frequency beneath each column. This shows what numbers the percentages are based on and enables the calculation of cell frequencies and the grand total, should this be necessary.
8 If column percentages are used, a 100 per cent figure can be placed beneath the column to provide a quick indication that percentages have been calculated within columns.

When to use tables

Although tables provide maximum information they are often inappropriate, especially when dealing with variables with a large number of categories. If one variable (say age) had 30 categories and the other had just five we would have a table with 150 cells. Such tables are uninterpretable. Depending on the sample size it can lead to many 'empty' cells or cells with only one or two cases which further complicate meaningful interpretation of the table. As a rule of thumb use tables only when your variables have less than seven to eight categories each. If your variables have too many categories you have the following options:

1 For *nominal* data combine some categories (see Chapters 14 and 16).
2 For *ordinal* data either combine categories or use rank order correlation (see Chapter 11).
3 For *interval* data combine categories, use a scattergram or the comparison of means approach (Chapter 11).

Using statistics to summarise association in tables

It is useful to summarise the information about association in a table by a single figure. This can provide a concise and easy overview of the character of the association in the table. This is done by using correlation co-efficients. There are many different types of correlation co-efficients, different ones being appropriate to particular situations. In essence a correlation co-efficient is simply an index which provides a succinct description of the character of the relationship between two variables. This section will outline the logic of these co-efficients and clarify how to select the appropriate one and interpret the answer correctly. It does not deal with their computation.

First, however, a number of characteristics of correlation co-efficients should be made clear.

1 The co-efficient will always be between 0 and 1.00: the higher the figure the stronger the association. Zero means no association; 1.00 means perfect association. Table 10.10 shows how the size of the co-efficient reflects the strength of the association.
2 Co-efficients for ordinal and interval data can have a minus sign in front. This simply means the association is negative; no sign means it is positive. The sign means nothing about the strength of the relationship. Thus 0.75 and −0.75 are equally strong relationships.
3 Some co-efficients only indicate whether there is a linear relationship while others are also good for measuring non-linear relationships.
4 Some co-efficients are affected by which of the two variables is treated as the independent variable. Such co-efficients are called

Table 10.10   Three tables indicating different strengths of association

	No association		Moderate association		Perfect association	
	Male	Female	Male	Female	Male	Female
Yes	65%	65%	30%	75%	0%	100%
No	35	35	70	25	100	0
Totals	225	175	225	175	225	175
	Correlation = 0.000		Correlation = 0.50		Correlation = 1.00	

asymmetric measures. Co-efficients which are unaffected by which variable is independent are called symmetric measures.

5 To establish an association between two variables does not prove that they are causally related (see Chapter 3).

6 Different measures of association are appropriate depending on the level of measurement of the variables being considered. It is this principle which provides the organising principle for the rest of this chapter.

Statistics when both variables are nominal

There are two broad types of co-efficients that can be used: chi square based and proportional reduction of error (PRE) measures. I will outline the *logic* rather than the precise computation of each of these approaches.

To calculate the chi square based correlation co-efficients we first have to calculate a statistic called chi square and then convert it into a correlation co-efficient. The logic of chi square is best explained using an example. We start off with a crosstabulation of the actual relationship between two variables. The figures in this table are called the observed frequencies (Table 10.11).

Then we work out what the table would look like if there was no association between the variables (these are called expected frequencies). Since 43 per cent of the sample (extreme right column) approved of disarmament we would expect, if there was no association, that the same percentage of left wingers, right wingers and moderates would approve of disarmament. Table 10.12 presents these expected frequencies.

Next we check to see the extent to which the observed frequencies

Table 10.11   Approval of disarmament by political orientation (observed frequencies)

		Political orientation				
		Right wing	Left wing	Middle of road	Total	
Approval of disarmament	Disapprove	75	35	60	170	57%
	Approve	25	65	40	130	43%
	Totals	100	100	100	300	

Table 10.12   Approval of disarmament by political orientation (expected frequencies)

		Political orientation		
		Right wing	Left wing	Middle of road
Approval of disarmament	Disapprove	57	57	57
	Approve	43	43	43
		100	100	100

differ from what we would expect on the assumption of no association. If the observed differs 'sufficiently' from the expected we can say there is an association.

One problem with calculating a chi square figure is that the result normally is not between 0 and 1. The size of the result is affected by sample size and table size (or degrees of freedom). Thus it is difficult to make much sense of the chi square result itself. To deal with this problem a number of statistics have been developed which convert the raw chi square figure into a correlation co-efficient between 0 and 1. The two most useful chi square based correlation co-efficients are phi and Cramer's V, the characteristics of which are outlined in Table 10.15.

The other main type of correlation co-efficients are called PRE (proportional reduction of error) measures. Since these calculate co-efficients using a different logic to the chi square measures it is worth explaining their general logic.

If two variables are associated we can predict people's characteristics on one variable given a knowledge of their characteristics on the other variable. Thus if we can predict more accurately given this

Table 10.13 Frequency distribution of faculty of enrolment

Faculty	N
Science	3791
Arts	3318
Total	7109

knowledge than without, the two variables must be associated. How much better we do so, acts as an index of the strength of association. The basic formula for all PRE measures is

$$\frac{E_1 - E_2}{E_1}$$

where E_1 represents the amount of error in guessing people's characteristics on the dependent variable without knowledge of a second variable, E_2 represents the amount of error in guessing when we know people's characteristics on a second variable and $E_1 - E_2$ gives us the reduction in error given knowledge of the second variable. Dividing this by E_1 (i.e. amount of original error) converts the reduction in error score to a proportion between 0 and 1.

The different PRE measures vary in how E_1 and E_2 are calculated and defined, but the logic of PRE measures will be clearer if we work through an example of one type of PRE measure. There are four basic steps.

1 *Calculate E_1:* Suppose we have a group of students and we know how the group was distributed on faculty of enrolment but we did not know the faculty of particular individuals (Table 10.13).

To guess the faculty of enrolment of any individual it would be safest to pick the single most typical faculty—science. If we did this for each person we would be correct 3791 times and make an error 3318 times. This is E_1: the number of errors we make.

2 *Calculate E_2:* Given information about individuals on another variable can we reduce the number of errors we make? Let us use gender as the second variable and assume we have the distribution in Table 10.14. If we knew someone's gender only, which faculty would we guess? For males and females we would be safest picking the most typical. For all males we would pick science but we would make 1264 errors (male arts students) and for females we would pick arts but make 846 errors. Given a knowledge of

Table 10.14   Faculty enrolment by gender

		Gender	
		Male	Female
Faculty	Science	2935	846
	Arts	1264	2054
		4209	2900

gender, the total error in guessing faculty would be 1264 + 846 = 2110 errors. This is E_2: errors made in guessing individual scores on the dependent variable given a knowledge of their scores on a second variable.

3   *Calculate $E_1 - E_2$:* This gives the reduction in error given a knowledge of the second variable. This is 3318 − 2110 = 1208.

4   *Divide $E_1 - E_2$ by E_1:* This gives a correlation co-efficient between 0 and 1 which enables us to easily see the proportional reduction in error or the strength of the relationship. This is 0.36. This means there is a 36 per cent reduction in error in guessing someone's characteristics on the dependent variable given a knowledge of their characteristics on another variable, over guessing without this knowledge. The higher the figure, the stronger the relationship must be.

There are many different measures based on this PRE logic. They differ only in their particular method of calculating E_1 and E_2. When dealing with nominal variables, the main PRE type co-efficients are Yule's Q, lambda, and Goodman and Kruskal's tau. The characteristics of each of these are summarised in Table 10.15.

To select the appropriate nominal level measure of association look at the characteristics of each in Table 10.15 and choose accordingly. It is not appropriate simply to look at which one gives you the highest co-efficient. For two-by-two tables, Yule's Q is probably the most widely used measure. For larger tables Goodman and Kruskal's tau is the most sensitive measure but since it is not available on SPSSX, Cramer's V is a satisfactory alternative. Lambda is the least useful measure.

Statistics when both variables are ordinal

The most common statistic when both the variables in a crosstabulation are ordinal level is gamma. Alternatives are Kendall's tau$_b$

Table 10.15 Characteristics of various measures of association

	Appropriate table size	Range	Directional	Symmetric	Linear only	Other features
Phi	2 × 2	0–1[2]	no	yes	no	Lower co-efficients than Yule's Q
Cramer's V	larger than 2 × 2	0–1	no	yes	no	More sensitive to a wider range of relationships than lambda
Yule's Q	2 × 2	0–1	no	yes	no	1. Higher co-efficients than phi 2. Same as gamma 2 by 2 case 3. Always 1.00 if an empty cell
Lambda	any size[1]	0–1	no	yes[4]	no	Insensitive and therefore not recommended
Goodman and Kruskal's tau	any size	0–1[3]	no	no	no	More sensitive than lambda but not available on SPSS
Gamma	any size	0–1	yes	yes	yes	Gives higher co-efficients than Kendall's Tau$_b$ or Tau$_c$
Kendall's Tau$_b$	square tables only	0–1	yes	yes	yes	
Kendall's Tau$_c$	any size	0–1	yes	yes	yes	
Eta	any size	0–1	no	no	no	
Pearson's r	any size	0–1	yes	yes	yes	see Chapter 11 'Pearson's Correlation'

Notes:
(1) i.e. given the qualifications in section 10.1.5
(2) Under certain conditions the maximum may be less than 1 (see Guilford, 1965:336)
(3) Will only be if there is perfect association and if the independent variable has the same number of categories as the dependent variable
(4) There is both a symmetric and asymmetric version

Table 10.16   The ranks of five individuals on two variables

	X	Y
	Rank on class	Rank on self-esteem
Case		
A	1	1
B	2	3
C	3	2
D	4	4
E	5	5

and tau_c. These three statistics all measure only linear association. If there is non-linear association use a nominal measure association.

Gamma is a PRE measure of association. To calculate gamma we rank all cases on one variable and then on the other. In Table 10.16 each case has been ranked from the highest social class to the lowest and the cases have been ordered accordingly. Then the self-esteem of each case has been ranked.

We then look for concordant pairs and discordant pairs. To do this we take a pair of respondents and look at their ranks on both variables. If the same case is of higher rank than the other on each variable this is a concordant pair.

Take cases A and B as an example. On social class, A has a higher rank than B. On self-esteem, A again has a higher rank than B. Therefore this pair of cases is concordant. If a case is ranked higher than the other on one variable but lower on the other variable this is a *discordant pair*: pair B and C are discordant. We look at each possible pair and work out the total number of concordant and discordant pairs. (If two people have the same rank on a variable they are tied.) If concordant pairs are greater than discordant pairs we have a positive association. If discordant pairs predominate we have a negative relationship. If concordant and discordant pairs are about equal there is no association. The greater the disparity between concordant and discordant pairs, the stronger the relationship. The actual formula by which gamma is calculated is

$$\frac{P - Q}{P + Q}$$

where
P = number of concordant pairs
Q = number of discordant pairs.

For an easy method of working out the number of concordant and discordant pairs by hand see Johnson (1977:97–9).

There are other statistics which can be used to measure association between two ordinal variables but gamma is preferred when variables have relatively few categories. When measuring association between two interval variables the usual statistic is Pearson's r. This will be discussed in detail in Chapter 11.

Statistics for mixed levels of measurement

When one variable is nominal and the other is ordinal or interval or one is ordinal and the other is interval, we can use one of three approaches to select the appropriate correlation co-efficient.

1 *Dichotomous variables:* If one variable has only two categories we can ignore its level of measurement and let the other variable determine the choice of the co-efficient. For example, if a dichotomous nominal level variable (e.g. gender) is crosstabulated with an ordinal level variable, we can treat them both as ordinal and select the appropriate statistic (gamma). In other words we can treat a dichotomous variable as being at the same level of measurement as the variable with which it is crosstabulated and select correlation co-efficients accordingly.

2 *Use a 'weaker' statistic:* We can always treat a higher level of measurement as though it is at a lower level (we cannot do the opposite). When neither variable is dichotomous, treat both variables as though they both are at the same level of measurement of the variable measured at the *lowest* level. Thus if one variable is nominal and the other is ordinal, treat both as though they are both nominal. If one is interval and the other is ordinal treat both as ordinal and select the co-efficients accordingly.

3 *Use a specially designed statistic:* There are specially developed statistics designed for various combinations of levels of measurement. These are not widely used but are listed in Table 11.5.

Summary

In this chapter I have outlined the idea of looking for relationships between two variables. For variables with relatively few categories, crosstabulations provide a good way of displaying such relationships. Principles of reading tables to detect and describe these relationships have been outlined in detail.

Correlation co-efficients provide a concise, single figure way of summarising the relationships displayed in crosstabulations. They are an index of the extent and way in which variables are related. Since there are many different correlation co-efficients, the principles of selecting these have been outlined. Essentially this involves working out the level of measurement of each variable and taking into account the number of categories in each of the variables. We can then select the most appropriate statistic. Table 11.5 assists with this.

Finally there are two principles when selecting appropriate correlation co-efficients.

1 Statistics designed for use with low levels of measurement can be used for analysis where the variables have been measured at a higher level (thus lambda can be used for interval data). In general this is not advisable since we lose information.
2 Statistics designed for high levels of measurement (e.g. gamma) should not be used when analysing data measured at a lower level (e.g. nominal level).

Further reading

An exceptionally well organised and clear account of the main measures of association depending on the level of measurement of variables is provided by Freeman in *Elementary Applied Statistics* (1965) in section C. Another helpful outline is in Chapter 6 of Johnson's *Social Statistics Without Tears* (1977). A brief but excellent overview of the range of statistics available is provided in Nie et al. in *SPSS: Statistical Package For the Social Sciences* (1975) pp. 218–30 and by Norusis in *SPSSX: Introductory Statistics Guide* (1983) Chapter 5. Clear but slightly more technical discussions are given by Loether and McTavish in Chapters 6 and 7 of *Descriptive Statistics for Sociologists* (1974) and in Mueller, Schuessler and Costner in Chapter 8 of *Statistical Reasoning in Sociology* (1977).

Two helpful outlines of how to use crosstabulations are available. Appendix A of Rosenberg's *The Logic of Survey Analysis* (1968) gives a guide to reading tables and Davis provides excellent guidelines about the presentation of both simple and complex tables in 'Tabular Presentation' (1968). Marsh (1988: 139–42) provides very useful guidelines about what to include in crosstabulations. Ehrenberg (1975) provides worthwhile ideas about effective ways of presenting tables.

For more complex treatments of measures of association used with crosstabulations see Chapters 1–3 of Davis' *Elementary Survey Analysis* (1971) in which the logic of these measures is clearly explained. More technical papers are by Reynolds in his paper 'Analysis of Nominal Data' (1977), Chapters 1 and 2, Hilderbrand, Laing and Rosenthal in 'Analysis of Ordinal Data' (1977), and by Liebetrau in 'Measures of Association' (1983) Chapters 1–4.

11 Bivariate analysis: alternative methods

Crosstabulations are a useful way of displaying relationships between variables but are of limited use when dealing with ordinal and interval data with many categories. This chapter will outline a number of techniques used in such cases. In particular it discusses scattergrams, regression, comparing means and rank order correlation. It concludes with a brief discussion of statistical inference which is relevant to both this and the previous chapter.

Scattergrams

Scattergrams provide an alternative way of displaying relationships between two interval level variables with a large number of categories. They are also easier to read at a general level than crosstabulations. In the same way that correlation co-efficients summarise the relationship displayed in a crosstabulation, a comparable statistic does this summarising function for scattergrams. This statistic is called Pearson's r.

The scattergram

A scattergram is a graph consisting of a horizontal and vertical axis and data points. The horizontal axis (called the X axis) represents the values of the independent variable and the vertical axis (the Y axis) represents the values of the dependent variable. The values of the two variables for any given case serve as the co-ordinates of the point representing that case (see Figure 11.1).

The way the points are scattered on a scattergram reflects the strength, direction and nature of the relationship between the two variables. Different sorts of relationships are reflected in the six scattergrams in Figure 11.2. A number of points about relationships can be noted from these scattergrams.

Figure 11.1 Scattergram of income by education

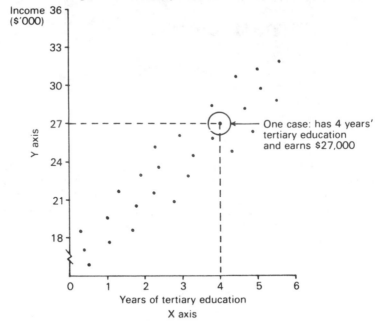

1 *Strength:* The more concentrated the points the stronger the relationship.
2 *Direction:* When the slope of the points is upwards moving from left to right (scattergrams a and b) the relationship is positive. A downward slope reflects a negative relationship.
3 *Nature:* When the points roughly form a straight line the relationship is linear. Where they form a curved line (f) it is curvilinear. Where there is no pattern (c) there is no relationship.

Pearson's correlation

Even though the character of a relationship is visually more obvious from looking at a scattergram than at a crosstabulation, it is still desirable to be able to summarise the relationship with a single figure. Pearson's r is the correlation co-efficient that is used for this with two interval level variables.

In the first five scattergrams in Figure 11.2 I have included a Pearson's r co-efficient beneath. This provides a single figure index of the strength and direction of any *linear* relationship between the two variables. You will notice that the more concentrated the points, the

Figure 11.2 Scattergrams illustrating different types of relationships

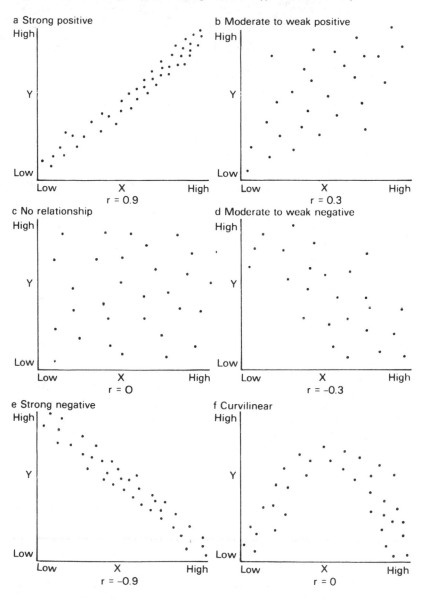

higher the co-efficient. In scattergram (f) the correlation is zero because Pearson's r only detects linear relationships.

When Pearson's r is squared (i.e. r^2) it is a PRE measure of association which is based on the logic of $\dfrac{E_1 - E_2}{E_1}$ as outlined in the previous chapter. It differs from other PRE measures simply in terms of how error is defined.

Here I only intend to explain the logic of r^2 rather than its precise computation. There are three main steps.

1   Calculate E_1. Given only a knowledge of the overall distribution of a group on the dependent variable (Y), our best guess of the score of any individual in that group would be the mean of Y. Thus if Y is annual income and the mean income of a group is $22 000 we would guess that each individual earned $22 000. To the extent that individuals earn less or more than $22 000 we make errors. The total extent to which we are wrong (the total amount wrong for all the cases) is expressed in terms of variance (see Chapter 9) and is called total variance. This is an index of the amount of error we would make in guessing the scores of individuals on Y without any knowledge of those individuals' scores on another variable. This error index is called E_1 or S^2y (variance given only knowledge of Y).

2   Calculate E_2. E_2 is the error we make in guessing individuals' scores on Y given a knowledge of individuals' scores on another variable (X). To calculate E_2 we first draw a regression line. This line serves to summarise the relationship between X and Y in a similar sense to that in which the mean summarises the distribution of Y alone. This line is also called the line of best fit and is the best single summary of all the points on the scattergram (see Figure 11.3). There are precise rules about how to 'fit' this line. These are discussed in Freeman (1965).

We can then use this regression line to predict individual scores on Y (income) given a knowledge of X (years of tertiary education). Using this regression line we would predict, for example, that anyone with three years' tertiary education would earn $26 000; anyone with five years of tertiary education would earn about $35 000 (see Figure 11.3). We need to know how accurate these predictions are for real cases. I have circled an actual case with five years of tertiary education whose actual income was $38 000. There is therefore some error ($3000) between the *predicted* value of Y and the *real* value of Y for that case. What is crucial though, is whether this prediction is more accurate than

Figure 11.3 An example of a regression line

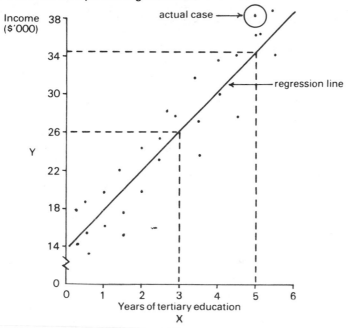

that made purely on the basis of knowledge of Y alone (see E_1). Using only Y our guess for this person was $22 000 (the mean of Y): we would have been $16 000 in error. Using the regression line we predict $35 000, only $3000 out. Thus for this case a knowledge of the individual's score on X (education) enables us to estimate their score on Y (income) more accurately than without this knowledge. If the two variables are related this will apply for most cases.

When calculating E_2 we would look at each case and make predictions on Y using each person's score on X and the regression line. We would then compare for each person their predicted score on Y with their actual score on Y. This would enable us to see how much total error we made in predicting Y from X. This error is expressed in terms of variance which acts as an index of error. This is E_2 or $Sy^{2'}$.

3   If the two variables are related, the amount of error in guessing Y with a knowledge of X will be less than without it. To see if this is so, simply subtract E_2 from E_1 (i.e. $E_1 - E_2$). This gives us the reduction in error given a knowledge of X. To express this as a correlation co-efficient with a range between 0 to 1, simply divide

this figure by the original error (E_1). This is reduction in error or $\dfrac{E_1 - E_2}{E_1}$. This produces a proportional reduction of error score which will range between 0 and 1. Thus an answer of 0.25 means that knowledge of X reduces error in guessing Y by 25 per cent. Since our index of error was variance this co-efficient is interpreted as a reduction of variance score (r^2). The size of the co-efficient tells us how much variance in Y is explained by X: this is referred to as explained variance. If r^2 is subtracted from one ($1-r^2$) we know the unexplained variance. The stronger the association between two variables the more variance is explained (i.e. the higher r^2 will be).

Put simply, what does explained variance actually mean? There is variation in Y: people vary in terms of how much they earn. If people earn different amounts because they have different amounts of education (or more correctly, if people who earn different amounts also vary in how much education they have) then we say we have explained why there is variation in income. To the extent that people have different incomes despite similar levels of education (i.e. income still varies even though education does not) we have unexplained variance.

So far I have talked about r^2. The problem with this is that the method of calculation means that there are no negative signs: r^2 is always positive. It is very useful in telling us how *strong* the relationship is but not its *direction*. Pearson's r tells us the direction. There are different ways of calculating r^2. I have only described the one that is clearest. We can first calculate Pearson's r (which gives us the direction of the relationship) and then square r to get r^2 which tells us the amount of variance explained which is the best indicator of strength. Typically people report only r since this provides information about the direction. To obtain a meaningful measure of the strength of the relationship we should square this figure: that is left up to us (to do this simply multiply r by r). This convention of reporting only r can be misleading since the r co-efficient is always larger than r^2 and if you forget to square r the strength of association can be exaggerated (e.g. if r = 0.6, $r^2 = 0.36$; if r = 0.4, $r^2 = 0.16$).

In summary, when we have interval variables with a larger number of categories it is most appropriate to display this in a scattergram. The statistic used to summarise the degree of relationship between these two interval variables is Pearson's r and r^2. These are calculated by using a regression line.

Regression analysis

The methods of analysis discussed so far allow us to work out whether two variables are associated: whether people who vary on one variable also vary systematically on the other. We also can determine how strongly these variables are associated. But we may want more information. For example, we may want to know how much someone with a given amount of education is likely to earn: in particular how much difference will staying on at school for another year make to someone's income level? Correlation will tell us how likely more education is to affect income (the higher the correlation co-efficient the more likely), but regression analysis tells us how much difference it is likely to make. It enables us to make predictions about people's scores on the dependent variable (e.g. dollars earned) if we know their score on the independent variable (years of education). It also enables us to say how much impact each unit change in the independent variable has on the dependent variable.

Regression analysis is linked closely to Pearson's correlation and scattergrams. Earlier in the scattergram we summarised all the points with a single line: the regression line or line of best fit. This line had two functions: to predict Y scores of individuals given a knowledge of X scores, and to estimate the strength of association between X and Y. The first function is the most relevant for regression and it is on this we shall concentrate.

Regression co-efficients

Earlier we looked at a scattergram showing a relationship between years of tertiary education and income. This scattergram is reproduced in Figure 11.4 without the data points. The regression line is used for prediction. To predict how much someone with five years' tertiary education would earn, we simply follow the vertical dotted line until we reach the regression line. Then we go horizontally until we reach the Y axis. This provides our prediction. In this case it is $34 000. If we do the same for someone with six years' tertiary education the prediction would be $38 000. If you look carefully, for every extra year of education the predicted income is $4000 higher. In other words for every 'unit' of the X variable (a year of education), we get an increase of 4000 units of Y (i.e. $4000). That is, *on average* a year of tertiary education has a 'payoff' of $4000.

The impact of X on Y (education on income) is 4000. This is variously called the regression co-efficient, the slope or the b co-efficient. The b co-efficient is always expressed in the units of

Figure 11.4 Predicting from a regression line

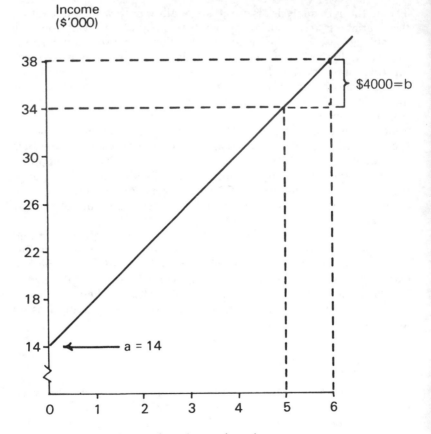

Years of tertiary education

measurement of the Y variable (the dependent variable). In this case
b is 4000, meaning $4000. It reflects the gradient of the regression
line: here it is 1 in 4000. In Figure 11.4 I have indicated how to work
out the slope and have shown why b is 4000. The other point to note
is the point at which the regression line passes through the Y axis.
This point is variously call the Y intercept or the constant and is
symbolised by the letter 'a'. It represents the predicted income of
someone with a value of zero on the X variable (i.e. no tertiary
education).

Using this scattergram with the regression line we could make predictions of income for people with varying levels of tertiary education. A more efficient way of presenting the same information and making the same predictions is to use the algebraic equation for the straight line. This is an important equation and is worth memorising. The equation is $Y' = a + bX$.

There are four parts to this. Y' means the value we would predict on the Y variable (e.g. income); a is the point at which the regression line crosses the Y axis; b is the slope of the line or the regression co-efficient; and X is any value of the X variable.

If we know the values of a and b we can predict Y values for any value of X. I am not going into how to calculate a and b without a scattergram. This is easily done by computer packages such as SPSSX. We know that in this case a $= 14\,000$ and b $= 4000$. Let us predict the Y value for someone who is six on the X variable (i.e. six years of education). We simply substitute these values in the above equation.

$$Y' = a + bX$$
$$= 14\,000 + 4000(6)$$
$$= 14\,000 + 24\,000$$
$$= \$38\,000$$

You will notice that this is the same prediction as would be made from the scattergram. To make a prediction for someone with five years of tertiary education (i.e. value of five on X), simply substitute five for six in the equation and thus multiply the b figure by five.

Knowing the equation, all we ever need then are the a and b co-efficients and we can make predictions. This is quicker and more efficient than using scattergrams. In most research reports only the a and b co-efficients are provided (see Table 11.1 for an example).

As well as enabling us to make predictions on Y for individuals, the regression co-efficient b provides a general measure of how much impact X has on Y. Even if we do not want to make specific predictions about how much we might earn if we take a three-year tertiary degree, we might want to know how much difference it might make to our earning power. To do this we simply look at the regression co-efficient. Alternatively, we might want to compare the b co-efficients for various subgroups. For example, we might want to see if tertiary education has the same impact or payoff for males and females or for people in the public service compared with those in private enterprise. In Table 11.1 we can simply compare the b co-efficients to see which types of people benefit most financially from tertiary education. This of course needs explaining by an appropriate theory.

Table 11.1   Regression co-efficients of years of tertiary education on income for various subgroups

	a	b
Male	15 000	4500
Female	13 500	3200
Public service	14 000	800
Private enterprise	12 000	1600

In summary, the regression co-efficient tells us how much impact one variable has on the other. Its interpretation is relatively straight-forward. The b figure is in the units of measurement of the Y variable. If Y = dollars income then b is dollars income. The precise interpretation is that for a change of one unit of X, Y increases by b amount (or decreases if b is a negative number). Typically, in reporting regression analysis for two variables just the a and b values are reported. The b values are emphasised most since these indicate how much impact one variable has on another.

Regression with non-interval variables: dichotomous variables

Although designed for interval level variables regression can be used for nominal or ordinal *independent* variables. A dichotomous (two-category) variable meets the requirements of interval level measurement. Even where the categories have no natural order they nevertheless satisfy the mathematical requirements of order: the categories cannot get out of order. The requirement of equal inter-vals between categories is also satisfied, since with only two categor-ies there can only be one interval which is, by definition, equal to itself. For this reason we can use any dichotomous variable, coded 0 and 1, in regression analysis (e.g. gender, native born/overseas born).

For example, we may use regression to predict income on the basis of gender. To do this we would use the formula

$$Y = a + bX$$

where
Y is the predicted income
a = \$14 000
b = \$5000
X = gender where female is coded 0 and male is coded 1.

Substituting these values we get

$$Y = 14\,000 + 5000(X)$$

Since females are coded as 0 their predicted income is $14 000 and since males are coded as 1 their predicted income would be $19 000. When using dichotomous variables the value of b represents the difference between the average income of females and males — in this case, $5000.

The difference between correlation and regression

Although linked, regression and correlation provide quite different but complementary information. If all the cases in a scattergram actually lay on the regression line there would be a perfect relationship between the two variables. If we knew someone's score on one variable we could use the regression line to predict with perfect accuracy scores on the other variable: there would be no discrepancy between the predicted and real values of actual cases. In this case the correlation co-efficient would be 1.00, indicating a strong relationship between the two variables. To the extent that cases do not lie on the regression line, the correlation co-efficient will be less than 1.00. The more the cases depart from the regression line, the lower the correlation co-efficient. This reflects the lower accuracy of predicting from the regression line. In other words the correlation co-efficient acts as an index of the accuracy of predictions from the regression line.

Regression uses the regression line to make predictions. It provides estimates of how much impact one variable has on another. Correlation co-efficients provide a way of assessing the accuracy of those estimates. Thus it makes sense to use a regression co-efficient and a correlation co-efficient together. Both co-efficients provide different information: the r^2 helps us work out how much reliance to place on our regression estimates. If we estimated using regression that another year of tertiary education would add $3000 to someone's earning power, we could use r^2 to provide an idea of how likely our estimate is to accord with reality. If r^2 is low we should not be too surprised if the extra $3000 does not eventuate. If r^2 is high we would have considerable confidence in the regression estimates.

A strong relationship (reflected in a high r^2) does not tell us anything about how much impact one variable has on another. For example, the b co-efficient of years of education on income might be only $300, which is a slight impact, but the relationship may still be strong in that most cases lie close to the regression line. This is illustrated in Figure 11.5 in graph c. To say that the relationship is strong simply means that if we predict an extra $300 for each year of education we can be fairly certain that this prediction will hold up in reality. Alternatively, there can be a high b co-efficient but this does not imply a strong relationship (see Figure 11.5 graph a). Our best estimate might be that b is $3000 but if cases are widely scattered (i.e. a weak relationship) predictions will not be very close to reality. Figure 11.5 illustrates that there is no necessary link between the size of the regression co-efficient and the strength of the relationship.

When can regression be used?

1 In general, regression can only be used when both the variables are interval level. Dummy regression analysis (see pages 221–4) can be used in certain situations with a nominal or ordinal independent variable.
2 It can be used when we wish to make predictions about the scores of individual cases or groups.
3 It can be used to measure the amount of impact or change one variable produces in another. It cannot be used to measure the strength of a relationship.

Finally a word of caution about regression co-efficients. They are asymmetrical: they will be different according to which variable is independent. When using them, make it very clear which variable is dependent and which is independent.

Comparing means

When dealing with an interval level dependent variable and an independent variable with only a few categories, it can be helpful to analyse the data by comparing the means of subgroups rather than using crosstabulations. This approach involves moving away from looking at the *categories* of the dependent variable and concentrating on its *distribution*. The logic of the approach is simple. If we want to know whether a person's gender makes any difference to their income we could create a crosstabulation (Table 11.2).

Alternatively, we could just look at the mean income for males and for females and compare them. Using the same data as in Table 11.2 we find the mean income for males is $12 048, and for females $6925. Obviously the means differ, so we would say gender makes a difference to income. This is a simple example because the independent variable has only two categories. The same logic applies if there are more categories: we simply have more means to compare. By

**Figure 11.5   Scattergrams displaying the relationship between correlation
and regression**

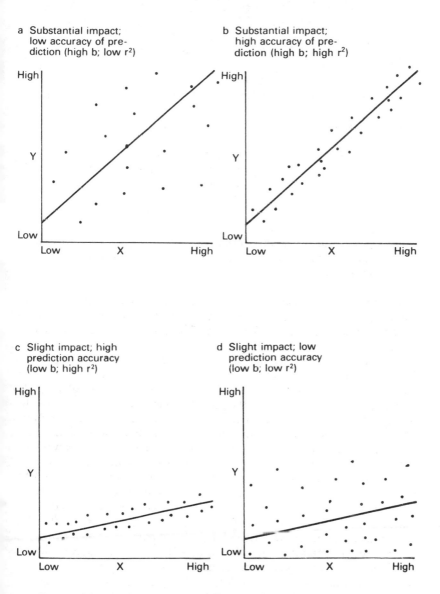

a Substantial impact;
   low accuracy of pre-
   diction (high b; low r^2)

b Substantial impact;
   high accuracy of pre-
   diction (high b; high r^2)

c Slight impact; high
   prediction accuracy
   (low b; high r^2)

d Slight impact; low
   prediction accuracy
   (low b; low r^2)

Note: Assuming that in each scattergram the same variables
and scales of measurement are being used

Table 11.2   Income by gender

	Male	Female
1 – 2000	2.5%	11.0%
2001 – 4000	12.5	27.0
4001 – 6000	6.4	13.7
6001 – 8000	7.3	12.3
8001 – 10 000	10.9	11.1
10 001 – 12 000	15.8	10.5
12 001 – 15 000	17.2	8.5
15 001 – 18 000	11.3	3.5
18 001 – 22 000	7.6	1.6
22 001 – 26 000	3.7	0.5
26 001 +	4.8	0.6
Totals	890 497	758 820

looking at a set of means we can see which subgroup means differ from one another.

A problem can arise when trying to interpret the differences between means. Are the observed differences in our sample 'real' or due simply to sampling error? (See the discussion on inferential statistics later in this chapter.) To answer this we use an inferential statistical technique called one way analysis of variance. This technique tells us whether the differences between our observed sample means are likely to exist in the population from which the sample was drawn. Computer programs are widely available to do analysis of variance. Their end product is to compute an F-statistic and a significance level (see pages 190–1). If the significance level is low (less than 0.05 or 0.01) it means that the variations between the sample means are 'real': they are likely to occur in the population.

When we are comparing three or more means (e.g. mean income for Protestants, Catholics and Jews), all an F-test can tell us is that at least two means exhibit a real difference from one another. To find out *which* means differ we can simply look at them or use a Scheffé test. These tests compare each possible pair of means and tell us which ones exhibit statistically significant differences (see Table 11.4 for references to these particular techniques).

To work out whether the comparison of means approach is appropriate you should note three points.

1 The dependent variable must be interval level.
2 The level of measurement of the independent variable does not

matter but the number of categories does. The more categories, the more means to compare, the more difficult it is to make sense of results. Where this variable has a lot of categories, either collapse them or, if the variable is interval, use another approach to analysis (e.g. scattergram and Pearson's correlation).

3 While comparing means provides a concise and often readily readable set of results, it leads to an enormous loss of detail (compare Table 11.2 with the two means below it). Crosstabulations provide much more detail. In deciding which approach to use consider how much detail is needed. You might use the means comparison approach in initial analysis to see if any patterns emerge and use tables later for more detailed examination.

Rank order correlation

When we have two ordinal level variables with a large number of categories and we wish to see if they are correlated, we have two options. We can combine categories and use the crosstabulation approach or we can use rank order correlation. Combining categories can lead to a loss of detail and distort patterns, so rank order correlation is often a desirable technique.

There are two main rank order correlation co-efficients: Kendall's tau and Spearman's rho. In many respects they are similar to gamma. They both involve ranking people on each variable and then comparing people's relative position on the two variables. (For a discussion of the procedures see Nie et al. 1975:288ff.)

Both Kendall's tau and Spearman's rho are normal correlation co-efficients. They range between 0 to 1, can have a negative sign, only measure linear relationships, and are symmetrical. There are no simple criteria for using one rather than the other of these two co-efficients. One of the main differences between the two is their method of dealing with tied ranks (i.e. when two or more people are on the same rank or category of a variable). It is suggested by some people (Nie et al. 1975:289) that this difference makes Kendall's tau more appropriate when there are likely to be a lot of tied ranks. In other words, if there are a lot of cases and relatively few categories in either variable use Kendall's tau. Where the ratio of cases to categories is smaller (i.e. fewer people and 'larger' variables), Spearman's rho may be more appropriate. In general, Spearman's rho produces co-efficients higher than Kendall's tau but close to Pearson's r.

Table 11.3 A correlation matrix

	Gender	Age	Income	Occupation	Importance of God	Interest in politics
Gender	1.00	−0.01	0.44	0.07	−0.17	−0.11
Age	−0.01	1.00	0.18	−0.02	0.26	−0.11
Income	0.44	0.18	1.00	−0.22	−0.13	−0.17
Occupation	0.07	−0.02	−0.22	1.00	−0.01	0.11
Imp. of God	−0.17	0.26	−0.13	−0.01	1.00	0.02
Interest in politics	−0.11	−0.11	−0.17	0.11	0.02	1.00

Notes: Gender is scored 0 = female, 1 = male; church attendance is scored from 1
to 9 with 1 indicating regular attendance; age is scored from a low (young)
to a high (old); occupation is scored 1 = high status through to 11 = low
status; importance of God is scored 0 = no importance through to 10 =
high importance; interest in politics is scored so that 1 = active interest
through to 4 = no interest.

Correlation matrices

A whole set of bivariate correlations can be presented in a very
efficient fashion by using correlation matrices as exemplified in
Table 11.3.

The variables across the top of this matrix are the same as those
down the side. The way to read the matrix is to map the co-
ordinates. Thus the correlation between occupation and income is
−0.22. To obtain this figure locate the occupation variable across
the top of the table and move down that column until you reach the
row that corresponds to the income variable. The same procedure
can be employed to obtain the bivariate correlation between any
two variables.

Since the variables on the side are the same as those across the
top you will notice that on occasions a variable is correlated with
itself. When this is done a correlation of 1.00 is obtained: a variable
will be perfectly correlated with itself. If you look down the diagonal from the top left-hand corner of the matrix you will see a series of
1.00 co-efficients representing variables correlated with themselves.
Above the diagonal is a triangle of co-efficients. Below it is a mirror
image of the same co-efficients. In the top triangle the correlation of
income (column) with gender (row) is 0.44. In the lower triangle the
correlation of income (row) with gender (column) is 0.44. Whenever
the variables across the top are the same as those on the side the
same pattern will occur. In fact all that is required to represent the
matrix is one of the triangles. The co-efficients of 1.00 and the mirror
triangle are redundant.

Given the way the variables are scored in Table 11.3 we can work out the substantive meaning of the co-efficients. A positive relationship means that people who obtained a *high* score on one variable tended to obtain a *high* score on the other variable. A negative relationship means that those who obtained a *high* score on one variable tended to obtain a *low* score on the other (page 159–60). Thus a *negative* correlation for the relationship between gender (where a low score of 0 = female) and the importance of God (where a low score = a non-religious response) means that women are more religious than men. That is, those with a low score or code on the gender variable (females) tended to get higher scores on the importance of God variable (i.e. rated God as important in their life). The *positive* correlation of 0.44 between gender and income (where a low score = a low income) means that women (low score of 0) tend to have low incomes.

Correlation matrices do not have to be balanced with the same variables on the side as across the top. When they are different there will not be a set of 1.00 co-efficients and the matrix cannot be divided into two triangles and there will be no redundant (repeated) co-efficients. While the co-efficients in Table 11.3 are Pearson correlations, the same format can be employed to present any set of correlation co-efficients whether they be gammas, Spearman's rho, Kendall's tau or whatever. A matrix is simply a convenient format for presenting a great deal of information. In the above example only the the co-efficients are presented, but additional information can also be included. Often significance levels are also included (normally represented by symbols such as * or ** to represent the level of statistical significance (see pages 190–1 ff.)). The number of cases on which the correlations are based can also be included.

Statistical inference

Once we have worked out whether two variables are associated in our sample, we will want to know whether they are likely to be as strongly associated in the population from which the sample was drawn; we need to know whether we can safely generalise beyond our sample. This is done by using inferential statistics (tests of significance).

What is the logic behind these statistics? It is standard to begin by assuming that in the population any two given variables are not associated (i.e. $r=0$). This is called a null hypothesis. If in our sample we observe an association between two variables (e.g. $r-0.4$), we have two ways of interpreting the discrepancy between our assumption of no association and our sample observation of association.

1   We have an unrepresentative sample. Despite random sampling techniques we can still obtain poor samples. This is called sampling error. Thus the discrepancy between the sample (0.4) and the population assumption ($r=0$) could be because our sample is not a fair representation of the population.

2   Our assumption of no association in the population is incorrect.

If we accept the first interpretation that the sample result ($r=0.4$) is due to sampling error, we would say that in the population the association is unlikely to differ from zero (i.e. we maintain our assumption of no association). Since we are normally interested in the population rather than the sample *per se*, we will work on the basis that the measure of association observed in the sample ($r=0.4$) is due to sampling error and is thus equivalent to no association ($r=0$), and interpret it on that basis.

If, on the other hand, we accept the second interpretation that our initial assumption of no association in the population is incorrect, we interpret our sample result as reflecting association that actually exists in the population; we act as though the association measured in the sample is 'real' and is not simply an artefact of a poor sample.

Tests of significance

To work out which interpretation is correct we use tests of significance. The logic of these is simple. If two variables are not associated in the population, how likely is it that we would obtain a random sample in which there was association between the two variables (i.e. our sample is inaccurate)? For example, if we drew 100 random samples how likely is it that we will get a faulty one, one in which we observe association which does not actually exist in the population? It is conventional to say that if there is a chance that more than five out of 100 samples would produce an association due simply to sampling error, this is too great a risk. Our particular sample could have been one of those five! Thus we would say that it is too likely that the observed association is due to sampling error and continue to assume that the 'real' association is zero.

Some people are tougher and say that if more than one out of 100 samples could produce by chance alone an association as strong as you have observed, this is too great a risk.

If, on the other hand, we find that only a very low number of samples could produce by chance our observed association, we will accept that our sample observation is 'real' and reflects an association in the population.

Since we never take 100 samples of the same population we have to estimate if 100 samples were taken how many by chance alone would give an association as strong as we have observed in our sample.

Probability theory provides us with an estimate of how likely our sample is to reflect association due simply to sampling error. (We will not go into this theory but we should be aware that it assumes we use simple random samples.) A test of statistical significance is the estimate of this likelihood. The figures obtained in these tests range from 0.0000 to 1.0000 and are called significance levels. What do they mean? Let us take a figure in between, 0.5000. This means that in 50 out of 100 samples (simply multiply the figure by 100) we would get an association as strong as we have observed purely because of sampling error (chance). Being cautious people we feel this is too great a chance that our observed association is not 'real'; we would not reject the assumption of no association in the population.

If we obtain a significance level of 0.05 this means that only five out of 100 samples would come up by chance with the association we have observed in our sample. A result of 0.01 means one in 100; 0.001 means one in 1000. Obviously the lower the significance level, the more confident we are that our observed association is 'real'.

I do not intend to go through how to calculate tests of significance. Again these are easily available on computer packages, and formulas are available in any statistics book, but there is one problem computer packages do not solve. Most packages will print out a significance level between 0.0000 to 1.000. At what level do we reject the assumption of no association in the population? Conventionally 0.05 or 0.01 are used at the critical point. These levels are, however, conventional and arbitrary.

The trouble with using the 0.05 level is that this can be too easy a test of the null hypothesis of no association: we might reject the assumption of no association in the population when there really is no association. Making this mistake is called a type I error and is most likely with large samples. Thus with large samples it is advisable to use the 0.01 level as the critical point. The trouble with using 0.01 consistently is that it can lead to type II errors—being too tough, that is accepting the null hypothesis when we should reject it. This is particularly likely with small samples. As a rule of thumb use 0.05 for small samples and 0.01 or lower for larger samples.

Tests of significance and measures of association

Different tests of significance have been developed for use with different measures of association and are thus used depending on the level of measurement of the variables being analysed. The tests appropriate for different levels of measurement are summarised in

Table 11.5. This table also indicates which measures of association should be used in conjunction with particular tests of significance.

It makes most sense to use measures of association and tests of statistical significance in conjunction. They provide different information but each set of information is most useful when seen in the context of the other. Thus a measure of association describes the extent of association between two variables. The significance test tells us whether that relationship is likely to be due simply to chance (sampling error) or whether it is likely to hold in the population from which the sample was drawn. Since we are not normally interested just in the sample, the test of significance provides very useful information. Even if we get a moderate or strong correlation in the sample, but the test of significance suggests it could be due to sampling error, we are not going to spend much time developing explanations for the relationship or putting much weight on it. In other words, it is important to look at both the correlation co-efficient and the test of significance to avoid misinterpreting the correlation co-efficient. But equally there is little value in just using the test of significance, since all this tells us is that a relationship in the sample exists (or does not exist) in the population. But it tells us nothing about the character of the association: its strength, direction or linearity. It is important to remember that a test of statistical significance does not say anything about the strength of a relationship. It simply tells us whether any relationship that does exist (be it weak or strong) is likely to occur in the population from which the sample is drawn. The links between measures of association and tests of significance are illustrated in Table 11.4.

We cannot assume that because we have a strong relationship in our sample this will necessarily hold in the population. It is true that given a similar sample size a strong association is more likely to hold in the population than a weaker one. However, the size of the sample is important. We might obtain a strong relationship in a small sample which will not be statistically significant: it is unlikely to occur in the population. This is because with a small sample the likelihood of sample error is much higher than with a large sample. Thus with small samples it is often difficult to achieve statistical significance. On the other hand, with large samples the probability of sampling error is much less. Any relationship we observe is less likely to be due to sample error. Thus with large samples it is easier to obtain statistical significance—even for quite weak relationships.

A number of critics have argued that far too much weight has been placed on statistical inference or tests of significance in data analysis (Selvin, 1957) and have suggested that such tests should be abandoned (Labovitz, 1970) or used only under very strict conditions. For

Table 11.4   The links between correlations and tests of significance

Correlation	Significance	N	Interpretation
0.35	0.27	100	Moderate association in sample but too likely to be due to sampling error. Continue to assume correlation of 0 in the population.
0.15	0.001	1500	Weak association but is very likely to hold in the population.
0.64	0.01	450	Strong relationship that is likely to hold in the population.
0.04	0.77	600	Negligible association. Highly probable that the correlation differs from zero due only to sampling error. Continue to assume correlation of 0 in the population.

example, tests of significance are really only appropriate when we have a simple random sample. Some tests assume that the variables are normally distributed. There is certainly merit in these criticisms and they highlight that the most important part of data analysis is that which takes place at the sample level where we try to detect relationships and search for explanations (see Chapters 12, 13 and 17). This is the realm of descriptive statistics on which this and subsequent chapters concentrate. Descriptive statistics help us make sense of our data and in social research this is crucial. Knowing that our sample results will hold in the population is useful additional information but is sterile unless we have first thoroughly and imaginatively analysed our sample data using descriptive statistics.

Summary

The focus of this (and the previous) chapter has been on outlining a range of methods of bivariate analysis. The emphasis has been on the logic of each approach and on interpreting results rather than on computational details. Considerable attention has been paid to criteria for choosing between alternative approaches and statistics. Table 11.5 provides a summary of the various methods and statistics and provides a guide to help select appropriate techniques for particular circumstances.

Table 11.5 Guidelines for selecting measures of association

Level of measurement of variables		Appropriate methods	Appropriate descriptive summary statistics		Reference for formula computation	Appropriate inferential statistic
1 Nominal/Nominal	'Shape' of variables 2 by 2	Crosstabulations	i Phi ii Yules Q iii Lambda iv Goodman & Kruskall's tau		[a]93 [e]264 [e]182 [a]90–3 [b]196, 179 [c]219–20 [e]184–5 [b]214–18 [c]194–7 [d]ch.7 [e]285–8 [a]94–7 [b]219–21 [c]196–206	chi square
2 Nominal/Nominal	3+ by 2+	Crosstabulations	i Lambda ii Goodman & Kruskall's tau iii Cramers V		as above [b]197	chi square
3 Nominal/Ordinal	Nominal variable with 3+ categories	Crosstabulations	i Theta ii Any statistics in 2 above		[d]ch.10	Mann–Whitney U-test (dichotomous nominal independent variable) K-sample median test Kruskal–Wallis
4 Nominal/Interval	Nominal variable independent	a Crosstabulations (if interval variable has only a few categories) b Comparison of means (esp. if interval variable has many categories)	i Eta (also called correlation ratio) ii Any statistics in 2 or 3 above but not very wise. i Eta		[b]248–51 [e]233–41 [d]ch.11	F-test (one-way analysis of variance) chi square F-test (one-way analysis of variance)

#	Variables	Method	Statistics	Page refs	Test for significance
5	Ordinal/Ordinal	Both with few categories	Crosstabulations	i Gamma ii Kendall's tau b (square tables) iii Kendall's tau c (any shape table)	[a]97–9 [b]228–9 [c]207–22 [d]ch.8 [e]280–82 [b]224–30 [e]283 [b]230	Test for significance of gamma Test for significance of tau
6	Ordinal/Ordinal	One variable with many categories	Rank correlation	i Kendall's tau	[a]101–2 [b]230 [e]158–61	Test for significance of tau
7	Ordinal/Ordinal	Both variables with many categories	Rank correlation	i Kendall's tau ii Spearman's rho	[a]100–101 [c]230–2 [e]152–6	as above Test for significance of rho
8	Ordinal/Interval	Both with few categories	a Crosstabulations b Comparison of means (if dependent variable is interval)	i Eta ii Any statistics in 5 above i Eta	[b]248–51 [c]233–41 [d]ch.11 as above	F-test F-test
9	Ordinal/Interval	Ordinal with few categories Interval with many	a Comparison of means b Rank order correlation	i Eta i Kendall's tau	as above [a]101–2 [b]230 [c]158–61	F-test Test for significance of tau

Table 11.5 (Continued)

Level of measurement of variables		Appropriate methods	Appropriate descriptive summary statistics	Reference for formula computation	Appropriate inferential statistic
10 Ordinal/Interval	Both with many categories	Rank correlation	i Kendall's tau ii Spearman's rho	as above [a]100–1 [b]230–2 [e]151–6	as above Test for significance of rho
11 Interval/Interval	Both variable with small number of categories	Crosstabulations	i Pearson's r		Test for significance of r
12 Interval/Interval	At least one variable with many categories	Scattergram	i Pearson's r ii Regression		

Reference key: [a]Freeman (1965)
[b]Loether and McTavish (1974) *Descriptive Statistics*
[c]Mueller et al. (1977)
[d]Johnson (1977)
[e]Cohen and Holliday (1982)

Further reading

Both Freeman, *Elementary Applied Statistics* (1965), Chapter 9 and Johnson, *Social Statistics Without Tears* (1977) pp. 100–13 provide exceptionally clear accounts of bivariate regression and r^2. Mueller, Schuessler
and Costner in *Statistical Reasoning in Sociology* (1977), Chapter 9 and
Blalock in Chapters 17 and 18 of *Social Statistics* (1972) give outlines
which are more advanced but still clear.

The outlines of regression, correlation and other bivariate techniques by
Nie et al., in *SPSS: Statistical Package for the Social Sciences* (1975),
Chapters 17 and 18 and Norusis *SPSSX: Introductory Statistics Guide*
(1983), Chapters 6–9 are excellent. For a slightly more advanced treatment of regression see Chapters 1 and 2 of the paper 'Applied Regression: An introduction' (1980) by Lewis-Beck.

For a more thorough treatment of statistical inference Freeman (1965)
provides a systematic introduction in section D of his book. All of Loether
and McTavish's *Inferential Statistics for Sociologists* (1974) is worth
reading but Chapter 8 is especially relevant. Johnson (1977), Chapter 12
and Mueller, Schuessler and Costner (1977), Chapters 14 and 15 cover
similar material. Henkel's paper 'Tests of Significance' (1976) provides a
very useful overview of statistical inference.

Hirschi and Selvin present a challenging critique of the value of statistical
inference in survey research in *Delinquency Research* (1967).

12 Elaborating bivariate relationships

Establishing relationships between two variables is only the beginning of analysis. We can elaborate these relationships to answer the following questions.

1 Why does the relationship exist? What are the mechanisms and processes by which one variable is linked to another?
2 What is the nature of the relationship? Is it causal or non-causal?
3 How general is the relationship? Does it hold for most types of people or is it specific to certain subgroups?

We need techniques to help us unpack the meaning and nature of bivariate relationships and to develop adequate causal and meaningful explanations. One set of techniques, referred to as elaboration analysis, is appropriate for limited analysis involving nominal and ordinal variables and is the focus of this chapter. Related, but more powerful, techniques appropriate for interval level variables are discussed in Chapter 13. Behind both sets of techniques lies the concept of statistical controls.

The logic of statistical controls

The reasoning underlying elaboration analysis is best understood within the context of the experimental and the cross-sectional research designs outlined in Chapter 3.

The experimental design relies on comparing change over time of two or more groups which initially were identical in all relevant respects. At the beginning of a study measurements are obtained on the dependent variable for at least two groups. After that one group will be exposed to some intervention or stimulus while the other will not. Any difference between the two groups after the intervention (time two) is interpreted as being due to the causal effect of the intervention. The intervention is the independent variable in the study. The groups are differentiated by their attributes on this variable (e.g. exposed or not exposed to the stimulus).

198

The strength of the experimental design, which lies in its usefulness for drawing conclusions about causal processes, is based on two things:

1 the use of a control group (the group not exposed to the experimental stimulus);
2 the assumption that in terms of all possible causal variables except the key experimental variable the two groups are identical.

If the groups were dissimilar to start with, we cannot be confident that differences between the two groups at time two are due simply to the effect of the experimental intervention. An example can clarify this. If we were testing the proposition that university leads to a loss of religious faith we would have two key variables:

1 attendance or non-attendance at university (the experimental or independent) variable;
2 level of religious faith (the dependent variable).

To establish whether the proposition is true we would obtain two groups — people about to commence university (the experimental group) and a comparable group who do not attend university (the control group) and collect data over time to see if the loss of faith among university students was greater than among the non-students. If the religiousness of the university group declined more than that of the non-student group we would be inclined to conclude that the university has been responsible for this. But this conclusion is warranted only if the two groups were identical at the beginning of the study and that with the exception of attending university they had other similar experiences over the time of the study. If the groups were different at the beginning then the greater religious change among the students could be due to the initial differences rather than university attendance.

Cross-sectional designs and statistical controls

In the cross-sectional design (page 41) a similar logic is employed. The sample is divided into groups on the basis of which category of the independent variable they belong to and these groups are compared with one another in terms of the dependent variable (see Chapters 10 and 11). Differences between the groups might be taken to be due to the influence of their different group membership. Thus differences between males and females (independent variable) in terms of income (dependent variable) might lead to conclusions about the causal effect of gender on income. We might detect income differences and take this as evidence of discrimination against women. But such a conclusion is only warranted if the men and women we compare are *alike in all other relevant respects.* To the extent that they differ then any variation between them on the dependent variable (income) could be due to these other differences.

With the experimental design the two groups are made similar by randomly assigning people to the two groups or by carefully matching the characteristics of people in each group so that at the beginning of the study the two groups are as alike as possible. This is not possible with the cross-sectional design where we collect all our data at the one point in time.

So we have to do this matching of the two groups after we have collected the data. This is done statistically by a process called *controlling.* The logic of this approach is to compare groups who are similar in other possibly relevant ways. For example, with the gender and income example we would want to make sure that the men and women we compared were the same in terms of their level of work involvement. Clearly it would be inappropriate to compare a group of women where many worked part time with a group of men where there were very few part-time workers and then observe income differences and draw some conclusions about income discrimination against women. We would need to ensure that we only compared men and women who had the same level of workforce participation: we would compare women who worked full time with men who worked full time and see if they had different levels of income. Then we would separately compare men and women who worked, say, 25 to 35 hours a week and so on. *Like must be compared with like.*

If the income differences still persist when the possible influence of other variables is removed by limiting comparisons to those who are alike on that variable, then we have at least eliminated one alternative explanation for the difference. It is not simply because of different levels of work involvement of men and women — the gender differences persist even when only full-time workers (or only part-time workers or whatever) are compared. Equally we would want to ensure that we compared men and women with similar types of jobs. The strongest evidence for discrimination comes when income differences persist amongst men and women who are *alike in all other respects.* We would compare the income levels of professional men and women, those of clerical men and women, men and women in the sales sector and so on. If men and women *at the same job level* have different incomes this would provide some evidence for the discrimination argument.

Multiple statisitical controls

We would also want to control *simultaneously* for other variables so that their effects could be removed as possible explanations for any differences between men and women. For example, we might think that income differences between men and women might be due to the cumulative effects of level of work involvement, types of jobs that men and women have, age differences, different amounts of workforce experience and different educational backgrounds. We would try therefore to remove the influence of these differences in any comparison of men and women. Thus we would want to divide our sample into many groups so that one group might be women who work full time in professional jobs, have tertiary qualifications, are between the ages of 35 and 40 and have at least 14 years' experience in the workforce. This group would be compared with a similar group of men. Another pair of groups might be similar to the above two except that both men and women were employed in trade jobs. Many other pairs of groups would be compared. By controlling or removing the effects of these other variables we are able to answer the question '*When other things are equal* does gender make any difference to income?' If men and women still have different incomes when all other things are equal we have evidence of discrimination: even when women have similar characteristics to men they still earn less.

Of course, it is not possible to control for every other possible variable so the possibility always remains that any income difference that remains could be due to the influence of uncontrolled variables rather than of gender. If the income differences between the two groups disappear when other differences between men and women are removed or controlled we would argue that the initial, observed differences in income must be due to the variables we controlled. Or, to put it differently, we would say that the variables we had controlled for *explained* the original relationship.

When statistical controls are introduced a variety of patterns of results is possible. In the example described above we might anticipate that income differences between men and women will disappear within each matched group of men and women. That is, men and women who have full-time professional jobs will earn the same amount; men and women in part-time professional jobs will have similar incomes and men and women working full time in clerical jobs will receive the same average income and so on. But other possibilities exist. In some comparisons (e.g. professionals and the unemployed) the income differences between men and women may be minimal but in other comparisons (e.g. tradespeople, factory workers) the differences between the incomes of similar men and women may persist or even be accentuated. A range of possibilities exists.

The remainder of this chapter outlines some of the potential results when statistical controls are introduced and examines ways of interpreting the different patterns. There is a variety of ways of introducing statistical controls. This chapter is mainly limited to controlling using crosstabulation analysis. This approach is useful but limited because it is difficult to control for more than one or two variables simultaneously. Because of the way in which these controls are introduced, we have to keep dividing the sample up into smaller and smaller groups of people that are alike in terms of the control variables. But this very quickly leads to very small groups of people for comparison with consequent problems of statistical reliability. In Chapter 13 we explore techniques for controlling for a whole set of variables simultaneously without having to face the same problems of sample size.

Detecting spurious relationships

Elaboration analysis can help detect whether an observed relationship is spurious. To demonstrate that two variables are correlated does not mean that one causes the other. When they are related but not causally related this is called a spurious relationship. For example, there is a correlation between the strength of peace movements and the outbreak of wars: the stronger peace movements are the more likely war is to break out. It is unlikely that this is a causal relationship. It is more probable that these are both consequences of a common cause, a third variable. In this case it is likely that both are a result of the common cause—international tensions. This is illustrated diagrammatically in Figure 12.1.

We can see how to detect spurious relationships more fully by using a more mundane example. Students in religious schools appear more religious (on given measures) than those in government schools (see Table 12.1). What is this relationship between type of schooling and religiousness due to? It could be that the school affects level of religiousness, but maybe both these are consequences of a third factor—level of parental religiousness. Religious parents might produce religious children and also tend to send their children to religious schools. Perhaps this is why those in religious schools are more religious, not because the schools cause them to become more

Figure 12.1 A spurious zero order relationship

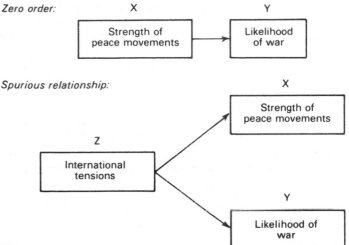

Table 12.1 Religiousness by type of schooling

		Type of schooling	
		Religious	Government
Level of	Low	48%	71%
religiousness	High	52	29
	N	800	800
		Q = 0.45	

religious. Put differently, if government school children had equally religious parents to those in religious schools they would be equally religious to those in religious schools.

Since there will be students in government schools who have religious parents we can compare the religiousness of these students with those religious-school students who also have religious parents. Similarly we can look at government and religious-school students who do not have religious parents and compare their religiousness with one another.

If our explanation is correct we would expect that equivalent government and religious-school students would reveal no difference

Table 12.2 Religiousness by school type controlling for parental religiousness (conditional tables)

		Child has religious parents			Child has non-religious parents	
		Relig. school	Govt school		Relig. school	Govt school
Level of child's religiousness	Low	35%	37%	Low	85%	82%
	High	65	63	High	15	18
	N	600	200	N	200	600
		Q = 0.04			Q = 0.10	

in religiousness. That is, we should compare government and religious-school students who are equivalent in terms of the explanatory variable: we hold this variable constant or control for it. Essentially we do this by looking at the relationship between the initial two variables within each subcategory of the new variable (see Table 12.2). We will call each of these tables a conditional table indicating a conditional relationship.

Here we see that type of schooling makes virtually no difference to religiousness. Amongst those with equivalent levels of parental religiousness the student religiousness is the same regardless of which type of school the person attended. The initial relationship between type of school attended appears to be spurious. On the other hand, had the original relationship persisted both for the children of religious parents and those of non-religious parents we could conclude that the initial relationship was not due to levels of parental religiousness.

We can detect a spurious relationship by comparing the initial bivariate relationship with the conditional relationships. If an initial relationship exists but there are no relationships in the conditional tables (see Tables 12.1 and 12.2) then we can say we have explained the original relationship.

To see if the initial and conditional relationships differ from one another in this way we may use either the various tables or the initial and conditional correlation co-efficients. The quickest and easiest way is to use the correlation co-efficients. If the conditional correlations are substantially lower (at least 0.10 lower according to Davis, 1971) than the initial bivariate correlation it may mean we have detected a spurious relationship.

The other test to use in conjunction with this is to draw a diagram as in Figure 12.1. If this diagram makes sense *and* we get the above pattern in initial and conditional relationships, the original relationship is spurious. In this case it makes sense to illustrate these three variables in that way.

Finally it is important to distinguish between completely and partly spurious relationships. When the conditional relationships disappear, the initial relationship is due entirely to the third variable: it is completely spurious (Tables 12.1 and 12.2). When the conditional relationships are weaker than the initial one (at least 0.10 lower) but not zero, the original relationship is only partly spurious.

Before proceeding with other applications of the elaboration technique it will be useful to introduce some technical terms. The variable for which we control is the test variable (parental support). The initial relationship without any controls is called a zero order relationship. The relationship between these variables when the effect of various test variables has been removed is called a conditional relationship (some books refer to it as a partial relationship but I will use this term in a more limited sense towards the end of this chapter). If we have controlled for only one test variable this conditional relationship is called a first order conditional; if two test variables are controlled simultaneously this is a second order conditional. The tables in which these relationships are displayed are called zero order tables and first, or second order conditional tables. The co-efficients used to summarise these relationships are called zero order and first order co-efficients.

Locating intervening variables

Even if two variables are causally linked we can use elaboration analysis to answer two related questions: is the causal relationship direct or indirect, and by what causal mechanisms are the variables linked?

As an example imagine a relationship between education level and expectations of obedience by one's children; people with low levels of education expect their children to obey set rules whereas those with higher education encourage their children to be more self-directed (see Table 12.3). Diagrammatically this is

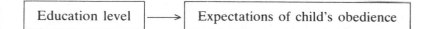

Table 12.3   Expectations of children by education level

		Education Level	
		Low	High
Expect children to be:	Obedient	66%	39%
	Self-directed	34	61
	Total	600	600
		Q = 0.50	

Figure 12.2   An indirect causal relationship with an intervening variable

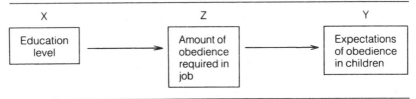

Instead of using Table 12.3 to display this relationship we could equally summarise it with a correlation co-efficient (e.g. Q = 0.50).

Why does this relationship exist? We might think that it has something to do with the sort of jobs people have. Specifically those with the lower levels of education might get jobs in which they have to obey a lot of rules, whereas those with higher levels of education might more often have jobs in which they are expected to be self-directed. In turn this may flow over to expectations of children. Those parents having jobs in which they must obey rules encourage the same traits in their children; those who must rely on self-direction encourage this in their children. In other words, the zero order relationship between education and expectations of children may be due to the type of job which education affects. The type of job in turn may affect expectations of children (see Figure 12.2).

To test this we would group people according to their type of job, that is according to whether it emphasises obedience or self-direction. If those with low and high levels of education have different expectations of children because of the sorts of jobs that education tends to lead to, then once we confine ourselves to people who have the same sort of job there should be no differences in expectations of children depending on level of education (see Table 12.4).

The figures in Table 12.4 show that when we look at those who are

Table 12.4 Expectations of children by educational level by type of work requirements

		Work requires obedience		Work requires self-direction	
		Educational level		Educational level	
		Low	High	Low	High
Expect children to be:	Obedient	72%	69%	35%	33%
	Self-directed	28	31	65	67
	Total	500	100	100	500
		Q = 0.07		Q = 0.04	

similar in terms of their type of job, educational differences make no difference to expectations of children. The reason for the zero order relationship is that education affects the type of job people get and it is *this* that affects people's expectations of children. Education has its effect on expectations through type of work. Job type is therefore called an intervening variable and knowing this helps clarify the process by which education affects expectations of children.

In order to say that our test variable is an intervening variable we must obtain a particular pattern in our results: weaker conditional relationships than the zero order relationship. This is exactly the same as when detecting spurious relationships. Since there are basic logical differences between a spurious relationship and an indirect causal relationship, we need some way of determining which one we have. The only way is to work out which interpretation of the links between the three variables makes most sense. This depends on our theoretical understanding of the variables. The simple guideline is that if the test variable is determined in time between the original two variables, the test variable is likely to be an intervening variable. If it is determined in time *before* the other two, we have found a spurious relationship. When in doubt try drawing diagrams comparable to those in Figures 12.1 and 12.2.

Replication

As well as elaborating the nature of relationships, we can test to see how robust the zero order relationship is. In the previous sections we have seen how the zero order relationship can disappear or decline when we look at people who are similar to one another on a third variable. If the zero order relationship persists even when people are similar in other respects (i.e. within the categories of the test variable), we have replicated the zero order relationship.

If, to use the earlier example, people with different levels of education differed in their expectations of children even though they had similar types of jobs (e.g. requiring self-direction), we would say that the original relationship between education and expectations of children is robust: it is replicated. Thus when the pattern in the conditional tables or the conditional co-efficients are much the same as the zero orders, the zero order relationship was not due to the influence of the test variable. The more control variables tested for, the tougher the test of the original relationship. If it persists despite these controls it increases our confidence that it is a real and general relationship and cannot easily be explained away.

Specification

So far we have seen patterns where each conditional table (or co-efficient) is similar to another: either all lower or all the same as the zero order. Often, however, these conditionals are split: you can get quite a different pattern according to which category of the test variable you are looking at. In other words, the relationship between the original two variables differs for various types of people. If we find this to be so we are specifying the original relationship: we pinpoint the specific types for whom it does or does not hold. Even if none of the conditional tables are similar to the zero order but are split (i.e. at least one is less than the zero order and at least one is the same as or higher than the zero order), we have still specified the relationship: we have shown how it varies for different types of people. The relationship is not general but subgroup specific.

This can be illustrated with an example I accidently found in my own research. I initially obtained the unsurprising result that Catholics in Catholic schools were more religious than those in government schools. I then controlled for sex and found that this applied only to boys; for girls it made no difference whether they went to government or Catholic schools (see Table 12.5). You will notice how the conditional co-efficients are split.

Another term that is given to the pattern where the relationship between X and Y differs according to the value of the control variable is *statistical interaction*. This means that the X variable does not have an effect on its own (or not just on its own to be precise) but when it occurs *in combination* with particular other characteristics it has a special effect. In other words the effect of X on Y is

Table 12.5 Religiousness by school type controlling for gender

Zero order relationship

		Type of school	
		Catholic	High
Religiousness	Low	39%	55%
	High	61	45
	N	899	144
		Q = 0.31	

Conditional relationships—controlling for sex

		BOYS		GIRLS	
		Catholic school	High school	Catholic school	High school
Religiousness	Low	37%	58%	41%	42%
	High	63	42	59	58
	N	579	65	320	79
		Q = 0.40		Q = 0.02	

partly dependent on additional characteristics of the person. It is when there is a particular 'brew' of characteristics that X affects Y.

Statistical interaction can be illustrated with the variables education (X), income (Y) and gender (Z). We have interaction if the relationship between education and income is different for males to what it is for females. If there was no interaction the relationship would be equally strong for both males and females. This can be illustrated with graphs (Figure 12.3).

In the graph where there is no interaction, education has the same effect for males as for females: the increase in education produces the same rate of increase for both men and women. In the graph that illustrates interaction we see that with men an increase of education leads to a greater increase in income than is the case for women. In other words, being male alters the effect that education has on income: it accentuates the effect of education. Being female reduces its effect.

Figure 12.3   Graphical representation of an interaction effect between gender and education on income

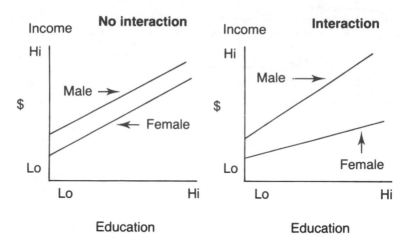

Partial correlations

So far we have only looked at test variables with two categories and consequently have had only two conditional tables and co-efficients to interpret. It is much more difficult when the test variable has a large number of categories. Imagine all the conditional tables and co-efficients if age was the test variable. One solution is to calculate a type of average of all the potential conditional tables. Such a table is called a standardised table (see Loether and McTavish, 1974a:290ff.). The normal solution, especially with interval level test variables, is to calculate an 'average' of all the conditional co-efficients. This leaves us with a single figure which is the partial correlation co-efficient.

It is interpreted in the same way as described in previous sections except that there is only one co-efficient to compare with the zero order (see Table 12.6). It tells us how much of the zero order relationship remains after the contribution of the test variables has been removed (partialled out). It indicates the 'pure' or independent relationship between the original two variables. Since the partial correlation is a single composite figure we cannot see whether the relationship between the original two variables varies across different categories of the test variable. Thus it is of no use for specification.

The partial correlation co-efficient is most widely used with interval variables and is based on Pearson's r (see Loether and McTavish, 1974a:300). Partial correlations also can be computed for

Table 12.6 Examples of patterns of partial correlations and their interpretation

Original variables

X	Y	Zero order correlation	Test variable	Partial correlation	Interpretation
Years of education	Income	0.45	Father's education	0.1	The original relationship was spurious
"	"	0.45	Respondent's (R's) occupation level	0.1	R's occupation is an intervening variable
"	"	0.45	R's age	0.45	R's age does not affect the relationship between education and income

Table 12.7 Interpreting conditional relationships

Conditional relationships compared with zero order	Interpretation
1 Same	Replication
2 Split	Specification
3 Less (test variable is determined in time before X and Y)	Spurious relationship
4 Less (test variable comes between X and Y timewise)	Indirect causal relationship between X and Y with test variable intervening

ordinal variables. Here a partial gamma (see Loether and McTavish, 1974a:298) or a partial Kendall's tau (Cohen and Holliday, 1982:171) are the most widely used. They are all interpreted in essentially the same way.

Summary

The basic procedure of elaboration analysis is

1   Look at the zero order relationship.
2   Select a test variable(s) and look at the conditional or partial relationships.
3   Compare the conditional or partial relationships with the zero order relationships.

4   Interpret the pattern. The ways in which the pattern can be inter-
    preted are summarised in Tables 12.6 and 12.7.

Elaborating zero order relationships is a crucial aspect of analysis.
It helps avoid misinterpreting relationships and as we shall see in the
next chapter is fundamental for developing reasonable theories and
understanding causal processes.

Further reading

Without doubt Rosenberg's *The Logic of Survey Analysis* (1968) is the classic
    treatment of the elaboration model. It is packed with examples, is
    comprehensive and very clear. Another excellent discussion is in Hirschi
    and Selvin's *Delinquency Research* (1967) part II where they illustrate the
    benefits of this approach and use it to highlight the shortcomings of much
    research.
For brief but very clear discussions see Johnson, *Social Statistics Without
    Tears* (1977); Chapter 7 or Chapter 8 of Loether and McTavish, *Descriptive
    Statistics for Sociologists* (1974).
Davis presents a more complex statistical treatment of the approach in
    Elementary Survey Analysis (1971) and Marsh, *The Survey Method* (1982)
    and Hellevick, *Introduction to Causal Analysis* (1984) highlight the value
    of the approach when trying to establish causal links with survey data.
    Davis' book *The Logic of Causal Order* (1985) provides a superb and
    very readable discussion of the logic of control variables in causal mod-
    els. Marsh's (1988) outline of some additional methods of controlling for
    third variables (in Chapters 14 and 15 on standardisation and median
    polishing) is also worth examining once you feel confident with the
    methods outlined in this chapter.

13 Multivariate analysis

This chapter deals with some quite sophisticated techniques for multi-variate analysis of interval level variables. The aim is to help develop an awareness of the potential of these techniques, but you will not become an expert on the basis of the chapter which gives the flavour of the techniques rather than being comprehensive. Five related techniques will be outlined. They all assume that we have only one dependent variable and two or more 'independent' variables. These techniques are all based on bivariate correlation and regression, so make sure you are clear about these before reading further. They also make use of the notions of controlling and intervening variables discussed in Chapter 12.

To illustrate these five techniques we will use an example for most of this chapter in which there is one dependent variable and three independent variables (Table 13.1).

The multivariate techniques I will outline enable us to answer several questions about the links between these variables. First, we can see which variables have the strongest relationship with the dependent variable (partial correlation). Second, we can work out which variable has the *greatest impact* on how much people earn (partial regression). Third, we can use a whole *set* of information (i.e. SES, IQ and EDUC) to predict people's income levels (multiple regression). Fourth, we can use several independent variables

Table 13.1 Variable names, descriptions and symbols

Independent variables	Abbreviation	Symbol
Parents' socioeconomic status	SES	X_1
Intelligence score	IQ	X_2
Years of education	EDUC	X_3
Dependent variable		
$ income per annum	INC	X_4

Figure 13.1   A diagrammatic representation of the variables in Table 13.1

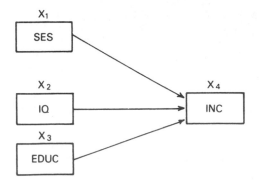

together to explain why people's income varies and to assess how accurately we can predict people's income (multiple correlation). Finally, we can specify the relationships between the independent variables to work out the *mechanisms* by which they affect INC and whether these effects are direct or indirect (path analysis).

Partial correlation

A correlation co-efficient for interval data (r) indicates how strongly two variables are related. It tells us how accurately we can predict people's scores on one variable given a knowledge of their score on the other variable (see pages 174–8).

The partial correlation co-efficient provides the same information except that the distorting effects of other independent variables have been removed (partialled out). It is as if we have looked at r for the two variables among people who are identical on all the other independent variables. A partial r can be computed between each independent variable and the dependent variable, and these can be compared to see which one enables the most accurate predictions of scores on the dependent variable (i.e. has the strongest relationship).

The following set of co-efficients illustrates these points.

$$INC(X_4) \text{ with } EDUC(X_3) \text{ controlling for } SES(X_1) \text{ and } IQ(X_2) = 0.4$$
$$\text{i.e. } r_{43.12} = 0.4$$

INC(X_4) with SES(X_1) controlling for EDUC(X_3) and IQ(X_2) = 0.3
    i.e. $r_{41.32}$ = 0.3
INC(X_4) with IQ(X_2) controlling for EDUC(X_3) and SES(X_1) = 0.1
    i.e. $r_{42.31}$ = 0.1

You will notice how these partial correlations are summarised. An r with subscripts indicates that it is a partial correlation. The subscripts mean that it is a correlation of the two variables before the dot with the effects of those after the dot removed. These co-efficients show which variable has the strongest 'pure' relationship with INC. Since EDUC has the strongest partial r (0.4), it is the best predictor of INC.

Partial regression co-efficients

A regression co-efficient is an estimate of how much impact an independent variable has on the dependent variable. Specifically, for each unit increase in the independent variable the score on the dependent variable will change by the number of units indicated by the regression co-efficient (b). Thus a b of 1000 between dollars income (dependent) and years of education (independent) means that for each additional year of education we estimate that income will increase by $1000: the 'payoff' of a year of education is $1000. The b co-efficient is measured in the same units as the dependent variable (see Chapter 11).

However, we cannot be sure that it is more education itself that leads to increased income or whether it is the influence of other things which tend to go with level of education (e.g. SES background). A partial regression co-efficient indicates how much impact education would have on income independent of education's links with other variables.

We will concentrate on the interpretation rather than the calculation of these co-efficients and this can be done using our previous variables. Here b with subscripts indicates a partial regression co-efficient. These subscripts are read as described earlier. Often the subscripts are abbreviated so that only the number of the independent variable is given with the rest assumed.

Regression of INC(X_4) with EDUC(X_3) controlling for SES(X_1) and
    IQ(X_2) = 1271
    i.e. $b_{43.12}$ = 1271 or b_3 = 1271
Regression of INC(X_4) with SES(X_1) controlling for EDUC(X_3) and
    IQ(X_2) = 5.0
    i.e. $b_{41.32}$ = 5.0 or b_1 = 5.0

Regression of INC(X_4) with IQ(X_2) controlling for EDUC(X_3) and
    SES(X_1) = 19.1
    i.e. $b_{42.31}$ = 19.1 or b_2 = 19.1

Each of these co-efficients indicates how much independent impact
each variable has on INC. To say that b_3 = 1271 means that for each
unit increase in EDUC(X_3), that is for each year of education, INC
will increase by $1271. This is independent of SES and IQ which
might be correlated with EDUC. Thus even though people have the
same IQ and SES the person with the higher education will earn more
at the rate predicted above. The same interpretation applies to each
of the other partial regression co-efficients.

The information provided by these partial co-efficients is useful but
is limited in that we cannot compare them to work out which factor
has the greatest effect. The reason is that each of the independent
variables is measured on a different scale. While one unit increase
on IQ leads to an independent increase of $19.1 and one unit increase
on EDUC (one year of education) leads to an independent increase
of $1271 on INC, we cannot talk of these units being of equivalent
size.

To see which factor has the greatest independent impact we must
standardise them. These standardised partial regression co-efficients
are called beta weights and are symbolised as b^* with appropriate
subscripts. We need not go into the formula for standardisation (see
Johnson, 1977:142) and can focus on their interpretation.

The b for EDUC was 1271. Standardised this might be 0.45. This
means that for each increase of the size of one standard deviation of
EDUC (e.g. s = 2 years) then INC will increase by 0.45 of a standard
deviation of INC (e.g. s = $5650). Since 0.45 of the standard
deviation of INC is $2542 ($5650 × 0.45) then a b^* of 0.45 means that
for each standard deviation increase of EDUC (i.e. two years) INC
will increase by $2542. Normally only the beta weights are given and
are used to pinpoint which variables have the greatest effect. Since
they are standardised we can look also at how much difference there
is in the payoff of two different variables. Thus if one variable has a
b^* of 0.9, it has twice the effect of one with a b^* of 0.45.

For our example we can provide the unstandardised (b) and
standardised partial regression co-efficients (b^*) (Table 13.2).

In this case the ranking is the same with both standardised and
unstandardised co-efficients, although this need not be so. You will
notice, however, that the relative importance differs. Using the b^*,
IQ and SES have roughly equal impact on INC whereas this is distorted when using the unstandardised co-efficients.

Another very useful way of applying regression co-efficients is to

Table 13.2 Partial regressions of three independent variables with INC

	b	b*
EDUC	1271	0.451
IQ	19.1	0.059
SES	5.0	0.053

Table 13.3 Partial regressions of three independent variables on INC separately for men and women

	Men		Women	
	b	b*	b	b*
EDUC	1424	0.49	1010	0.41
IQ	28.0	0.066	13.0	0.04
SES	3.0	0.031	8.8	0.09

calculate them separately for different subgroups and then compare whether each variable has the same payoff for the different groups. This can be done with either unstandardised or standardised regression co-efficients as long as the use of the unstandardised ones is confined to comparing the same variable across groups.

For example, we might calculate the co-efficients separately for men and women (Table 13.3).

According to these figures men get a greater 'payoff' than do women for each year of education ($1424 cf.$1010) and each IQ point ($28 cf.$13).

In summary, partial regression co-efficients indicate how much independent impact or 'payoff' each independent variable has. When standardised we can tell which one has the greatest impact. Partial regression differs from partial correlation. Partial regression enables us to predict how much impact one variable has on another, while partial correlation enables us to assess the accuracy of those predictions.

Multiple regression

Most discussions of partial regression are under the heading of multiple regression. I have treated them separately to emphasise the different sorts of uses to which regression co-efficients can be put. The emphasis above has been on interpreting b or b* co-efficients individually or in comparison to one another. They also can be used together so that the joint impact of a set of variables can be assessed.

Multiple regression works on the principle that the more we know about a person the more accurately we can guess other attributes of that person. It makes use of the information provided by partial regression. To estimate someone's income I could use my knowledge of their EDUC. But IQ and SES have unique effects additional to EDUC so it makes sense to use this information as well to obtain a better estimate than that provided by EDUC alone.

To be statistical we can do this by simply extending the bivariate regression formula of $\hat{Y} = a + bX$ into

$$\hat{X}_4 = a + b_1X_1 + b_2X_2 + b_3X_3 \text{ etc.},$$

where each X represents a particular variable and each b represents the partial regression co-efficients of that variable on the dependent variable.

When standardised b co-efficients are used, this equation is changed slightly. The X values are transformed into standard scores (z scores) and the 'a' term is dropped as it is always zero. The standardised formula becomes

$$\hat{Z} = b_1^*z_1 + b_2^*z_2 + b_3^*z_3 \text{ etc.}$$

Normally when making predictions the unstandardised equation is used. Standardised figures are used more when trying to assess the relative impact of each independent variable. The following discussion will use the unstandardised equation.

Using our example we can translate this formula into

$$\text{Predicted INC} = a + b_1(\text{SES}) + b_2(\text{IQ}) + b_3(\text{EDUC}).$$

Assuming $a = 1000$, we can substitute the partial regression co-efficients (unstandardised or standardised can be used depending on your purpose) to get

$$\text{Predicted INC} = 1000 + 5.0(\text{SES}) + 19.1(\text{IQ}) + 1271(\text{EDUC}).$$

For any particular person we can take their scores on each variable and put them into the formula to predict that person's income. For example we might have a person with these values: SES = 12; IQ = 100; EDUC = 12. For this person we would get the equation

$$\text{Predicted INC} = 1000 + 5.0(12) + 19.1(100) + 1271(12)$$
$$= 1000 + 60 + 1910 + 15\,252$$
$$= \$18\,222.$$

For sociologists who often want to make predictions about groups

Table 13.4 Subgroup means and b co-efficients for men and women

	Men		Women	
	$\bar{X}$	b	$\bar{X}$	b
SES	16	3.0	15	8.8
IQ	100	28	100	13
EDUC	16	1425	11	1010

rather than individuals, multiple regression can be used in another productive way. Using the same basic procedure we can estimate the mean score for a group (e.g. the mean INC) rather than an individual score. To do this we use the group mean for each variable in the regression equation to predict from rather than individual scores.

If we had the following group means for the whole country, $X_{SES} = 16$, $X_{IQ} = 100$, and $X_{EDUC} = 13$, we could estimate the mean income for people in this country. Assuming that the earlier partial regression co-efficients were representative we can put these group means into the equation with the result

$$\text{Predicted } X_{INC} - a + 5.0(16) + 19.1(100) + 1271(13)$$
$$= 1000 + 80 + 1910 + 16\,523$$
$$= \$19\,513.$$

If we wished we could use this application of multiple regression in useful ways. We could calculate partial regression co-efficients and group means separately for different subgroups (e.g. men and women) and make estimates of the X_{INC} for each subgroup (see Table 13.4).

Using the figures from Table 13.4 we can develop a separate regression equation and estimate mean incomes for men and women.

Men: Predicted $X_{INC} = a + 3.0(16) + 28(100) + 1424(16)$
$$= 1000 + 48 + 2800 + 22\,784$$
$$= \$26\,632.$$

Women: Predicted $X_{INC} = a + 8.8(15) + 13(100) + 1010(11)$
$$= 1000 + 132 + 1300 + 11\,110$$
$$= \$13\,542.$$

The male and female income estimates vary for two reasons. The group means differ—women have lower mean EDUC and SES. The payoff or impact (b) of these variables differs for the two groups. Women, for example, get less benefit in terms of income for each unit of IQ and EDUC. Not only do they have less EDUC, they are rewarded less *pro rata* for what they have.

We could go further here and demonstrate the disadvantage that women suffer. If women got the same income benefits for their IQ, SES and EDUC that men do, we could look at women's income compared with what they would earn under the benefits men get. To test this we can simply put the male b co-efficients in the female equation to get

$$\text{Women: Predicted } X_{INC} = a + 3.0(15) + 28(100) + 1424(11)$$
$$= 1000 + 45 + 2800 + 15\,664$$
$$= \$19\,509.$$

This means that even given female means on SES, IQ and EDUC, women would earn \$19 509 rather than \$13 542 if they were rewarded at the same rate as men per IQ point and year of education.

In summary, multiple regression can be used in a variety of ways. Apart from the use to which partial regression co-efficients can be put, multiple regression can be used so that a set of variables is used to make predictions for particular individuals, whole groups or sub-groups. These procedures can be applied to a wide variety of research problems.

Cautions

Care needs to be taken when using multiple regression analysis. The technique is based on various statistical assumptions and is only sensitive to certain types of relationships between variables. The form of regression described above is only sensitive to linear relationships between variables: it does not detect *curvilinear* relationships (see pages 160–1). Furthermore, it does not detect *interaction* effects between independent variables (see pages 208–10). Thus it does not detect relationships where education, for example, affects income for males more than it does for females. There are ways of doing regression analysis that are sensitive to these types of relationships, but it is beyond the scope of this book to discuss them.

Multiple regression also assumes that the variance in the dependent variable is constant for each value of the independent variable (technically called *homoskedasticity*). If this is not so, then regression results can be distorted. Another problem to be on the lookout for is called *multicollinearity*. This is a problem caused by independent variables that are highly correlated with one another. When independent variables are highly intercorrelated, it is impossible to distinguish between their separate effects and regression estimates can become unstable. One simple way of detecting multicollinearity is to look at the zero-order correlations between each of the independent variables. Correlations over 0.70 in large samples are likely to reflect multicollinearity. It is beyond the scope of this book to discuss methods of detecting these problems or ways of dealing with them. They are dealt with in detail in Lewis Beck (1980), Norusis (1985), Berry and Feldman (1985) and Schroeder, Sjoquist and Stephan (1986).

A further problem with multiple regression is that it assumes that variables are measured at the interval level. This can severely limit the range of situations in which it can be used. Fortunately, a variation on normal regression overcomes this problem.

Multiple regression with non-interval variables: dummy regression

Multiple regression can be extended to analyses when the dependent variable is interval but one or more *independent* variables are nominal or ordinal and have more than two categories. We can, for example, use variables such as religious affiliation, country of birth, political preference as independent variables. It is easiest to explain how this is done by using an example. Since the variables in the example used so far in this chapter are all interval we will use quite a different example in which the independent variables are non-interval.

Suppose we wanted to look at the effect of religious denomination on the frequency of attendance at religious services. We have two variables: number of times religious services are attended each year (ATTEND) and denomination (DENOM) with five categories —

1 Catholic;
2 Protestant;
3 Jewish;
4 non-Christian; and
5 no religion.

Since DENOM is a nominal variable we cannot do regression in the normal way. Instead we can 'trick' regression by breaking up the nominal variable into a number of dichotomous variables. Since dichotomous variables can be treated as interval variables (see pages 182–3) we can then quite legitimately perform a regression analysis. These variables which are called *dummy variables* are created by taking a category of the variable DENOM and creating a new dichotomous variable from that category. This task is easily accomplished by computer packages such as SPSSX. When creating the dummy variable from a category the people from that category will be coded as 1 and everyone else as 0.

In this case we might end up with the following dummy variables:

1   CATH: 1 = Catholic, 0 = everyone else;
2   PROT: 1 = Protestant, 0 = everyone else;
3   JEW: 1 = Jewish, 0 = everyone else;
4   NONXIAN: 1 = other non-Christian, 0 = everyone else.

In this example there is no dummy variable for the 'no religion' category of the original variable. This is important. *The number of dummy variables must always be one less than the number of categories of the original variable.* This is necessary to avoid the technical problem with multiple regression—multicollinearity. The category for which we do not create a dummy variable becomes a baseline against which we compare the other categories. As will be seen shortly, omitting a particular category does not stop us obtaining regression information for that category.

Using these dummy variables our regression equation will be:

$$\text{N of services attended} = a + b_{\text{Cath}}(\text{CATH}) + b_{\text{Prot}}(\text{PROT}) + b_{\text{Jew}}(\text{JEW}) + b_{\text{Nonxian}}(\text{NONXIAN})$$

If we obtained the following b figures from our analysis:

$$a = 2;\ b_{\text{Cath}} = 15;\ b_{\text{Prot}} = 5;\ b_{\text{Jew}} = 7;\ b_{\text{Nonxian}} = 10$$

we get the following:

$$\text{N of times attended} = 2 + 15(\text{CATH}) + 5(\text{PROT}) + 7(\text{JEW}) + 10(\text{NONXIAN})$$

Using normal regression procedures we can predict how often, on average, Catholics attend religious services in a year. Since Catholic is coded as 1 and a Catholic will necessarily receive a code of 0 on each of the other dummy variables (Table 13.5) we can estimate that for Catholics:

$$\text{N of times attended} = 2 + 15(1) + 5(0) + 7(0) + 10(0)$$
$$= 17 \text{ times a year}$$

Table 13.5 Constructing dummy variables and codes

Category on DENOM	Code on DENOM	Dummy variable codes			
		CATH	PROT	JEW	NONXIAN
Catholic	1	1	0	0	0
Protestant	2	0	1	0	0
Jewish	3	0	0	1	0
Non-Christian	4	0	0	0	1
No religion	5	0	0	0	0

Using the same approach, estimates can be made for every other group *except the omitted group* — those with no religion.

In dummy regression the estimate for the omitted category is obtained by using the intercept (a). In this case the intercept (a) is 2 so this means that those with no religious affiliation attend religious services, on average, twice a year. Given that the intercept represents the regression estimate for the omitted category it also means that the b figures for the groups represented by the dummy variables can be interpreted as being that much higher (or lower) than the omitted category. That is, the figures for Catholics, Protestants and others is the average attendance of these groups *relative* to the attendance of the omitted category. Thus, Catholics attend church on fifteen more occasions per year than those with no religion; Protestants on five more occasions and so on.

Given that this type of interpretation is possible, it makes sense, when selecting the base category (that which is omitted), to choose a category against which we want to compare other groups. Thus if the variable was country of birth and our main interest was to compare differences between native born and those born in various overseas countries it would make sense to make native born the base category and create dummy variables to represent various overseas birth places. A useful guideline, when using ordinal variables, is to use one of the extreme categories as the base category.

In the end however the choice of the base category makes no difference to the final estimates we obtain. Had we chosen Catholics as the baseline in the above example we would have obtained the following results:

$$a = 17; \ b_{Prot} = -10; \ b_{Jew} = -8; \ b_{Nonxian} = -5; \ b_{None} = -15$$

When these figures are placed in the regression equation we obtain exactly the same estimates as when NONE was the omitted category. Thus

$$\text{N of times attended} = 17 + -10(\text{PROT}) + -8(\text{JEW}) + -5(\text{NONXIAN}) + -15(\text{NONE})$$

The estimate for Protestants is still seven times a year or ten times less than Catholics; for those with no religion the estimate is still two times a year or fifteen times less than Catholics.

Dummy variables can be included in regression analysis together with interval level dependent variables and their interpretation remains essentially the same. If age was added to the above equation the figures would change and the interpretation of the figures would simply be that these are the effects of denominational membership with the effect of age controlled.

If more than one set of dummy variables is used in the one equation the value of 'a' will represent the value for the *combination* of omitted categories. If gender was added to the earlier equation with males being coded as 0 and females as 1, the value of 'a' would represent the attendance levels of *males* with *no religious affiliation*, the 'b' value for Catholics would be the attendance frequency of *male Catholics* relative to males without a religious affiliation and so on. Thus in an equation with the following figures:

$$\text{N of times attended} = 1 + 14(\text{CATH}) + 4(\text{PROT}) + 6(\text{JEW}) + 9(\text{NONXIAN}) + 3(\text{FEMALE})$$

males with no religious affiliation attend religious services on average once a year and male Catholics attend fifteen times a year. Females with no religious affiliation would attend four times a year on average (a + b(female) = 1 + 3). Female Catholics would attend, on average, eighteen times a year (1 + 14 + 3).

In summary, by converting nominal and interval independent variables into a series of dichotomous or dummy variables coded 0 and 1 it is possible to extend the power of multiple regression to problems where not all the variables are measured at the interval level.

Multiple correlation

We have already seen the difference between regression co-efficients and correlation co-efficients for bivariate analysis. Regression (b) enables prediction of people's score on a dependent variable. Correlations (r) enable us to assess the accuracy of those predictions.

When we are making predictions using a set of variables in a regression equation, we can use the multiple correlation co-efficient (R) to assess how accurate this set of variables is in predicting people's actual values on the dependent variable. It is interpreted in the same way as the bivariate correlation co-efficient (r). If we obtain a low R we do not place too much weight on the predictions. Be cautious of regression equations and predictions without R, since there is no way of evaluating their usefulness.

Earlier we saw that when r is squared (r^2) it tells us how well variation in the independent variable accounts for variation in the dependent variable. For example, do differences in education account for why people have different incomes? An r^2 of 0.60 means 60 per cent of the variance is explained, leaving 40 per cent to be explained due to factors other than educational differences.

The same applies when we have two or more independent variables. R^2 tells us how much variation in the dependent variable is explained by a set of independent variables. In other words, R^2 tells us how well a combination of people's characteristics helps explain why they differ from one another on the dependent variable. Apart from applying to a set of independent variables, R^2 has the same interpretation as r^2. The more variance explained by a set of independent variables (i.e. the higher R^2), the more powerful the model is.

Path analysis

Path analysis is a procedure for analysing and presenting results, which draws heavily on the techniques already outlined in this chapter. It is used for testing causal models and requires that we formulate a model using a pictorial causal flowgraph (Figure 13.2) and helps us see what we are trying to say. It makes use of R^2, thus enabling us to evaluate how good the model is, and by using beta weights (called path co-efficients in path analysis) also enables us to specify how much effect each variable has. In addition it enables us to work out the mechanisms by which variables affect one another; it can pinpoint the extent to which a variable's effect is direct or indirect. As such, path analysis provides a lot of information about causal processes in an easily understandable way.

Using our earlier variables we can draw a path diagram. Learning how to develop and read these diagrams is the key to path analysis.

In a path diagram we must place the variables in a causal order. The variables we include, the order in which we place them and the causal arrows we draw are up to us. We will develop the model on the basis of sound theoretical reasoning. We could, of course, develop such a model even if we did not intend to use path analysis. These

Figure 13.2   A path diagram

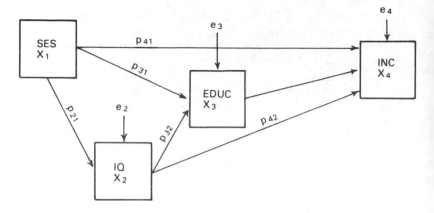

diagrams provide a useful way of specifying what our theory is and for keeping several ideas in the air at once. The point of path analysis is to provide one means of evaluating how well a set of data fits that model. The key point is that we must develop the model and do it before any fancy statistical analysis. Statistical analysis will not do it for us. Sophisticated statistics and analysis do not substitute for sound careful theoretical reasoning: rather they rely on it. Marsh argues that

> It is the model that stands between the researcher and unbridled empiricism in the attempt to draw causal inferences, for it forces researchers into explicit theory making activity. (1982:72)

When drawing a path diagram, causally prior variables will be placed on the left and we progressively work across to the most 'recent' variable. This is the dependent variable. The arrows specify the assumed direction of causal influence.

Each arrow is given a name which is a p with a subscript. The subscript reflects the numbers of the variables joined by the arrow; the number of the 'dependent' variable is placed first. Thus p_{41} in Figure 13.2 refers to an arrow from variable 1 (SES) to 4 (INC). In this case p_{41} is a direct path. SES also influences INC indirectly through the route—SES(1) → EDUC(3) → INC(4). This path would be named $p_{31}p_{43}$. The indirect path SES(1) → IQ(2) → EDUC(3) → INC(4) would be $p_{21}p_{32}p_{43}$.

In a path diagram each path is given a path co-efficient. These are beta weights and indicate how much impact variables have on various

Figure 13.3 A path diagram with path co-efficients

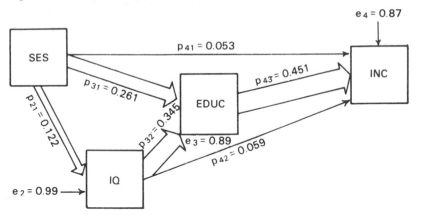

other variables. In Figure 13.3 the path diagram has been redrawn with path co-efficients. For the sake of clarity some arrows have been enlarged roughly proportionate to the size of each path co-efficient. To clarify the idea of the direct and indirect paths and the relative importance of each path, it is helpful to think of the arrows as water pipes of varying diameters depending on the size of the path co-efficient (p_{43} is 'wider' than p_{41}). If you poured water in at, say, SES, by which path would the most get through? By looking at the diagram in this way we can track down by what mechanisms variables have their effect and evaluate the relative importance of each mechanism. This is extremely helpful in developing a sophisticated understanding of causal processes.

In path analysis we can work out how much a variable affects another variable and compare this effect with the effects of other variables to work out which is the most important. The effect of a variable is called the *total effect*. It consists of two different types of effects: *direct effect* and *indirect effect*. Using SES and INC as an example the indirect effects are those where SES affects INC via some other variable (e.g. via EDUC) while direct effects are un-mediated effects. The total effect of SES on INC is the sum of these two sets of effects. The indirect effect of SES can be further broken down between the various indirect paths. The process of working out the extent to which an effect is direct or indirect and in estab-lishing the importance of the various indirect paths is called *decom-position* and this is illustrated in Figure 13.4.

In path analysis these various effects are calculated by using the

Figure 13.4   Calculating direct and indirect effects from SES to INC

Direct	
SES ————————→ INC	= 0.053
0.053	

Indirect	
SES → EDUC → INC	
= (0.261) × (0.451)	= 0.1178
SES → IQ → EDUC → INC	
= (0.122) × (0.345) × (0.451)	= 0.019
SES → IQ → INC	
= (0.122) × (0.059)	= 0.007

Total indirect effect	= 0.1438

Total causal effect	= 0.1968

path co-efficients. Since these are standardised they can be compared directly with one another. Working out the importance of a direct effect between two variables is done simply by looking at the path co-efficients. To assess the importance of any indirect effect or path just multiply the co-efficients along the path. You can do this separately for each indirect path. To get the total indirect effect between two variables simply add up the effect for each indirect path that joins those variables. To find the total causal effect (to use the water analogy, to find how much water would get through), simply add the direct and indirect co-efficients together (see Figure 13.4).

To interpret the various answers in Figure 13.4 refer back to the earlier outline of the meaning of beta weights. By simply looking at the figures, it is easy to see which path is most important and to state by what means SES affects income.

The other important figures in the path diagram are the 'e' figures coming out of nowhere which point at the variables. These are called 'error terms' and help us evaluate how well the whole model works. The error term tells us how much variance in a variable is unexplained by the prior variables in the model. To indicate unexplained variance this figure has to be squared. To work out how much variance is explained (i.e. R^2) simply subtract the squared error term from one. In this case e_4 is the crucial error term since it tells us about how well variance in INC, our dependent variable, has been explained. Here e_4 is 0.87. The unexplained variance is $(0.87)^2$ which is 0.76. Since 76 per cent of variance in INC is unexplained by the model, 24 per cent is explained (i.e. R^2).

This R^2 figure provides a useful way of evaluating how well the model works, that is how well it fits a set of data. If we can come up with another model with either a different ordering of variables or different variables that explained more variance (i.e. higher R^2), it would be more 'powerful'. It is worth noting that regardless of the size of the path co-efficients, if R^2 is low it is not a great model.

Summary

A number of multivariate techniques have been outlined in this chapter.

1 *Partial regression co-efficients—unstandardised:* These tell us how much independent impact an independent variable has on the dependent variable with the effects of other variables removed.

2 *Standardised partial regression co-efficients (beta weights):* These provide the same information as above except that they can be compared with one another to work out which variable has the greatest impact.

3 *Multiple regression:* This makes use of the information provided by a set of independent variables to predict values on the dependent variable. Normally, unstandardised partial regression co-efficients are used to work out the joint impact of a set of variables. The technique can be applied to individuals, groups or subgroups.

4 *Partial correlation:* This tells us which variable has the strongest independent relationship with the dependent variable. As such it helps assess the accuracy of predictions based on partial regression co-efficients.

5 *Multiple correlation:* This helps assess how well a set of variables together explains variation in the dependent variable (R^2). As such it helps evaluate the accuracy of predictions based on multiple regression and is useful in evaluating the fit between a model and data.

6 *Path analysis:* This enables us to evaluate the relative importance of various direct and indirect links between variables and as such helps us to understand the causal mechanisms between variables. It also helps evaluate how well a model fits a set of data.

The importance of these multivariate techniques lies not in their statistical sophistication but in their value in testing complex theoretical models. Their potential is realised when they are preceded by careful, theoretical reasoning. It is not much use having insights about possible intervening variables in a causal process after data are collected and then realising that this information has not been collected. These techniques help us evaluate our models and encourage us to specify our model clearly but they do not create them.

Of course they can help refine models, but the validity of the co-efficients we calculate is dependent on the correctness of the causal model. If the model does not make sense, any co-efficient, no matter how impressive, is meaningless (Marsh 1982:79).

The sophistication of the techniques is no substitute for theoretical sophistication. The importance of the answers they provide is a function of the questions we ask and the models we test, not the sophistication of the technique we apply. The value of these techniques is that we can ask the complex questions and propose complicated models and know that there are systematic ways of analysis to help answer them. They enable us to take the notion of multiple causation of phenomena seriously and to escape analysis that reflects Durkheim's idea that each effect has only one cause. Enabled to unpack causal mechanisms, we can achieve a better understanding of causal processes that underlie simple correlations and do not have to rely on our stock of plausible, *ad hoc* explanations of these correlations. As such these multivariate techniques can be used (but do not by any means guarantee) to help develop explanations which in Weber's sense are adequate at the level of both cause and meaning.

Further reading

A very clear non-technical introduction to the multivariate techniques outlined in this chapter is given by Johnson in Chapter 8 of *Social Statistics Without Tears* (1977). Kerlinger provides a very good conceptual and non-statistical explanation of a range of multivariate techniques in *Behavioural Research: A Conceptual Approach* (1979), Chapters 4, 11–13. Mueller, Schuessler and Costner in *Statistical Reasoning in Sociology* (1977), Chapter 10 and Loether and McTavish's *Descriptive Statistics for Sociologists* (1974), Chapter 9 and Blalock in *Social Statistics* (1972), Chapter 19 give slightly more advanced outlines. Perhaps the best moderate level discussions are in Nie et al. in *SPSS: Statistical Package for the Social Sciences* (1975) pp. 301–5, 320–42, 383–97 and in Norusis in *SPSSX: Introductory Statistics Guide* (1983).

For advanced, statistical treatments of a fair range of multivariate techniques see Tabachnick and Fidell's *Using Multivariate Statistics* (1983) for a very well organised discussion which gives a great deal of practical advice. Kerlinger and Pedhazur present a very thorough discussion of multiple regression techniques in *Multiple Regression in Behavioural Research* (1973). An excellent set of books that deals with both the theoretical and practical aspects of multiple regression is published in the Sage series on Quantitative Applications in the Social Sciences (Berry and Feldman, 1985; Achen, 1982; Schroeder, Sjoquist and Stephen, 1986 and Lewis-Beck, 1980).

Part IV   THE PROCESS OF ANALYSIS

14 Coding

Computer analysis typically requires that people's answers to questions or our own observations be converted into numbers. This conversion process is called coding. This chapter deals with the coding of questionnaire data, but the principles also apply to data collected in other ways.

Coding involves four main steps: allocating codes to the answers to each question (or variable); allocating computer columns to each question; producing a codebook; and checking codes. Each of these is considered in turn and the chapter concludes with a discussion of some of the complexities of coding.

Allocation of codes to each variable

Each variable has at least two categories and any person must fit into one and only one category. The essence of coding is to give a number to each answer to a question. Each answer to a particular question must be given a distinctive code. This code is fed into the computer and the number thereafter represents a particular response to a given question. Codes can be allocated either before the question is answered (precoding) or afterwards (postcoding).

Precoding

With forced-choice questions it is possible to allocate codes to answers before people fill in the questionnaire since we have determined beforehand what range of answers we will get. To make it easier to code someone's actual responses, the codes that represent each answer are printed on the questionnaire itself. This can be done in different ways (Figure 14.1).

Postcoding using fixed coding schemes

For some variables, excellent sets of codes exist and, where possible

Figure 14.1   Two methods of precoding questions

Are you: (tick box)	1 [ ] Married 2 [ ] Never married 3 [ ] Separated 4 [ ] Divorced 5 [ ] Widowed 6 [ ] Other	Are you: (circle number)	1 Married 2 Never married 3 Separated 4 Divorced 5 Widowed 6 Other

and appropriate, these should be used. Not only do they save a lot of work, but they are normally very well worked out and enable greater comparison between the findings of various studies. Census Offices and codebooks from major surveys have many coding schemes and these should be consulted for variables such as occupation, educational qualifications, country of birth, ethnicity and religious denomination.

Table 14.1 provides an example of a pre-established scheme for coding an open question. This example illustrates how codes can be assigned at various levels of generality. These codes are used for answers to the question 'What is your highest qualification?' where interviewers obtained detailed information including the name of the qualification and the field in which the qualification is obtained.

This question could be coded at one of three levels. We could use the general category level, but each of the general categories could be coded more precisely. I have listed a second level of codes for only one of the general categories (graduate diploma level). These reflect more detailed information about the type of qualification at each of the general levels. Further distinctions within each of these second-level codes are possible and these are reflected in the specific level codes that detail the second-level code of 'teacher training' much more precisely. If you decided to code only at the general level, then single-digit codes from 0 to 9 could be used. If you coded at the second level, a two-digit coding level could be used, while a three-digit code would be used in coding at the specific level.

Clearly the specific level code provides more information. Knowing that someone has a postgraduate diploma in special education is much more informative than simply knowing that they have a postgraduate diploma or even a postgraduate diploma in teacher training. Coding at the specific level is preferable. Although it is more time consuming and requires the collection of more specific information, it allows the greatest flexibility at the analysis stage. While these fairly specific codes will probably need to be collapsed into broader categories later on, there is great flexibility in how various

Table 14.1   Part of a pre-established code for an open question on highest qualification

'What is your highest qualification?'

General Category Codes

Code	General Category
001–099	Higher degree level
100–199	Graduate diploma level
200–299	Bachelor degree level
300–399	Diploma level
400–499	Certificate, trade level
500–599	Certificate, other level
600–799	Not classifiable by level
800–899	Inadequately described
900–999	Other codes

Second level codes

Graduate diploma level

101–104	Management, administration and related fields
105–110	Natural, mathematical and applied sciences
111–113	Mathematical and computer sciences
114–120	Engineering and technology
121–125	Architecture and building
126–133	Social sciences
134	Humanities
135	Religion and theology
136–141	Teacher training
142	Education (other)
143–151	Medicine
152–153	Dentistry
154–159	Paramedicine
160	Vetinary science
161–163	Artistic, library and performing arts
164–168	Agriculture and forestry
169	Transport and communication
170	Unclassifiable field of study
171	Field of study not specified

Specific level codes

Teacher training

136	Pre-primary and early childhood
137	Primary education
138	Secondary education
139	Special education
140	Education librarianship
141	Teacher training, not specified

Source: Australian Bureau of Statistics Information Paper 2149.0

categories are combined. If only broad codes are used initially, it is not possible to retrieve the original detail or to change the broad categories into which specific qualifications are placed.

Developing a set of codes from the answers given

Often we will need to develop our own set of codes based on the responses obtained in the survey. For example, we might ask people to indicate what they think will be the major problem facing the country in ten years' time. We might be able to anticipate some answers and develop a partial coding scheme beforehand, but there will be many responses that we probably could not predict.

The first step in developing these codes is to be clear about the purpose of the question. This is followed by the examination of between 50 to 100 questionnaires and seeing if these fall into broad groupings. Once this is done, the more specific responses should be placed under the broad headings and assigned specific codes. For example, we might be able to group responses about major problems in ten years' time under headings such as social, economic, moral, military, environmental, political, religious and so on. Having done this, we can develop specific codes for responses under each heading. Under the environmental heading, we might have responses that fall into categories such as overcrowding, air quality, water quality, scarcity of resources, extinction of species, greenhouse problems, ozone problems, etc.

When developing these codes, try to make the categories and codes flexible so that additional codes can be added later as more questionnaires are examined. Use multiple-digit codes so that there are plenty of spare codes if they are needed. A system something like that in Table 14.1, where a range of codes are allocated initially to a broad category (e.g. environmental problems) and more specific codes are allocated to specific answers under this broad heading, is desirable.

Multiple answers

When coding open questions, one problem is that people often provide several answers to the one question or the same answer could be coded under two different headings. Even though we might have asked only about what people think the major problem will be in ten years' time, a person might nevertheless give three problems. How do you decide which answer to code? One method is to select only the first answer and ignore the rest. But this seems rather arbitrary, and means that valuable information is lost. Another approach is to use a *multiple response* coding strategy (see below).

The other problem is that the same answer can be coded under several different codes. For example, someone might say that the biggest problem will be 'overpopulation that will lead to greater air pollution and increase the problems of poverty'. This could be coded using a code for overcrowding, a code for air pollution or under a social problems code that relates to poverty. If only one code is allocated, the coder will have to make a decision. This needs to be done in consultation with other coders. Sometimes codes can be allocated according to a preset order of priorities. You might decide that in cases where a response could be given both an environmental and some other code, the environmental code will take priority. Clearly this sort of decision can produce distortions in the data and any such policy will depend on the purposes of the survey and needs to be made very clear to readers.

Coding multiple responses to closed questions

Where respondents provide several responses, the best method of coding is to develop a *set* of variables to represent those responses. There are two approaches for developing these variables. Either the *multiple dichotomy method* or the *multiple response method* can be used. The difference between these two methods can be illustrated using a question about the qualities people think are important in children. These qualities are listed in Table 14.2.

We might provide 500 respondents with a list of these qualities and ask them to indicate which two of twelve qualities they felt were

Table 14.2 Multiple codes using the multiple dichotomy method

Variable number	Is this quality important?	Yes (code = 1)	No (code = 2)	Total N
1	Good manners	60	440	500
2	Tries hard to succeed	103	397	500
3	Honesty	89	411	500
4	Neatness and cleanliness	213	287	500
5	Good sense and sound judgment	30	470	500
6	Self-control	54	446	500
7	Gets along well with other children	69	431	500
8	Obeys parents	149	351	500
9	Responsibility	21	479	500
10	Considerate	70	430	500
11	Interested in why and how things happen	40	460	500
12	Is a good student	102	398	500

most desirable in children. This would provide us with 1000 responses (500 people each giving two responses).

We could develop two sets of variables from this. The first approach is called the *multiple dichotomy method*. This involves creating a separate variable for each of the categories of the question. Since people can select more than one category, we reflect this by creating twelve variables. A person will be given a 'yes' code for the two variables they selected and a 'no' code for the ten variables they did not select. Thus we would develop a variable for 'manners' which would have two categories to indicate whether or not it was selected. Another dichotomous variable would be created for 'tries hard', another for 'honesty' and so forth until we had twelve dichotomous variables. We could then obtain frequency distributions for each variable to see how often it was selected.

The alternative approach is to use the *multiple response method*. Instead of creating a separate variable for each category of the question, we would create only two variables into which we would place a respondent's two choices. Each of these two variables would have twelve categories to reflect each of the possible choices. Thus the variables might be called 'choice 1' and 'choice 2'.

Regardless of which way we code the answers, we record the same number of people giving each response. The difference is in the way we break the answers up into variables and in the codes we give each of these variables.

Table 14.3   Multiple codes using the multiple response method

Code		Variable 1 (Choice 1)	Variable 2 (Choice 2)
1	Good manners	40	20
2	Tries hard to succeed	65	38
3	Honesty	32	57
4	Neatness and cleanliness	108	105
5	Good sense and sound judgment	4	26
6	Self-control	30	24
7	Gets along well with other children	20	49
8	Obeys parents	60	89
9	Responsibility	3	18
10	Considerate	42	28
11	Interested in why and how things happen	8	32
12	Is a good student	88	14
	Total N	500	500

Multiple responses to open questions

Open questions can often produce multiple responses that require the creation of several variables to capture the responses. A survey of recently divorced people might ask respondents what they feel were the main factors that contributed to their marital breakdown. No doubt many people will list a variety of factors.

When coding responses it will normally be best to construct a number of variables into which to code responses. We still have to choose between the multiple dichotomy approach and the multiple response method. Which approach is chosen will depend on the number of different answers that are given and on the particular focus of the study. If there are a large number of factors given, this could lead to a very large and cumbersome number of dichotomous variables.

In such cases it might be best to use the multiple response method. This would involve finding the case with the largest number of factors listed and creating that many variables. Each of these variables will have the same number of identical codes. Each person will then be given a code on each of the variables.

For example, the largest number of factors that any respondent listed might be five. Accordingly we would create five variables that we might call factor1, factor2, factor3, factor4 and factor5. We would then develop an exhaustive list of factors given and give each of those factors a unique code. We might find 25 different factors listed over all the respondents. Thus we might give alcohol a code of 1, unfaithfulness a code of 2, financial pressures a code of 3, violence a code of 4 and so forth (see Figure 14.2). The same set of codes would be used for each of the five variables (factor1 to factor5). The first case we come across might list only one factor— alcohol—so that case would receive a code of 1 on the factor1 variable and a missing value code on the remaining four variables. The second case might list three factors—violence, alcohol and unfaithfulness. They would be given a code of 4 on factor1, 1 on factor2, 2 on factor3 and a missing value code on factor4 and factor5. The third case might only mention parental interference and financial pressures, and would thus be coded as 25 on factor1, 3 on factor2 and 99 on the remaining variables (see Figure 14.2).

Using the multiple response approach can lead to some difficulties with analysis. If we wanted to find out how many people gave a particular response (e.g. violence), we would have to look at the information contained in five variables. For any given person, this factor could have been coded into any of the five variables. One way of analysing data coded in this way is to use a method called

Figure 14.2   Coding multiple responses to an open question

List of codes

Code	Response
1	Alcohol
2	Unfaithfulness
3	Financial pressures
4	Violence
. . .	. . .
25	Parental interference
99	No answer

Case 1:
Alcohol

Case 2:
Violence
Alcohol
Unfaithfulness

Case 3:
Parental interference
Financial pressures

Coded cases

	Factor1	Factor2	Factor3	Factor4	Factor5
Case 1	01	99	99	99	99
Case 2	04	01	02	99	99
Case 3	25	03	99	99	99
. . .	. . .	. . .	. . .	. . .	. . .

MULTRESPONSE in the SPSSX program. This provides a way of analysing responses to all five multiple response variables at the same time. (It counts across all the variables and adds up how many times a given response is given over all the variables.) This method is useful for relatively simple analysis (frequencies and crosstabs), but is of no use for the more advanced multivariate techniques and makes the calculation of summary statistics such as correlations impossible. If a particular factor (e.g. violence) is to be the focus of the analysis and multivariate analysis and summary statistics (e.g. correlations) are required, multiple dichotomies would be used rather than multiple responses.

Other approaches for open-ended questions

The methods described above for the analysis of data from open-ended questions represent ways of reducing answers to a form that can be placed in a variable-by-case matrix and which is thus amenable to survey methods of data analysis.

These data can be handled in other ways with various types of text-based computer packages. These range from the relatively simple approaches which simply search through text for particular words and thus locate answers that use these words or phrases (e.g. Gofer) to the more complex and powerful packages such as NUDIST and Ethnograph.

Coding numerical data

For some variables such as age, income, number of children and so on, people's answers are already in numerical form so it is not necessary to convert the answer into a code. We can simply code their exact answer. Thus if someone is 39 years old we would simply give them the code 39. Often people are asked to tick a particular income or age category (e.g. 25–35; 36–45). In these cases it is best to give people a code which represents the midpoint of the category. Thus for someone in the category 36–45 we would code them as 40. Where people are asked to respond in this way it is worth putting the midpoint next to each category to make the coding easier later on.

Dealing with missing data

Each variable for each case should have a code even if a person does not answer a question. These codes are called missing data codes and are done in the same way as normal coding. The main thing to ensure when working out how to code missing data is to allocate a distinctive code for missing data. That is, make sure that the code you allocate is different from a valid code (i.e. one which represents an actual answer to the question).

Since there are different reasons why people do not answer questions, different codes are often given to different types of missing data. There are four main types of non-response to questions.

1 The respondent was not required to answer the question (e.g. a question asking about the ages of someone's children would not be appropriate to someone who had already answered that they have no children).

2 Not ascertained: maybe the interviewer missed the question, or the respondent missed it, or it was not clear what someone's answer was.

3   The respondent refused to answer.
4   The respondent did not know the answer or did not have an opinion. Sometimes this response is treated as a valid response while on other occasions the researcher will want to treat it as missing data.

It may be desirable to give a different missing data code to each of these different types of non-response. There are no set rules about what particular codes should be allocated to missing data as long as the missing data code will not be confused with a valid code. Which codes are 'available' for missing data depends on how many valid codes there are for the question. If 'available', either 0 or 9 is often used.

It is worthwhile trying to give the same missing data code to as many variables as possible to avoid confusion and make computer programming simpler. This is not always possible. For example, where both 0 and 9 could be valid codes (e.g. a question on ages of children), we would have to give another missing data code—perhaps 99 or −1.

Allocation of column numbers to each variable

To enter codes on to a computer they must be put on a record. The codes for a respondent are placed on one or more records. The records for each respondent are then put together so that the first record or set of records represents the first respondent, the next record(s) represents the second respondent, and so forth. Put together in this way the set of records is called a data file.

Each record can contain only a limited amount of information. Usually only 80 characters can be placed on each record; if all the codes for a particular case will not fit on to one record we simply start on another until we have entered all the codes for that case. We then start on the next case. Since a record will contain 80 characters, it is referred to as having 80 columns—each character takes up one column. Thus a number with one digit (i.e. any number from 0 to 9) will take up only one column. A two-digit number (10 to 99) will take up two columns; a three-digit number (100 to 999) will take up three columns, and so forth.

When putting codes from a questionnaire on to the computer we have to put the code which represents the response to a particular question in the same position on the data record for each case. For example, we might put the code for 'paid job' in column 5 for each case, 'type of work' in columns 6 to 7 and so forth (see Figures 14.3

and 14.4). To avoid confusion and to assist keypunch operators it is normal to work out in which column each variable is to be coded before the questionnaire is printed. This enables the printing of the columns in which a variable is to be coded on the questionnaire (see Figure 14.3) and means that keypunch operators can enter data on to the computer straight from the questionnaire. Normally, the right-hand margin of the questionnaire is reserved for this purpose: next to the question the columns allocated to that variable are printed and beside that are spots in which the code for that question can be entered. The keypunch operator can then just look down this margin, enter the codes into the computer and keep a constant check that they are entering the codes in the correct columns.

When allocating columns to a variable we have to anticipate the highest code of the variable. If this is a single digit allocate one column; if the maximum value is a two-digit number allocate two columns and so forth. If unsure how many columns will be needed (e.g. with an open-ended question), play safe and allocate more columns than needed—empty columns do not matter. Make sure that you anticipate your missing data codes when working out what the highest code will be. If we have allocated, say, two columns for a variable but a particular code only needs one column we must ensure that we right justify the codes. Thus if we have two columns (e.g. columns 6–7) in which to place a code of 4 we should code this as 04 not as 4 blank (i.e. 04 not 4).

If all the codes for one case will not fit on to one record, simply continue on to the next record. When allocating codes in a question-naire allocate columns to variables sequentially. Thus allocate the first column(s) to the first variable (question) in the questionnaire, the next columns to the next question and so on. If we have to go on to another record for that case simply start again at column 1 of the next record (see Figure 14.3). Normally the first few columns are allocated to an identification number, each case being given a unique number. In the example in Figure 14.3 three columns have been allocated for identification numbers thus allowing up to 999 different identity codes to be used. For a sample of more than 999 people, more columns would be allocated for identification numbers. Fol-lowing this a column is reserved to indicate which record of that case a particular record is.

Figure 14.4 illustrates part of a file deck which would be produced from the set of questions in Figure 14.3. You will notice that for each case there are two records. For each case the same information is coded in the same columns of a given record. Thus on record 1 for each case we have an identification number (001,002); age is in columns 8–9 and so forth. Thus for each case we know that the codes

Figure 14.3   Example of allocating computer columns to questions and coding

	Ident	_ _ _ 1–3
	Record	_ 4

Q.1   Do you currently have a paid job?   Yes [ ] 1   _ 5
                                          No [ ] 2

Q.2   What kind of work do you do? _____   _ _   6–7

_____

Q.3   How old are you? _____ years   _ _   8–9

.
.
.

Q.69   Generally speaking how would you describe your   _ 80
       political views?
                    Traditional   [ ] 1
                    Middle of the road   [ ] 2
                    Progressive   [ ] 3
                    Other (specify)   [ ] 4
                                    Ident   _ _ _   1–3
                                    Record   _ 4

Q.70   How do you feel about the Government's current   _ _   5–6

       immigration policy? _____

_____

Q.71   Are you: Male   [ ] 1   _ 7
                        Female [ ] 2

Q.72   Are you currently: _ 8
             Married   [ ] 1
             Never married   [ ] 2
             Divorced   [ ] 3
             Separated   [ ] 4
             Widowed   [ ] 5
             Other (specify) [ ] 6

Figure 14.4   Example of a data file for questions in Figure 14.3

Columns	1	2	3	4	5	6	7	8	9	80	
case 1	0	0	1	1	1	0	1	3	9	1	record 1 of case 1
	0	0	1	2	0	3	1	2		. . . .	record 2 of case 1
case 2	0	0	2	1	2	0	0	1	8	2	record 1 of case 2
	0	0	2	2	1	1	2	2		. . . .	record 2 of case 2

(2 cases only)

Figure 14.5 An example of a codebook (for one question only)

Q.1   Does R have paid job?
Variable name: PJOB
Record: 1
Columns: 5
Valid codes: Yes   1
No   2
Missing data: Inappropriate   0
Not ascertained   9
Special instructions: If respondent helps spouse in jobs (e.g. on farm,
bookkeeping, etc., but does not specifically get paid,
code as having paid work)

in particular columns on given records represent a person's response
to a particular question.

Producing a codebook

Having decided how to code each response to each question, it is
worth making a systematic record of all the decisions made. This
record is called a codebook and the following points are normally
included (see Figure 14.5).

1   List the question asked.
2   Most computer programs require that a variable has a short name
by which it is referred to in the program. In the codebook list the
name given to each variable.
3   List the record on which the variable is located.
4   List the columns in which the variable is located.
5   List the valid codes for each question.
6   List the missing data codes for each question.
7   List any special coding instructions which were used for coding
particular questions.

Checking for coding errors

No matter how much care is taken there will always be some errors
either in coding or in entering a set of codes on to the computer.
Many of the problems in entering codes on to the computer are now
being minimised by sophisticated data entry checking programs.
Nevertheless it is still necessary to check that coding has been
correctly done. This will be done with the aid of a computer pro-

gram and is easily achieved with SPSSX. Three main checks are made.

1 *Valid range checks:* For any variable there are only certain codes which are legitimate either as valid codes or as missing data codes. Any code outside this range indicates a wrong code and needs to be corrected. For example, if a code of 6 was found for the question in Figure 14.5 this would be a wrong code. The easiest way to check for this is to set up valid range checks at the data entry stage or to write an SPSSX FREQUENCIES program after the data have been entered.

2 *Filter checks:* If contingency questions are used, some questions should only be answered by certain people depending on how they answered a previous question. For example, we might have asked people whether they had any children. If people had children we might have asked what their ages were. Someone who said they had no children should not have answered the question about ages. If they did the coding to one of the questions is wrong. Such errors can be detected with SPSSX by using a series of IF statements or the CROSSTABS procedure.

3 *Logical checks:* Certain sets of responses will be illogical. The above is one sort but others can occur. For example, if someone's age is coded as 50 it seems illogical if the age of their eldest child is coded at 48. Detecting these sorts of illogical codes takes a lot of time and requires careful thinking about illogical combinations of codes.

It is tempting to avoid a lot of this checking of coding: it is time consuming and often finds relatively few mistakes. In my view it is still worth doing. Certainly the most important stages are in initial coding when it is best to carefully draw up a codebook and know beforehand how answers are to be coded, but it is also important to use experienced keypunch operators who use data checking procedures.

Complicating issues when coding

Often a particular question in a questionnaire contains a lot of different information and is in effect tapping a number of different variables. When this is so we must conceptualise each of the variables contained in the question and allocate codes and computer columns to each variable. Figure 14.6 provides a question in which respondents are asked to record information about their brothers and sisters.

Figure 14.6 A multivariable question

In the table below please put the age and sex of each of your brothers and sisters in the order in which they come in your family.
Put yourself in the table too and indicate which person you are by an asterisk (*).

Position	1st	2nd	3rd	4th	5th	6th	7th	8th	9th
Sex									
Age									

Figure 14.7 Another type of multivariable question

Within the last year have you helped your mother in any of the following ways? (tick all that are appropriate)

Loaned or given money (over $200)	[ ]
Helped during illness	[ ]
Provided comfort in difficult times	[ ]
Given valuable gifts (over $200)	[ ]
Given a hand when needed	[ ]

In this question there are a large number of possible variables: the number of sibs someone has, the number of brothers, the number of sisters, the respondent's position in the family, the age gaps between sibs, the respondent's age and sex, the age and sex of each sib, position of the respondent among the same sex and so on. Depending on which of these variables are of interest, codes and columns will need to be allocated accordingly.

There are other questions which are in fact multivariable questions. For example, where someone is allowed to tick more than one response to a question, each possible response becomes a variable to which people are effectively answering yes (by ticking) or no (by not ticking). In the question in Figure 14.7 each possible response would be a separate variable and would have to be allocated a separate column (see earlier discussion of multiple dichotomies).

Another complexity when coding is the opposite to the above: instead of extracting several variables from the one question several questions can be used to establish the code on one variable. Scaling is one example of this but there are others. For instance, when trying to code someone's social status we will not rely on just one characteristic of a person but a particular mix. If we were using only occupation to establish social status how would we code this for a married woman since in our society a married woman tends to take on the status of her husband. It would be misleading to code the status of a woman who did some part-time clerical work but was married to a doctor as having clerical status. We could give married women their husband's occupational status score. But is this accurate? What if a woman had a higher status job than her husband—how would we code this? The aim here is not to resolve these problems but to point out that often a code involves a mix of information contained in various questions. Often we can just code each question individually and use the computer to create a new variable out of all the pieces of information. But where judgment is involved it is often not possible or very difficult to do this complex coding by computer and it is best to do it before entering data on to the computer.

Summary

In this chapter a number of practical issues involved in coding questionnaires and in preparing data for computer analysis have been considered. Many decisions have to be made before data are collected and before the questionnaire is printed. Planning ahead, clarifying the variables, precoding where possible and allocating computer columns before printing the questionnaire save a lot of work and eliminate many opportunities for clerical errors later on.

Further reading

There are very few comprehensive treatments of coding. Each of the following provide useful chapters which are very readable. Perhaps the best are Warwick and Lininger *The Sample Survey* (1975), Chapter 9 and Moser and Kalton's *Survey Methods in Social Investigation* (1971), Chapter 16. Babbie's discussion in Chapter 13 of *The Practice of Social Research* (1983) is very down to earth and Hoinville and Jowell's *Survey Research Practice* (1977), Chapter 8 covers similar material. Bateson's *Data Construction in Social Surveys* (1984) approaches the issue of coding from a more theoretical perspective and highlights the theoretical rather than technical issues involved in the coding phase.

15 Building scales

The basic principle of scaling is part of everyday life. When we meet people for the first time we try to build up a picture of them: we develop impressions of their friendliness, intelligence, trustworthiness and so forth. These impressions rarely rely on one piece of information but are a composite picture based on a number of clues.

In survey research a scale is simply a more formalised and systematic version of this everyday activity. It is a composite measure of a concept, a measure composed of information derived from several questions or indicators. To create a scale we simply convert the information contained in several relatively specific variables into one new and more abstract variable. Thus, instead of measuring conservatism simply by asking what political party someone votes for, we would ask about a range of issues which we think tap conservatism. These questions are then combined into a single index of conservatism.

Why bother building scales?

There are several reasons why it is desirable to measure a concept by using multiple indicators rather than one. First it helps get at the complexity of the concept. Unless we have defined a concept very narrowly we need multiple indicators to tap the complexity of most concepts. To measure religiousness we could ask how often someone attends church, but if we see religiousness as more complex than this we would also ask about beliefs or ritual observance, and work out how important religion is in a person's life. Taken together these questions provide a better measure of religiousness than a rather barren and partial single measure.

Second, it assists in developing more valid measures. Often one observation on its own can be misleading and we need to see it in the context of other observations to avoid misinterpretation. For example, if we only look at how someone votes we might treat those who vote for the more conservative political parties as conservative and those voting for progressive parties as less conservative. But many of those who vote for progressive parties will be politically conservative in many respects so we need to interpret a person's vote within the context of other political attitudes. Multiple-item scales can then help us avoid some of the distortions and misclassification which can arise by using only single-item measures of complex concepts.

Third, it helps increase reliability. The way in which a question is worded can affect substantially the way people answer it. If we rely on only one question people's answers could be largely a function of the wording of the question. Using a number of questions should minimise the effect of one which is badly worded.

Fourth, it enables more precision. A single question does not allow us to differentiate between people with much precision. For example, to use suburb of residence as a measure of people's status would lead to a very crude classification. We would classify residents from wealthier suburbs as higher status than those residents from poorer suburbs but we are treating a lot of people whose status varies (e.g. those in wealthier suburbs) as though they were the same status. Additional questions about, say, occupation, education and income would help differentiate between the status levels of those whom we had treated as of equal status. Thus we get a better ranking of people according to their status and can distinguish between small status variations. With a single indicator this precision is not possible.

Fifth, by summarising the information conveyed by a number of questions into one variable the analysis is simplified considerably. Instead of analysing each question separately we can do a whole lot in one attempt.

Summated scaling: the logic

A scale consists of answers to a number of questions. For each question people receive a score depending on their answer. The score is allocated to particular answers depending on how favourable the answer is to the attitude being measured. The scores for each question are then added together to provide each person with an overall score for that set of questions (scale score). This scale score is taken to indicate a person's 'position' on the abstract dimension which the individual questions are intended to tap.

The following questions designed to measure traditionalism will illustrate this process.

		Strongly agree	Agree	Undecided	Disagree	Strongly disagree
a	If you start trying to change things very much you usually make them worse.	[ ] 4	[ ] 3	[ ] 2	[ ] 1	[ ] 0
b	If something grows up over a long time period, there will always be much wisdom in it.	[ ]	[ ]	[ ]	[ ]	[ ]
c	It is better to stick by what you have, than to try new things you do not really know about.	[ ]	[ ]	[ ]	[ ]	[ ]
d	We must respect the work of our forebears and not think that we know better than they did.	[ ]	[ ]	[ ]	[ ]	[ ]
e	A person does not really have much wisdom until he is well along in years.	[ ]	[ ]	[ ]	[ ]	[ ]

Depending on how an individual answers the set of questions the scale score for that person will vary (see Figure 15.1). Since strong agreement with traditionalist statements receives high scores then high scale scores indicate high traditionalism.

Figure 15.1 An illustration of scale scores

Person			Item			Scale score	Interpretation
	a	b	c	d	e		
1	4 +	4 +	4 +	4 +	4 =	20	Very highly traditionalist
2	4	2	1	0	3 =	10	Moderate
3	2	1	2	1	1 =	7	Moderate
4	0	0	0	0	0 =	0	Very non-traditionalist

Although the previous question format is common, it is not the only style appropriate for summated scaling. The following are also used

1 A different number of response categories. Sometimes only two (agree/disagree) are used; sometimes seven or ten are used.
2 Rather than asking people to agree or disagree with a statement, respondents are asked to put a mark on a continuum. For example, we might want to assess someone's relationship with

their mother. We could ask them to describe the relationship on each of the following continua:

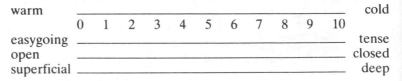

warm _____ cold
0 1 2 3 4 5 6 7 8 9 10
easygoing _____ tense
open _____ closed
superficial _____ deep

These types of questions are scaleable in the same way as described later.

3   Even if the 'statement format' is used, it need not be limited to asking about agreement or disagreement. Instead you could ask how important certain things are or how true something is of them.

Summated scales simply require that we measure the strength of some opinion on some matter by assessing 'position' on a number of questions. There are many means by which we get at strength of opinion on particular items and these have been discussed in some detail in Chapter 6.

Likert scales

The problem common to all scaling techniques is how do we know which questions to include in the scale? We cannot simply add together the scores from any set of questions: we must be confident that they all tap the same underlying concept. To work out which items legitimately belong to the scale there are two main stages.

Construct a rough scale

At this stage there are four steps:

1   *Develop a set of questions* which on the face of it seem to measure the relevant concept. These questions usually consist of a mixture of favourable and unfavourable statements to which people are asked to express their extent of agreement and disagreement. The statements are selected to reflect orientation to the attitude of interest.

   Since one aim of scaling is to be able to distinguish between people who fall at different points along an attitude continuum (e.g. radicalism/conservatism), there is no point in developing extreme items with which everyone will agree (or everyone disagree). For example, if we wanted to assess people's attitude to mothers working, the following item would not be very good:

It would be better to develop a less extreme question such as:

> There are no circumstances in which mothers should leave their children to get a paid job.

It would be better to develop a less extreme question such as:

> It's normally better for mothers of young children to stay at home rather than go out to work.

The process of constructing the rough, initial scale is illustrated below with a set of items designed to measure the extent to which people are oriented towards the future as opposed to being preoccupied with the present.

	Strongly agree	Agree	Undecided	Disagree	Strongly disagree
Eat drink and be merry for tomorrow we may die.	− 0	1	2	3	4
I am a fairly ambitious person.	+ 4	3	2	1	0
If people thought ahead more we would not be facing many of today's problems.	+ 4	3	2	1	0
I try not to think about the future very much.	0	1	2	3	4
Conserving our resources for the future is one of the most important issues facing the world today.	+ 4	3	2	1	0
I try to save money for a rainy day rather than spend it as soon as I get it.	+ 4	3	2	1	0
I prefer to enjoy the present rather than plan ahead.	− 0	1	2	3	4
The trouble with many people is that they are not prepared to wait for things.	+4	3	2	1	0
It is all very well to develop plans for the future but the first priority should be to deal with current problems.	− 0	1	2	3	4
I mainly take life as it comes rather than always planning ahead.	−0	1	2	3	4

	Strongly agree	Agree	Undecided	Disagree	Strongly disagree
Zero population growth is an important goal given the likely overpopulation in the future.	+ 4	3	2	1	0
There is so much to worry about in the present that I do not give the future that much thought.	− 0	1	2	3	4
It is important to make plans for the future and not just accept what comes.	+ 4	3	2	1	0

2 *These questions are then answered* by a group of people similar to those to whom we finally want to give the questions.
3 *Score each person's response* to each question. It is important to score consistently so that a 'favourable' response to the attitude always gets a high score. Thus for 'positive' statements (i.e. future oriented) *strongly agree* will get a high score (see questions marked +) while for 'negative' statements (i.e. present oriented) *strongly disagree* will get a high score.
4 *Add up each person's score* on each item to obtain their scale score. In this case the highest score could be 52 (four on each of thirteen items) and indicates high future orientation. The minimum score of zero equals a very low future orientation.

Selecting scale items in secondary analysis

When doing secondary data analysis we will often want to construct scales for which the initial investigators did not specifically design questions. Nevertheless there may well be questions in the data set that enable us to produce satisfactory scales. When doing this, two complementary approaches — one conceptual and one empirical — are helpful. First, we can get an idea of which items might go together by looking at their content. For example, we might be interested in developing a scale of conservatism. By examining the questions in a survey we will identify a number which, on the face of it, would probably tap this concept as we understand it. The second step to assist with this initial selection of scale items is to obtain a correlation matrix (page 189) of the items that might conceivably belong together. This will provide correlations of each item with each other item. Items that belong together in a scale will normally have at least modest correlations with each other item in the scale. When selecting items from a matrix it is important not to rely only on the correlations. The items must also belong together conceptually. A correlation between gender and measures of self-esteem does not mean that gender should be part of our measure of self-esteem. By examining which items seem to be correlated and which conceptually belong together we will obtain an initial set of items from which to construct an initial scale using the techniques described above. We will then need to refine the scale and select only the best of these initial items.

Selecting the best items

We need to look at each item to see if it really belongs to the scale. This is known as item analysis and there are two aspects to consider—unidimensionality and reliability.

1 *Test for unidimensionality:* A unidimensional scale is one in which each item measures the same underlying concept. We need to eliminate items which do not measure this concept. To do this, check to see if the responses to a particular item reflect the pattern of responses on other items. If it does not we can assume it is because the item is measuring something different from the other items and thus drop it from the scale. For example, if people who tend to be future oriented on most questions do not seem to be future oriented on a particular question we would drop that question. The way to work out whether the responses on a particular item reflect the responses on other items is to calculate a correlation co-efficient between people's score on the item with their score on the rest of the scale. Correlation co-efficients range between 0 to 1. This co-efficient is called the item-to-scale co-efficient. The higher it is the more clearly the item belongs to the scale. As a rule of thumb, if it is less than 0.3 then the item is dropped from the scale. Testing all the initial items in this way and dropping the inappropriate ones should result in a unidimensional scale. A further test for unidimensionality can be done with factor analysis where a unidimensional scale should result in a factor solution with only one factor (see discussion below).

2 *Test for reliability:* A reliable scale is one on which individuals would obtain much the same scale score on two different occasions. An unreliable scale is the result of unreliable items, so we need to test each item for its reliability. Since it is often not

Table 15. 1   An illustration of scale testing co-efficients

Item	Item-total correlations	Alpha if item deleted
1	0.27*	0.72
2	0.48	0.62 .
3	0.61	0.60
4	0.40	0.65
5	0.21*	0.68
6	0.52	0.58
7	0.34	0.77*
8	0.60	0.64
9	0.49	0.68
10	0.33	0.60
11	0.23*	0.72
12	0.49	0.66
13	0.57	0.59

Alpha for scale = 0.65

possible to get people to answer the same questions on two occasions to assess reliability, an alternative approach is to look at the consistency of a person's response on an item compared to each other scale item (item–item correlations). This provides a measure of the overall reliability of the scale. The index of this is given by a statistic called 'alpha'. This ranges between 0 and 1. The higher the figure the more reliable the scale and as a rule of thumb alpha should be at least 0.7 before we say the scale is reliable. The size of alpha is affected by the reliability of individual items. To increase the alpha, and thus the scale's reliability, drop all unreliable items. To do this we would need to calculate what the alpha would be if a particular item was dropped.

The figures in Table 15.1 illustrate how items are selected for a final scale. These figures would be generated by SPSSX procedures. Looking at the item-total correlations, items 1,5 and 11 do not form part of a unidimensional scale. These should be deleted. With all the items included the scale is not sufficiently reliable (alpha=0.65). If item 7 is deleted the scale alpha would rise to 0.77. This means that item 7 is unreliable and therefore would be dropped.

Having decided which items are worth including in the final scale we would recalculate people's scale score and recheck the scale using the statistics outlined above. Assuming these are satisfactory we can now use these items in the main data collection phase of the study.

Using the method discussed we began with a concept and developed questions to tap that concept. An alternative approach is to ask a wide range of questions and see if there is a pattern to the way people answer sets of questions. Then look at what sets of items people answer in a consistent way. By looking at which items 'go together' we can try to see what more general concept they might reflect. The statistical technique used in this more inductive approach to scaling is called factor analysis (see Kim and Mueller, 1978a, 1978b).

Factor analysis

Factor analysis is an appropriate method for scale development when you have a set of interval-level, non-dichotomous variables. It is a mathematically complex method of reducing a large set of variables to a smaller set of underlying variables referred to as factors. Fortunately computer packages can handle the complex computations, so this section focuses on the logic and steps of factor analysis.

The basic aim of factor analysis is to examine whether, on the basis of people's answers to questions, a smaller number of more general factors that underlie answers to individual questions can be identified. For example, we might ask people about what attributes they consider to be important in children (e.g. good manners, obedience, neatness, imagination, independence and self-control). By observing the pattern of answers, we might see that some people emphasised good manners, obedience and neatness and placed little weight on imagination, independence and self-control and vice versa. In other words, some variables tended to cluster together.

Factor analysis helps us identify this sort of patterning in the overall set of responses to these questions. For example, despite having answers about six attributes in children, these answers might reflect or be caused by two more general, underlying attitude dimensions or factors. We might say that the first set of variables represents an attitude dimension about *conformity*, while the second set reflects the dimension of *autonomy*. Answers to the six individual questions are caused by these two underlying factors. If our aim is to reduce data, it is desirable to be able to identify which variables belong together and to have a method of combining these variables into scales.

Table 15.2   Variables used in the factor analysis example

Variable name	Extent to which each characteristic is considered important for a job
PAY	Income from job
INIT	Opportunities to use initiative
RESPONS	Having responsibility
ACHIEVE	The feeling of achieving something
PRESSURE	Not too much pressure
HOLIDAY	Generous holidays
HOURS	Good hours
SEXBOSS	Having a boss of the same sex

There are four main steps in forming scales using factor analysis. At each of these stages there are a variety of ways of doing the factor analysis, but only one main method will be discussed here. The four steps are:

1   Select the variables to be factor analysed.
2   Extract an initial set of factors.
3   Extract a final set of factors by 'rotation'.
4   Construct scales for use in further analysis.

To illustrate these steps I will use eight variables that relate to the job characteristics that people value (see Table 15.2).

Selecting variables for analysis

A problem with factor analysis is that, regardless of the variables used, a set of 'underlying' factors will be produced—whether they make sense or not. Indeed, factor analysis is particularly prone to the GIGO (Garbage in, garbage out) problem. Since the 'solution' (i.e. extraction of factors) is based on correlations between variables, we can produce factors that have nothing in common conceptually. We might find that the variables education, age and income are empirically correlated and they might therefore be identified as a factor in factor analysis. But this does not mean that they are really measuring the same underlying dimension. The variables might be *causally related* rather than *reflecting* some underlying factor.

When selecting variables to be factor analysed, it is important to be able to assume that correlations between the variables will *not* be causal. Instead, correlations between the variables are assumed

Table 15.3   Correlation matrix of variables in the factor analysis

	Pay	Init	Respons	Achieve	Pressure	Holiday	Hours	Sexboss
PAY	1.00							
INIT	.17	1.00						
RESPONS	.2	.40	1.00					
ACHIEVE	.16	.40	.33	1.00				
PRESSURE	.18	.08	.12	.07	1.00			
HOLIDAY	.31	.14	.21	.07	.32	1.00		
HOURS	.38	.14	.17	.10	.32	.39	1.00	
SEXBOSS	.12	.06	.07	.00	.04	.14	.06	1.00

KMO = .75

to be produced by some third, common factor (see Figure 15.2). In practical terms, this means that when selecting variables to be analysed we should avoid including variables that are likely to be causes of others in the analysis.

We should also ensure that the variables to be analysed have at least reasonable correlations with some other variables in the analysis. At the variable selection stage it is helpful to obtain a correlation matrix, inspect it and exclude those variables that do not correlate with any others in the analysis.

As Table 15.3 shows, some variables correlate well with some others, but not with all variables. For example, INIT is correlated with RESPONS and ACHIEVE but not with PAY, HOURS, HOLIDAYS, PRESSURE or SEXBOSS. A close examination of the pattern of correlations shows that certain clusters of variables correlate with each other but not with other clusters of variables. It is this clustering that factor analysis detects.

There are a number of ways of assessing whether a set of variables in a correlation matrix is suitable for factor analysis (see Norusis, 1985:128–9). Among these is a statistic called KMO which ranges from 0 to 1. If this statistic yields high values above 0.7, then the correlations, on the whole, are sufficiently high to make factor analysis suitable. More care should be taken if they lie between 0.5 and 0.69, and KMO values below 0.5 mean that factor analysis would be inappropriate for that set of variables. Dropping some variables that do not correlate well with any others (e.g. SEXBOSS) should help. Measures similar to the KMO value can also be obtained for each variable to give some indication of which variables might be dropped from further analysis (see Norusis, 1985: 129–30).

**Figure 15.2   Graphic representation of the causal assumptions
underlying a two-factor factor analysis**

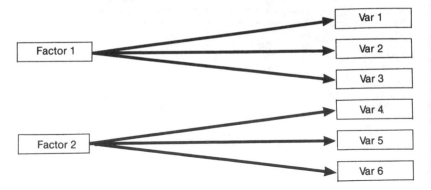

Note: To be complete, this model should have arrows to the right hand side over the variable boxes to represent the variation in each variable that is not due to the influence of the factors.

Extracting an initial set of factors

The main aim of exploratory factor analysis is to see whether a smaller number of common factors can account for the pattern of correlations in a larger number of variables. Do the individual variables covary because they have underlying factors in common? To extract factors, two decisions are necessary. The first is to decide on which of a number of methods of extracting the factors is to be used. Kim and Mueller (1978a and b) discuss these alternatives.

The second decision is to work out *how many* factors to extract. Since the aim of factor analysis is to represent a set of variables as simply as possible, the best factor analysis will have as few factors as necessary. A factor analysis can extract as many factors as there are variables, but a lot of these factors will be meaningless and are of no value. We should retain only the best factors. But what *are* the best factors?

One common way of determining which factors to keep is to use a statistic called the *eigenvalue*. In factor analysis we are testing a causal model in which unknown factors are the independent variables and the individual variables are dependent (see Figure 15.2 for a representation of this). Since we do not know, initially, how many

Table 15.4 Communalities, eigenvalues and per cent of explained variance in the unrotated solution

Variable	Communality	Factor	Eigenvalue	% of variance	Cum pct
PAY	.43	1	2.39	29.9	29.9
INIT	.62	2	1.38	17.3	47.2
RESPONS	.54	3	.99	12.6	59.6
ACHIEVE	.59	4	.80	10.0	69.6
PRESSURE	.40	5	.68	8.5	78.1
HOLIDAY	.55	6	.61	7.6	85.7
HOURS	.57	7	.58	7.3	93.0
SEXBOSS	.07	8	.56	7.0	100.0

Note: The initial extraction has two parts: initial and final. In the final stage, the figures for the selected factors (e.g. those with an eigenvalue above 1.0) are listed. I have listed all the figures here for the sake of completeness.

factors 'exist', then any number of models could be used. (Factor analysis will initially create as many factors as there are variables.) The problem is to work out which one is best. The best model will be the simplest (i.e. with the fewest factors) and explain the most variance in the original set of variables. If we are to work out which factors to keep, we should keep those that explain most variance in the set of individual variables.

The *eigenvalue* is a measure that attaches to factors and indicates the amount of variance in the pool of original variables that the factor explains. The higher this value, the more variance it explains. To be retained, factors must have an eigenvalue greater than 1. In the initial phase of extracting factors, a number of tables are produced. One of these provides various figures, including eigenvalues for each factor (see Table 15.4).

In this example, only two factors have an eigenvalue greater than 1. This means that we will use only two factors to summarise the eight variables. Once the number of factors has been determined, a *factor matrix* is produced for the factors that qualify for further analysis (Table 15.5). In this matrix, each column represents a factor and the figures in the column represent the correlation (*factor loading*) between that factor and the particular variable (in the row).

The eigenvalue of a factor is the amount of variance in all the variables that is explained by that factor. This figure is obtained by squaring the correlations in the factor matrix (to obtain proportion of explained variance for each variable) and then adding each of these squared figures in the column. Thus for factor 1 the total variance explained by factor 1 is $(.63)^2 + (.56)^2 + (.60)^2 + (.48)^2 +$

Table 15.5   Unrotated factor matrix for variables and factors in Table 15.4

	Factor 1	Factor 2
PAY	.63	−.20
INIT	.56	.56
RESPONS	.60	.43
ACHIEVE	.48	.60
PRESSURE	.49	−.40
HOLIDAY	.63	−.40
HOURS	.64	−.39
SEXBOSS	.22	−.15

$(.49)^2 + (.63)^2 + (.64)^2 + (.22)^2 = 2.39$. This is the same figure as the eigenvalue for factor 1 in Table 15.4. The factor that explains most variance will be factor 1, with factor 2 explaining the second most variance and so on.

One measure of a good factor analysis is the amount of the total variance in the original variables that is explained by the factors. The greater the explained variance, the better the solution. But to increase the total variance explained we have to increase the number of factors. This is one reason why the rule of only using factors with an eigenvalue of 1 or higher is used.

Sometimes we may have a large number of factors with eigenvalues greater than 1, but for the sake of simplicity we do not wish to retain all the factors. How do we decide which of the factors with eigenvalues greater than 1 to retain? One way is to look at the *total amount of variance explained* in the whole set of variables by various numbers of factors. This information is provided in the Cum pct column in Table 15.4. As the number of factors increases, the total amount of variance explained increases. But it increases by smaller amounts with each additional factor. You have to make a decision when the additional factors do not lead to sufficient increases in the explained variance and only use the factors up to this point. Other methods for deciding how many factors to keep are discussed in Kim and Mueller (1978: 41–5).

Clearly we can maximise the amount of variance explained overall by increasing the number of factors used. But since this is often undesirable, we can try to maximise explained variance by eliminating the odd variable whose variance the main factors do not account for. We can detect which variables are problems in this respect by calculating a statistic for each variable called its *communality*.

In our example, two main factors have been extracted. The communality figure for each variable is obtained by using the correlation between each of these two factors and the variable and calculating the proportion of variance in that variable that is explained by the combination of the two extracted factors. This is obtained by squaring each of the co-efficients for a particular variable in the factor matrix (Table 15.5) and adding them together. The answer is called the *communality* of the variable. Communalities range from 0 to 1. The higher the figure the better the set of selected factors explain the variance for that variable. The communality for PAY is calculated by $(.63)^2 + (-.20)^2 = 0.43$.

If the communality figure is low, it means that the variance for that variable is not explained by the selected factors. Normally it is best to drop variables with low communalities and thus increase the total variance explained by the two factors. In this example, dropping SEXBOSS with a low communality of .07 increases the total variance explained by the factors from 47 per cent to 54 per cent. The rest of this analysis is based on the exclusion of the SEXBOSS variable.

In summary, the initial extraction stage enables us to work out how many factors we will need for our final solution. The number of factors selected will be affected by the eigenvalues and the amount of total variance accounted for. There is a tradeoff between the desirable goals of maximising total explained variance and minimising the number of factors needed. One way of both maximising explained variance and minimising the number of factors required is to drop variables with very low communality figures.

Extracting the final factors—rotation

Once we know how many factors to use, we need to clarify which variables most 'belong' to each factor. Except when we have a single-factor solution (i.e. only one factor emerges) we expect that some variables will 'belong' to one factor and others will 'belong' to another.

The initial extraction of factors does not make it clear which variables belong most clearly to which factors. Often, as in the unrotated example in Table 15.4, many variables will 'load' on several factors and some factors will have almost every variable loading on them. To clarify which variables belong to which factors, and to make the factors more interpretable, we proceed to a third stage called factor rotation. Ideally rotation will result in factors on which only some variables load and in variables that load on only one factor.

There are a number of methods of 'rotating' variables, but these

Table 15.6   Rotated factor matrix

Variable	Factor 1	Factor 2
HOURS	.76	.09
HOLIDAY	.74	.08
PRESSURE	.65	−.01
PAY	.61	.22
INIT	.09	.78
ACHIEVE	.01	.76
RESPONSE	.20	.71

will not be discussed here. (See Kim and Mueller 1978b for a discussion of the concept of rotation and the differences between the various methods.) One of the most widely used methods of rotation is *varimax* rotation. The following example is based on this.

Table 15.6 provides a rotated factor matrix. This is the matrix that is crucial to interpreting the results of the factor analysis.

High loading variables 'belong' to the factor on which they load. The pattern of high and lower co-efficients in the rotated matrix makes it much clearer which variables belong to which factor. Although there is no absolute rule as to how high a co-efficient should be before it is said to load on a factor, it would be unusual to use co-efficients below 0.3.

Before interpreting the pattern of co-efficients in Table 15.6 it is worth mentioning a few problems you might come across at this point:

1 *Variable loads on more than one factor:* If a variable loads relatively highly on two or more factors, there are several options. A different method of rotation might resolve the problem. Alternatively, you might leave things as they are but when creating factor-based scales from the analysis (see below), only include the variable in the factor for which it loads most highly. Another approach is to include the variable in the construction of all scales on which it loads but to take particular care if you are correlating factors with one another in subsequent analysis. The inclusion of the same variables in two scales will inflate the correlation between the two scales. Finally, you might decide that the variable that loads on several factors contaminates the analysis too much and drop it from the factor analysis.

2 *Variable loads only weakly on all factors:* If this is the case, then the communality of the variable will be low and the variable should be dropped from the analysis.

3 *Negative loadings:* The sign on a factor loading does not mean anything about the strength of the relationship between the variable and the factor. A negative sign only has meaning relative to the signs on the other variables: different signs simply mean that the variables are related to the factor in opposite directions. For this reason you should consider coding the variables in the same direction before the analysis.

At this stage the main statistical work of a factor analysis has been done and the researcher needs to interpret the results. Having located factors that go together empirically, you need to try to infer some conceptual commonality from the empirical commonality of the variables that load on that factor.

In our example, the factors make some sense. The variables that load on the first factor seem to have something in common. They relate to *conditions* of work—pay, generous holidays, no pressure and good hours. By contrast, the variables that load on factor 2—sense of achievement, responsibility and initiative—emphasise the *content* rather than the conditions of the job. The first factor might be called *extrinsic* work orientation and the second might be called *intrinsic* work orientation.

Reducing the initial eight variables to two meaningful factors has two benefits. It may alert us to groupings of variables that we would not otherwise have thought of and thus enables us to work at a more sophisticated conceptual level. It also greatly simplifies subsequent analysis. For example, we might be interested in gender differences in job orientation. Rather than examining gender differences in each of the eight job variables we can look at gender differences on the two factors. As a result of the factor analysis, we might rephrase our original question and ask questions such as whether men look for intrinsic rewards in jobs while women look for extrinsic rewards.

To use the identified factors in subsequent analysis, we can construct scales based on the information provided by the factor analysis.

Factor scores and scales

There are at least three different ways of forming scales using the information gained from a factor analysis. We can create:

1 unweighted factor-based scales;
2 weighted factor-based scales; and
3 factor scales.

Table 15.7   Weighted factor-based scores for one person

Variable	Weight	Individual's original score	Weighted score (weight × raw score)
HOURS	.76	3	2.28
HOLIDAY	.74	4	2.96
PRESSURE	.65	5	3.25
PAY	.61	3	1.83
INIT	.09	2	.18
ACHIEVE	.01	2	.02
RESPONSE	.20	1	.20
Scale score		20	10.72

Unweighted factor-based scales are the easiest and are very similar to the summated scales discussed earlier in this chapter. They are based on only some of the information gained from the factor analysis and can be illustrated in relation to the extrinsic work orientation factor. To construct a scale in this way, we simply identify the variables that will form the scale by selecting variables with a reasonable loading on that scale (e.g. variables with loadings above 0.3) and then add up people's raw scores on each of the selected variables to obtain their scale score. For the extrinsic work orientation score we could construct an additive scale from the variables HOURS, HOLIDAY, PRESSURE and PAY. If desired, we could then transform the scale to have upper and lower limits as discussed elsewhere in this chapter.

Alternatively we can construct a *weighted factor-based scale* using some or all of the variables and taking their factor loadings into account. Using this approach we can include all the variables or only the variables above a certain value. Instead of simply adding up people's scores on each of these variables, we *weight* their score by the factor loading. We do this by multiplying their score by the loading. Table 15.7 provides an example of this for one person. You should note that including the variables that load weakly on the scale does not make much difference one way or another. Because the weights on these variables are so low, they contribute very little to the final scale. If only the heavily loading factors are used, the scale score drops only from 10.72 to 10.32.

The third type of scale is the most complex and is called a *factor scale*. The two types described above are *factor-based* scales (i.e. they use information supplied by the factor analysis). Factor scales are normally created by computer programs as part of the factor analysis routines.

Table 15.8 **Producing an individual's score on a factor scale**

Variable	Factor score for variable	Individual's standardised score	Weighted score (factor score × std score)
HOURS	.40	.22	.09
HOLIDAY	.39	.74	.29
PRESSURE	.36	1.11	.40
PAY	.30	.17	.05
INIT	−.07	−.25	.02
ACHIEVE	−.11	−.30	.03
RESPONSE	.003	−.61	.002
Factor scale score			.882

Note: The standard scores and factor scores are automatically calculated by programs such as SPSSX, as are the final factor scales and individual factor scale values. In this example the standard scores are the standard scores for the raw values in Table 15.7.

This approach uses respondent's standardised scores on each variable rather than their raw scores (see pages 148–9). Instead of multiplying these standardised individual scores by factor loadings (as in the approach-weighted factor-based scales), *factor scores* are used. These are computed by factor analysis programs and supplied in the output. Programs then create a new variable to represent the factor. The values of this new variable are calculated by the factor-analysis program by multiplying a person's standardised score for each variable with the factor score for the same variable. The resulting figures for each variable are then added up to form that person's score on the new factor scale variable. The factor scale that is produced in this way will have a mean of 0. Fortunately, all this is done by the computer. An example of the creation of scores on a factor scale is provided in Table 15.8.

Complicating issues

There are three important problems which can complicate the construction and use of scales.

Interpreting scale scores

Since a scale score is a summary of a person's responses to a number of questions, there is some loss of detail. This leads to a number of difficulties. First, we do not know how a person has responded to any particular question. Second, even though two people have the same scale scores it does not mean that they have answered particular questions identically. The same scale scores can be achieved with quite different sets of answers. Although two people might be similar in their overall attitude they might differ markedly on particular questions. There are scaling techniques which do not have this problem: Guttman scaling enables us to work out from someone's scale score how they have answered particular questions and we can be quite confident that two people with the same scale score answered the questions in the same way (see McIver and Carmines, 1981).

Third, scale scores must be interpreted in relative rather than absolute terms. This is so in two senses. Someone with a score of 30 on a conservatism scale with a range of 0 to 40 cannot be described as 75 per cent conservative or as twice as conservative as someone with a score of 15. Since scale scores do not have a precise interpretation, all we can say is that the higher someone's scale score is, the more conservative they are likely to be.

There is another sense in which scale scores are relative. We often want to know whether someone's score is 'high' or 'low'. This can be best worked out relative to the distribution of scale scores for other people in the sample. For example, on a scale with a 0 to 40 range, how do we interpret a score of 30? If nearly everyone else got between 30 to 40 then a score of 30 is relatively low. If nearly everyone got below 30 then 30 is a relatively high score. Often researchers say that the scores of the third of the sample with the highest scores will be called high and the scores of the third with the lowest scores will be called low. The scores of the middle third will be called moderate (see Figure 15.3). This technique is discussed in more detail in Chapter 16.

Equivalence of items

As outlined so far, each item in a scale contributes equally to the final scale score. In the examples used each item has had a score range of zero to four. Sometimes researchers feel an item is more important than others and want strong agreement with it to contribute more than four points to the final scale. To do this the item can be weighted. To make an item twice as important as other items, we might score strong agreement as eight, agreement as six and so forth. Apart from difficulties in working out how much extra weighting a particular item should have, researchers normally find little merit in this procedure and treat all items in a Likert scale as being equally important and develop what are called equal weight scales.

Figure 15.3 **Relative classification of scale scores as low, moderate and high in three samples**

	Individual scale scores								
Sample 1:	5	9	12	15	20	23	29	32	38
		low			moderate			high	
Sample 2:	5	9	10	11	13	15	17	18	20
		low			moderate			high	
Sample 3:	27	29	32	34	35	36	37	39	40
		low			moderate			high	

Two main problems emerge when developing equal weight scales. These are caused by variables that have very different distributions and by variables that have a different number of response categories.

Combining items that have quite different *distributions* into a scale will mean that different items will be, in effect, weighted differently in the final scale score. The problem here revolves around the meaning of particular scores or answers on the various items used to build the scale.

Suppose we want to develop an index of life satisfaction based on five items, each of which is designed to measure people's feelings of satisfaction with various aspects of their life — with their job, marriage, education, standard of living and social life. For each question people are required to indicate, on a range of 0 to 10, how satisfied they are with that particular aspect of their life. The higher the score, the more satisfied people are with that part of their life. For the sake of the example, imagine that on the marriage satisfaction question most people indicated that they were satisfied with their marriage, with everyone indicating a satisfaction level somewhere between 4 and 10 with the average being 7.5 and the standard deviation being 1.5. In contrast, imagine that on the standard of living question most people indicated that they were dissatisfied, with everyone giving a score of 6 or less with the average being 2.5 and a standard deviation of 1.5 (Figure 15.4).

The question is whether a score of 5 on the marriage question is to be regarded as equivalent to a score of 5 on the standard of living question. Should it carry the same weight? Does it reflect an equivalent amount of satisfaction if we are constructing a general measure

Figure 15.4   Different distributions for two variables

of satisfaction? Although they are the same number, they have quite a different meaning when viewed in the context of the rest of the people who answered the question. In the case of marriage it indicates relative dissatisfaction, while it reflects relative satisfaction in relation to the standard of living. The point is that scores that people obtain have no *absolute* meaning but are *relative* to the distribution in which they occur.

One way of ensuring that the weight a score is given reflects the information provided by the distribution of the variable is to re-express the raw score that someone has by looking at it in the context of how other people answered the question. This is done by *standardising* the scores on the variable. The notion of standardisation was discussed earlier in Chapter 11. The general procedure for standardising scores is to subtract the average score from the individual's raw score and divide the result by a measure of spread of the distribution. In this way the person's score is re-expressed, taking into account where it lies relative to the rest of the distribution. This can be done with *ordinal* or *interval variables*. With ordinal variables the median will be subtracted from the raw score and the result will be divided by the decile range or other appropriate measure of dispersion. In the case of interval variables the mean will be subtracted from a person's raw score and the result will be divided by the mean. The person's raw score would be re-expressed in terms of the number of standard deviation units that it lay from the mean.

Thus a person who scored 5 on the marriage question where the mean was 7.5 and the standard deviation was 1.5 would have their score re-expressed as -1.67. The same score of 5 on the standard of living question which has a mean of 2.5 and a standard deviation of 1.5 would be re-expressed as $+1.67$.

This would be accomplished using the following transformation for each item on the scale:

$$\text{Newitem} = (\text{olditem} - \bar{x})/s$$

where,
$\bar{x}$ = the mean of the untransformed item
s = the standard deviation of the untransformed item
$/$ = divide by

The second problem with constructing equally weighted scales arises when we wish to combine items with different numbers of response categories. Unless adjustments are made, the different length of scales will mean that some items are automatically more important. For example, one item may have two categories (agree/disagree) with codes 0 and 1, another with five categories (strongly agree to strongly disagree) with codes 0, 1, 2, 3 and 4 while another might have ten categories with finer gradations of agreement and disagreement and be scored 1 to 10. In this case strong disagreement with the ten-category item would give someone a score of 10, strong disagreement with the four-category item a score of 4, and disagreement with the two-category item a score of 1. Clearly disagreement with the ten-category item contributes much more to a final scale score than it does with the other items.

One solution is to rescore items so that they become equivalent. In this case we could multiply the scores on the two-item scale by 10, thus making the equivalent to strong disagreement on that item equal 10, while agreement would remain as 0. On the item with scores 0 to 4 multiply scores by 2.5 thus making strong disagreement (code 4) equal 10. By weighting scores in this way the strongest disagreement on all three items will be scored as 10 thus making all the items equivalent.

Another and better way of adjusting for different-length items is to use a form of standardisation as described above. If people's scores on each of a set of different-length items are converted into a standard score of one sort or another the problem is solved. If the scores are expressed in standard deviation units (z scores) then all the items on the scale will have the same potential length, thus ensuring that each item has an equal potential weight in the final scale score. Alternatively, if we wished all item scores to be positive, we could simply divide the raw scores for each person by the standard deviation of the item (Newitem = olditem/s). This method would provide equally weighted items but would not adjust for different distributions of each variable in the way that z scores do.

Forcing scales to have meaningful upper and lower limits

A difficulty when dealing with scales made up from either standardised items or from raw scores is in knowing what the lower and upper limits of the scale are. Depending on the number of items in a scale, their distribution, the number of categories in each item and the minimum and maximum scores of each item, the lower and upper values of a scale can vary between any two values. Thus a score of say, 56 or minus 12 has no immediate meaning without first looking at the minimum and maximum values of *that* scale, its distribution and so forth. The problem is compounded when, in the same piece of analysis, one is dealing with several scales, each with different minimum and maximum values.

In order to overcome these problems and to make the meaning of scale scores a little more intuitive, it is desirable to convert the scales so that they have a specified minimum and maximum value.

One way of achieving this is to use the following formula.

New scale = ((old scale − minimum scale value)/range) ∗ n

Where,

New scale	= score on scale with upper and lower limit.
Old scale	= score on old scale (using standardised scores)
Minimum scale value	= lowest score observed on old scale
Range	= range of observed scores on old scale
n	= upper limit for new scale
∗	= multiplied by
/	= divided by

Using this formula the scale scores will be forced between 0 and the number indicated by n. The following examples show how this is done for a scale where:

Minimum observed score on old scale = 5
Maximum observed score on old scale = 20
Range = 15

Example 1

Individual score on old scale = 20 (i.e. highest observed score)
Desired upper limit on scale = 10

New score = ((20 − 5)/15*10
　　　　　= (15/15)*10
　　　　　= 1*10
　　　　　= 10

Example 2

The individual's old score is 5 (lowest observed score). Thus:

$$((5 - 5)/15)*10 = (0/15)*10$$
$$= 0*10$$
$$= 0$$

Example 3

Individual's old score is 7.5. Thus:

$$((7.5 - 5)/15)*10 = (2.5/15)*10$$
$$= 0.17*10$$
$$= 1.7$$

If we wanted the scores to be on a 0 to 100 scale we would simply multiply by 100 rather than 10. If we wanted everything between zero and one we would multiply by one. The effect of subtracting the minimum value from the old scale score is to ensure that the maximum value of the scale is set by the multiplication factor (e.g. 10). For example, in the above example of the person who scored 20 on the old scale, the effect of not subtracting the minimum score from the person's score would have produced a new scale score for that person of 13.3. In other words, there would be no upper limit for the scale.

The effect of dividing by the range is to ensure that people who obtained the highest and lowest observed (as opposed to theoretically possible) score on the old scale get the highest and lowest possible scores respectively on the new, transformed scale. For example, a score of 60 might have been possible had a person obtained the maximum score on each item, but in fact the highest *observed* score might be 44. With this transformation the score of 44 (not 60) would be given the maximium value on the transformed scale. This has the virtue of allowing the distribution to define what is high and low as opposed to the researcher's arbitrary notions.

The problem of missing data

A scale score is arrived at by adding up a person's score on each item. However, if a person has not answered all the questions how is a score obtained for each item for that person? When coding answers for survey analysis a person must receive a code or score for every question—even if they have not answered it. When they have not answered it they are given a special code called a missing data code

Figure 15.5   Problems of missing data for scaling

Person	Item										Scale
	1	2	3	4	5	6	7	8	9	10	score
A	1	1	1	9	9	9	1	1	1	1	34
B	1	1	1	1	1	1	1	1	1	1	10

(see Chapter 14). This can be any code except the code for a legitimate answer (a valid code). However, this creates problems when trying to create scale scores.

The problem of missing data is illustrated in Figure 15.5. In this example missing data have been coded as 9. When this score is included in the addition to arrive at a scale score it distorts the scale score by inflating it. Had zero been used it would have deflated it. On the basis of questions answered person A and B are identical but the missing data in the scale score hides this. Methods of dealing with missing data are discussed on pages 282–6.

Summary

I have outlined what scaling is and pointed out that scaling in social research is simply a formalised version of an everyday process. A number of reasons for bothering to develop scales have been considered. The focus has been on only one type of scales—Likert scales. These are the most common type of scale and rely on combining people's responses to a number of questions into one variable. Since the principle of scaling is to combine only questions which tap the one underlying dimension we cannot add together just any questions. I have outlined a number of procedures to help determine whether it is legitimate to combine certain measures. Finally, I have outlined a number of practical difficulties in developing satisfactory scales and suggested ways of dealing with these.

Further reading

An old but still useful introduction to scaling is Bert Green's paper 'Attitude Measurement' (1954). *Techniques of Attitude Scale Construction* (1957) by Edwards is also an old but useful book. Some of the issues of scaling are addressed in section one in Lazarsfeld, Pasanella and Rosenberg's collection of papers in *Continuities in the Language of Social Research* (1972).

The Sage University Paper series on Quantitative Applications in the Social Sciences has published a number of technical papers on a wide range of scaling techniques. A very good one on the scaling techniques discussed in this chapter is provided by McIver and Carmines in their paper 'Unidimensional Scaling' (1981). Papers on a range of other scaling techniques are provided in this publication. The collections of questions listed at the end of Chapter 6 provide some useful scales. Very good treatments of factor analysis are provided in Kim and Mueller (1978a and 1978b) and in the *SPSSX Advanced Statistics Guide* by Norusis (1985).

16 Initial analysis

Data analysis is a process, not simply a matter of applying data about a crude set of variables to test a set hypothesis. The variables with which we work normally have to be refined both conceptually and empirically. Often we have to create variables from our data and collapse and reorganise the categories of variables. Initial analysis will reveal various patterns: some will be anticipated, others will surprise or puzzle us. These initial results will not be the end of analysis but should stimulate other questions which can be explored with the data.

While the process of analysis will vary depending on the style of research—explanatory or descriptive, theory testing or theory building, degree of focus in the research question—there are a number of common stages. This chapter considers two main stages, preparing variables for analysis and doing the initial analysis.

Preparing variables for analysis

Often data are not collected or coded in precisely the required form so they need to be adapted to our purposes, a process which can be quite time consuming. Decisions made at this stage require considerable judgment and can affect the patterns detected during analysis. There are two main aspects to this preparation: recoding existing variables and creating new ones.

Recoding existing variables

Recoding involves changing the codes which were allocated initially and is easily achieved by computer programs. There are three main uses of recoding. First, it can be used to rearrange the order of the categories of a variable. Most computer programs will put the categories of a variable in the order suggested by their numerical code. For example, we might initially have given industry groups particular codes as in Table 16.1, but for our analysis we might want

Table 16.1 Recoding to rearrange the order of categories

Initial code	Industry	% in unions	New code
1	Agriculture, forestry, fishing	20	1
2	Mining	64	5
3	Manufacturing	54	4
4	Electricity, gas, water	78	6
5	Construction	50	3
6	Wholesale and retail	28	2

Figure 16.1 An illustration of the need to reverse code when scaling

Considering the words below how would you say *you* generally feel towards those in authority over you?

1	Rebellious	1	2	3	4	5	6	7	Conforming
2	Obedient	1	2	3	4	5	6	7	Disobedient
3	Disrespectful	1	2	3	4	5	6	7	Respectful

them ranked in terms of degree of unionisation of the industry group so that they are ranked from lowest unionisation to highest. The extreme right-hand column indicates how we would need to recode to achieve this ranking.

A second purpose of recoding is to change the value of a variable. This is particularly important when developing scales (see Chapter 15). You will recall that a scale is normally developed by adding together people's scores (codes) on a set of variables. Each variable needs to be coded in a consistent direction so that the score obtained by adding together a set of variables is interpretable.

Imagine that we wanted to form the three questions in Figure 16.1 into a scale. The difficulty here is that on questions one and three a low score reflects someone who does not defer to authority, but on question two a high score reflects such a person.

To create an interpretable scale score all the items must be coded in the same direction; we would want a low score on each variable to mean the same thing in terms of the overall dimension they are meant to measure. When this is so the scale score which is simply the addition of scores on individual questions is meaningful. Thus we might want a low scale score to represent non-deference to authority and a high score to reflect deference. As the items are coded in Figure 16.1 a non-deferential person would have obtained a score of 1 on items one and three but a 7 on item two thus not producing a low scale score. To eliminate this problem we would need to reverse code question two to make the items additive. Thus we would change 7 into 1, 6 into 2, 5 into 3 and so forth.

The third main purpose of recoding is to collapse categories of a variable into fewer categories. For example, when coding a question about country of birth we might have a separate code for each country but for analysis purposes need only to distinguish between industrialised and non-industrialised countries or between broad categories of countries (e.g. North America, Central and South America, Australasia, South-East Asia, Middle East, Northern Europe, Southern Europe, etc.).

There are a number of reasons why it is often desirable to collapse categories of variables.

1   The detailed coding may not reflect the variable which is relevant to the research problem. As such recoding can be used to create a 'new' variable. For example, we might recode detailed occupational codes into simply blue-collar and white-collar categories. Or we might have asked people how they feel about the mining and export of uranium and initially have coded responses as 1 = strongly in favour of export; 2 = moderately in favour; 3 = mildly against; 4 = strongly against. If we wanted to use this question to measure not whether people were for or against but to measure strength of feeling on the issue we would put codes 1 and 4 into the same category (strong opinion) and 2 and 3 together (more ambivalent).

2   For analysis in which crosstabulations or frequency tables are used it is extremely helpful to avoid using variables with too many categories. The more categories, the more difficult a table is to read; I try to keep to a maximum of seven or eight categories. By collapsing categories, tables become easier to read. However, the enthusiasm to enhance readability by 'compressing' a variable must be tempered by common sense. Avoid so compressing a variable that it becomes too crude for the research question being addressed.

3   If there are very few people in a category it can be worth combining it with another suitable category. Very low frequencies can produce misleading tables and distort some statistics.

4   Collapsing categories can highlight patterns in the data that might otherwise not stand out. However, collapsing should not be done simply to create relationships. There should always be a sound justification for the way categories have been combined. Table 16.2 provides an illustration of recoding a variable in a justifiable way so as to highlight but not create a relationship between two variables.

5 When elaborating bivariate relationships a separate table is produced for each category of the test variable. If the test variable has a lot of categories it becomes extremely difficult to make sense of patterns since there are endless tables and co-efficients to interpret.

Of course collapsing categories is not by any means always necessary. Many methods of analysis are best done without collapsing categories, for example, scattergrams, comparison of means, regression, Pearson's correlation, partial correlation, rank order correlation and the advanced multivariate techniques discussed in Chapter 13.

Table 16.2 Relationship between education and gender with education in both its uncollapsed and collapsed form

	Uncollapsed			Collapsed	
	Male	Female		Male	Female
Completed university	13	7 ⎫			
Other tertiary	7	6 ⎬ At least some tertiary		40	27
Some university	20	14 ⎭			
Trade	16	21	Trade	16	21
Completed secondary	22	5	Completed secondary	22	5
Some secondary	17	39 ⎫			—
Primary only	5	8 ⎭ Some secondary or less		22	47
N	244	243		244	243

Approaches to recoding

There are two main approaches to working out which categories should be combined. The first is to use the 'substantive approach' by which we combine categories that seem to fit together. Normally this is a matter of common sense: if we cannot give a sensible name to the combined category then it is probably a meaningless category. Which categories go together depends in part on what we are using the variable for. For example, occupations could be collapsed into industry-based categories so that all jobs associated with a particular industry are grouped together (e.g. health, natural science, metal working, transport, chemical, agriculture, construction, etc.). Alternatively occupations could be collapsed into prestige groupings so that those with high prestige are combined in one group and so forth. Or they could be classified according to the amount of training involved so that those which require a degree are put in one category, those requiring a diploma in another and so on. When collapsing categories make sure that you do not collapse them in such a way that nearly everyone ends up in the same category.

With ordinal and interval variables which have ranked categories, collapsing is mainly a matter of working out cutting points along a continuum. Thus with age it is a matter of deciding on age groupings and recoding to establish these groupings.

The second approach is to use the distribution of the variable to recode by. When collapsing the categories of ordinal or interval variables this approach may be used. Often the meaning of a particular response to a question is best interpreted in relative than in absolute terms. For example, how are we to regard the income level of a person who earns $20 000 a year: is this low, medium or high? It depends on what other incomes we compare it with. If most people earn less then it is relatively high; if most earn more it may be relatively low. We can classify a particular value of a variable as high or low depending on the values of other people in the sample.

To recode in this way we first work out into how many categories we want to collapse the variable. Let us say we want to divide it up into three categories: low, medium and high. We will then divide the sample into the third with the lowest scores, the middle third, and the top third with the highest scores. To do this we look at the frequency distribution of the variable in its unrecoded form and then use the cumulative percentage column. Look for the cumulative percentage closest to 33 per cent (a third of cases). Then look across to the code which corresponds to this cumulative percentage. All people who obtained this code or lower will be put in one category of the recoded variable. Then look for the cumulative percentage closest to 67 per cent to get the next third and so forth (see Table 16.3).

This process of dividing a variable into three groups is called trichotomising. A variable may be divided into two groups (dichotomising) by using the cumulative percentage closest to 50 per cent or divided into four groups using the 25 per cent, 50 per cent and 75 per cent marks. In fact any number of divisions are possible. Once we have collapsed a variable in this way it is up to us to label the new categories appropriately.

You will notice that in Table 16.3 the sample has been divided into approximately three equal groups as opposed to dividing the categories of the variable into three equal lots (0 to 3, 4 to 6 and 7 to 10). This avoids categories with very few people in them and the problems which flow from this. For example, if most people were bunched towards one end of the continuum (e.g. from 7 to 10) then very few people would be in two of the three categories. Collapsing the sample

Table 16.3   Illustration of trichotomising a variable

Question: On a scale of 0 to 10 how would you rate your relationship with your father?
(0 = terrible; 10 = excellent)

	Score	%	Cumulative %	
Terrible	0	9	9	
	1	3	12	
	2	3	15	First 'third' = poor
	3	7	22	
	4	3	25	
	5	9	34	
	6	9	43	
	7	14	57	Second 'third' = moderate
	8	15	72	
	9	18	90	Third 'third' = good
Excellent	10	10	100	

into groups avoids this problem. Collapsing categories in this way also has the advantage of letting the data define what is low, medium or high rather than imposing some external, unrealistic definition.

It is a matter of judgment whether to use the variable's distribution or the content of the categories to recode by. Which method is selected depends on the variable itself and the purpose of the analysis.

Creating new variables

As well as recoding variables, new variables can be created from existing ones by combining the information contained in a set of questions. In this way some very useful and sophisticated variables can be developed. Normally this is done in one of two ways.

1   *Developing scales:* Techniques of scaling and the purpose of scales have already been outlined in Chapter 15.
2   *Using conditional statements:* Often the information contained in a number of variables provides the information needed to create a new variable even though there is not initially a single question that taps that variable. For example, we may wish to estimate the age difference between a husband and wife. We may have a question asking about the age of a person and another on the age of that person's spouse. From these two pieces of information we can create a third piece, the age difference between the two people. When we wish to determine someone's ethnicity we have to use a number of different pieces of information. It would be simplistic only to ask in what country someone was born. We

would probably also want to know in what country their parents were born, how long they had lived in their current country, what language was spoken at home, background of friends, ethnic self-identification and so forth. We would classify people's ethnicity in terms of particular mixes of all these pieces of information: the new variable would be a conglomeration. This new variable could be created manually at the initial coding stage by looking at each piece of information for a person and then allocating a code for the ethnicity variable or with SPSSX it could be done later on with a set of IF statements.

In summary the first stage of analysis involves preparing variables so that they are in a form suitable for addressing the research question and the methods of analysis to be used. Recoding is part of this preparation and can be used to change the order of categories, change their value or collapse categories. When collapsing categories either the content of the categories or the distribution of the variable can provide the basis for recoding depending on the nature of the variable and the research problem. The other aspect of preparing variables is to create new variables based on an amalgam of information contained in other variables.

The problem of missing data

Almost always survey data have missing values: answers to some questions will be missing. This presents several problems:

1 How can questions be improved to minimise missing values?
2 How are missing values coded?
3 Do missing values introduce a bias in the analysis?
4 How are missing values to be taken into account during analysis? Are there ways of substituting valid values for missing values?

Since the first two issues have been dealt with elsewhere in this book (chapter 6, pages 101, 241–2, 273–4) this section focuses on handling missing values at the data analysis stage.

Checking for missing data bias

Are people for whom we have missing values on a variable different from those with valid values? For example, is there a tendency for those who refuse to answer questions about income to have other characteristics such as ethnic background or education level in common? If missing data come from certain types of people, then either the variable on which data are missing should be dropped or considerable care should be taken with the analysis.

The simplest way of detecting any such bias is to divide the sample into two groups: those with missing values and those with valid values on a particular variable. (Care must be taken to exclude cases who were *not required* to answer the question from the analysis.) Having divided the sample into these two groups, you examine how the two groups answered other questions. Crosstabulations or comparison of means can be useful ways of conducting this analysis.

For example, if we have missing data on the income variable, we would divide the sample into those who did and those who did not give their income. This results in a dichotomous variable. We can then crosstabulate this variable with other variables (e.g. other key variables that will be examined in the analysis, or with variables that we suspect might reveal a bias, such as ethnicity). A relationship between the 'missing data on income variable' and the other variables (e.g. ethnicity) indicates that the missing data are not randomly distributed and that use of that variable may introduce bias into the sample.

Minimising the effect of missing values

There are a variety of methods for dealing with missing data at the data analysis stage. When deciding which method to use:

1   Try to minimise the loss of cases and data.
2   Avoid distorting sample variance and correlations.
3   Strive for simplicity.

Missing values are a problem because they reduce the number of cases available for analysis. In scale construction, bivariate and multivariate analysis, this can lead to an unacceptable loss of cases. For example, take a simple crosstabulation between age and income. Imagine that for each question, 10 per cent of people refused to answer but suppose that they are a different 10 per cent for each variable. That means that we have lost 20 per cent of cases. In multivariate analysis where we are dealing with a number of variables simultaneously, the loss of cases from missing values can increase as we add more variables. In scale development, missing cases can be a particular problem. We may wish to create an additive scale from 10 items but if a person has not answered one of the ten questions it is difficult to construct a scale score for that person, thus losing all the information supplied by his/her answers to the other items. In a set of 10 items there is a considerable chance of many people not answering at least one of the 10 items. This can result in being unable to construct a scale score for a large proportion of the sample.

Hertel (1976) has outlined a number of alternative ways of dealing with missing values.

1   *Delete cases:* Using this approach, any case that has missing data on any of the *set* of variables being analysed is eliminated from further analysis. This method, called *listwise* deletion of missing data, can lead to the loss of a lot of data: valid answers on many questions are disregarded simply because of a non-answer on one question. Because many people will have failed to answer one question in a set, this approach can lead to an unacceptable reduction in sample size. Hertel recommends that this method of handling missing data ought not to be used if it leads to a loss of more than 15 per cent of cases. However, if the missing data are clustered in a small number of cases, then you might wish to eliminate those cases as the quality of the data from those cases may be suspect.

2   *Delete variables:* If a particular variable is responsible for a large number of the missing values, that variable can be dropped from the analysis. The advantage of this is that we do not lose any cases and may lead to the elimination of an unreliable item. The advisability of this approach depends on how important that particular variable is for the analysis.

3   *Pairwise solution:* This frequently used approach can be used when analysis is based on a zero-order correlation matrix as is the case with many multivariate techniques (e.g. factor analysis, regression, reliability, etc.). When calculating the correlation between any two variables, we include all cases that have non-missing values for those two variables even if those cases have missing values on other variables being used in the analysis. Using the pairwise approach we would get a correlation matrix in which each co-efficient may be based on a different number of cases. The disadvantage of the pairwise approach is that it leads to some loss of cases, but this is not nearly as marked as with the listwise approach.

4   *Sample mean approach:* If we do not know the value on a variable for any given person, then the best guess for that person is the same as the measure of central tendency for that variable. With interval level variables we would replace missing values with the value of the mean for the sample. Although we will make errors in our guesses, this method produces fewer errors

than by guessing any other value (see discussion of PRE measures on pages 166–8, 176–8). The problem with this approach is that it reduces the variability of the sample on the variable for which missing data are being estimated, thus reducing the level of association between this and other variables.

5 *The group means approach:* One way of overcoming this problem is to use group means rather than the overall sample mean. To do this we would divide our sample into groups on a background variable (e.g. ethnicity, gender, education) that is well correlated with the missing value variable. We would then obtain the mean for the 'missing data variable' within each category of the selected background variable. For example, if we were trying to estimate income for people who refused to answer the question, we might divide the sample up into groups according to their education level and then within each education level further divide it by gender. We would then obtain the mean income for non-missing cases within each group. Thus we might find that the mean income for tertiary educated females is $27 000 and the mean for tertiary educated males is $32 000 and so forth. Using the group means approach we would simply substitute these mean values for missing values for people according to the group into which they fell.

The disadvantage of this approach is that it exaggerates homogeneity within groups and thus can overestimate the variance between groups and for the sample overall. This can lead to an inflation of correlations when using the variable for which the missing data have been estimated.

6 *Random assignment within groups:* This approach is similar to the group means approach in that it relies on dividing the sample into groups on the basis of background variables that are likely to be correlated with the missing data variable. But it differs in that it does not involve substituting the group mean for any missing data. Instead, when we locate a case with missing data on a particular variable we would simply look at the value on the same variable of the nearest preceding case and give the same value to the case with the missing value. This method means that missing values are replaced by a variety of different values. This method does not affect sample or group variability and has no effect on the strength of correlations and avoids any loss of cases. Despite being somewhat more complex to execute, it is a highly desirable way of handling missing data.

7 *Regression analysis:* This is a more complex method that involves the use of regression to predict the value of a person on the

missing data variable. Since the regression will be based on a matrix in which the pairwise method will be used, this approach leads to a loss of cases.

Which method should be used to handle missing data? Of the methods that involve estimating valid values for missing values, the random assignment of numbers is the least likely to lead to data distortions but it is more complex. Of the approaches that involve losing data or cases, the pairwise solution is generally best and is easily accomplished with most computer packages. On occasions, however, other approaches are more appropriate. If most missing data is due to a few cases or a particular variable we might question the quality of responses from those cases or for that variable and decide that it is better to eliminate what may be unreliable data.

Doing the initial analysis

There is no recipe for analysing data but there are a few useful guide-lines. The actual analysis will of course depend on the research problem.

I have just emphasised the necessity of preparing variables for analysis. The first step in analysis should be to obtain a frequency distribution of each variable to make sure they are as we intend them to be. With SPSSX this can be done simply with a FREQUENCIES program. From this we can check that all the codes are valid, that recoding and the creation of new variables has been done in the intended way.

It is then useful to try to build up a picture of what the sample 'looks' like. To do this, look at the frequency tables of the important variables. If the study is about conservatism look at all the variables designed to measure this and develop a picture of the extent of conservatism, the differences on the different measures and so forth. This can help achieve more creative analysis later on. Also look at how the sample is distributed on various sociodemographic variables such as sex, age, ethnicity, class and education. This may reveal certain biases in the sample which may help us account for patterns we observe later on (see page 299).

Before proceeding any further with the analysis we need to make sure we know in detail exactly what questions we are trying to answer. For example, we might want to find out about people's attitudes to the in vitro fertilisation program. As well as specifying which aspect of the program we are interested in, we would work out what we want to know about. Do we simply want to know what percentage approve or disapprove? Or do we want to know which types of people approve and disapprove. If so we must be specific. Do we want to see whether age, religion, class, education, sex and so on affect attitudes? When we can break down the research topic into these sorts of very specific questions we will have a very good idea of precisely what analysis is required. If we simply wish to know what percentage approve of fertilising multiple embryos or implanting embryos in surrogate mothers, a frequency table on that variable will do. If we want to know whether Catholics and other religious groups have different attitudes, a crosstabulation of the attitude by religion will answer the question. With computers the mechanics of analysis are easy: any number of tables can be generated with relative ease. The difficulty is being clear about which tables we need. This can only be done by thinking first. The alternative is to get bogged down trying to work our way through endless and irrelevant tables.

Try to keep this stage of analysis simple. The focus will probably be on simple univariate analysis and examining bivariate relationships. Marsh observes

> If you look at the way sociologists actually work, they often ask of the bivariate relationship, why is there a correlation here, and work productively by gradually elaborating the relationship at the kernel of the model, thinking, refining their ideas, rejecting and including variables one at a time. (1982:85)

The next chapter considers ways of doing this. The focus of the initial analysis, however, should be on the 'relationship at the kernel of the model'. Initially focus on seeing whether this relationship exists and what it looks like. Avoid doing fancy analysis until this has been done.

Once having worked out what analysis is needed, do it and then read the tables produced. As we do so we need to build up an overall picture of each table and keep asking 'what is this telling me?' and 'why these results?' and 'what else do I need to find out?'

When reading frequency tables try to get an overview of the distribution of the variable before becoming preoccupied with details. Look to see if people are clustered in certain categories or whether they tend to be spread evenly over them. Are there any patterns? What might they mean?

The same approach applies when reading crosstabulations: first get an overview and then look at details. When reading and describing a crosstabulation, move from the general to the particular. I try to do three things when looking at a crosstabulation. First, I look to see if there is a relationship between the two variables. To do this I look at the appropriate correlation co-efficients and then the relevant per-

Table 16.4   Level of deference to people in authority by highest level of education

		Education					
		Primary	Some secondary	Completed secondary	Trade	Other tertiary	University
Level of deference	Low	4%	7%	7%	7%	18%	33%
	Medium	22	55	42	62	56	47
	High	74	38	51	31	26	20
	N	27	122	59	82	73	119

Gamma = −0.40

centages in the table. It is helpful to ask four questions: Is there a relationship? How strong is it? Is it positive or negative? Is it linear or curvilinear? (see pages 160–1). Second, I try to explain in plain English what the relationship is, and finally I provide illustrative figures from the table.

The figures in Table 16.4 can be used to illustrate this. This table could be described as follows: 'There is a moderate negative linear relationship between education and level of deference (G = −0.40). That is, the higher the level of education, the lower the level of deference. For instance, only 4 per cent of those with primary education alone were non-deferential compared to 33 per cent of those who had completed university.' Having provided this overview we might wish to highlight a few particular points of importance, but the focus will be on providing an overview of what the table tells us.

Once we have done this sort of analysis we can start to ask questions which will lead onto further analysis. The further analysis depends both on the initial results and the ability to probe them.

Summary

This chapter has considered the first stage of the process of analysis. It has outlined some ways in which variables can be prepared for analysis and how the first dip into the data might procede.

Normally, the initial stage of data analysis produces more questions than answers. The patterns are often unexpected. Variables that we thought would be related are not and correlations are weaker than anticipated. Some patterns seem to contradict each other and others are simply inexplicable. Research that ends at the point of simply looking at a number of frequency distributions and bivariate relationships will normally not go far enough. The best analysis is that which tries to account for the initial set of observations. We are then forced to think, and develop explanations. The data extends us and stimulates analysis. Some of the ways in which this can be done are discussed in Chapter 17.

Further reading

Remarkably little is written explicitly about the initial analysis of data. Chapter 9 of Hoinville and Jowell's *Survey Research Practice* (1978) deals with some issues on how to classify values of variables. Warwick and Lininger outline some things to do when preparing for analysis in Chapter 10 of *The Sample Survey* (1975). Huff's classic book *How to Lie With Statistics* (1954) is well worth reading as it shows what not to do in initial analysis. Further aspects of variable preparation for more advanced analysis are discussed in Chapter 4 of Tabachnick and Fidall (1983).

17 Moving beyond initial analysis

The patterns that are observed in the initial analysis of data provide the basis for the next stage of analysis. There are countless ways in which this stage of analysis can proceed; what we do depends on the initial patterns, research problem and theory. However, it is desirable to do at least four broad things at this stage.

1 Clarify the nature of the initial relationships.
2 Account for unexpected findings.
3 Check the robustness of the initial findings.
4 Eliminate alternative explanations of the findings.

This chapter deals with each of these aspects of analysis and concludes with a discussion of two further issues, the role of Deviant Case Analysis (DCA), and the value of *ex post facto* theorising and its implications for the nature of the research process.

Clarifying relationships

It is one thing to establish that two variables are related but quite another to establish why they are related. Is the relationship causal or spurious? If it is causal, is it direct or indirect? If it is indirect, what are the causal mechanisms? It is normally when trying to answer these sorts of questions (i.e. once the initial bivariate relationships have been examined) that the elaboration procedures discussed in Chapter 12 are best employed.

When using these elaboration techniques we always need to use test variables. The problem in such analysis is knowing which test variables to use. It is both impractical and undesirable simply to control for every possible test variable in the hope that something might turn up. This lazy form of analysis mainly produces endless tables which defy meaningful interpretation, and leads to boring and ill-focused research.

To avoid such data dredging, test variables should be selected on the basis of theoretical reasoning, previous research and commonsense. For example, initial analysis might reveal that women attend church more often than men. A search of the literature would reveal various 'explanations' for this. One is that women are less involved in the paid workforce and therefore have more time, fewer social outlets, feel more deprived and are protected from the secularising pressures of the workplace. This might be why women attend church more than men.

Using elaboration techniques this explanation of the initial relationship could be tested by looking at the relationship between gender and church attendance controlling for level of workforce participation.

Alternatively I might have a hunch that the over-representation of women among church attenders is restricted to older groups of people rather than being a general pattern. I could use age as a test variable. If I found that it was only among older people that more women than men attend church, I would have to ask what is it about older people in particular that would lead to this distinctive pattern.

The central point is that the selection of test variables should be directed by good reasoning rather than being haphazard. Careful selection of test variables and the use of elaboration techniques provide one way of clarifying the nature of relationships. The techniques discussed in Chapter 13 also can be used for this purpose.

Dealing with unanticipated results

More often than not the patterns revealed in the initial analysis are not what are expected or hoped for. Anticipated patterns either do not exist or are weaker than expected. Sometimes they are stronger than expected and on other occasions they seem contradictory. The real world never fits our theories as neatly as we would like. The point of research ought not to be to fit reality to some pet theory but to develop a theory which fits empirical reality. The mark of a good researcher is not the ability to formulate hypotheses or hunches that turn out to be correct but the ability to make sense of data and to analyse them intelligently.

Understanding weaker-than-expected patterns

A weaker-than-expected relationship may be due to many things, the most obvious being that the initial expectations were wrong. But before accepting this interpretation check to make sure it is not due to something else.

First, check to make sure the results are not due to faulty indicators. For example, we might not have found an anticipated relationship between age and political conservatism. It could be that we have not really been tapping political conservatism very well. If there are several different indicators of the same concept, it is worth doing separate analysis with the various indicators to see if there is a consistency in the patterns regardless of which indicators are used. If we got no relationship when conservatism was measured by vote, but get the expected relationships when measuring conservatism by asking about attitudes to political change (e.g. abolition of the position of governor-general, constitutional reform), it may be that vote is not a valid measure of political conservatism. In other words, before accepting that no relationship exists check that you were initially measuring what you thought you were.

Second, check to see whether the answers to the question are affected by a social desirability factor. People's responses to questions such as 'Do you believe in freedom of speech?' or 'Is it important to try to reduce unemployment?' are likely to be affected by this factor. If people's answers reflect 'acceptable' answers rather than their real attitudes, the question does not enable us to distinguish between people whose real attitudes differ. The result is that any analysis using such a question is unlikely to show relationships between the non-discriminating variable and other variables. To check whether the lack of an expected relationship could be due to this problem, look at questions which could produce these socially desirable responses. If most people have given much the same answer then the question may not discriminate adequately between any differences that might exist between people. In such cases try using another question if one is available.

It is also worth checking to see whether the way variables have been collapsed is masking a true relationship. Table 17.1 illustrates in an extreme way how recoding a variable can do this.

Table 17.1   An illustration of how recoding can mask a relationship

	Unrecoded version			Recoded version	
	Male	Female		Male	Female
Strongly agree	50%	15% ⎫	→Agree	60%	60%
Agree	10	45 ⎬			
Disagree	30	5 ⎫			
Strongly disagree	10	35 ⎬	→Disagree	40	40
N	500	500	N	500	500
Gamma = 0.37			Gamma = 0.00		

On the other hand we may not have recoded a variable and this may be masking a relationship (see Table 16.2). This is not to say that variables should simply be recoded to 'create' the desired relationship. The way a variable is recoded must be defended in terms of what system of classification makes sense. What we must avoid is hiding relationships simply because of the way a variable is coded.

A fourth check to make is the relationship within various subgroups. The anticipated relationship may be conditional and only apply to particular subgroups, and this may be hidden when everyone is combined in the initial analysis. For example, among older people education might be positively related to conservatism (the higher the education the more conservative) but among younger people the opposite may be true. When both old and young people are analysed together, the opposite patterns of old and young would cancel each other out and make it appear that there was no relationship when in fact there was under certain conditions.

Fifth, it is worth checking to see if the lack of relationship is due to various characteristics of the sample. For example, more people than expected might say the level of migration into the country ought to be reduced dramatically. A close look at the make-up of the sample might show that those who have migrated to the country are grossly under-represented (as is typically the case) and this might account for the unanticipated finding. In other words, check the characteristics of the sample. If distortions are evident then control for that variable. In this case we would check to see if the under-representation of migrants is affecting the result by analysing those from migrant and non-migrant backgrounds separately. If both groups had similar attitudes then this bias in the sample would not account for the initial unexpected finding. However, if the attitudes of the under-represented group were different, this could help explain the initial results. We could then adopt analysis procedures to eliminate this problem (see page 299).

Sixth, correlations can be lower than expected because of low variance in the variables. This calculation of co-efficients such as Pearson's r use variation in one variable to explain variation in another variable (see pages 174–8). If a variable has very little variation, it is less able to explain variation in another variable and correlations will be low. For example, we may have a sample in which there is considerable variation in income and we wish to explain this variation in terms of gender. But if virtually all the sample were male then the high variation in income could not be due to gender (i.e. to variations in gender) since this variable barely varies in the sample. The correlation between gender and income in this sample would therefore be very low. Before doing correlations it is therefore worth checking the level of variation in each of the variables to ensure that low variance will not be a problem.

A final thing to check is the nature of the relationship. Most correlation co-efficients only indicate whether a linear relationship exists. Two variables may be related but in a non-linear pattern. When this is the case the linear measures of correlation will be low but this does not mean there is no association. An examination of correlation co-efficients which are sensitive to non-linear relationships is always desirable: Cramer's V and eta are useful for this purpose. Also look at the appropriate crosstabulation or scattergram as well as the summary statistic since these can reveal important patterns which are not reflected in the summary statistics.

Of course, relationships might be weaker than expected because of unrealistic expectations. Relationships between social science variables—particularly those involving attitudes—are normally weaker than social science and popular stereotypes would have us believe. For example, these stereotypes produce images that males have one set of attitudes and females have a quite distinct set; that young people have totally divergent views from older people; that those from higher status groups are markedly different from those from lower status groups. A real problem with the way social science research is used is that relationships and trends get translated into stereotypes that overemphasise group differences. In reality, even though groups may differ overall, there is invariably a great deal that they have in common and a great many people in different categories who are very similar to one another. Although a greater percentage of males than females might express a particular opinion, there will normally be far more men and women who share the same opinion.

There are many reasons why correlations will often be weak. Social behaviour and attitudes are highly complex and influenced by many factors, so we should not expect any one variable to be strongly related to another. A weak relationship between age and conservatism, for example, should not be surprising, since many factors other than age affect conservatism. If, as social scientists, we accept the notion of multiple causation and understand something of the complexity of human social behaviour, we should mainly anticipate fairly weak correlations.

It is better to accept that most relationships are weak than to overinterpret results. Table 17.2 shows percentage figures on a range of attitudes broken down according to gender, education, age and job status. For this table I selected the variables because popular stereotypes would lead us to expect many strong relationships between these sociodemographic variables and the attitudes involved.

Table 17.2 Percentage differences on a range of attitudes

Attitude	Job prestige		Education		Age		Gender	
	Low	High	Tertiary	Less	Under 30	30 +	Male	Female
Approves of legalising marijuana	25	26	32	23	40	19	27	22
Has positive attitude to self	78	82	83	79	76	81	80	78
Highly competitive	48	45	41	47	49	45	58	37
Votes for left-wing party	48	41	48	41	44	41	43	41
Believes in personal God	61	58	54	61	53	62	52	67
Approves of abortion if can't afford child	60	63	62	61	61	62	64	59
Give women preference in jobs	31	19	17	29	30	25	24	28
Defence—should be a very high priority for govt	46	32	16	44	31	43	37	43
Royalist	44	42	32	47	28	50	37	51
Favours death penalty	61	53	39	60	54	59	62	53

Source: National Social Science Survey, Australia, 1984
For most of the analysis, n is greater than 2500

The table shows that most differences are only modest at best. Most are less than 10 per cent, and only five are greater than 20 per cent. While the direction of most of the differences are predictable, the size of the differences are nowhere near as great as both sociological and popular stereotypes would have us believe. The same applies with correlations. These are normally lower than we would expect (see Table 17.3).

It is important to realise that correlations and relationships, in general, will be weak. Recognising this should help reduce the sense of despair some people experience when all their correlations are weak or non-existent and hopefully will reduce the temptation to overinterpret results or to use various devices to increase correlations to 'respectable' levels.

Finding stronger-than-expected relationships

On occasions variables are more strongly related than expected. Apart from checking that we have used the correct variables the same sorts of checks as outlined above can be used.

Table 17.3   Correlations for a range of variables

	Redistribute wealth	Economic conservative	Anti trade union	Feels military threat	Anti environment	Christian belief
Age	.13	−.00	.09	−.02	.14	.01
Education	−.01	−.04	.10	.25	.08	.06
Gender	−.06	−.04	.07	.23	−.08	.18
Occuptional prestige	.17	.14	.07	−.21	−.01	−.02
Income	.05	.11	−.07	−.19	.00	−.10

Source: National Social Science Survey, Australia, 1984
The variables age, education, prestige and income are coded so that a high score indicates they have more of this characteristic. Gender is coded 0 = male; 1 = female. The variables across the top are coded so that a high score reflects the characteristic indicated by the labelling of the variable. Thus a high score on 'redistribute wealth' indicates that the respondent is in favour of redistributing wealth

In addition, it is worth checking for 'outlier effects'. When a few very atypical cases or groups are included in a sample they can 'create' a pattern. For example, we might be examining the level of industrial disputes over the last ten years and expect that it has been stable. Having collected data from ten different industry areas (e.g. transport, building, manufacturing, mining), we may find that there has been an overall increase in disputation. It would be necessary to check whether this increase was general or specific to just one or two groups. For example, if disputes had increased dramatically in one industry but not in others, this idiosyncratic industry could, when combined with the others, create what appears to be a general pattern. In other words, when you find an unanticipated relationship, check to see what it is composed of so that its meaning can be interpreted properly.

The same effect can occur with regression: outliers can create seriously distorted regression lines and co-efficients. In Figure 17.1 the two outliers create a higher b co-efficient than is warranted by the bulk of the cases. Without the two outliers the regression line would be horizontal and b would be 0. With the outliers, b is about $100 which is a distortion of the real pattern. In order to detect these sorts of outlier effects it is worth displaying data fully in either a scattergram or crosstabulation to see what is going on.

Care must also be taken not to misinterpret tests of statistical significance: a test of significance tells nothing about the strength of a relationship but only indicates the probability that the observed relationship is due to sampling error (see Chapter 11, Tests of significance). With large samples very weak relationships can be statistically significant: in a sample of 2000 an r^2 or 0.002 is statistically significant at the 0.05 level but this is not much of a rela-

Figure 17.1 The distorting effect of outliers on regression

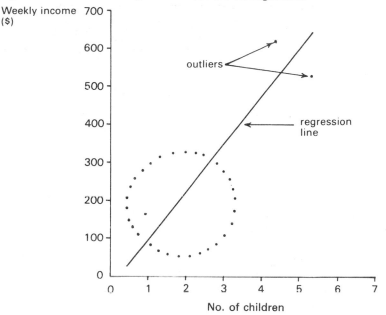

tionship! So do not simply look at significance levels and think that you have an unexpected relationship that needs explaining.

It is always worth examining significance levels and correlation co-efficients together. With small samples it is common to obtain unexpectedly high correlations due entirely to sampling error. Whenever you obtain a correlation, check the significance level. This will provide an estimate of whether it is likely to be due to chance. If it is due to chance then the explanation of the unexpectedly high correlation is unproblematic and does not require developing new theories to account for the new findings.

Finally, whenever you obtain any strong relationship check to make sure it is not spurious. If, despite all these various checks on the relationships, the pattern persists, we have to start trying to work out at a theoretical level why the relationship exists and how important it is.

Dealing with contradictory results

It is not unusual to discover apparently contradictory findings within the same study and thus it is necessary to try to account for them.

Often they may be more apparent than real. For example, we might ask a question designed to measure prejudice to which people give socially desirable 'non-prejudiced' responses, but more subtle questions might make the same people appear prejudiced. To help resolve this sort of contradiction look closely to see if it is caused by the way the questions have been asked.

Contradictions also can arise when comparing responses to broad questions with those to more specific questions. For example, people might say they strongly support nuclear disarmament but responses towards particular proposals to disarm or specific forms of disarmament (e.g. unilateral) may produce quite different answers. Here people's responses may appear contradictory but probably reflect answers to quite different issues and thus there is no real contradiction.

Contradictions also may simply be the researcher's own view of what constitutes a contradiction. For example, people may support nuclear disarmament but support the mining of uranium. To some people it is inconceivable that someone can hold both these attitudes at the same time, while for other people there is no contradiction. Thus when apparent contradictions occur in the data we should ask ourselves what we can learn from them about the nature and structure of people's attitudes and the meaning of their answers.

Using very broad concepts also can produce apparently contradictory results. For example, middle-class people attend church more than do working-class people and in this sense are more religious. In contrast working-class people are more likely to pray and in this sense are more religious. If we take church attendance and prayer equally as indicators of the broad concept of 'religious' there appears to be a contradiction. But if the concept is refined so that we distinguish between public and private religiosity, the contradiction is resolved. Often 'conflicting' findings simply reflect poor conceptualisation on our own part.

Of course, some contradictions in results reflect real contradictions: they reflect inconsistencies between attitudes and actions, within a world view and so forth. Finding inconsistencies in data is often a positive thing: it helps avoid simplistic interpretations of data and can highlight the complexity of social life and of people's attitudes. These contradictions can stimulate curiosity and encourage different and innovative analysis to help resolve such puzzles.

Checking relationships

Even when the expected patterns turn up it is important to analyse the data further to see how 'robust' the initial pattern is. There are at least three questions to ask.

Is the pattern likely to apply only to this sample?

We need to have an idea of whether the results simply reflect quirks in the particular sample or are likely to be more general. There are two broad ways of dealing with this question: using another sample in one form or another and using inferential statistics.

Ideally the first approach would involve obtaining another sample to see if the same patterns reoccur. Since this is normally impractical other techniques can be used. When a sample has known biases (e.g. education, class, sex, ethnicity) we can statistically remove these biases and see what the results would have been like without them. For example, highly educated people may be over-represented so we can look at the patterns amongst the highly educated separately from the rest of the sample. If the pattern in the highly educated group is much the same as for the others, the bias in the sample does not matter as it is not responsible for the initial pattern.

If the pattern for the over-represented group is different to the rest of the sample we will need to 'reweight' various groups to remove the effect of the bias and redo the analysis. The principle of reweighting is simple. If there are twice as many highly educated people in the sample as there ought to be then their contribution to the final results should be halved. This is easily achieved by computer packages such as SPSSX.

Inferential statistics provide another way of assessing whether patterns are likely to be peculiar to the particular sample or general to most samples. Tests of significance provide an estimate of how likely it is that the pattern found in a particular sample could occur in a random sample when in fact it did not exist in the population from which the sample was drawn (see pages 190–1). Rather than having to draw other samples against which to compare our own results, we can use inferential statistics to provide an estimate of how likely it is that the results we have found would approximate those in other samples if they were drawn. Thus when dealing with random samples, inferential statistics provide a simple and efficient way of estimating how general the results are likely to be.

Does the pattern hold for subgroups within the sample?

It is worth checking to see if the initial patterns we find are conditional on other factors. If the initial relationship holds across a wide range of subgroups we can be more confident that it is both real and general. For example, we might initially observe that the higher people's education, the less prejudiced they are. But does this persist regardless of other characteristics such as age, sex, social class and so forth? If the initial relationship persists across age, class and sex groups we can be more confident that it is real and general rather than being due to the influence of a few heavily represented groups in the sample.

If, on the other hand, it only holds amongst certain types of people (e.g. women, younger people, working class), any explanation of the links between education and prejudice will have to be refined sufficiently to account for its patchiness. The procedures by which this sort of testing can be done are outlined in Chapter 12.

Does the pattern persist with different indicators?

The value of checking results using different indicators of key variables has been discussed already. When we obtain the results we anticipated, this procedure is still warranted to ensure that they are not simply 'indicator dependent'. If there is a consistency regardless of which indicator is used, we can be more confident that the relationship is real. If it varies with different indicators then our interpretation of the initial pattern must take this into account.

In summary, even when we obtain the results we expected we should still check the initial results to see how robust they are. The three approaches outlined are all based on the principle of replication. If the initial results can be replicated in 'different' samples, across various subgroups and with different indicators, we can be more confident that the initial relationship is real and not due to an idiosyncratic sample or indicator. If we cannot easily replicate the results, the interpretations of the initial results must take that into account.

Eliminating alternative explanations

In Chapter 2 I argued that it is necessary to develop convincing explanations of results, not just plausible ones. To do this we need to eliminate competing explanations to that which we have developed. This is done partly during analysis.

One way to achieve this is to list as many plausible explanations as are consistent with the facts. Then try to work out what additional information and analysis is needed to enable us to choose between the alternatives. Often there are crucial tests which make the elimination of certain explanations easy. This process can be best illustrated with an example.

Some people argue that fewer people are doing well at university now than ten years ago and argue that this is reflected in a smaller percentage of students passing now than previously. Assuming for the moment that this is correct, there are a number of ways of interpreting such a finding.

1 Students are not being prepared adequately for university by secondary schools.
2 There has been a decline in student motivation rather than abilities and this causes fewer to pass.
3 More students are withdrawing from courses for economic reasons thus leaving fewer to pass the course.
4 The standard of teaching has declined.
5 The difficulty of university courses or the expectations of university teachers have increased.

Rather than simply selecting one of these explanations because we like it, we would need to think carefully to work out what additional information we require to see which of these explanations holds. Unfortunately we may find that we do not have the crucial information which helps test particular explanations. If so, state what the alternative explanations are and what further research would be required to test them. Careful planning at the data collection stage can reduce this problem: it involves thinking ahead and anticipating results and collecting information which can help test them.

Deviant case analysis (DCA)

DCA refers to a way of looking at data once the initial analysis has been completed (see Rose, 1978; Denzin, 1978) and is similar in logic to analytic induction (Denzin, 1978). The initial analysis may reveal certain trends or patterns but normally there will be some 'deviant' cases which run counter to the major trends. For example, it is generally true that jobs with high income have high status and those with low income have low status. But there are deviant cases such as the tradesman on a very high income or the clergyman on a low income. Rather than these exceptions to the rule being ignored, they can provide a basis for refining theories and avoiding simplistic explanations.

The process of DCA can be illustrated with a simple example in which we find that on the whole people marry people with a similar level of education to themselves (Table 17.4). In this example the two groups of fifteen represent 'deviant' cases. The approach of DCA is to find out what it is about the 'deviant' cases which distinguishes them from 'normal' cases. We might find that most of the men with low education who marry women with high education

Table 17.4   Relationship between husband's education and wife's education

		Husband's education	
		Low	High
Wife's education	Low	85	15
	High	15	85
	N	100	100

have characteristics which explain their 'deviance'. They might be highly successful or may have other characteristics which 'compensate' for their lack of formal education. Thus we might argue that rather than equality of education level affecting who people marry, it is equality of status which is important. As such an examination of the deviant cases has led to a refinement of the argument.

DCA is not always an appropriate method of analysis. It is most appropriate when looking at the relationship between two variables both with a small number of categories where there are clear trends. When two variables are strongly related it is easy to identify deviant cases but when the relationship is weak it is less clear which cases are deviant. The same is true when dealing with interval variables with many categories: it is by no means clear which cases are deviant except at the extremes.

The role of *ex post facto* theorising

Ex post facto explanations are those which are inductively developed after making observations. This is in contrast to the hypothesis testing approach where predictions are deductively derived from theory and then data are collected to test the hypothesis. If the data fit the predictions, the hypothesis is accepted (see Chapter 2).

The problem with the *ex post facto* approach is that there are often a number of alternative explanations of a set of observations and without further evidence it is impossible to choose between these competing *ex post facto* explanations. All explanations should be falsifiable: unless we can say what possible findings would constitute disconfirmation of an explanation then the explanation is useless. This is the advantage of the hypothesis testing approach: evidence which could potentially disconfirm the hypothesis is specifically collected. With *ex post facto* explanations, the evidence which could disconfirm the explanation is often unavailable or not examined so we are in no position to evaluate the explanation.

These problems have often led to injunctions against *ex post facto* explanations in favour of the hypothesis testing approach. Many of the suggestions in this chapter, however, require the use of an *ex post facto* approach. My view is that there is nothing wrong with developing such explanations as long as those explanations are then tested. In other words, look at the data and develop explanations of the observed patterns. These explanations, however, must only be regarded as possibilities—in effect hypotheses to be tested. We must then go on to see what evidence we can use to test this (see Chapter 2). The *ex post facto* explanation is conditional upon finding further key evidence. It is only a step in arriving at an explanation.

This approach to analysis has a number of advantages over simply adopting the deductive hypothesis testing approach. First, it reflects that data analysis is a continuing process which involves moving backwards and forwards between theory and data. This results in analysis and theories which take account of the complexities in the data more than does a ritualistic hypothesis testing approach. Secondly, it encourages researchers to look at patterns in the data and to develop explanations of these regardless of what they might be. The danger of the hypothesis testing model is that patterns which do not confirm the hypothesis often are simply ignored rather than seen as requiring explanation. Thirdly, it can help avoid the sterility of a purely hypothesis testing approach. There will be important patterns in some data which would not be anticipated beforehand and thus hypotheses would not be developed to test them. Accordingly, a researcher may never be sensitised to them. In contrast, the more inductive *ex post facto* approach encouraged here can provide more scope for researchers to discover quite new patterns in data and develop some quite innovative ideas (see Rosenberg, 1968: chs 8, 9). Marsh has argued for this approach to research when she writes

> It is not unscrupulous to have a good idea, an insight into the possible way in which one variable is having an effect on another, or a pang of doubt that a plausible prior variable may be entirely responsible for the visible correlation. In fact, such ideas may actually be inhibited by rushing at a dataset with one's head lowered, model polished and gleaming in one's hand. (1982:85)

It is not that there is only one approach to research. The traditional hypothesis testing approach is valuable but has its limitations. The same is true of the more inductive *ex post facto* approach. My own view is to use whatever approach is appropriate to the problem at hand. The model outlined in Chapter 2 emphasises using both approaches at different stages of research.

Summary

I have emphasised the importance of asking questions about the results obtained from the initial analysis. There is a flow to analysis which involves looking at the results and asking '*why* is this pattern occurring?' and 'what does it mean?' and then doing further analysis to answer these questions. This will probably throw up further results of which we will ask the same questions. This chapter has provided some clues about how this analysis might proceed. Persisting with these questions can help avoid misinterpreting the initial results. It is a helpful way of arriving at a fuller understanding of initial results which can lead to more convincing and exciting explanations and interpretations of the data.

Further reading

There is a shortage of books which provide clues about the process of analysis. One excellent discussion is in Chapters 8 and 9 of Rosenberg's *The Logic of Survey Analysis* (1968). Another classic discussion is Hirschi and Selvin's *Delinquency Research: An appraisal of analytic methods* (1967) in particular part II on causal analysis although the whole book is of relevance. Silvey also provides a brief discussion in Chapter 5 of *Deciphering Data* (1975). Merton's discussion of the interaction of theory and data and of serendipity in Chapters 4 and 5 of *Social Theory and Social Structure* (1968) are certainly worth reading. Huck and Sandler's *Rival Hypotheses: Alternative Interpretations of Data Based Conclusions* (1979) is an exceptionally readable account of how to avoid overinterpreting data. Three papers in section II C of Lazarsfeld and Rosenberg's *The Language of Social Research* expand on the discussion of deviant case analysis in this chapter.

18 Putting it into practice: a research example

As well as describing the various stages of research and techniques of data analysis it is helpful to see how these are applied. This chapter, which is based on a piece of research in which I was involved (de Vaus and McAllister, 1987), provides an example of various stages and decisions involved in the research process.

The research question

Throughout this book the importance of specifying the research question has been emphasised (Chapter 3). The study on which the example in this chapter is based arose out of the observation in the sociology of religion literature that on whatever measure you choose to look at, women seem to be more religious than men. While the *descriptive* data showing that women are typically more religious than men are available no one has tried to *explain* empirically why this is so (pages 28–9). So our research question was: why are women more religious than men? Does the gender difference have a sociological basis?

Having formulated the question the next step was to see what sorts of explanations other people had put forward in the literature (pages 22–4). We were anxious to put our own research within a theoretical framework both so that the analysis would have direction and the results would have some significance for broader theoretical and sociological issues (Chapter 2). We were able to detect some *ex post facto* explanations in the literature (page 12). These included explanations that emphasised the role of psychological processes and differences between men and women and those that interpreted the religious differences as the result of different sex role socialisation.

There were also hints of another type of sociological explanation. Rather than focusing on sex role socialisation, some people drew attention to the different roles and the different position occupied

305

by men and women in society. We called this a *structural location* explanation. Reference to different aspects of structural location was detected in the literature: these included the different roles of men and women in *child rearing*, their different rates of *workforce participation* and different degrees of *focus on the family* among men and women. It is not possible here to go into the reasons why people suggested that these differences could account for religious differences between men and women. This is dealt with at some length in our original article.

But in essence the proposition was that if it was not for the fact that women have greater child rearing responsibilities than men, are less likely to be involved in the workforce and have a greater family focus than men, then gender differences in religion would not exist. Presumably therefore, amongst men and women where these structural location differences are not evident there should be little evidence of gender differences in religious orientation.

Because of the data to which we had access (see below) we could not directly test the socialisation explanation, so we narrowed the focus of the research still further. We decided to concentrate on the extent to which structural location factors (child rearing role, workforce participation and family focus) accounted for the greater religiousness of women. This process of progressively narrowing a research topic is typical in social research. We started with a broad topic but eventually narrowed down the topic to a defined and manageable question (pages 28–33). The model that we ended up testing is represented diagramatically in Figure 18.1.

Figure 18.1   Theoretical model to test structural location theory

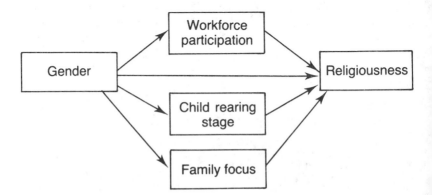

Hypotheses

In order to test each of the three 'paths' in this model at least seven hypotheses can be developed:

1 The differences between the religious orientation of men and women will disappear once the effect of stage in the child rearing cycle is removed.

2 Amongst men and women who have no children and those whose children are grown up there should be fewer religious differences than among men and women still in the active child rearing stage.

3 Women in the workforce will be less religious than women out of the workforce.

4 The religious orientation of women in the workforce will be more similar to males in the workforce than to females out of the workforce.

5 When the effects of gender differences in workforce participation are removed (controlled), gender differences in religious orientation will be reduced markedly.

6 Those who are focused more on the family than work will be more religious than those with less family focus.

7 When the effects of gender differences in family focus are removed, gender differences in religious orientation will be markedly reduced.

Clarifying and operationalising the concepts

We were fortunate enough to have access to data from the Australian Values Study Survey (part of an international study conducted in over 25 countries worldwide) which provided a national probability sample for Australia ($N = 1228$) that had questions which enabled us to tap the main concepts required for this research. Rather than collecting our own data we were able to do a secondary analysis of these data (pages 74–6). Had we been collecting the data we would have collected additional information and asked some of the questions differently but the advantages of a large, representative data set far outweighed these disadvantages.

The variables that were used in the study can be divided into three main groups: measures of the *dependent variable* (religion), measures of the *independent and intervening variables* (gender, workforce participation, stage in child rearing cycle and family focus) and measures of *background variables* including age, country of birth, education, family income and occupation (page 81).

Religion

Religion is a concept that can be divided into a number of dimensions (pages 50, 52). Glock and Stark have distinguished between public and private religious practice, belief, experience and knowledge. Others have added dimensions such as commitment and the salience of religion in people's lives. A number of questions regarding religion were included in the data set. On the basis of the distinctions made by others and on the basis of a correlation matrix of the various religious questions (page 188) we initially distinguished between four dimensions of religiousness and decided to look at gender differences on each of these dimensions. Other dimensions would have been included had the data been available but four dimensions were considered adequate for the purposes of the research. These were:

1   *Church attendance*: The question was 'Apart from weddings, funerals and baptisms, about how often do you attend religious services these days?' The response categories were ordered in such a way that the variable was measured as a nine-category ordinal scale.
2   *Belief*: Respondents were asked to indicate whether or not they believed in: a soul, devil, hell, heaven and sin. Each of the questions simply had yes/no answers and thus can be classified as interval-level variables.
3   *Commitment or salience*: Two questions were used: 'How important is God in your life?' Respondents were asked where, on a scale of one to ten, they would place themselves. The second question asked 'Independently of whether you go to church or not, would you say you are a religious person, not a religious person or a convinced atheist?'
4   *Revelation or experience*: Two questions were asked: 'Next, about being aware of, or influenced by, a presence or power, either God or something else—but different from your everyday self—have you been aware of such a presence or not?' and 'Have you ever felt as though you are very close to a powerful, spiritual force that seemed to lift you out of yourself?' Both these ques-

tions were answered using an ordinal-based scale indicating the frequency with which they had had such experiences.

Independent and intervening variables

A variable to measure stage in the child rearing cycle was constructed from a number of variables in the data set. Using separate questions about marital status, number of members of the household, age of each child and whether or not the children had left home, we developed a composite variable (page 281) with four categories: single, married without children, married with children at home and married with all children having left home. Workforce participation was based on a single question which originally had nine categories. We collapsed it into five categories: working full time, working part time, unemployed, home duties and retired. Because of the small numbers involved we excluded students and those with some other employment status because their small numbers would create problems of statistical reliability (pages 276–81). Family focus was a scale constructed from four questions measuring the relationship between work and family values and was intended to reflect the degree of family focus. These questions asked how important it was to have a job that did not disrupt family life, did not interfere with the spouse's career, did not require having to move home and that the family thought was worthwhile. Each of these questions was answered with either a yes or a no answer. Each dichotomous variable can therefore be treated as though it is interval. The composite variable had a range of 0 to 4 (consisting of four items each scored as either 0 or 1) with 4 indicating the highest level of family focus.

Background variables

To ensure that any observed effects of variables such as workforce participation were not contaminated by other background characteristics associated with workforce participation (e.g. age, living in cities, education, etc.) we introduced these variables so that their effect could be removed (controlled) in the analysis (page 198).

Preparing the variables for analysis

Having selected the variables we intended to use it was necessary to reduce the number of variables to a manageable number and to try to simplify the form in which they were presented so that the analysis and presentation of results could be simplified. The initial preparation of the independent and intervening variables was relatively straightforward and has been described above. It simply involved constructing composite variables or collapsing the categories of extant variables. Further modifications will be discussed shortly.

The preparation of the measures of religion involved a number of steps. Proper unidimensional scales were required to reduce the number of variables to be analysed (Chapter 15): we had to ensure that the items in each scale belonged together, that each variable in each scale was scored in the same direction and we had to construct the scales so that the scoring or number of categories of one variable did not bias the overall scale. We also wanted to transform each scale so that they have the same upper and lower limits so that scores on each of the four dimensions of religiousness could be compared easily.

Producing the scales

The first task was to ensure that each item was *scored in the same direction* (page 277) both so that the scores on the scales could be compared and so that the items within each of the scales could be combined to form the scale in the first place. We first had to make a decision about what a high score was to mean (page 254). We decided that all variables should be coded so that a high score indicated a religious response while a low score represented the less religious response. Because some of the selected items (the five belief questions and the religious person question) were originally coded so that a low code indicated a religious response, they had to be reverse coded (page 277).

The second step was to decide how to treat missing data (pages 273–4, 282–6). Because missing data can lead to an unacceptable loss of cases, especially when constructing scales, we decided to substitute the mean of the variable for missing data. To do this we first had to obtain the mean of each variable and then recode the variable so that the missing data code was recoded to the mean. Thus, if the mean was 1.23 and missing data were coded as -1 then all people who had missing data on that variable would be recoded to have the valid code of 1.23 and would thus be included in the analysis. This approach to handling missing data is relatively straightforward and, because it uses the mean, avoids biasing the results and eliminates problems caused by a loss of cases.

Table 18.1 **Reliability statistics for the three religion scales**

Belief		Commitment		Revelation	
Soul	0.57[a]	Importance	0.67	Experience 1	0.56
Devil	0.71	of God		Experience 2	0.56
Hell	0.72	Religious	0.67		
Heaven	0.67	person			
Sin	0.60				
Alpha	0.84		0.80		0.72

Note: [a] These are corrected item–total correlations. The total scale score against which they are correlated does not include the item in that total.

The third step was to ensure that each of the items in the scale contributed equally to the final scale score. To adjust for variables with different numbers of categories, the scale scores were adjusted by dividing each person's score on each scale item by the standard deviation of that item (we obtained this when we calculated the mean of each item in the above step). In this way each item has an *equal weight* in the final scale (pages 268–71).

The fourth step was to see whether the now-equally weighted items we had selected for each scale actually belonged together empirically. Was the scale *unidimensional* and had the questions been answered *reliably*? We had earlier obtained a correlation matrix (pages 188, 254–5) of all the religion variables, which gave us a rough idea that they would probably form a unidimensional scale: the items we had selected for the scales all correlated quite highly (0.45 or higher). But a reliability analysis is a more rigorous way of ensuring that each scale is unidimensional (page 255). The results of this are reported in Table 18.1 and show that each of the scales was highly reliable (alpha co-efficients) and unidimensional (item–total correlations). For each scale the alpha co-efficient was well above 0.7 and no item–total correlation fell below 0.3. Since the items met the criteria of a good scale we created a summated scale (pages 255–6) by simply adding together the already weighted scores for each item in the scale.

But since each of the scales had a different number of items, the final scale scores of each of the items varied considerably. The measure of church attendance ranged from 0.000 to 2.67, belief ranged from 8.53 (least religious) to 17.06 (most religious), commitment from 2.10 to 8.47 and revelation from 0.78 to 7.03. (The scores have these decimal places because the raw item scores in each scale have been divided by the item's standard deviation.) To make scores on the scales comparable we decided to transform them so that each scale had a minimum of 0 (least religious) to 10 (most religious). This transformation was made using the formula described on page 271 and resulted in four religion variables or scales ranging from 0 to 10.

Finally, because these scales potentially have many categories since there can be any number of possible scale scores between 0 and 10 (e.g. 5.54, 5.55 etc.), it is desirable to have a collapsed version of the scale for crosstabulation analysis (page 278). Because the transformed scale was needed in its detailed form for interval-level analysis it was necessary to create collapsed versions of the scales in addition to the uncollapsed versions. To do this, frequency distributions of the transformed scales were obtained and, using the cumulative percentage column for each scale, the distribution of each scale was collapsed into thirds. Because the items had previously been recoded so that low scores indicated low levels of religiousness, the bottom third of each distribution was categorised as being non-religious, the middle third as moderately religious, the top third as being highly religious (pages 280–1).

Preparing variables for regression analysis

Since we planned to use regression analysis we had to get variables in an appropriate form. This meant that all variables had to be either interval level or dichotomous, but since most of our variables were not initially in this form we had to change their character. The workforce participation, family stage and family focus variables were each converted into sets of dummy variables. Workforce participation was a five-category variable (full time, part time, unemployed, home duties and retired). This variable can be represented by creating four dummy variables and omitting one category — full-time workers (pages 221–4). Family stage was converted into three dummy variables with those who were single and childless being the omitted category, and family focus produced four dummy variables with the most focused being the omitted category.

The background variables also needed to be modified to make them appropriate for regression analysis. Country of birth and the occupation of the head of the household, which were measured at the nominal and ordinal level respectively, were recoded to create two dichotomous variables coded 0 and 1. This necessarily led to a loss of information but was the simplest way of including these variables in the analysis. Education was originally measured in terms of the level achieved rather than as an interval level based on the number of years. One way of coping with this is to estimate the number of years of education that would normally be required to reach a certain highest level. Thus someone who had completed year 10 would normally have completed eleven years of schooling and thus their education code was recoded to reflect this. This can be done for each level of education, thus producing an approximation to an interval scale. A similar process can be applied to grouped numeric data. Family income was collected in income groups such as $0 to $1999, $2000 to $3999 and the like. To convert this to an interval scale in which income was coded in terms of thousands of dollars earned, the midpoint of each category can be used as an average of the income of people in that category. Thus the income category $2000 to $3999, which originally had a code of 2, was recoded to 3 to indicate that on average people in this category would earn $3000. Those in the income category $15 000 to $19 999 would be recoded to a code of 17 to reflect an average income of $17 000. The selection of the midpoint of the category is based on the assumption that precise incomes of people in each category are evenly distributed through the category. The midpoint thus represents the average income of those in that category.

Initial analysis

The central aim of the project was to see if gender differences in religious orientation were open to a sociological explanation. The first step was to establish the extent to which there were gender differences in religion.

The first stage of most analyses is to obtain a picture of how each of the variables is distributed. Not only does this provide a useful picture to guide the analysis, but it often provides crucial information that is required in later analyses. In this case these figures were helpful in part of the regression analyses. These results are summarised in Table 18.2.

The first decision to make was how to analyse the data to answer this question. The problem was that only one of the four scales (belief) was, strictly speaking, an interval-level scale. Although the other scales had the appearance of being interval through the various transformations (and the transformations had assumed that they were measured at the interval level) they were in fact based on questions which were measured at only the ordinal level. Two points should be made at this stage. There is considerable disagreement about how scales such as these ought to be treated. While, strictly

Table 18.2   Variables, definitions and means

Variable	Definition	Means Male	Means Female
Ascribed characteristics			
Age	Years	41.1	38.2
Australian born	1 = yes, 0 = no	0.77[a]	0.78
Lives in urban area	From a low of 0 to high of 1.0	0.80	0.80
Socioeconomic status			
Education	Years	12.20	11.20
Head of household non-manual worker	1 = yes, 0 = no	0.44	0.41
Family income	$1000's	21.50	21.50
Life cycle stage			
Single		0.21	0.13
Married, no children		0.09	0.09
Married, children in home	1 = yes, 0 = no	0.45	0.58
Married, children not in home		0.25	0.20
Workforce participation			
Working, full time		0.76	0.23
Working, part time		0.03	0.22
Unemployed	1 = yes, 0 = no	0.05	0.04
Home duties		0.00	0.48
Retired		0.15	0.03
Family focus			
Very important		0.10	0.15
Fairly important		0.13	0.19
Indifferent	1 = yes, 0 = no	0.27	0.26
Fairly unimportant		0.31	0.27
Very unimportant		0.19	0.13

Note: [a] The figures in this table that are based on dichotomous variables (those coded 0 and 1) will be expressed in decimal points. These can be converted to the percentage of people in that category. Thus the figure of 0.77 for Australian-born males means that 77 per cent of the males in the sample were Australian born.

speaking, they are ordinal, the convention is to treat scales with many categories such as those in this study as being close enough to interval level to justify interval-level statistics. While few people would be prepared to do this with single-item, Likert-style questions, the convention is that scales based on *summated* ordinal questions can safely be treated in this way. The reality is that in most cases the same patterns occur regardless of whether the variable is treated as ordinal or interval (see Table 18.3). Given this, the argument is that interval-level analysis ought to be used since it opens up a whole range of more powerful and sophisticated techniques that allow us to control more readily for the effect of extraneous variables.

Table 18.3 Gender differences in religion using different methods of analysis

Method of analysis	Scale			
	Attendance	Belief	Commitment	Revelation
Kendall's tau[d]	0.10[a**c]	0.14	0.16**	0.12**
Spearman's rho[d]	0.11**	0.17**	0.18**	0.13**
Crosstabs[e]				
Male %[b]	26.3	26.0	23.2	20.8
Female %	35.3	35.8	38.1	30.0
Gamma	0.18**	0.25**	0.29**	0.23**
Comparing means[d]				
Male mean	3.2	5.2	7.1	1.8
Female mean	4.0	6.0	6.2	2.3
Difference (F–M)	0.8**	1.4**	0.9**	0.9**

Notes: [a] Positive co-efficients mean women are more religious than men.
[b] % = Per cent high on scale
[c] ** significant at 0.001 level. Significance test of tau and rho are those designed for these measures, chi square is used for gamma, while F-tests are used for the comparison of means (pages 194–6).
[d] Calculated using uncollapsed scales
[e] Based on trichotomised scales

The data can be analysed in at least three different ways to see whether there are gender differences in religiousness:

1 *Kendall's tau and Spearman's rho*: On the assumption that the scales are ordinal, either Kendall's tau or Spearman's rho provide appropriate measures of correlation between religiousness and gender. They are appropriate because gender is a dichotomous variable and thus can be regarded as being at any level of measurement (page 171), and the scales are at least ordinal level. Since gender is only dichotomous, Kendall's tau is probably more appropriate than Spearman's rho (page 187), but the pattern of the results is the same regardless of which of the two co-efficients are used (see Table 18.3): the statistically significant correlation means that gender differences exist on all the scales with women being more religious than men.

2 *Crosstabulations with gamma*: While treating the scales of religiousness as ordinal, an alternative approach is to crosstabulate the scales with gender and calculate gamma co-efficients as measures of association (page 170). Because crosstabulation results become both unreliable and difficult to interpret if the variables have too many categories, it is necessary to collapse variables with too many values (page 278). Accordingly, each of the scales was trichotomised as described earlier and yielded

gamma co-efficients which showed the same pattern of gender differences as described above (Table 18.3).

3   *Breakdown*: If the scales are treated as interval-level variables it is appropriate to calculate the means of males and females on each of the scales and to estimate whether the means differ from each other (pages 184–7). When this was done (Table 18.3), the same pattern as described above occurred. In other words, regardless of which method was used, exactly the same pattern emerged: women were consistently more religious than men. In all cases the differences were statistically significant: they are highly likely to reflect real patterns in the wider population from which the sample was drawn (pages 189–93).

Testing the explanations

Since the above results show that there is something to explain we can proceed to the next stage of the analysis to test the hypotheses. Again we could adopt various methods, depending on the assumptions made about level of measurement. However, the same pattern of results was obtained regardless of whether we treated the scales as ordinal or interval.

Workforce participation: crosstabulation analysis

One way of looking at the data was to treat the scales as ordinal and to do crosstabulations using the collapsed scales by gender controlling for the effect of workforce participation. Zero and first order partial gammas were obtained (pages 210–11). According to our hypotheses, women who work will be less religious than those not in the workforce and women in the workforce will have levels of religiousness more similar to those of working men than of non-working women. Furthermore, when level of workforce participation is controlled, the gender differences in workforce participation should disappear or at least decline. That is, the zero-order correlation should be significant while the partial correlation will be statistically insignificant. Table 18.4 shows that each of these hypotheses is strongly supported.

That is, the relationship between gender and religion is virtually non-existent when level of workforce participation is controlled. On each of the scales there are significant zero-order relationships indicating that women are more religious than men. The partial gammas, from which the influence of different levels of workforce participation has been removed, show that without this effect there is virtually no difference between the religiousness of men and

Table 18.4   Religious scales by gender controlling for workforce participation (crosstabulation analysis)

Scale	Full time M	F	Home duties M	F	Zero gamma	Partial gamma
	%	%	%	%		
Attendance	25[a]	21	100[c]	38	0.19**[b]	0.01
Belief	27	23	100	43	0.25**	0.05
Commitment	21	20	100	46*	0.29**	−0.02
Revelation	47	43	0	55*	−0.22**	−0.02

Notes: [a] These percentages represent the percentage *high* on these dimensions.
[b] Positive gammas indicate that women on the whole were more religious than men.
[c] Percentages in this column are based on an N of 1 and are therefore totally unreliable.
** Statistically significant at the 0.001 level

women with comparable levels of workforce participation. This is reinforced by looking at the religiousness of men and women in the full-time workforce. There are virtually no differences in the percentages of men and women who are highly religious: if anything, men are slightly more religious than women. The same picture emerges when we compare women who work full time with those engaged in home duties full time: working women are markedly less religious. All of these results support the three hypotheses relating to the effect of workforce participation on gender differences in religiousness.

Workforce participation: multiple regression analysis

The difficulty with this crosstabulation analysis is that we have not controlled for any other variables. For example, we do not know whether the lower religiousness of working women relative to non-working women is because of differences in the age, education and social class profile of the two groups of women. We do not know whether the similarity of working women to men is because of the similarity of their age and education profiles. Ideally, if we are to assess the importance of variables such as workforce participation on gender differences, we should ensure that the comparisons made between the various groups of men and women are comparisons of men and women who are alike in all relevant respects (pages 198–202).

It is very difficult to do this with crosstabulation analysis. The more variables that are controlled at once, the more we confront problems with small sample sizes and statistical reliability. One way around this problem is to use analysis techniques that allow us to control for a whole set or background variables simultaneously without running into the problem of small sample sizes. Multiple regression is such a technique.

We therefore tested our hypotheses by using multiple regression. This enabled us to estimate the scores of people on each of the religious scales after the effects of other variables had been controlled. These scores are those we would expect if people were alike on all the variables that are controlled. Since our interest was in gender differences in religiousness, we did the analysis separately for men and women and then calculated the differences between the male and female estimates of religiosity under various controlled conditions.

Treating each of the scales as interval, our stategy was to estimate the mean score separately for men and women according to their level of workforce participation whilst controlling for the background variables of age, whether Australian born (Aust), whether an urban resident (Urban), occupation of head of household (HHocc) and family income (Faminc). As previously described, a set of four dummy variables was created to reflect the five categories of workforce participation: part-time workers (WrkPT); the unemployed (WrkUEMP): those engaged full time in home duties (WrkHD); and the retired (WrkRTD), with full-time workers being the omitted category.

This was done by using an equation of the following form:

$$\text{Belief score} = a + b_1(\text{Age}) + b_2(\text{Aust}) + b_3(\text{Urban}) + b_4(\text{Educ}) + b_5(\text{HHocc} + b_6(\text{Faminc}) + b_7(\text{WrkPT}) + b_8(\text{WrkUNEMP}) + b_9(\text{WrkHD}) + b_{10}(\text{WrkRTD})$$

Using the multiple regression procedure in SPSSX we were able to calculate the unstandardised regression co-efficients (b figures) for each variable (pages 179–82, 215–17). This procedure was run separately for men and for women, thus yielding separate b figures for men and women. Since the aim was to calculate the mean belief of men and women according to their level of workforce participation, we simply obtained the mean value for each of the variables (Age to Faminc) and multiplied the means by the b value of the appropriate variables. Using the mean of a group provides estimates for groups rather than individuals and is appropriate for a great deal of social science analysis (pages 218–20). Since workforce participation was broken down into a set of dummy variables and full-time workers were the excluded category (page 222), the mean belief score for full-time workers was obtained simply by summing the 'a' value with each of the 'b' values for each variable after they had been multiplied by the mean of the variable. For full-time workers the value of the other workforce participation variables necessarily was 0 (page 223).

The estimate for those who worked part time was obtained by giving the WrkPT variable the value of 1 and multiplying it by the b value for WrkPT and adding this figure to the estimate gained for full-time workers (the omitted category). That is, the b value for WrkPT was simply added to the value obtained for full-time workers. This procedure is illustrated in Figure 18.2 and is worth working through carefully to understand how the regression estimates in the following tables were obtained. This procedure was repeated for each of the categories of workforce participation and for each of the scales. This provided us with separate estimates for men

Figure 18.2 Calculating regression estimates for the belief scale

Variable	Males		Females	
	b	Mean[d]	b	Mean
Age	−0.002[d]	41.1	−0.002	38.2
Aust'n	−0.287	0.77	−0.132	0.78
Urban	−0.373	0.80	0.37	0.80
Education	−0.073	12.1	−0.057	11.2
Occupation	0.357	0.44	0.12	0.41
Family income	−0.025	21.5	−0.02	21.5
Part timers	0.31		0.71	
Unemployed	−0.59		0.80	
Home duties	.[c]		1.55	
Retired	−0.32		0.58	
Constant (a) = 7.34			Constant (a) = 6.96	

Equation for males
Belief score = 7.34 + −0.002(41.1) + −0.287(0.77) + −0.373(0.80)
 + −0.073(12.1) + 0.357(0.44) + −0.025(21.5) + 0.31(WrkPT)
 + −0.59 (WrkUNEMP) + 0.00(WrkHD) + −0.32(WrkRTD)
 = 7.34 + −0.08 + −0.22 + −0.298 + −0.88 + 0.157 + −0.537
 + 0.31(WrkPT) + −0.59(WrkUNEMP) + 0.00(WrkHD)
 + −0.32(WrkRTD)

For male full-time workers (the omitted category) we estimate that:

Belief score = 7.34 + 0.002(41.1) + −0.287(0.77) + −0.373(0.80)
 + −0.073(12.1) + 0.357(0.44) + −0.025(21.5)
 = 5.48

Figure 18.2 Calculating regression estimates for the belief scale (Cont'd)

For the other categories of workforce participation we simply add the estimates for b co-efficients for these groups to the estimate obtained using the omitted category (full-time workers) and get the following:

Full-timers		= 5.48
Part-timers	5.48 +	0.31	= 5.79
Unemployed	5.48 +	−0.59	= 4.89
Home duties	5.48 +	0.00	= 5.48
Retired	5.48 +	−0.32	= 5.16

Equation for females
Belief score = 6.96 + −0.002(38.2) + −0.132(0.78) + 0.371(0.80) + −0.057(11.2)
+ 0.120(0.41) + −0.020(21.5) + 0.71(WrkPT) + 0.80(WrkUNEMP) +
1.55(WrkHD) + 0.58(WrkRTD)
= 6.96 + −0.076 + −0.103 + 0.297 + −0.638 + 0.049 + −0.43
+ 0.71(WrkPT) + 0.80(WrkUNEMP) + 1.55(WrkHD) + 0.72(WrkRTD)

For female full-time workers (the omitted category) we estimate that:

Belief score = 6.96 + −0.002(38.2) + −0.132(0.78) + 0.371(0.80) + −0.057(11.2)
+ 0.120(0.41) + −0.020(21.5)
= 6.06

For the other categories of workforce participation we simply add the estimates for b co-efficients for these groups and get the following:

Full-timers		= 6.06
Part-timers	6.06 + 0.71	= 6.77
Unemployed	6.06 + 0.80	= 6.86
Home duties	6.06 + 1.55	= 7.61
Retired	6.06 + 0.72	= 6.78

To estimate the *differences* between the belief estimates of males and females in the various workforce participation categories we simply subtract the male scores from the female scores.

	Female	Male	Difference
Full-timers	6.06	5.48	0.58
Part-timers	6.77	5.79	0.98
Unemployed	6.86	4.89	1.97
Home duties	7.61	5.79	.[c]
Retired	6.78	5.16	1.62

Notes: [a] The b values in this example are approximations only since at the time of writing I did not have access to the results from the weighted sample that we used in our paper. They represent the *patterns* in the weighted sample but the precise figures are estimates only. They are used here to illustrate the method of calculation rather than to provide precise figures.
[b] Since these workforce participation variables are dummy variables it is not their mean that is relevant for the calculation of regression estimates. Instead the b co-efficient would be multiplied by 1 to arrive at its contribution when we are trying to estimate the religious belief of people in that category of workforce participation.
[c] Because of too few N it was not possible to calculate a figure for males involved in full-time home duties.
[d] These are the same as in Table 18.2.

Table 18.5 Workforce participation and religious orientation: differences in regression estimates for men and women

Workforce participation		Church attendance	Scale			
			Belief	Commitment	Revelation	(Mean)
Working full time	(1)	−0.1	0.6	0.2	0.2	(0.2)
Working part time	(2)	1.5	1.0	1.3	−0.5	(0.8)
Home duties	(3)	na	na	na	na	
Unemployed	(4)	1.2	2.0	1.8	1.2	(1.6)
Retired	(5)	−0.1	1.6	0.0	1.6	(0.7)
(Mean)	(6)	(0.8)	(1.4)	(0.9)	(0.5)	(0.9)

Notes: Positive values indicate that women are more religious than men.
All religious scales are scored 0 to 10.
The regression estimates were calculated by evaluating the regression estimates at the mean (see above).

and women on each of the scales controlling for the relevant set of background variables. To see whether there were differences between the estimates for men and women in each of the workforce participation categories we simply subtracted the male estimate from the female estimate and obtained the values in Table 18.5. Positive values indicated that women would have higher levels of religiousness.

Similar conclusions can be drawn from this table as from the crosstabulation analysis. The bottom row (6) indicates the overall differences in the means of men and women regardless of their level of workforce participation. Thus on a 0 to 10 scale of church attendance there was a difference of 0.8 of a point in the average for males and females. The first row indicates the difference amongst men and women who work full time. For each of the scales these values are very low and much lower than the overall men/women differences (see Table 18.3).

Another hypothesis developed to test the workforce participation argument was that women in the workforce will be less religious than those engaged in full-time home duties. Although the figures in Table 18.5 did not allow us to estimate this, the original regression estimates obtained from the analysis described above did. The means for women who worked full time were lower on each of the scales than for women engaged in home duties. On all four scales, full-time female workers had an average score of 4.4 compared with 5.2 for those engaged in home duties—a difference of 0.8 points, which is much more than the average difference between men and women who worked full time (0.2 points—see Table 18.5).

Table 18.6   Stage in child rearing cycle by religious orientation: differences in regression estimates for men and women

Family stage	Church attendance	Belief	Commitment	Revelation	(Mean)
		Scale			
Single	(1) 1.5	2.0	0.8	0.8	(1.3)
Married, no children	(2) 0.6	1.2	0.3	0.9	(0.8)
Married, children in home	(3) 0.7	1.3	1.0	0.5	(0.9)
Married, children left home	(4) 0.1	0.6	0.5	−0.1	(0.3)
(Mean)	(5) (0.8)	(0.9)	(0.9)	(0.5)	(0.8)

Stage in the family life cycle: multiple regression analysis

Because of the advantages of regression analysis and the fact that it yields a similar picture to the crosstabulation analysis it is not necessary to report further results from the crosstabulations.

To examine the stage in the family life cycle model we conducted a similar regression analysis to that described above. The only difference was that instead of using the four dummy variables for workforce participation we used three dummy variables for family stage with single people being the omitted category.

The results in Table 18.6 were obtained in this way. What they show is that stage in the family life cycle does not generally affect the extent of religious differences between men and women. The hypothesis that gender differences will be smaller among men and women who no longer have child rearing responsibilities was not supported. The figures in row 3 represent those still rearing children and show that the gender differences are much the same for other people as for those whose children have left home. The extent of gender differences declines over the life course rather than being related to the presence or absence of children.

Family focus: multiple regression analysis

The same type of regression analysis was undertaken to examine the extent to which the different levels of family focus among men and women might account for their different levels of religiousness. Dummy variables were created for the family focus scale which had a range of 0 through 4. A comparison of the figures in Table 18.7 with those in Table 18.3, where no variables are controlled, shows a

Table 18.7 Family focus and work by religious orientation: differences in regression estimates for men and women

Family focus		Church attendance	Scale			
			Belief	Commitment	Revelation	(Mean)
Very unimportant	(1)	0.8	2.0	0.8	0.3	(1.0)
Fairly unimportant	(2)	0.9	1.1	0.8	0.5	(0.8)
Indifferent	(3)	0.6	0.9	0.2	0.0	(0.4)
Fairly important	(4)	0.8	1.4	0.9	0.4	(0.9)
Very important	(5)	0.4	1.8	1.8	0.5	(0.9)
(Mean)	(6)	(0.8)	(0.9)	(1.3)	(0.2)	(0.8)

very similar pattern in both tables in relation to family focus. This means that the variables which have been controlled in Table 18.7 are not responsible for the gender differences observed in Table 18.3. The family focus hypothesis therefore was not supported.

So far our analysis, which was designed to test the extent to which gender differences in religious orientation are due to structural location factors, has shown that one structural location variable— workforce participation—is responsible for virtually all the gender differences. The other two were relatively unimportant.

Decomposing the gender gap

So far we have examined the initial (zero-order) gender gap and tested the extent to which each of the three structural location explanations, *on its own*, helps explain the gender differences. But each of these explanations is not entirely independent of the other. Workforce participation of women is tied to stage in the child rearing cycle and the degree of family focus is linked with both workforce participation and child rearing stage. To work out how important these factors are relative to each other (that is independent of their joint relationship) is is desirable to look at the effect of each, controlling for the effect of the other variables. This also enables us to work out which of the structural explanations has the greatest independent impact on religious orientation (pages 215–17). We need a way of evaluating their relative importance.

In addition, the regression estimates in the three tables above do not provide us with one easy-to-interpret figure to estimate how much overall effect these variables have on gender differences. The zero-order and partial gammas reported earlier provided a simple way of comparing the uncontrolled relationship with that when the structural variables are controlled (pages 210–11). A similar thing can be accomplished with regression analysis. To do this we had to solve a *series* of regression equations. This was accomplished by obtaining a bivariate regression figure for the relationship between gender and a religious scale. This figure was the same as the difference between the means for men and women on that scale (Table 18.2) and will not have the effects of any variables controlled.

Next the variables representing each of the *sets* of independent variables were entered into the regression equation in blocks. Thus all the ascribed characteristics (age, country of birth and urban residence) were entered as a block followed by the socioeconomic variables (education, occupation and family income). Then the set of dummy variables representing stage in the family life cycle were entered as a block followed by the labour force participation dummy variables and then the family focus variables. The order in which these blocks of variables were entered reflected our assumptions about causal order. We assumed that ascribed characteristics came before socioeconomic status which precedes family stage which itself influences workforce participation and in turn affects the level of family focus.

This procedure can be illustrated with church attendance.

Equation 1

The first regression equation involved only the gender and church attendance variables and produced a 'b' figure of 0.8 which represents 0.8 points on the 0 to 10 scale of church attendance. The value of 0.8 is the unstandardised regression co-efficient for the zero-order relationship between gender and church attendance. Since gender was coded 0 for men and 1 for women, a positive value indicates that women are more regular attenders than men.

Equation 2

In the second equation we forced in the block of variables designed to measure ascribed characteristics. To ascertain the extent to which the original value of 0.8 was due to the effect of the ascribed characteristics we simply compared the 'b' co-efficient for gender in the first equation with the 'b' co-efficient for gender in the second. Any difference between the two represents the extent to which the original 'b' co-efficient of 0.8 was due to the effect of ascribed characteristics. In this case the value of b for gender in the second equation was 0.8—exactly the same as in the first equation when

Table 18.8 **Decomposing the gender gap in religious orientation**

	Church attendance	Belief	Commitment	Revelation
1 Total effect (lines 2 + 3)	0.8	1.4	0.9	0.5
2 Direct effect	0.3	0.7	0.4	0.1
3 Indirect effect (lines				
(a) + (b) + (c) + (d) + (e)	0.5	0.7	0.5	0.4
(a) Ascribed characteristics	0.0	0.0	0.1	0.0
(b) Socioeconomic status	0.1	0.1	0.0	0.0
(c) Life stage	−0.1	−0.1	−0.1	0.0
(d) Workforce participation	−0.5	−0.6	−0.5	−0.6
(e) Family focus	0.0	−0.0	0.0	0.0

the effects of ascribed characteristics were not included. This means that none of the original, overall relationship was due to differences in the ascribed characteristics of men and women in the sample. This is indicated by the value of 0 in column 1 row 3(a) of Table 18.8.

Equation 3

In this equation we added the block of variables designed to measure socioeconomic status in addition to those already entered in equations 1 and 2. We compared the 'b' co-efficient for gender with that obtained in equation 2. Any change represents the effect of socioeconomic status on the original relationship between gender and church attendance with the effects of ascribed characteristics removed. In this case the 'b' value for gender was 0.9 which yields a difference value of 0.1 as indicated in column 1 of Table 18.8. That is, if it were not for socioeconomic status differences between men and women in the sample, the initial gender difference would have been slightly greater.

Equation 4

Next we added the dummy variables for stage in the family life cycle to those added in the previous equation. Again the focus is on the b value for gender and how it changes from the previous value. We are not interested in the b values of the variables entered in this step. In this case the b value for gender was 0.8, indicating that the effect of life-cycle stage to the overall relationship was only 0.1 points.

Equation 5

Here we added the dummy variables for workforce participation as a block. The b value for gender dropped to 0.3 indicating that of the previous 0.8 points difference 0.5 was due to gender differences in workforce participation. If it was not for these differences the original gender difference would have been only 0.3 points.

Equation 6

Finally we added the variables for family focus and found that the b value of 0.3 for gender was the same as in the previous equation, indicating that once other variables were controlled, different levels of family focus did not contribute anything to the overall gender differences.

This procedure enabled us to work out how much of the overall gender difference in church attendance is due to various sets of factors and how much remained after these effects were removed. The logic is akin to comparing zero-order correlations with first, second and third-order partial co-efficients and interpreting the drop in the co-efficient as being due to the effect of the variable that is being controlled. The remaining correlation is seen to be due to the direct effects of the original two variables (pages 210–11). Using this procedure we can calculate how much of the original (total) effect is due to the influence of the control variables (indirect effect) and how much remains (direct effect).

The step-by-step procedure also enables us to work out how much of the indirect effect is due to the influence of the various control variables. All that we have to do is to compare the size of the co-efficients. The meanings of the terms total, direct and indirect effect are outlined on page 227 in the discussion of path analysis, although the method of arriving at the figures is different to the method described here.

In this case we can see that the bulk of the original total effect of gender on church attendance is indirect. Of the indirect effect, by far the most important factor was gender differences in workforce participation. Other variables had virtually no effect on the gender difference in church attendance.

Exactly the same sort of analysis was conducted for each of the other indices of religion. Since each of the scales had been converted to a scale ranging from 0 to 10 we were able to compare the effects of gender on each of the scales even though unstandardised co-efficients were used (page 216). These results are presented in Table 18.8. For each of the four dimensions of religiousness at least half of the original gender gap disappeared once the effects of these structural location variables were removed (compare line 1 with line 2). On each of the scales workforce participation was responsible for the bulk of the initial effect (line 3(d)), while the other variables had virtually no effect.

Discussion

There were many other things that we could have looked at. We could have conducted further analyses to locate the groups amongst which gender differences in religion are greatest (e.g. among which age groups, which denominations and so forth) but such analysis would have diverted us from our main goal. The analysis outlined above was directed to answering specific questions.

Once the results have been analysed and described it is useful to do a number of things.

Summarise relevant results

Having obtained results that bear directly on the original hypotheses it is valuable to briefly summarise the main findings insofar as they relate to hypotheses and theory. In this case three main points could be made.

1 Gender differences in religiousness exist across at least four dimensions of religious orientation.
2 A large amount of these differences can be accounted for in terms of gender differences in structural location.
3 Of the three structural location factors examined, only one was important—gender differences in levels of workforce participation. If it was not for the fact that women are less likely than men to be in the full-time workforce, then religious differences would be either non-existent or much less pronounced than they currently are.

Ex post facto *explanations for further examination*

The results will not always be quite what were anticipated. Some might be in accord with expectations while others might be more surprising. It is useful to suggest possible explanations for the observed patterns. In this case we have identified that workforce participation is an important explanatory variable, but it is not clear precisely *why* this is so. Some possible explanations might be offered that could be pursued in further research using appropriately collected data. It is possible that working *displaces* the need for religion: that it provides activities, interests, friendships, meaning and identity that some people otherwise might gain from religion. The greater religious similarity of working men and women might be due to *conformity* pressures in the workplace that reduce the religion of women to that of men. Alternatively the greater religiousness of women out of the workforce might be due to a greater sense of *deprivation* among those not participating in an activity that is valued by society thus encouraging a religious response as a way of relieving this feeling. Whatever the explanation might be, it is worthwhile speculating about some possibilities that other people might pursue in the future.

Implications

The results can have both theoretical and practical implications and these are worth spelling out briefly in the discussion section of a report.

In this case the results have implications for important sociological questions and *theories* in areas such as value formation, attitude change, gender differences and for secularisation theories. These should be spelt out in the final part of the paper.

Results can also have important *policy implications* and careful thought should be given to these. These results should be of direct relevance to church policy makers. Because of the increasing involvement of women in the workforce, the church can anticipate a decline of women in the church.

Finally, suggestions for *future research* that flow from the current research are always desirable. Is the basis of gender differences in religion applicable to other gender-based value differences (e.g. does it also account for political differences, differences in attitudes to war, sexual morality and the like)? Suggestions for more detailed research with a different design may be warranted. A longitudinal study of women who return to the workforce might help clarify whether it is workforce participation that actually produces religious change and, if so, clarify the processes and reasons. Suggestions for future research with a different research design, alternative data collection techniques and different types of sample are often appropriate.

Summary

In this chapter I have shown how we have moved from a broad research topic to a much narrower and more manageable question that has been placed within a theoretical context. The concepts have been operationalised within the limits imposed by the available data. The number of variables have been reduced by creating reliable, unidimensional, equal-weight scales all ranging from 0 through 10 to enable easy comparison across scales. Variables were modified by recoding, combining information from various questions and creating dummy variables to facilitate the later analysis.

A range of analysis techniques were employed. The first step was to obtain the distributions and summary statisitics on all the final variables. A range of methods of bivariate analysis were employed on the basis of different assumptions about the level of measurement of the variables but all showed exactly the same pattern in the data. The same was done with the initial multivariate analysis in which the influence of other key variables was controlled. This showed that, regardless of the assumptions about whether the indices of religion were ordinal or interval, the same substantive patterns emerged. Because of this we felt confident in treating the scales as being appropriate for interval-level analysis and employed a variety of more complex multiple regression procedures.

The final point to make is that these more complex methods, while very helpful in helping us draw firmer conclusions because they enable us to control for the effects of many variables simultaneously, and to easily decompose the zero-order relationship into its component parts, are not indispensible. Analysis can be undertaken at many different levels. In this case similar substantive conclusions would have been drawn had we only done the first-order crosstabulation analysis. The more complex procedures improve the analysis and our confidence in the final results and can help eliminate alternative explanations of the initial results. The aim should be to try to learn to use these more powerful methods. But in the meantime a lot can be accomplished with simpler methods and careful, systematic thinking.

19 Ethics in survey research

Any survey will be shaped by three broad sets of considerations: technical, practical and ethical. Technical considerations involve ensuring that matters such as sample design, questionnaire construction, scale development and the like are as rigorous as possible. Practical considerations mean that the survey design must take account of realities such as budgets, deadlines and the purpose of the research (e.g. student project, PhD thesis, government report). Ethical considerations must also shape the final design of a survey. These issues are the concern of this chapter.

Ideally a survey will be technically correct, practically efficient and ethically sound. In reality, however, these matters frequently conflict and require careful balancing. We can design a technically sophisticated and feasible project but it may need to be changed so that it is ethically sound. For example, we could devise ways of obtaining close to 100 per cent response rates by compelling people to participate or by giving the impression that participation was compulsory. But such compulsion would encounter ethical issues such as invasion of privacy, and run counter to societal norms regarding voluntary participation. Participation in surveys might be higher if we obscured the purposes of the research but this raises issues of honesty and compromises principles of informed consent.

There are two broad approaches to making ethical decisions about research. One is to establish a *set of rules* and follow these regardless of the consequences for the research (Kimmel, 1988: 46). For example, you might adopt the rule that you should tell the truth regardless of the consequences or that you will only collect information from or about people with their fully informed consent. However, following such rules rigidly will mean that you cannot conduct a lot of research or, if you do, the results will be so contaminated that they would be of little value. For example, suppose you adopt the rule that people should be fully informed about the purpose of research before they participate. This sounds fine but a detailed explanation of these purposes can distort the way people answer questions. If you explain that you are exploring the hypothesis that people with low levels of education are more prejudiced and authoritarian than those with high levels of education it is highly probable that this will affect the way people answer the questions and thus invalidate the scientific merit of the survey. Furthermore, if you rigidly keep to the rule that you should not collect information without a person's informed consent this may prevent you from asking a person for any information about, say, other family members (a common occurrence in surveys) without the consent of those other family members.

Another way of making ethical decisions in research is to follow ethical guidelines but to use judgment far more than the rule based approach would allow. Using this approach you would take account of the *consequences* of a particular course of action and judge whether the potential benefits of the research outweighed the risks to the participants.

While using your judgment might be more realistic than the rule based approach it does have its problems. As a researcher you are an interested party who has a certain self interest in seeing the research completed. In these circumstances it is easy to develop justifications whereby you believe that any short-term harm to study participants is outweighed by possible long-term benefit to society at large. No doubt some of the more outrageous misuse of human subjects in medical research have been justified in these terms. One can always justify all sorts of dubious research by anticipating *potential* long-term benefits which in reality are never realised.

Another problem is that the assessment of costs to the participants and the benefits to society are subjective decisions based on the researcher's own moral position of what is good or bad and what is important or unimportant. Our own beliefs or prejudices about the relative importance of some people can also unintentionally influence the way we judge the harm to certain people. Medical and social research is full of examples where people from disadvantaged groups (e.g. black Americans, homosexuals, working class gang members) have been afforded a lower level of privacy or care than would have been acceptable had the participants been more socially advantaged.

I am not going to prescribe a set of ethical rules to be followed when conducting surveys. I do not believe that this is either possible or helpful. Since you will conduct research in different settings and use different methods you will need to make judgments based on the situation. The most useful thing I can do is to highlight the key issues so that you can anticipate these and develop solutions ahead of time. I can outline some principles and dilemmas, but as a researcher you will need to provide the solutions in particular research settings.

As researchers, our ethical responsibilities extend to various types of people—all of whom might be affected by the research itself or by the research results. Among these are:

1   the research participants
2   your profession and professional colleagues
3   sponsors and funders of the research

Research participants

Voluntary participation

This principle means that people should not be required to participate in a survey study. Even though surveys do not involve physical risks to people that participation in medical experiments might, we are nevertheless invading people's privacy and will normally be seeking personal information and private views. At the very least we are taking up their time.

Voluntary participation, however, conflicts with the methodological principle of representative sampling. Given the choice certain types of people (e.g. those with lower levels of education, from non-English-speaking backgrounds) are more likely than others to decline to participate in surveys and can produce biased samples. However, compulsory participation in surveys is not the solution. Although compulsion might minimise bias it will undermine the quality of the answers respondents provide. Since there are ways of statistically adjusting for known sample biases it is best to maximise the quality of responses and do all we reasonably can to encourage voluntary participation.

Some unscrupulous survey researchers have pretended that participation is compulsory. By posing as government officials they have tried to give the impression that participation is required. Others simply neglect to tell people that participation is voluntary and hope that respondents will assume that they are required to participate.

One way of ensuring that participants understand that participation is voluntary is to tell them explicitly. For example, at the beginning of a questionnaire respondents can be told:

> 'Although your participation in this interview will be greatly valued, you are not required to participate. You can stop at any point or choose not to answer any particular question. Just let the interviewer know.'

There are a number of difficulties when applying the principle of voluntary participation. One of these is whether the principle should be different for governments and their agencies. Governments often *require by law* that citizens participate in certain surveys. In some countries citizens are required to participate in household expenditure surveys (presumably because of the bias that would be introduced by non response if participation was voluntary) and participation in the national census is typically compulsory.

A further difficulty arises from the blurred boundaries between research and bureaucratic form filling. At what point does the collection of information for official records become research? Many universities need to have a clear picture of where their student population comes from, what their educational background is and so forth. Universities find this information helpful for the purpose of planning and in dealing with access and equity issues and policies. To obtain this valuable information they often *require* students to complete a questionnaire when they enrol. Their enrolment is not considered complete until the questionnaire is returned with their enrolment form. In the cases of which I am aware students certainly do not believe that they have any choice. Is this research or is it something else? Is participation voluntary or not?

The universities will argue that although participation is not voluntary the confidentiality with which the results are handled means that the benefits of the information outweighs the negligible risks to the participants. This is probably true but it highlights the blurred line between compulsory form filling and research and the fact that research data are frequently collected in the guise of record keeping, thus ignoring the principle of voluntary participation.

The context in which surveys take place can give the impression that participation is required. Surveys conducted in first year psychology classes by the lecturer or among social welfare recipients by welfare officials introduce a power differential that can make people feel obliged to participate, either from a concern about the consequences of non-participation or simply out of deference. In situations where there is a 'captive audience' the researcher needs to be especially careful to stress that participation is truly voluntary.

Researchers cannot always ensure that participation by all people is voluntary. Some questionnaires involve the 'indirect participation' of people. For example, a questionnaire that asks about the income, education and occupation of a person's parents or partner can be an invasion of the privacy of those people and means that these people are 'participating' involuntarily. A survey in which children are asked about parental behaviour is clearly one in which the parents are 'involuntary participants'.

Informed consent

Informed consent is a close cousin of voluntary participation. Voluntary participation implies that participants make a choice, and true choice requires accurate information if it is to be truly voluntary.

Typically the requirement of informed consent in a questionnaire or interview survey means that participants are informed about:

1   The purpose of the study and its basic procedures.
2   An outline of any reasonably foreseeable risks, embarrassment or discomfort (e.g. some questions may deal with very private or sensitive matters).
3   A description of the likely benefits of the study.
4   A description of how the respondent was selected for the study.
5   An offer to answer any questions.
6   A statement that participation is voluntary and that the respondent is free to withdraw at any time or to decline to answer any particular question.
7   The identity of the researcher and the sponsor.
8   Some information about the way in which the data and conclusions might be put.

While the issue of informed consent seems entirely reasonable and desirable it is not entirely straightforward. *How much* information should we provide before a participant can be considered informed? How *fully* informed should participants be? What does it mean to be informed? Providing more information does not mean that people will be any better informed. Simply providing detailed descriptions of the study does not mean that respondents will be any more enlightened as a result. Indeed, detailed technical information may confuse, distract and overwhelm rather than inform. Too much detail may discourage participation—not because people are better informed but because they are bored to distraction.

Furthermore, providing details about the study—especially detailed information about the study design, the hypotheses and theories we are testing—can distort the way people answer questions and undermine the validity of the findings.

One solution is to provide basic information and to offer to answer further questions. While few people might ask questions, we should be prepared to answer them. If the information might distort the way people answer questions we can tactfully explain that this is a concern and offer to deal with the questions *after* the interview or questionnaire has been completed. In some psychological research in particular, participants are deliberately deceived since accurate knowledge would invalidate the study. Where this is warranted it is critical that participants be fully debriefed after the study.

This raises the question of when consent should be obtained. Most ethics committees[1] require that consent is obtained *before* participation.

However, in the case of surveys at least, participants have little idea as to what they are really agreeing to until they have seen the actual questions. There is a good case for arguing that people can really only provide *informed* consent *after* they have completed the questionnaire or interview.

How should informed consent be demonstrated? A common way is to ask participants to sign a written informed consent form. However, a signed informed consent form is not always necessary nor possible. For example, it would be extremely difficult to obtain a signed informed consent form for a telephone interview. A postal survey could ask that a signed consent form be returned with the questionnaire but it seems rather unnecessary. In the case of both telephone and postal surveys it is important that a record is kept of the information provided to participants, but it seems reasonable to assume that continuing with the telephone interview or returning the postal questionnaire demonstrates consent.

There are problems with asking people to sign consent forms. Not only does it formalise the interview unduly and lead to a loss of rapport, it can also make some people more suspicious about the research. I recall one survey of refugees from a country racked by civil war where there was a great deal of fear for the fate of relatives back home. When they were asked to sign a form in writing they were terrified and simply refused to participate further. This was not because they were any more informed about the content of the survey but because they feared signing the form—any form. The same problem can be anticipated for many minority groups or for surveys involving sensitive issues.

Research sheds some light on the effect of informed consent on participation in social surveys. Singer (1978) found that detailed, truthful information provided before completing questionnaires had little effect on the response rate overall or to particular questions. Singer and Frankel (1982) found a similar pattern with telephone surveys. However, Singer has found that when participants were asked for *signed* consent the response rate dropped by about 7 per cent regardless of whether signatures were requested before or after interviews.

Other issues complicate the matter of informed consent. Should consent include an agreement regarding the uses to which the data might be put? Some people would prefer not to participate in a study if they were aware of the conclusions that might be drawn or the purposes to which it might be put. For example, welfare recipients might prefer to avoid participating in surveys that could lead to the reduction of welfare payments. Even if researchers explain the purposes of their own research this does not deal with the fact that survey data are frequently deposited in data archives and made available to other researchers for secondary analysis. In such cases it is not possible for the primary researcher to anticipate the purposes to which the data might be put.

Finally, *who* should give consent? In research of young children, intellectually disabled and others who may not be in a position to fully understand the implications of participating in a survey, who should give permission? Participation still ought to be voluntary but consent may need to be obtained from other people as well as the participant. The consent of parents and guardians should be sought and, in the case of students, the consent of the school should also be sought.

No harm to participants

In some experimental studies participants are potentially exposed to harm because of the intervention of researchers. For example, in medical experiments in which new drugs are trialed, participants are exposed to danger. In psychological experiments participants might be exposed to stimuli or be induced to behave in ways that they later regret and find distressing.[2]

The dangers are less evident in surveys. Since survey researchers rely on natural variation in samples rather than induced variation, and rely on natural change over time rather than deliberately creating change, there is little danger that surveys will create the harm that experimental studies can. This is not to say that surveys are without their dangers. The questions that survey researchers ask—such as those about family relationships, sexual behaviour, unpopular attitudes—can distress and embarrass respondents and may create psychological harm.

Simply selecting a person for a survey can be harmful. I recall one study of domestic violence victims in which the researcher wanted to know why women who issued complaints to the police about a violent husband later withdrew their complaint. The study was well intentioned and was designed to help women facing domestic violence. Names of women who withdrew complaints were obtained properly through the Magistrate's Courts where such complaints were lodged as public documents. Questionnaires were then sent to these women. A number of women were extremely distressed by the simple fact that they had been selected for the survey. They had mistakenly believed that their complaint was secret and they were hurt and humiliated by the fact that the researcher knew their name.

Where surveys are administered through third parties (e.g. to students via their teacher; to employees through their supervisor) these third parties must not see the responses before the questionnaires are returned to the researcher. In one study I conducted of religious attitudes among school students the questionnaires were returned in sealed envelopes to the school office. When I collected the questionnaires from one Catholic school I discovered that the sealed envelopes had been opened. I never knew who opened them or whether the individuals who completed particular questionnaires were identifiable, but the potential of this breach of confidentiality is clear. In many universities where students are now required to complete subject evaluation questionnaires, special care is required to ensure that lecturers do not see individual students' responses. To ensure this, completed questionnaires are placed in sealed envelopes and collected by people other than the lecturer.

Anonymity and confidentiality

The most obvious way in which participants can be harmed in survey research is if the confidentiality of responses is not honoured. Typically, survey participants are assured that their answers will either be anonymous or confidential. As part of the process of obtaining informed consent it should be clear to respondents how their responses will be treated. Sometimes researchers fail to distinguish between anonymity and confidentiality and can thus inadvertently mislead respondents.

Anonymity means that the researcher will not and cannot identify the respondent. Confidentiality simply means that the researcher can match names with responses but ensures that no one else will have access to them.

Postal surveys that use identification numbers are not anonymous. Face to face interviews rarely are anonymous. Telephone surveys may or may not be anonymous—it depends on the method of obtaining telephone numbers. If the researcher has contacted a person using random digit dialling the interview is probably anonymous.

It is the *perception* rather than the *fact* of anonymity that is important. If respondents are likely to suspect your assurances of anonymity it is better to assure them of the confidentiality rather than the anonymity. This must be a matter of judgment. On sensitive matters such as drug use and sexual behaviour people tend to respond differently depending on whether anonymity or confidentiality are assured. On more innocuous topics, assurances of anonymity rather than confidentiality do not make any difference.

There are three main reasons for assuring confidentiality. The first is to improve the quality and honesty of responses, especially on sensitive issues. The second is to encourage participation in the study and thus to improve the representativeness of the sample. Finally, we offer confidentiality to protect a person's privacy.

Do not promise confidentiality unless you can keep the promise. It is inappropriate to promise confidentiality when you know that other people outside the study will have access to the information and can identify the respondents. You can face very difficult ethical dilemmas. Sometimes, after a promise of confidentiality is given, you might discover information that you feel requires action but which would betray the promise of confidentiality. For example, in a study of school children you might learn the identity of a drug pusher or a teacher who is sexually molesting students. In a study of prisoners you might learn of plans for an escape or the identity of a person who murdered an inmate. In such cases you face the problem of your promise of confidentiality against the harm caused to others by respecting that promise. Make sure that you do not make unrealistic promises of confidentiality.

When promising confidentiality make sure that you are aware of the legal situation. Depending on the context in which data are collected it may be subject to Freedom of Information legislation. In many countries research data collected with the guarantee of confidentiality do not enjoy legal privilege and can be subpoenaed by courts. In this context it is important to clarify your rights to maintain the confidentiality of data when working in government agencies or under contracts. Contracts frequently make explicit statements about the ownership of data and it is important to ensure that these provisions do not compromise your undertakings regarding confidentiality.

There are a number of steps that you can take to protect the confidentiality of data. As mentioned earlier, it is imperative to guard against 'third party data collectors' (e.g. teachers, supervisors etc) who might have access to the completed questionnaires before they are returned to you. Other people working in a research team, including those who code and enter the data, must be made aware of their ethical responsibilities in this regard.

Once data are collected there are two broad strategies to ensure that confidentiality is guarded. The first is to separate identifying information from a respondent's answers. This can be done by providing cases with ID numbers and having a separate file in which these ID numbers are linked with the person's name. In many cases you will not need to keep any record of the person's name at all. If you do not need to follow up respondents after they have returned their questionnaire you can simply give each person an ID and destroy any identifying personal data (name and address). If follow up is required then a separate file can be created in which the ID number is attached to personal data. Access to this file can be tightly restricted so as to avoid its misuse. Standard procedures for limiting access to computer files (passwords on files, encryption etc) should make these data extremely secure.

Another danger to confidentiality arises when data come from a particular locality, group or organisation. For example, a census of a small township could be used in such a way as to breach confidentiality. If unit record data (i.e. data with a separate record for each case) for such a census were made available and the particular town was identified it would be a simple matter to identify particular people and learn how they answered questions in the census. If the town had one doctor and the census data indicated people's occupations it would be easy to locate the doctor and identify that person's responses. Other people in small sub-groups in known localities can be identified by a set of crosstabulations. For example, there may be twenty teachers in the town but because we also know the age, gender, marital status, and educational qualifications of people it would not be difficult to identify individuals who had a unique set of these characteristics (e.g. female teacher, aged 35, married, with two children and holding a Bachelor of Science degree).

There are a number of ways of minimising breaches of confidentiality when releasing data. One is to restrict the release of unit record data and to ensure that where these data are released people sign undertakings to respect the confidentiality of individuals. Another technique is to remove information that could help with such identification. For example, when census authorities release any unit record data, detailed locality identifiers are removed so that it is not possible to identify where any individual comes from. A related approach is to recode variables to remove very detailed codes (e.g. exact occupation, precise age, exact country of birth, precise education qualification) and to place individuals into broad groups thus making it almost impossible to obtain highly specific information about any case. In some cases—especially in the release of tabular data from the census rather than in the release of unit record data—cells with fewer than twenty cases are randomly assigned a cell frequency in order to make it impossible to reliably identify individuals via a complex crosstabulation.

Colleagues and profession

With the increasing commercialisation of research it is important to recognise the effects of what we, as individuals, do and to reflect on the effect that this has on other researchers and on their capacity to make credible contributions to social science understanding. If we perform our research role poorly it is not just we who suffer but the whole discipline of which we are members. We can undermine the capacity of other researchers to make a contribution to debates in which social scientists ought to be involved. If we claim greater expertise than we possess, if we underanalyse or misinterpret data, we bring the discipline and our fellow professionals into disrepute.

It is critical that we resist the temptation to claim greater expertise than we possess. This is not easy. Jobs are scarce and in a job market where employers can call the shots employers frequently ask for unrealistic skills and thus invite applicants to misrepresent their expertise. A great deal of research is now done under contract where researchers have to tender competitively to win the work. I have seen many situations in which social researchers have been placed in or have accepted positions in which they are responsible for research way beyond their competence. In universities and elsewhere great store is placed on researchers winning grants and contracts and this can lead to researchers overestimating their skills or, if they are successful in winning the grant or contract, employing research assistants who do not have the necessary skills. This problem is made far worse by the fact that there is a serious shortage of graduates with sufficiently refined research skills.

Analysis and reporting

It is not difficult to analyse and report results in ways that distort the underlying patterns. It is easy to use selectively 'juicy' quotes from in-depth interviews to support almost any proposition you might want to suggest. It is barely more difficult to report statistical data in such a way as to mislead readers. Selective reporting and selective, distorted analysis can readily paint a highly misleading picture. Huff's book *How to Lie with Statistics* provides plenty of lighthearted examples of how this can be done.

Although it should go without saying that falsification of results is unacceptable, there are plenty of examples in scientific literature where people have either fabricated results entirely or changed figures to make them appear more impressive. The pressure to publish in academia, the temptation to cut corners, to save money or to be politically correct, can tempt people to fabricate results. Those who do fabricate results no doubt expect that the chances of detection are slight. They are probably correct.

Replication of results has been one of the key safeguards against falsification. Replication requires that another researcher can collect comparable data in the same way and thus check the veracity and reliability of any set of results. This is an important safeguard in experimental research where it is possible to reproduce the conditions under which another researcher has conducted an experiment. However, true replication is less achievable in survey research. This is because social surveys rely on samples in a particular place and time, and to the extent that the time and place of two surveys (and thus the sample) are different then any variation between results can be defended in terms of sample differences. This makes true replication extremely difficult. An unscrupulous person could fabricate or at least modify results and claim that any differences between these and those of other researchers are due to differences in time and place. If all else fails they could claim that the differences are due to sampling error. Results can be misrepresented without fabricating them. You can distort results by inappropriately analysing data. It is really quite easy. You can recode variables to produce the desired results. You can choose to analyse only certain variables and thus produce a misleading picture. You might fail to test the reliability of scales, use significance tests inappropriately (or not at all), neglect appropriate multivariate analysis or fail to control for relevant variables. It is not difficult to mislead the consumers of social research. In the end we must rely on honesty rather than the fear of detection to produce good research.

Inappropriate analysis may not be deliberate but may mislead nonetheless. It is therefore important that researchers ensure that they have the necessary skills to analyse data thoroughly and appropriately. To do otherwise is hardly different from the surgeon who may be able to perform an appendectomy undertaking brain surgery. The pretence of greater expertise than one possesses is, in my view, misrepresentation and therefore unethical behaviour.[3] Ignorance of appropriate methodology—or at least the representation of greater expertise than one, in fact, possesses—is just as unethical as falsification of results. Inappropriate analysis can be just as misleading as deliberate falsification of data.

Perhaps the most common way in which researchers mislead is by only reporting convenient or 'positive' results. Rather than fabricating results or manipulating data to achieve the desired results, a misleading impression can be achieved easily simply by not reporting inconvenient results. Data are usually complex and some results will support a particular hypothesis while others will contradict it. The appropriate course of action when one comes up with 'negative' results is to modify the hypothesis to accommodate them and thus reflect the complexity of social life. However, the temptation is to have one's simple hypotheses supported and to report only the data that do this. In science and social science few people achieve fame by finding that two variables are unrelated or by having their ideas disproven. It is the discovery of patterns and relationships rather than the discovery of chaos and complexity that wins attention. No doubt some results are misreported or flawed for this reason.

An important safeguard against misreporting or misanalysis of results is to make data sets publicly available through data archives in which researchers deposit their data sets and make them available to other researchers for secondary analysis. In Australia this is done via the Social Science Data Archives at the Australian National University;

in Britain it is done via the ESRC data archives at the University of Essex and in the USA via the ICPSR archives at the University of Michigan. Making data available for analysis by others is perhaps the survey researcher's closest approximation to replication. While it does not prevent falsification of the original data set, it does act as a check on misanalysis.

There are those who argue that this plea for full and fair analysis and presentation of results is impossible. They argue that all research is necessarily subjective and that our values and assumptions inevitably affect the questions we ask and the way we analyse and interpret data. Instead of allowing the facts to speak for themselves, they argue, we make the facts speak for us. There is some merit to this view. However, it is an abrogation of responsibility to argue that because our judgments are clouded by our values and background we can give up trying to be thorough and demanding in our analysis. The best antidote to this sort of subjective analysis is to acknowledge our own position and to deliberately look for evidence that might *disprove* our own theory.

Some of those who are more idealistic might argue that full and thorough analysis does not really matter. Some will assert that values are all important and that the primary role of the researcher is to bring about worthwhile change in the society we study. That is, we should be social activists rather than social researchers. To the extent that 'research' and analysis can achieve worthwhile change then subjective analysis is justifiable, even if it is incomplete and partial.

Others, who are more cynical, argue that social policy is affected by political and financial considerations and that good quality research is irrelevant to the policy process. In the end, they argue, it does not matter what social researchers 'discover' as it does not make much difference. In fact, coming up with the 'right' results is more important since these are more amenable to being used in the political process and these can therefore be influential and achieve desirable ends. However, to the extent that social research affects social policy, poor research will have very direct effects on the lives of people. Furthermore, misreporting or shoddy analysis affects one's colleagues as it will eventually bring the discipline into disrepute and undermine the capacity of good research to influence social policy.

We should acknowledge that data collection and analysis are affected by our values and that this may cause us to fall short of the ideal of full and thorough analysis. But this is not to say that we should give up our attempts to stand back from our values and assumptions and to test them against the data. We should look at all the data we collect rather than that which suits our purposes. We should rigorously test our scales and evaluate the validity and reliability of our variables. We should look for 'negative' results and do all we can to report inconvenient results. It is only by doing this that we can extend our knowledge beyond that which our beliefs and prejudices dictate. If there is one lesson to be learned from history it is that those who believe that they have the final truth and that they know what is good and right for the rest of us are almost certain to be mistaken. It is therefore important that the social scientist be involved in *testing* the beliefs of ourselves and of others as to what the 'real' world is like.

How does all this relate to our ethical responsibility to our profession and colleagues? My own view is that to give up attempting to *learn* new things from our research is to discredit the whole exercise of research. If research is simply an exercise in supporting our own subjective views then there is no point to it except as a political exercise. If we *use* research rather than *learn* from it then we ultimately discredit our fellow researchers and reduce their efforts to subjective and political exercises and make it easy to dismiss the results of their work.

Collaboration and assistance

A great deal of research is a joint effort. This raises the problem of acknowledging whose research it is. This is not a trivial issue since authorship is the key means by which a person's research expertise and contribution is measured and acknowledged. Consequently, some people have claimed authorship unjustifiably. Cases where the name of the professor of a department is automatically included on all publications from the department regardless of his or her contribution to the research is such an example. However, in other cases those who have made substantial contributions (e.g. research assistants who are employed to do the bulk of the research itself) are simply acknowledged in a footnote.

Authorship is an ethical issue since it relates to the accurate representation of research contributions. Misrepresentation has important implications for people's careers. When researchers of equal status contribute equally to a research project there should be little problem in recognising their contribution. Typically this is done by acknowledging them as joint authors in publications that flow from the research project.

However the matter is often not quite this simple. The nasty reality of power and status differences intrude and complicate the issue. Whose contributions ought to be recognised by joint authorship? Which sorts of contributions ought to be recognised in this way? There is no simple answer to this and the conventions of different disciplines vary widely.

We should start by acknowledging that unequal power relations are involved in the process of authorship. Frequently this means that powerful people who have made only modest contributions are acknowledged, while the contributions of junior people who are being paid specifically to do the research are taken for granted and remain unacknowledged by authorship.

Of course the evaluation of contributions is a subjective matter. Is it to be measured by the amount of time a person spends on the project or by the type of contribution? How do we evaluate the contributions of the person who suggested the initial idea and a possible hypothesis but then had little further involvement, compared with the research assistant who conducted all the interviews or the typist who transcribed all the interviews in the study? One could argue that they have all made contributions without which the study could not have proceeded. Should all be acknowledged as authors?

Authorship is not the same as being the *writer* of a report or article. In my view there is no reason why the person who writes up the research that results from many contributions should be especially privileged. The writer could not write the article or report without the contributions of others. If we properly recognise the multiple contributions to research then multiple authorship would become more common in the social sciences.

Some people will argue that you cannot acknowledge all contributors as authors as it would make the list of authors too long and would provide no way of recognising the relative contributions of various people. They are no doubt correct in many circumstances and their solution is to acknowledge the contributions of many people in footnotes. This is often a sensible approach but it is not without its problems. There is still the matter of which contributions are acknowledged by joint authorship and which are acknowledged by a footnote. In career and reputational terms, authorship matters while an acknowledgment in a footnote stands for naught, so the way this is resolved is important for the particular individuals involved.

It is probably not possible to establish hard and fast rules in relationship to authorship and I do not propose to try. Instead I have listed the types of contributions people frequently make to research projects. Ask yourself the question of how these contributions should be recognised. What principles are you using when coming up with your answers?

Should people who make the following contributions be acknowledged as joint authors?

1   The initiator of the original idea who does little beyond formulating the research problem/question/hypotheses.
2   A person of high status whose name is crucial in winning a grant/contract (without which the research could not proceed) but who contributes little to the research.

3   The head of a department or a research manager who organises and enables the research to take place.
4   The person or agency that funds the project but makes no contribution to the intellectual content of the project.
5   The person or agency that formulates the research problem and puts it out for tender but makes no contribution thereafter except monitoring the project.
6   People such as interviewers who collect research data according to a pre-defined schedule/questionnaire.
7   Those who formulate the questionnaire or research instrument but are not involved in data collection, analysis or writing.
8   Those who make the data analysable by coding, transcribing or entering data onto a database.
9   Research assistants who collect and analyse data under the close instruction and supervision of the principal researcher.
10   Those who write up the data.
11   In the case of secondary analysis, what recognition should be given to the person responsible for collecting the primary data, developing scales and the questionnaire?

In the end I would prefer an approach to authorship that goes beyond simply recognising the person who writes the report, and for this reason multiple authorship will be appropriate. We need to be sensitive to the power dimension of authorship. In my experience the more influential people are the more likely they are to be acknowledged, and the less influential they are (e.g. research assistants, field workers, students) the less likely they are to be acknowledged as a joint contributor.

In all this there is a danger of 'inverted snobbery'. In the effort to avoid 'freeloaders', those who have initiated the core ideas of a project but have not been very involved thereafter are not recognised while those who carry out the research initiated by others take the glory. Supervisors of postgraduate students face a similar problem. Should supervisors who play an important role in shaping a research thesis but do not collect or analyse the data be recognised as joint authors of work that flows from the thesis?

Even if we can resolve the matter of establishing which contributions should be acknowledged through authorship, the problem of order of authorship remains. Where there are multiple authors the order often reflects the seniority or relative contributions of authors. Most of the same issues outlined above are involved in resolving this problem.

In summary, we cannot escape the fact that research, as with most other human enterprises, is laced with the issues of inequality and power. Many people contribute to the research enterprise but not all are recognised—or not recognised equally. Some people are 'overacknowledged' in the authorship stakes because of their positions of influence while other, less powerful people on whom the whole research enterprise depends are simply noted in a footnote. The solutions are neither obvious nor simple. It is, however, critical that these matters are clearly specified and agreed at the *beginning* of research projects and at the time of hiring staff so that everyone enters the situation knowing the ground rules.

Funding

When reporting research, it is conventional to provide readers with methodological details about data collection, sampling, and the ways in which data were prepared for analysis. The principle is to provide the reader with sufficient information so that they can evaluate the results in the light of the methodological quality of the research.

Although most researchers will try to collect, analyse and report data without fear or favour, we would be making a mistake to pretend that the political context in which data are collected, the source of funds, contractual obligations and sponsorship of the research have no impact on what data are collected and the way they are interpreted. If you were reading research on the effects of smoking on health you undoubtedly would want to know if the research was sponsored and funded by the tobacco industry. If research showed that doctors did not over-service or over-charge you would want to know if the research was funded by the Medical Association. If crime research highlighted an increasing crime rate and the need for more police we should know if the research was sponsored by the Police Association.

This is not to say that such research is necessarily flawed, but readers and consumers of research should be provided with sponsorship and funding information so that they have a context within which to look at the research. In the end, the research should be evaluated in terms of its quality but sponsorship information alerts us to possible biases of which we might otherwise be unaware.

Sponsors and funders

As more and more research is funded by governments, and funds are competitively won by tender and are performed under contract, it is important that the relationship with the sponsor and funder is clearly specified and that the researcher then honours the agreed undertakings. In specifying the relationship with the funder we should be mindful of our responsibility to conduct the research to the highest standards and as objectively as possible and to analyse and report the data without fear or favour.

It is important to clarify your rights and obligations *before* contracts are signed or funds are accepted. Ensure that you work out who owns the data and who has access to it. If the funder retains ownership you need to clarify what guarantees and procedures will be adopted to ensure the confidentiality of respondents. If the funder retains ownership you should clarify what access other people will have to the data once the contractual obligations have been met.

As a researcher you should also clarify your right to publish the research. Can you publish independently? Does any publication require the approval of the funder? Are there conditions on publication, such as meeting certain contractual obligations or waiting a certain period of time? Whether you are prepared to accept restricted rights of publication is a matter for your own choice but it can mean that you are participating in a most undesirable form of censorship where publication would clearly be in the public good.

A common problem with contracted research is that the funders are not researchers and are unaware of what can and cannot be achieved. It is important therefore that researchers are clear about the limits and appropriateness of methods and that these are clearly explained to funders. Frequently funders do not specify their research questions sufficiently and the researcher needs to spend time clarifying these. These should be clarified *before* the research begins, since the failure to be clear and specific beforehand can lead to misunderstandings and accusations of bad faith later on. Funders should know what they are funding and researchers should use their professional expertise to alert funders to what is realistic and achievable. This will frequently involve a collaborative refinement of research questions.

Sometimes you will face the opposite problem. Some funders may try to specify the research far too much. Some will either hint at or specify the results or conclusions they expect. Any professional researcher should not accept contractual conditions that require a particular outcome or set of findings. Some funders wish to specify particular methods and research designs. While this may be appropriate, the researcher should be satisfied that these specifications are for methodological reasons rather than as a way of achieving the desired results. Where funders require specific methods you should be satisfied that these are appropriate and that you are happy to undertake the research on these conditions.

Difficulties can arise where funders or contractors retain the right to approve research instruments, data analysis methods and the like. Funders who retain the right to approve questionnaires can object to the inclusion of certain questions and require that questions be asked in particular ways. Great care should be taken in accepting conditions that give funders the right to censor or dictate as this leaves the researcher open to undue influence and can compromise their capacity to conduct professional research fully and fairly. This does not mean that you should not seek comment and input from sponsors. As the researcher, you should develop a consultative relationship but you should be in a position to make the final methodological decisions.

As well as establishing your rights as a contracted researcher it is also important to recognise your responsibilities. Since there is strong competition for research funds it is tempting for those who tender for research to promise more than they can deliver and to make claims beyond their expertise. Researchers have an obligation not to misrepresent their expertise. Where you do not have the required expertise, specify the arrangements you have made to address these gaps (e.g. through sub-contracting, consultants). Similarly, you should be careful about undertaking the research if you know beforehand that the funds are inadequate or the timelines are inappropriate. To my mind it is misrepresentation to accept a research contract in the knowledge that the funding and time do not allow you to deliver.

It is also important to respect your access to and to be discrete with privileged information obtained from sponsors. If you have agreed to a particular research design and terms of reference you should discuss any departure from these with the body that agreed to fund the research. Where research contracts have agreed timelines the researcher should make every effort to keep to those timelines and to deliver reports as agreed. In the past many academic researchers have not performed well in this regard and have given academic researchers a bad reputation with funding bodies.

Summary

Research design involves more than sorting out the technical and the practical aspects of a project. We must pay careful attention to the ethical issues involved. Often ethical considerations will conflict with technical and practical considerations but these compromises must be made. We should not put technical or practical considerations above the interests of the people who participate in the research. We should also be careful to pay proper attention to the effect of our research on other researchers, funders and on society at large.

In survey research there are three main factors to consider when protecting the interests of participants. The first is that participants participate on the basis of informed consent. While it may be difficult to decide what constitutes *informed* consent, and *when* and *how* to obtain the consent, it is nevertheless important to obtain the agreement of participants. Second, participants should be volunteers and should not be made to feel that they must participate. Third, participants who participate should not be harmed as a result of participating. One way of ensuring this is to make sure that respondents are able to participate anonymously or if this is not possible that the information they provide is confidential.

A researcher's responsibility extends to his or her fellow researchers and professional colleagues. We can bring the practice of social research into disrepute by falsifying results, misanalysing results or by misrepresenting our own expertise. We also have a responsibility to properly report our own contribution and that of others in the research enterprise. While taking and attributing credit for research is often tangled up with issues of power and status, it is nevertheless important to properly represent the relative contributions of research participants. Consumers of our research also have a right to know who funded the research so that they can take this into account when they read and evaluate our results.

Finally, we have a responsibility to our funders and sponsors. If we undertake to do research we should be sure that we can meet our obligations, that we can do what we claim we can and that we meet deadlines. We also need to be clear about our rights and obligations to our funders. Issues of the ownership and confidentiality of data, methods to be used and rights to publish need to be resolved before embarking on the research. We need to ensure that we respect privileged information that we come across in the course of the research. Any suggestion that we will make certain findings or only report favourable outcomes must be avoided. As professional social science researchers we should ensure that we are able to conduct and report the research we undertake without fear or favour.

Notes

1   Most research institutes, government departments, universities and hospitals have ethics committees, the purpose of which is to ascertain whether a research proposal meets ethical guidelines. Typically, funding and approval is not available until the approval of an ethics committee has been given.

2   The Milgram experiments on obedience are classic examples of this. See Baumrind (1964) and Milgram (1964).

3   It is worthwhile distinguishing between misrepresentation and diffidence or lack of confidence at this point. Many people will lack confidence about their capacity to undertake some analysis. Sometimes this is well based but in others it stems from undue modesty.

Further Reading

An excellent overview of the ethical issues involved in social science research
is Kimmel's book *Ethics and Values in Applied Social Research* (1988).
Seiber's collection of papers in her book *The Ethics of Social Research:
Surveys and Experiments* (1982) and Reynolds' book *Ethical Dilemmas
and Social Science Research* (1979) both provide thorough discussions of
a wide range of issues. Ritzer's 1974 edited collection *Social Realities:
Dynamic Perspectives* presents a series of views and lively excerpts that
highlight some of the ethical issues involved in real life research. Seiber's
book *Planning Ethically Responsible Research* provides very useful guidelines to students for conducting ethically responsible research.
Issues of informed consent are thoroughly dealt with in *A History And Theory
Of Informed Consent* by Fadden and Beauchamp, (1986) while Singer's
papers (1978 and 1982) provide a thorough analysis of the effects of informed consent.
Although they are now getting somewhat old the books by Barnes *Who Should
Know What? Social Science, Privacy and Ethics* (1979) and by Boruch and
Cecil *Assuring the Confidentiality of Social Research Data* (1979) both
provide useful overviews of confidentiality issues.

20 The potential of surveys

Catherine Marsh (1982) has described the prevailing *Zeitgeist* in British sociology as regarding survey research as 'hopelessly empiricist, the product of vulgar American sociology, atheoretical and generally a waste of time'. She argues that by the current orthodoxy among sociologists:

> the survey is rejected out of hand as being incapable of producing any information worth having. Some go further and argue that in fact science is ideology, measurement a fiction and rigour a joke. The stereotype of the survey researcher is of a senescent, plodding servant of the establishment who hasn't yet quite caught up with the new and devastating revolutions that have taken place in the philosophy of science. (1982:3)

No doubt there are many reasons for this antipathy. Many of the 'fundamental criticisms' of surveys, rather than being informed and sober evaluations, are I believe reactions to poorly designed, executed and analysed surveys and are not in fact fundamental criticisms of the method itself. The training and support for survey research has often been poor and has predictably led to many poor surveys. Many of those who reject surveys have encountered and participated in surveys before they were sufficiently trained to do so. It is hardly surprising that such people have become disappointed in their results and are particularly aware of the deficiencies that can confront the poorly done survey. Good survey research cannot be done without a thorough understanding of the method.

I am convinced that much of the prejudice against surveys is based on a misunderstanding of what survey research is and can achieve, and that survey research need not be as mindless nor as limited as much 'sociological prejudice' would have us believe.

In Chapter 1, on the nature of surveys, a number of specific criticisms of surveys were outlined. Marsh (1982) provides a thorough, extremely readable and forceful discussion and evalution of these criticisms. I urge readers to look closely at her book. At this point I can only make a few comments in passing.

351

Surveys are frequently criticised because of the difficulty of establishing causal links with correlational data. This is the favourite criticism of experimentalists who, you will recall, create differences between people by their own intervention and then see what effect this has on some other variable. Through the use of randomisation, control groups and other ways of eliminating the influence of extraneous factors, the experimentalist hopes to draw unambiguous causal inferences. The survey researcher relies on existing differences between people and checks to see if these differences are related to some other variable. The problem is that people who differ in one respect may differ in others too, so we can never be certain what a correlation between two variables is due to. The techniques of elaboration analysis and multivariate analysis are designed to avoid drawing faulty causal inferences from correlational data. These techniques are used to compensate for the lack of randomisation and control groups used by the experimentalist by statistical simulation: they effectively create *post factum* control groups.

With these techniques the researcher can go a long way towards avoiding drawing faulty causal inferences. They eliminate a simplistic reliance on simple bivariate correlations. There are of course those who use simple correlations to draw causal inferences without doing even basic analysis to test their robustness. But these misuses of correlational data are easily avoided and should not damn the method itself.

In the final analysis, however, we can never be absolutely sure that we have controlled for every relevant variable. Some unmeasured factor may account for the correlation. However, the better the researcher, the less likely this is to be a problem.

Surveys are often criticised for being inherently positivistic. The label of positivism has become a term of abuse but like most sins means different things to different people. Marsh develops a forceful attack on the view that surveys are inherently positivistic and I refer readers to her discussion (1982: ch. 3).

A related accusation about surveys is that they are incapable of getting at the meaningful aspects of social behaviour. I have argued that simply to establish a correlation between two variables is not to explain why they are linked. This is Weber's point when he argues

Without adequacy at the level of meaning, our generalisations remain mere statements of *statistical* probability, either not intelligible at all or only imperfectly intelligible; this is no matter how high the probability of outcome ... and no matter how precisely calculable in numerical terms it may be. On the other hand, from the point of view of its importance for sociological knowledge, even the most certain adequacy on the level of meaning signifies an acceptable *causal* proposition only to the extent that evidence can be produced that there is a probability ... that the action in question *really* takes the course held to be meaningfully adequate with a certain calculable frequency or some approximation to it (whether on average or in the 'ideal' case). (Runciman, 1978)

In other words, to find that women tend to be more religious than men, for example, is not to establish what *makes* women more religious. Sociological knowledge will only come when a plausible account of the connection is given. On the other hand, a plausible account cannot be accepted simply because it makes sense or is meaningful. The correlations must also exist.

The question is, can surveys collect data which permit meaningful explanations or is there some reason in principle why this type of data is closed to the survey researcher? Marsh concludes her consideration of this question as follows:

Making sense of social action in a valid manner is very hard, and surveys have not traditionally been very good at it. The earliest survey researchers ... [brought] the meaning from outside ... by making use of [their] stock of plausible explanations ... or from subsidiary in-depth interviews, sprinkling quotes derived from there liberally on the raw correlations ... Survey research became much more exciting when ... it began to include the meaningful dimensions in the study design.

This was done in two ways. First by

asking the actor either for her reasons directly or to supply information about the central values in her life around which we may assume she is orienting her life. [Secondly by] collecting a sufficiently complete picture of the context in which the actor finds herself that a team of outsiders may read off the meaningful dimensions. (1982:124)

In the end researchers will disagree about how much information is needed to develop satisfactory meaningful explanations and about the source and type of this information, but these problems are not peculiar to survey research.

Throughout this book a range of techniques which enable the development of meaningful explanations has been discussed. These include 'reason analysis' (Kadushin, 1968), elaboration, multivariate analysis, *ex post facto* theorising, the emphasis on the ongoing process between theory testing and theory construction, the techniques of theory construction and the insistence on establishing the meaning of particular variables for particular cases by seeing them within the context of other variables. It has also been argued that survey research is not restricted to structured questionnaires. Other techniques such as postcoding unstructured in-depth interviews or systematic observation are valuable sources of survey data.

This is not to pretend that developing meaningful explanations is an easy task for the survey researcher, or anyone for that matter. It involves careful collection of data and skilful analysis. The explanations will not be perfect but the meaningful aspects of behaviour are accessible to the survey researcher. In my view these efforts are preferable to a reliance on the unverifiable and unsystematic introspection of some styles of sociological research.

In the same vein, surveys are accused of looking at 'bits' of behaviour and specific opinions out of the context in which they occur. The 'wholeness' in which attitudes are held and behaviour performed is lost and so their meaning and significance is misunderstood (Blumer, 1956). To greater or lesser extents all data collection techniques will encounter this problem. Techniques have been developed to minimise it although the practice of much survey research still suffers. The point of scaling techniques, factor analysis, elaboration, multivariate modelling, sophisticated coding schemes and the creation of complex composite variables is to provide the context which surveys are accused of ignoring. Depending on how information is collected, how much is collected and the way it is analysed the survey researcher who is conscious of the problem of context can go a long way towards interpreting the meaning of behaviour and opinions in light of their context.

A related charge is that surveys are inherently atomistic:

> Their fundamental source of information is a sample of individuals. The questions asked in these studies are put in terms of the psychological reactions of individuals. Accordingly, the assumption is required that the historical study of society ... can be understood by means of such data about individuals. (Mills, 1959:79)

Several brief comments can be made. There is no reason why surveys must look only at individuals. Other units of analysis are used which deal with collectivities and are not guilty of atomism. Even where individuals are the units of analysis, structural constraints and determinants on behaviour can still be located. Using individuals as units of analysis does not restrict us to psychological explanations. The danger of looking at collectivities only is that 'it reifies social processes, and suggests that there is something real and tangible about social forces independent of individual actions' (Marsh, 1982:60). I would wish to argue that examining the actions of various types of individuals can provide a useful window through which to see some of the workings of our social structure. Finally, new methods of structuring data collected from individuals enable its aggregation into various units of analysis from individuals through to very complex collectivities. These methods are referred to as hierarchical and relational data handling techniques. Computer packages such as SIR (Scientific Information Retrieval) are making these techniques more widely accessible.

C.W. Mills also has contended that the design, implementation and analysis of surveys requires no sociological imagination. His view has been repeated by many people since. However, the truth is that good surveys require creative imagination, reflection, puzzling, interpretation and insight. There is no way that good survey research is accomplished by following a set recipe. Of course there are sterile surveys but there is nothing about the nature of the method that precludes creative thinking or a sociological imagination.

Mindless empiricism is another criticism levelled at surveys. Throughout this book I have argued that it is only the poor survey that is atheoretical. A good survey is based on theory. Theories ought to be and can be the basis of the research design and the analysis. Without theory, surveys, like any other research method, produce a mindless mess. Like so many of the criticisms of surveys this criticism is of a common practice but not of the method itself.

Other criticisms focus on techniques that are often used in surveys. Since structured questionnaires are frequently used the critics think that to criticise questionnaires is to damn the survey method. This is simply wrongheaded. Questionnaires are but one way of obtaining a rectangular data matrix. They are probably the easiest way of collecting large sets of data and this accounts for their popularity—not any logical requirement that surveys must use questionnaires. The history of surveys clearly demonstrates the use of a wide variety of data collection techniques.

It is true that questionnaires are too readily used on inappropriate topics and are often very poorly designed and piloted. Survey researchers need to pay very careful attention to developing and selecting appropriate data collection techniques. In passing, Marsh notes the irony of questionnaires being criticised because minor variations in question wording can affect people's answers. She argues that this is no less problematic in 'more informal, "negotiated" interactions in a pub over a pint of beer' (1982:56).

The statistical techniques used by survey researchers lead to a great deal of criticism. Survey analysts and the critics would do well to focus more on the logic of the statistics and evaluate their use from this point of view. Statistics are simply tools to implement various logical operations. I suspect that if the emphasis of reports was to focus on the logic and meaning of statistical results rather than on displaying the latest statistical toy some of the criticism of statistics would go. Survey researchers ought to try to demystify statistics and not hide behind them. A determined attempt by survey researchers to communicate results and make them accessible is sorely needed.

In conclusion, these comments are not meant to imply that surveys do not have their weaknesses. Many of the weaknesses are made much worse by the practice of many surveys and they are not as serious as many of the critics would have us believe. It does mean, however, that surveys need to be conducted by trained and informed researchers. In the end, methodological pluralism is the desirable position. Surveys should only be used when they are the most appropriate method in a given context. A variety of data collection techniques ought to be employed and different units of analysis used. The method should suit the research problem rather than the problem being fitted to a set method.

Further reading

The most useful reference here is Marsh's *The Survey Method* (1982).

Appendix A   AREAS OF THE NORMAL CURVE

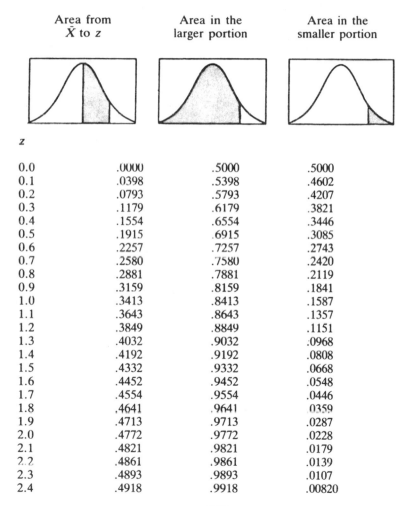

	Area from $\bar{X}$ to z	Area in the larger portion	Area in the smaller portion
z			
0.0	.0000	.5000	.5000
0.1	.0398	.5398	.4602
0.2	.0793	.5793	.4207
0.3	.1179	.6179	.3821
0.4	.1554	.6554	.3446
0.5	.1915	.6915	.3085
0.6	.2257	.7257	.2743
0.7	.2580	.7580	.2420
0.8	.2881	.7881	.2119
0.9	.3159	.8159	.1841
1.0	.3413	.8413	.1587
1.1	.3643	.8643	.1357
1.2	.3849	.8849	.1151
1.3	.4032	.9032	.0968
1.4	.4192	.9192	.0808
1.5	.4332	.9332	.0668
1.6	.4452	.9452	.0548
1.7	.4554	.9554	.0446
1.8	.4641	.9641	.0359
1.9	.4713	.9713	.0287
2.0	.4772	.9772	.0228
2.1	.4821	.9821	.0179
2.2	.4861	.9861	.0139
2.3	.4893	.9893	.0107
2.4	.4918	.9918	.00820

357

2.5	.4938	.9938	.00621
2.6	.4953	.9953	.00466
2.7	.4965	.9965	.00347
2.8	.4974	.9974	.00256
2.9	.4981	.9981	.00187
3.0	.49865	.99865	.00135

Source: L.C. Freeman (1965) *Elementary Applied Statistics* New York: Wiley

Appendix B   EXERCISES

1   The nature of surveys

1   Draw a variable by case matrix for six people and five variables of your choice. Fill in characteristics for each case.

2   Draw three variable by case matrices each using a different unit of analysis from the following list: countries, years and conversations. In each matrix use four cases and five variables appropriate to the selected unit of analysis.

3   Different methods of research (survey, experiment and case study) have different characteristics. Next to each characteristic below indicate the method having the particular characteristic.

   a   Can use questionnaires.
   b   Can use unstructured interviews.
   c   Can use observation.
   d   Can use content analysis.
   e   Uses a variable by case matrix.
   f   Is based on 'natural' variation between cases.
   g   Researcher creates variation between cases.
   h   Compares the 'treatment' with the 'no treatment' group for analysis.

4   Imagine you wish to see whether being unemployed leads to a loss of self-esteem. Briefly contrast how the case study, the experiment and the survey would differ in their basic procedure for testing this proposition.

2   Theory and social research

1   For each of the following studies say whether it is a descriptive or explanatory study.

   a   A study to assess the level of alienation in society.
   b   A study to assess voting intentions for the next election.
   c   A study to assess whether divorce is linked to the affluence of a family.
   d   A study to see whether the age at which people are getting married is increasing.
   e   A study to discover people's attitude to computers and other new

359

technology.

f A study to test whether worker-participation schemes increase productivity and quality of work.

2 In your own words explain the following terms:
theory, inductive, deductive, *ex post facto*, operationalisation, empiricist, rationalist.

3 Below is a theory which you might hear in everyday conversation.

Our affluent society leads to the decline of the self help ethic which in turn leads young people to expect things to be done for them which creates laziness and this leads to youth unemployment.

a Translate it into a 'box and arrow diagram' as in Chapter 2 in the section 'Six stages in theory testing'.

b Develop at least four conceptual propositions for the theory.

4 What is the difference between a sociological perspective and a theory?

5 It was argued that the role of theory is central to research. Explain what its role is.

3 Formulating and clarifying research questions

1 For each of the following statements say what unit of analysis is being used.

a Most people in this country are conservative.

b Within any one year about 13 per cent of families move.

c Australia has one of the lowest rates of participation in tertiary education amongst developed countries.

d Within any one year 18 per cent of Australians move.

e In each of the past ten years the level of foreign aid has declined.

2 You wish to see whether increases in income actually make people happier. Forgetting for the moment how you would measure happiness, design cross-sectional and panel studies to test this idea. Then design a study that avoids the problems inherent in these two.

3 You wish to do a descriptive study on prejudice. Using the guidelines suggested in Chapter 3, focus this topic into a much more specific research problem.

4 Try putting the theory which is diagrammed in Figure 3.1 into words.

5 For each of the following statements of research findings indicate the type of research design that appears to have been employed and explain what is wrong with the conclusions that are drawn. Concentrate on problems that arise from research design problems.

a Sixty-eight per cent of married people scored high on our index of conservatism while only 38 per cent of single people scored high. Obviously getting married causes people to become conservative.

b After observing a sample of childless married couples over a ten-year period we observed that the level of marital happiness declined over this period. Childlessness works against people being happily married.

c In the early 1970s, before the end of the Vietnam War, surveys showed that tertiary students had strong anti-American attitudes. Recent surveys have shown that these feelings are no longer evident among students. Ending the Vietnam War certainly improved the attitudes of students to the United States.

d Old people attend church more often than young people. For example, 58 per cent of those over 60 attend church regularly while only 22 per cent of those under 25 do so. From this we can conclude that as people get older they become more religious.

e The average number of children per family now is 2.2. Families are obviously getting smaller these days.

f To test the idea that having children makes people happier, a group of parents were asked how happy they felt now compared with how happy they were before they had children. Eighty-seven per cent said they were happier now than before they had children. From this we can conclude that having children improves people's happiness.

g A HEADSTART program (a preschool educational program to help disadvantaged children have a head start by the time they commence school) was used to test the effectiveness of HEADSTART. A group of four-year-olds from disadvantaged backgrounds were chosen to enter the program. IQ tests were given at the beginning of the program and again at the end. There was an average gain of ten IQ points over the period of the program. HEADSTART increases children's IQ.

4 Developing indicators for concepts

1 Explain why indicators must be developed for concepts.

2 Why might different people develop quite different indicators for the same concept?

3 Why is developing a nominal definition both problematic and important?

4 Throughout the U.S. and in a number of other countries a Scholastic Aptitude Test (SAT) is used for selection into tertiary education. This is basically a multiple choice, short answer, 'content free', unsighted, limited-time test. What do you think these results are meant to indicate? What reliability and validity problems might there be with this measure? How might you find out how reliable and valid SAT tests are?

5 List six variables for which single item indicators would be adequate and six for which multiple indicators would be more appropriate.

6 Develop a set of questions to measure conservatism. Explain the steps you have taken to move from the concept to your set of questions.

7 In exercise 3 for Chapter 2 you developed a diagram and conceptual propositions for a theory. Using the same theory and propositions

a   Clarify the concepts in your propositions.
b   Develop indicators for each concept.
c   Develop testable propositions.

5 Finding a sample

1   Find a page of your telephone directory with relatively few businesses and draw a simple random sample of 20 people from the first column. Use the table of random numbers (Table 5.1). List *all* your workings used to draw this SRS.

2   Using the same page of the directory select a systematic sample of 40 people using the whole page. Show all your workings.

3   Turn to Figure 4.1. Assume that cases 11, 05, 20, 38, 17, 18, 40, 49, 12, 01, 20, 21, 44, 46, 14, 23, 48, 14, 22 are female. Draw a stratified sample of fifteen people using sex as the stratifying variable. Show all your workings.

4   Using a street directory of your city, select a multistage cluster sample. For the first stage use the directory's key map in which you can see that the whole city is divided up and each area has a map number. Select fifteen areas and list them showing your workings. Then randomly select only *one* of these areas. Divide it into sixteen equally sized units (use a 4 × 4 grid) and randomly select a sample of four of these units. For this exercise select only *one* unit and then proceed to draw a sample of individuals from this unit. Assume for this exercise that each residential block has exactly the same number of households (e.g. 50). Show all your workings and list the problems you have encountered.

5   For the above exercise describe two ways in which you could have increased the likely accuracy of the sample without increasing the final sample size.

6   How would you go about obtaining a probability sample of members of Rotary in your country? Assume there is no access to a national list of members and you want to personally interview people but wish to minimise costs.

7   Outline the difference between:

a   bias and sampling error;
b   probability and non-probability samples;
c   quota and systematic samples;
d   a representative sample and a random sample;
e   a sample and a census.

8   You want to draw a simple random sample of voters in your electorate to see how they intend to vote. Assume there are about 70 000 voters in your electorate. How large a sample would you need? Explain the assumptions you have made in determining your sample size.

9   Think of two research topics in which you would need to use non-probability sampling techniques and explain why a probability sample would not be feasible.

10 What does it mean to have a sampling error of 4 per cent at the 95 per cent confidence level?

6 Constructing questionnaires

1 Design four questions on the topic of smoking tobacco products. One question should tap beliefs about smoking tobacco products, the others should be designed to measure attitudes, attributes and behaviour respectively in relation to this topic.

2 Examine the questions in Figures 6.4, 6.5, 6.6, 6.8, 14.2, pages 253–4 and in exercise 3 below and indicate whether the question is tapping attributes, attitudes, beliefs or behaviour.

3 Describe what is wrong with each of the following questions.

a How often do you have contact with your mother? (tick one box for each type of contact)

	See	Phone	Write
Daily			
Weekly			
Monthly			
Yearly			
Never			

b Do you feel that the contact you have with your mother is:
[ ] Too much
[ ] About right
[ ] Too little
[ ] Not important

c Do you feel that your relationship with your mother is affected by'her desire to obtain vicarious gratification from your achievements?
[ ] Yes
[ ] No
[ ] Cannot tell

d Do you agree or disagree that your mother does not treat you as an adult?
[ ] Agree
[ ] Disagree
[ ] Undecided

e   Overall how do you get on with your parents?
    [   ] Very well
    [   ] OK
    [   ] Not so well
    [   ] Badly
f   What is your present income?
g   Most people in this country say they are opposed to Asian migration.
    How do you feel about Asian migration to this country? (Mark on the
    scale between 0 to 10)
    Opposed _____ Agree
                0   1   2   3   4   5   6   7   8   9   10
h   [Ask married women only]
    Many women who stay at home full-time looking after young children
    say they feel frustrated. What frustrations did/do you feel at this
    stage?
i   Why did you drop out of your course at university?
    [   ] Lecturer was hopeless
    [   ] I was too lazy to put in a reasonable amount of work
    [   ] I got sick and got too far behind

4   Develop a brief questionnaire designed to test the proposition that con-
    servatism is a product of four factors: stage in the life cycle, social class,
    level of conservatism of one's parents and level of religiousness. Take
    care with both your questionnaire wording and layout. Try administering
    it to two or three people to see how it works.
5   Set out your version of the above question using the principles of layout
    for a telephone survey.

7   Methods of administration

1   Which method of questionnaire administration would you select to best
    deal with the following:

    a   a topic likely to be of only marginal interest to most respondents;
    b   highly personal or controversial questions;
    c   a survey that needs to be completed quickly;
    d   boring questions;
    e   it will be difficult to find the respondent at home;
    f   a survey of a particular organisation;
    g   respondents are unlikely to have the required information at hand;
    h   finances are very limited;
    i   the questionnaire is difficult to follow;
    j   the researcher is the only person conducting the survey — trained
        interviewers are either unavailable or too expensive;
    k   the questionnaire is relatively long;
    l   no satisfactory sampling frame exists;
    m   a high response rate is particularly important;

n   the sequence in which questions are answered is important;
o   responses are likely to be affected by social desirability factors.

2   Explain the reasons for your choice in each of the above situations.
3   Imagine that you had to obtain people's views about reducing taxation and about their attitude to the government cutting, maintaining or increasing social welfare and environment programs. Produce an introduction that you would use to convince people to participate in the survey. Prepare a different introduction for each of the methods of questionnaire administration.

8   Overview of analysis

1   List ten nominal, ten ordinal and ten interval level variables. Try to select variables that are sociological. If the level of measurement of the variable could differ depending on response categories, make it clear why you are treating it at the level you are.
2   What level of measurement are the variables in the traditionalism scale in chapter 15?
3   What level of measurement is each variable in Figure 14.3?
4   Develop three questions which tell us something about a person's religiousness. One question should yield nominal data, another will yield ordinal data and the third will produce interval data.
5   For each of the following problems which analysis technique would you use: univariate, bivariate or multivariate?

a   To determine the proportion of males and of females in your sample.
b   To determine the income distribution in the sample.
c   To see if sons get on better with their fathers than do daughters.
d   To see if ethnic background is related to frequency of contact with siblings.
e   To see if education level affects income differently for males and females.
f   To see if the income levels of older people differ from those of younger people.

6   In your own words describe the different functions of inferential and descriptive statistics.
7   List the advantages and disadvantages of obtaining interval level data.

9   Univariate statistics

1   From the data below construct three properly labelled frequency tables. The first will be a frequency table for marital status, the second for age grouped in five-year categories (15–19, 20–24; 25–29; 30–34, etc.) and the third will be of age without using categories. Calculate percentages

by excluding missing data. Where appropriate calculate cumulative percentages. In this data the age and marital status are grouped in cases. Age is given in years and for marital status, M = married; W = widowed; N = never married; S = separated; D = divorced. Thus the first case is 32 years old and married. A dash means missing data.

32M, 48W, 68M, 83N, 60M, 29M, —N, 68M, 56M, 54M, 22M, 72M, 25M, 58M, 48M, 43M, 23M, 43M, 52M, 32M, 76W, 33M, 43M, 30M, 27M, 86S, 49—, 44M, 42M, 50M, 30M, 44M, 64—, 28M, 44M, 26M, —D, 19M, 51M, 40D, 36M, 38M, 66M, 56M, 71W, 34M, 59M, 27M, 29M, 30M, 45M, 36M, 64M, 39M, 36—, 66S, 43M, 56W, 58M, 35S, —M, 63M, 41M, 82W, 45M, 43M, 23M, 27S, 42M, 36M, 24M, 33M, 37M, 57M, 38M, 39D, 29M, 53M, 58M, 50M, 41M, 45M, 38M.

2   Explain briefly in words the pattern contained in each frequency table you have produced.
3   For each frequency table put underneath which measure of central tendency and dispersion you would use.
4   Calculate the appropriate measure of central tendency for each table.
5   For the third table the variance is 240.52. What would be the standard deviation for this table? Explain precisely what this standard deviation figure tells us.
6   Assuming the data is from a random sample, what statistics would you use to help generalise from this sample to the population for each table?
7   For the third table, within what range of ages would you estimate the population mean to be (at the 95 per cent level of confidence)?
8   For the first table 81 per cent are married. In the population from which the sample is drawn what percentage would you estimate are married (estimate at the 95 per cent confidence level)?
9   Explain why it is normally desirable to use a measure of dispersion in conjunction with a measure of central tendency.
10   Explain in your own words some potential advantages and disadvantages of using summary statistics in univariate analysis.
11   In the third table what is the z-score of a 57-year-old (assume age is normally distributed)? What percentage of people would be younger than such a person?
12   What measure of central tendency and dispersion would be most appropriate for each of the following variables? Number of sibs; country of birth; crime rate (crimes per 100 000 of population); marital status; age (young, middle-aged and old).

10   Bivariate analysis: crosstabulations

1   Construct a crosstabulation from the following 50 people. In this data there are two variables: sex (M = male; F = female) and vote (O = Other; L = Labor). When constructing this table include the count, row, column and total percentages in each cell and include column and row marginals.

```
M–L  F–L  F–O  M–L  M–O  F–L  F–O  F–O  M–L  M–O
M–O  F–O  M–L  M–O  F–O  F–L  M–L  M–L  F–L  F–O
M–L  F–O  M–L  M–O  F–O  F–O  M–L  M–L  F–O  M–L
F–O  M–L  M–O  F–O  F–L  F–O  M–O  F–O  M–L  M–L
F–O  F–O  M–L  F–L  M–L  F–O  M–L  F–O  F–O  M–L
```

2 Explain what the following figures in your table mean:
   75%; 12%; 76%; 26

3 Reconstruct your table showing only the necessary information to detect
   whether the two variables are related.

4 Describe the character of the relationship in the table you have
   produced.

5 Describe the relationship in Table 17.1 (unrecoded and recoded) and
   Table 16.2 (collapsed version).

6 For each of the following statements indicate whether it is true or false.

		True	False
a	When dealing with interval data you can use only statistics specifically designed for interval level variables.	[ ]	[ ]
b	Statistics which can be used for nominal level variables also can be used for interval level variables.	[ ]	[ ]
c	Statistics designed for use with low levels of measurement also can be used for higher levels of measurement but not vice versa.	[ ]	[ ]
d	Statistics designed for use with ordinal data can be used for nominal data.	[ ]	[ ]

7 Describe the nature of the association in the following table.

		Social class		
		Low	Medium	High
Number	None	11%	28%	45%
of	Few	23	18	35
arrests	Many	66	54	20
	N	129	260	73

8 Which measure(s) of association would you use for each of the following
   pairs of variables?

a Age (in years)/income (in $).
b Number of sibs/social class (upper, middle, lower).
c Level of education (primary, secondary, tertiary)/IQ score.
d Sex/self-esteem (high, low).

e   Desired number of children/religion (Protestant, Catholic, Jewish, none, other).

f   Sex/marital status (married, widowed, divorced).

g   Quality of relationship with mother (good, neutral, poor)/social class (upper, middle, lower).

9   Which measures of association would you be likely to use for the various combinations of variables in the matrix below?

x variable

	Nominal (dichotomous)	Nominal (3+ categories)	Ordinal (few categories)	Interval
Nominal (dichotomous)				
Nominal (3+ categories)				
Ordinal (few categories)				
Interval				

y variable

10 Draw crosstabulations to illustrate the following types of relationships. (Use only percentages for this exercise and be sure to label your tables properly.) Select whatever variables seem appropriate.

a   A 2 × 2 table reflecting a strong negative relationship.

b   A 2 × 2 table reflecting a very weak positive relationship.

c   A 3 × 2 table reflecting a moderate, linear, positive relationship.

d   A 3 × 2 table reflecting a moderate, linear, negative relationship.

e   A 3 × 2 table reflecting a curvilinear relationship.

11 If a table reflects a clear curvilinear relationship, linear measures of association will be (circle one):
     high   moderate   low   can't tell

12 If there is a non-linear relationship between two ordinal variables which measure of association would you use?

13 What does it mean to say two variables are independent of one another?

14 Explain in your own words why it is worth using correlation co-efficients rather than simply looking at crosstabulations.

15 a   What do the following co-efficients mean?
         0.05; 0.25; 0.5; −0.85; 0.8.

     b   Which of the above co-efficients reflects the strongest relationship?

11 Bivariate analysis: alternative approaches

1 Below is a scattergram of the relationship between number of years in the job (X) and income (Y) for people in a private enterprise industry (hypothetical data)

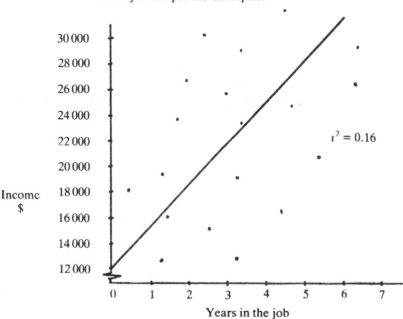

Relationship between income and years in the job for private enterprise

a Describe the character of the relationship in this scattergram.
b What income would you predict someone with two and three years on the job would earn respectively?
c What is the b co-efficient for this scattergram?

2 The following regression equation applies to the same variables as in exercise 1 but for people in the Public Service (hypothetical data): $Y = 15\,000 + 1000X$; $r = 0.56$.

a What is the impact of years on the job on income?
b How accurately can we predict Y from X?
c How much variation in income is explained by X?
d Compare as thoroughly as you can the relationship between years on the job and income for the public service sample and the private enterprise sample in exercise 1?

3 Draw two scattergrams. Draw the first so that the relationship is strong and negative but the impact of X on Y is relatively low. Draw the second

so that the relationship is positive, the impact of X on Y quite high and in which X provides an accurate basis for predicting Y. Select whatever variables you feel are appropriate.

4   Explain in your own words why it is valuable to report both a regression co-efficient and a correlation co-efficient.

5   Examine the regression equation which represents the relationship between years of education of a person's father (X) and the number of years education they receive themselves (Y): $Y = 4 + 1.2X$; $r = 0.40$. Briefly explain

   a   The equation as a whole.
   b   The meaning of each symbol.
   c   The meaning of r.
   d   If someone's father had thirteen years of education, how much would you estimate they would have?

6   Imagine the comparable equation when X is mother's years of education: $Y = 4 + 1.5X$; $r = 0.22$. Compare this with the relationship in exercise 5.

7   In what sense is a regression line or a line of best fit similar to a mean?

8   Think of a situation (i.e. specify the dependent and independent variables) in which the comparison of means approach would be appropriate.

9   If you obtained the following figures for the mean annual income levels of three groups (based on random samples) what else would you find helpful before drawing conclusions? Professional workers = \$28 263; clerical = \$23 261; manual workers = \$21 036.

10   What is the difference between a measure of association and a test of significance?

11   Why is it desirable to use tests of significance?

12   If in a random sample we obtain a correlation of 0.30 between two variables, what does this tell us about their correlation in the population?

13   What does it mean to say that a relationship is significant at the 0.05 level?

14   Interpret each of the following sets of results

	Correlation	Significance
a	−0.45	0.001
b	0.15	0.001
c	0.64	0.37
d	0.24	0.05
e	0.05	0.66

15·   In the above question why might the correlation of 0.64 be non-significant but the much weaker correlation of 0.15 be significant?

16   What is wrong with the following statements?

   a   'There was a significant relationship between sex and income (correlation = 0.60).'
   b   'Age is strongly related to prejudice (significance = 0.001).'

17 Why should tests of significance and correlation co-efficients be used in conjunction?

18 Using the correlation matrix in Table 11.3, explain in simple English what the following co-efficients mean:

a 0.17 (column 6, row 3);
b −0.13 (column 3, row 5);
c 0.44 (column 3, row 1);
d −0.001 (column 5, row 4).

19 We have two variables: years of education (Y) and country of birth (X) which is coded 1 for native-born and 0 for overseas-born. Regression analysis produces an 'a' co-efficient of 9.5 and a 'b' co-efficient of 2.2. What do these figures tell you about the education levels of native-born and overseas-born people? How many years of education do native-born people have on average? How many years of education do over-seas-born people have on average?

12 Elaborating bivariate relationships

1 a Briefly interpret the following set of tables.

Zero order

		Workforce participation	
		In	Out
Level of	Low	63%	42%
religiousness	High	37	58

First order

		MALE		FEMALE	
		In workforce	Out of workforce	In workforce	Out of workforce
Level of	Low	63%	62%	43%	42%
religiousness	High	37	38	57	58

b Represent the relationship between these three variables diagrammatically.

2 a Below is a zero order table showing a relationship between social class and IQ score. Examine it and then select a test variable and draw

hypothetical first order tables which illustrate that the test variable is an intervening variable.

		Class	
		Lower	Middle
IQ score	Low	60%	35%
	High	40	65

b   Represent the relationship between the three variables diagrammatically.

3   We find a zero order relationship between two variables X and Y (correlation = 0.60). Imagine we have a dichotomous test variable. What would the conditional co-efficients be if:

a   The test variable is an intervening variable which completely accounts for the zero order relationship?
b   The zero order relationship was partly spurious?
c   The test variable specifies the zero order relationship?
d   The test variable is an intervening variable which partly accounts for the zero order relationship?
e   The test variable is irrelevant to the zero order relationship?

4   Explain in your own words the purpose of elaboration analysis.
5   Explain in your own words the logic of controlling for third variables. In particular explain why, if the test variable is responsible for the zero order relationship, the first order relationships should be zero.
6   Below is a zero order and two first order tables and co-efficients. Examine them and select the correct statements from those which follow.

		Relationship with mother is	
		Poor	Good
Visits mother	Often	29%	43%
	Moderately	25	23
	Infrequently	46	34
	N	274	295

Gamma = −0.25	Significance = 0.001

Controlling for sex

Relationship with mother is

		MALE		FEMALE	
		Poor	Good	Poor	Good
Visits mother	Often	31%	38%	26%	46%
	Moderately	30	26	20	21
	Infrequently	39	36	54	33
		N 142	131	N 132	164

Gamma   = −0.10   Gamma   = −0.38
Significance = 0.46   Significance = 0.0004

a   The zero order relationship was spurious.
b   Regular visiting by women is affected by the quality of the relationship with their mother whereas this is not true for men.
c   The zero order correlation is largely due to the contribution of the correlation between visiting and the relationship with mother among women.
d   Overall, people visit their mother more when the relationship is poor than when it is not.
e   Among men a poor relationship does not make much difference to the frequency with which they visit their mother.
f   Sex is an intervening variable.
g   Sex specifies the zero order relationship.

7   What is the difference between:

a   A zero order and a first order relationship.
b   Conditional correlations and partial correlations.
c   Specification and replication.
d   A spurious relationship and an indirect causal relationship.

8   Draw a graph that shows that the relationship between age (X) and conservatism (Y) interacts with level of social class (working, middle and upper).

13   Multivariate analysis

1   In multivariate analysis, which statistics or techniques are used to:

a   work out which independent variable has the greatest independent impact?
b   see how well a set of independent variables jointly explains the variance in our dependent variable?

  c   estimate the indirect effects of independent variables on dependent
      variables?
  d   determine which independent variable has the strongest independent
      relationship with the dependent variable?
  e   work out the joint impact of a set of independent variables?
  f   estimate the independent impact of a variable?
2 Examine the path diagram below and explain what it means as fully as
   you can.

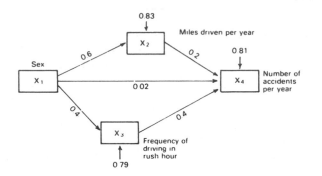

3 Examine the following figures and answer the questions which follow.

Independent variables	b	b*
Education	0.141	0.395
Occupation	0.009	0.221
Income	0.030	0.260
Age	−0.231	−0.176
Constant (a)	3.520	
Dependent variable		
Prejudice		
R = 0.6221	$R^2 = 0.3870$	

  a   Which independent variable has the greatest independent impact on
      prejudice? (Give figures to support your answer.)
  b   What would be the predicted prejudice score of someone with ten
      years of education, a score of 60 on the occupation scale, a score of
      100 on the income scale and who was 35 years old? What would be the
      prejudice score for a similar person who was 40 years old?
  c   What does the minus sign in front of the b and b* co-efficients mean?
  d   How satisfied would you be with your explanation of prejudice given
      the above figures? Why?
  e   Why would b* for education be the highest of the four b* co-efficients
      whereas it is not as a b co-efficient?
  f   For what purpose would you use the b co-efficients? What would you
      use the b* co-efficients for?

4 Examine the path model below and answer the questions which follow.

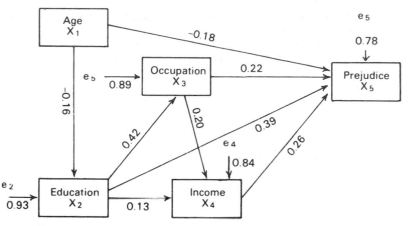

a By what paths does education affect prejudice?
b By which path does education have most effect on prejudice?
c Which variable has the greatest total effect on prejudice: education or age?
d How much variance in prejudice is explained by this path model?
e What is the single most important direct effect on prejudice?

5 Explain in your own words the differences between:
a Multiple correlation and partial correlation.
b Multiple correlation and multiple regression.
c Partial correlation co-efficients and partial regression co-efficients.
d Partial regression co-efficients and beta weights.
e Indirect effects and direct effects.
f Path analysis and regression analysis.

6 Examine the following multiple regression equations (there is a separate one for men and women). The co-efficients are not standardised.

$$\text{WOMEN: } Y = 2.4 + 7.8X_1 - 11.2X_2 + 3.6X_3 + 0.04X_4$$
$$R^2 = 0.34$$
$$\text{MEN: } Y = 4.3 - 3.5X_1 + 6.9X_2 + 2.5X_3 + 3.9X_4$$
$$R^2 = .46$$

a In which group does X_2 have the greatest independent effect: men or women?
b In which group are X_1, X_2, X_3 and X_4 together best at predicting Y?
c Among men, which variable is the best independent predictor of Y?

7 Explain the purpose and value of multivariate analysis.
8 What role does theory play in these complex multivariate statistical methods of analysis?
9 We initially have two variables: years of completed education (Y) and type of secondary school attended (X). Type of school attended has five

categories: government only, Catholic only, private (non-government) only, a combination of government and Catholic and a combination of goverment and private. To do regression analysis the type of schooling variable needs to be formed into a set of dummy variables. When this was done the following results were obtained:

Variable	b
Catholic education only (EdCATH)	1.01
Private school education only (EdPRIV)	1.61
Combination of government and Catholic schooling (EdGOVCAT)	1.61
Combination of government and private schooling (EdGOVPRV)	1.10
Constant	10.30

On the basis of these results answer the following questions:
a What is the omitted category?
b What are the average years of completed schooling of students who went only to government schools?
c Which type of schooling leads to the greatest number of years of completed education? Provide estimates for each type of schooling.
d On average, how many years do students who only attend Catholic schools complete?

10 If we add gender (coded 0 = male; 1 = female) to the above equation we obtain the following results:

Variable	b
EdCATH	1.04
EdPRIV	1.64
EdGOVCAT	1.60
EdGOVPRV	1.05
Gender	−0.46
Constant	10.06

a Given that all the variables are dummy or dichotomous variables what does the figure 10.06 for the constant represent?
b How many years of completed education would you estimate that males who attended Catholic schools only would have?
c Which groups of people would have more completed years of education than the above group?
d When the type of school attended is the same, who has the greatest number of years of completed schooling — males or females?

11 When age (coded in years) is added to the above equation, the following results are obtained:

Variable	b
EdCATH	0.97
EdPRIV	1.67
EdGOVCAT	1.32
EdGOVPRV	1.03
Gender	−0.44
Age	−0.04
Constant	11.70

a What does the figure of 11.70 for the constant represent?

b Looking at the results for the above equation, which type of schooling results in the greatest number of years of completed schooling? How many years is that?

c Do older people tend to have more or less years of completed schooling than younger people when other things (gender and type of schooling) are taken into account?

d How many years of schooling would you predict the following would have:

- 25 year old male who exclusively attended a private school;
- a comparable female;
- a male who attended a combination of Catholic and government schooling;
- a male who attended only Catholic schools.

14 Coding

1 For an earlier exercise on questionnaire design you will have developed a short questionnaire. Develop a full codebook for this questionnaire.

2 Do the same with any other questionnaire you can get hold of.

3 Ask a wide range of people an open-ended question (e.g. what do you think of university?) and develop a coding scheme from the answers given.

4 Formulate one multivariable questionnaire item.

5 Under what circumstances would you precode questions?

6 What are the advantages and disadvantages of precoding?

7 Explain, with examples, how you would check that data have been coded and entered onto the computer correctly.

8 You have used an open-ended question in a survey asking people about the conditions under which they believe that capital punishment is justifiable. Imagine that no one listed more than four different conditions, but overall there were 10 different situations mentioned by va-

rious respondents. For the purpose of this exercise you will need to imagine what these 10 conditions might be (it does not matter what conditions you come up with). Show how you would go about coding the responses to this question using both the multiple dichotomies method and the multiple response method of coding.

15 Building scales

1 In your own words explain why it is desirable to build scales.
2 What is the difference between reliability and unidimensionality?
3 Use the questions in Chapter 15 designed to test future orientation and administer them to some people (if done as a class obtain about 100 cases). Using the steps described, test to see which items belong to the scale. You will need to use the SPSSX reliability program for this. Make sure that you work out what to do with missing data.
4 From the correlation matrix below decide which items you would select to include in a scale (or scales).

	Variables						
	A	B	C	D	E	E	F
A	1.00	0.05	0.00	0.21	−0.03	0.09*	0.32*
B	0.05	1.00	0.21*	0.10	0.44*	0.17*	0.01
C	0.00	0.21*	1.00	0.03	0.26*	0.11	0.09
D	0.21*	0.10	0.03	1.00	−0.04	0.00	0.18*
E	−0.03	0.44*	0.26*	−0.04	1.00	0.30*	−0.02
F	0.09	0.17*	0.11	0.00	0.30*	1.00	0.04
G	0.32*	0.01	0.09	0.18*	−0.02	0.04	1.00

* = significant at the 0.01 level

5 Imagine a set of ten questions designed to measure conservatism. Each item is scored from 1 to 4 with 4 being given to the most conservative response to each question. Non-answers were coded as 9.
   a What would be the scale score of someone who was most conservative on every question?
   b What is the minimum scale score possible?
   c What would a scale score of 48 suggest?
   d If two people both obtained a scale score of 25 what conclusions can you draw about how they answered each question?
   e If one person obtained a scale score of 15 and another a score of 30, what conclusions would you draw from this?
6 Imagine you obtained the following co-efficients when testing the ten items for the previous scale. What would you do on the basis of these? Why?

Item	Item-total correlations	Alpha if item deleted
1	0.56	0.59
2	0.20	0.68
3	0.33	0.67
4	0.47	0.62
5	0.21	0.71
6	0.51	0.62
7	0.72	0.60
8	0.43	0.73
9	0.50	0.64
10	−0.57	0.61

Overall alpha 0.62

7   Explain using an example why missing data cause problems when scaling.

8   Explain using an example why items with a different number of response categories can cause problems when building scales.

9   Below are some details about a set of questions we want to form into an equal weight scale. As they are, would they form an equal weight scale? Why or why not? If they would not form an equal weight scale as they are, how would you go about ensuring that each of the items had an equal weight in the final scale?

Item	N of categories	Minimum possible value	Maximum possible value	Mean	Standard deviation
A	2	0	1	0.59	0.13
B	10	1	10	3.51	2.04
C	4	1	4	3.13	0.78
D	5	0	4	3.03	0.86
E	7	1	7	3.49	1.99
F	10	0	9	7.56	3.24
G	5	0	4	1.98	1.12

10 Below are some details about three composite scales, each of different lengths, in which the items have been equally weighted. Each of the scales had the following characteristics:

Scale	Lowest observed score	Highest observed score	Lowest possible score	Highest possible score
A	5.5	8.9	2.5	11.6
B	0.7	10.5	0.6	11.5
C	6.5	0.5	5.5	23.0

a A person obtained the following scores on the three untransformed scales: Scale A = 6.0; Scale B = 2.2; Scale C = 9.0. Using the formula in Chapter 13 convert these scores to scores on transformed scales that would have a minimum value of 0 and a maximum value of 10. What do the transformed scores tell you when you compare this person's score on the three transformed scales?

b A person obtained the following scores on each of the untransformed scales: Scale A = 7.0; Scale B = 7.2; Scale C = 7.3. Convert these scores to scores on scales that would have a minimum value of 0 and a maximum of 10. What does a comparison of the transformed scores tell you?

11 Below are statistics produced for a factor analysis of eight variables. Your task is to inspect the statistics and answer the questions that follow.

People were asked how justifiable they felt certain behaviours were. Each variable is scored on a scale from 1 to 5 with 1 meaning that the action was never justifiable and 5 indicating that it was always justifiable. The eight variables are: AFFAIR = Married person having an affair; UNSAFE = Accepting unsafe work conditions even if for higher wages; HOT = Buying something you knew was stolen; DIVORCE = Divorce justifiable; ABORT = Abortion justifiable; BENEFITS = Claiming government benefits to which you are not entitled; LIE = Lying in your own interest; HOMO = Justifiability of homosexuality.

Zero-order correlation matrix

	AFFAIR	UNSAFE	HOT	DIVORCE	ABORT	BENEFITS	LIE	HOMO
AFFAIR	1.00							
UNSAFE	.28	1.00						
HOT	.35	.29	1.00					
DIVORCE	.38	.17	1.00					
ABORT	.38	.18	.21	.55	1.00			
BENEFITS	.31	.28	.50	.12	.14	1.00		
LIE	.49	.30	.41	.25	.30	.36	1.00	
HOMO	.40	.14	.20	.44	.45	.14	.26	1.00

KMO = 0.81

Communality, eigenvalues and variance figures before rotation

Variable	Communality	Factor	Eigenvalue	% of variance	Cum pct
AFFAIR	.55	1	3.14	39.3	39.3
UNSAFE	.35	2	1.39	17.4	56.7
HOT	.61	3	.78	9.7	66.4
DIVORCE	.65	4	.68	8.5	74.9
ABORT	.65	5	.58	7.3	82.2
BENEFITS	.61	6	.51	6.4	88.6
LIE	.53	7	.47	5.9	94.5
HOMO	.57	8	.44	5.5	100.0

Unrotated factor loadings

Variable	Factor 1	Factor 2
AFFAIR	.74	−.02
LIE	.69	.23
ABORT	.65	−.48
DIVORCE	.62	−.51
HOT	.62	.48
HOMO	.61	−.44
UNSAFE	.49	.33
BENEFITS	.55	.55

Rotated factor matrix

Variable	Factor 1	Factor 2
BENEFITS	.78	−.00
HOT	.77	.09
LIE	.65	.32
UNSAFE	.58	.11
DIVORCE	.07	.80
ABORT	.12	.80
HOMO	.12	.75
AFFAIR	.50	.54

a   If you were redoing this factor analysis, are there any variables that
    you would omit? Give reasons for your decision.
b   On the basis of the figures in the zero-order correlation matrix, what
    variables would you anticipate will cluster together into factors?
    Explain your answer.
c   Examine the second table. On the basis of these figures, what is the

Factor scores for variables on factor 1
(includes the raw and standardised scores for a particular
individual for each of the variables for a given individual)

Variable	Factor score	Raw score	Standard score
AFFAIR	.15	2	.30
UNSAFE	.28	4	.85
HOT	.38	4	.68
DIVORCE	−.12	3	.15
ABORT	−.10	5	1.10
BENEFITS	.40	4	.4
LIE	.27	5	.9
HOMO	−.09	1	−.2

    optimal number of factors needed to represent this set of variables?
Explain in your own words the meaning of the following figures in
the second table: 0.55 (communality); 3.14 (eigenvalue); 39.3 (% of
variance); 56.7 (cum pct). Show how the figures of 0.55 and 3.14
would have been calculated.

d   Examine the rotated factor matrix. What name would you give each
factor? What do the high figures mean? What do the low figures
mean?

e   On the basis of the information in the fourth and fifth tables, calculate:
   (i)   the unweighted factor-based scale score for the individual
whose scores are provided;
  (ii) the weighted factor-based scale score;
 (iii) the factor scale score.

16   Initial analysis

The best way to learn to do analysis is to actually do it. Only a few exercises
have been provided because it is hoped that you will have a set of data on
which to apply the principles in Chapter 16.

1   List the steps you would normally take during initial analysis.

2   What will be the main focus and role of initial analysis?

3 a   Turn to Table 9.3 and collapse it into four categories on the basis of
the variable's distribution.

   b   Collapse Table 9.3 using the substantive approach. Justify your
classification.

   c   Compare the advantages and disadvantages of the two approaches.

5   Dichotomise the variable in Table 9.4.

6   How might you recode marital status in Table 10.2? Give reasons for your
answer.

7 Explain why reverse coding may be necessary.

8 Make up two crosstabulations. The second table will be a collapsed version of the first (e.g. Table 16.2). Develop the two tables so that in one there is a relationship but in the other it is masked.

9 Here is the list of religious groupings and in brackets following each is an approximation of the percentage of people in each grouping (Australian figures). Draw two frequency tables in which the categories are arranged in a sensible order. List alternative ways in which they could also have been ordered. The second table will have fewer categories. Use the guidelines in Chapter 16 to combine categories.

Anglican (11%); Baptist (2%); Brethren (0.2%); Catholic (28%); Churches of Christ (1.2%); Church of England (17%); Congregational (0.5%); Greek Orthodox (2.6%); Indefinite (0.4%); Jehovah's Witness (0.3%); Hebrew (0.6%); Lutheran (1.7%); Muslim (0.4%); No religion (2.6%); Not stated (9.8%); Presbyterian (3%); Salvation Army (0.50%); Seventh Day Adventist (0.3%); Uniting (12%)*; Other Christian (2.7%); Protestant (undefined) (3.2%).

* a combination of Methodist, Presbyterian and Congregational churches.

10 Below is a set of data for 10 people for seven variables. In each cell of the table the numbers represent codes for each variable. The * symbol indicates missing data. The seventh variable is gender where M=male and F=female. All the other variables are interval level variables.

CASE	Var 1	Var 2	Var 3	Var 4	Var 5	Var 6	Gender
1	7	*	2	2	4	4	M
2	4	9	*	1	1	2	M
3	6	2	2	2	*	7	F
4	*	9	7	1	6	4	F
5	0	4	8	4	6	3	F
6	5	1	7	3	*	8	M
7	6	7	*	5	3	9	M
8	5	*	4	2	*	6	F
9	*	7	*	7	*	1	M
10	6	4	6	*	8	5	F

a If you correlated var 1 with var 4, how many missing cases would you have if you used the pairwise method of handling missing data? How many missing cases would the listwise method result in?

b Without substituting new values for missing values, what steps would you take to minimise the influence of missing values for this set of data?

c Using the sample means approach, develop substitute scores for the missing values scores for var 1.

d   Using the group means approach (use gender as the grouping variable), develop substitute scores for missing values for var 2.
e   Use the random assignment of values within groups approach (use gender as the grouping variable) to develop substitute values for missing values for var 1.

17   Moving beyond initial analysis

As with initial analysis the best exercise is to do some actual analysis.
1   You find a relationship between gender and self-esteem: males have a higher self-esteem than females. You wish to find out why this relationship exists. Explain what steps you would take to do this.
2   You expect gender to be related to income but find that it does not seem to be.
    a   Outline what steps you could take to check why the expected relationship was not found.
    b   If despite all your checking you cannot explain the absence of the anticipated pattern, what should you do then with the results?
3   You expect to find no relationship between gender and intelligence but find a moderate association with females being more intelligent than males.
    a   Outline the steps you could take to check why these results were found.
    b   If despite your checking the relationship remains, what would be your next course of action?
4   You have found, as expected, that education is positively related to tolerance: the more education, the greater the tolerance. You are tempted to go no further since you have found the results you want.
    a   Why is further analysis necessary?
    b   What analysis might you do?
5   You suspect your sample is biased.
    a   How would you go about checking this?
    b   How would you check to see if the bias is affecting your results?
    c   How would you minimise the influence of bias in the sample?
6   a   Explain in your own words what Deviant Case Analysis is.
    b   What is the point of DCA? Illustrate your answer with an example.   .
    c   When is it helpful to use DCA?
7   a   What is *ex post facto* theorising?
    b   What are the dangers of *ex post facto* theorising?
    c   How are these dangers best avoided?
    d   In Chapter 2 in the section on plausibility and theory testing there are five *ex post facto* explanations for why women are more religious than men. Select any two of these and explain briefly what sort of data you would collect to test them.

18 Putting it into practice

1 Explain what the figures in the two right-hand columns of Table 18.1 mean.
2 Based on Table 18.2, what percentage of women in the sample worked full time?
3 Put each of the figures in column 1 of Table 18.3 into words.
4 What do the partial gammas in Table 18.4 tell you? Why are they not sufficient on their own to evaluate the extent to which workforce participation accounts for the relationship between gender and religiousness?
5 The figures below represent the regression estimates for church attendance for females using the same data and variables as used in Figure 18.2. Remember that church attendance has been converted to a score on a 0 to 10 scale and that the workforce participation variables are dummy variables.

Variable	b
Age	0.05
Australian	−0.79
Urban	−0.53
Education	0.18
Occupation	0.75
Family income	−0.02
Part timers	1.63
Unemployed	1.25
Home duties	1.25
Retired	0.70
Constant	1.25

a Using the regression equation on page 318 estimate the church attendance score for females in each of the five workforce participation categories.
b Explain, in simple English, what the co-efficient 1.63 for part timers means.
c Explain, in simple English, the meaning of the figure 1.25 for the constant.
6 Explain as clearly as you can why the figures in Tables 18.6 mean that the greater overall religiousness of women is not due to their child rearing responsibilities.
7 Examine Table 18.7 and answer the following questions
a What does the figure 1.4 in the belief column represent?
b What does the figure 0.7 (direct effect) in the belief column mean?
c What does the figure 0.7 (indirect effect) in the belief column mean?
d Explain how the figures in the belief column support the view that workforce participation is the most important single reason for gender differences in religious belief.

19   Ethics

1   As part of a survey on the way parents raise their children you ask about discipline. In the process you discover that a parent is using discipline techniques that you believe constitute child abuse. However, you have guaranteed confidentiality. What should you do?

2   In this study, as part of the informed consent procedures, you outline to respondents the areas about which questions will be asked. You are aware that you are obliged by the law to report any instance where you suspect child abuse may be taking place. The law adopts a definition of child abuse that is much stricter than many parents would accept (e.g. hitting a child with an object) and it is likely that some parents will report behaviour that they see as innocent but which falls under the definition of child abuse. You fear that if you tell them of your obligation to report and explain the types of behaviour that are reportable many people will either refuse to participate or will not report their actual methods of discipline thus invalidating the findings. What should you do?

3   On pages 344 and 345 is a list of ways in which people might contribute to a research project. Which of these people should be recognised as authors? By what principles are you making your decisions?

4   After carefully informing a person of the purpose and content of a project a person agrees to participate in an interview for the project and signs an informed consent form to indicate this. Some time later the person indicates that on reflection they do not want to be part of the study and they want their information to be destroyed. However, you have spent both time and money on this case and are well advanced with your data analysis. What should you do? Why?

5   A team of interviewers has collected data for your survey of 2000 adults. After publishing your results in a journal you discover that one interviewer did not administer the questionnaires but fabricated answers. What should you do? You decide to reanalyse the data and find that no patterns are changed significantly. What should you do?

6   In the course of interviews among marijuana users to whom you have promised confidentiality you learn of the identity of a person who is distributing hard drugs. What should you do?

7   You obtain the membership list of a secretive religious sect and wish to obtain their views on a number of political, ethical and religious matters. You believe that they would be unwilling to participate in a study of the views of members of that sect so you send them a survey questionnaire telling them that they have been selected at random as part of a nationwide survey of opinions? Is this a justifiable way of obtaining data that would otherwise be inaccessible? Why, or why not?

8   A researcher wants to obtain information about the way university affects the attitudes of students about the roles of males and females. The first step is to measure their attitudes when they come to university and to this end the researcher obtains permission to include a set of questions in the questionnaire that the university requires all new students to complete when they enrol. The university questionnaire includes questions about the student's background, their parent's background, their educational aspirations and

their reasons for attending this particular university. Do you see any ethical problems with this research exercise?

9 A university requires that all lecturers administer a student evaluation questionnaire at the end of each subject to measure the level of satisfaction of students with the particular subject. What ethical issues arise in this exercise and what measures would you take to ensure that ethical guidelines were adhered to?

10 List methods by which one can minimise the chances of researchers misrepresenting their data through misanalysis or fabrication.

Glossary

acquiescent response set: the tendency of some respondents to automatically agree with 'agree/disagree' questionnaire statements.

availability sample: a form of non-probability sampling in which the sample units are selected simply because they are available.

average: a general term that refers to statistics (mode, median and the mean) measuring normality. The choice of which average to use depends on the variable's level of measurement and distribution.

beta weight: a standardised regression co-efficient that represents how many standard deviation units the dependent variable changes for each standard deviation unit change of the independent variable.

bias: where error tends to go in one direction more than another.

bivariate analysis: a general category of analysis in which two variables are analysed simultaneously in order to examine the relationship between the two variables.

census: the collection of data from *all* the population elements rather than from a subset (a sample).

central tendency measures: see **averages**

closed response questions: questions in which the respondent is asked to select from a set of pre-defined responses.

cluster sampling: a form of probability sampling in which sample elements are concentrated in selected geographic areas (e.g. census collectors' districts, city blocks).

codebook: a listing of the contents of a data file that identifies the characteristics of each variable. It contains the variable's column location, name, codes, labels, the form of the data (e.g. numeric or alphanumeric) and its frequency distribution.

coding: the symbols used to represent categories of a variable (e.g. 1 = male; 2 = female). Although these symbols are usually numeric (numbers), alphanumeric (letters) characters may be used.

concept: general and abstract notion that is not directly measurable or observable. Concepts are the building blocks of theories but need to be operationalised before being used in empirical research.

conceptual proposition: a statement of a relationship between two concepts. Conceptual propositions may be *causal* (religiousness produces conservatism) or *non causal* (religiousness is related to conservatism). They may be *directional* (the greater the religiousness the greater the conservatism) or *non directional* (religiousness is related to conservatism).

conditional relationships: a relationship between two variables that varies depending on the presence of other conditions. For example, if the relationship between education and income is stronger among males than among females the relationship between education and income is conditional because it depends on a third factor (gender). This is also known as statistical interaction.

confidence interval: the range of values between which the population parameter is estimated to lie. The confidence interval should be used in conjunction with the *confidence level*.

confidence level: indicates how *likely* it is that the population parameter will lie within the range specified by the confidence interval.

construct validity: the evaluation of the validity of a measure by comparing results using that measure with the results expected on the basis of theory. If the results do not conform to theory it is usually assumed that the measure rather than the theory is at fault.

content validity: the assessment of validity based on whether the measure of the concept covers the concept's full meaning (e.g. does a test of mathematical skills cover the full range of mathematical operations?).

contingency question: a question which is asked of only some respondents depending on their answers to previous filter questions.

control variable: a variable, often called the Z variable or the test variable, that is held constant when exploring the nature of the relationship between other variables. By holding a variable constant we can ascertain the extent to which the control variable is responsible for the initial relationship.

controls/controlling: the process of removing the effect of control variables on the relationship between other variables.

correlation co-efficient: an index of the extent to which two variables co-vary within the same sample (e.g. are differences in income linked to educational differences?). There are many different correlation co-efficients (e.g. gamma, Person's r, Spearman's Rho) and most range between 0 (the two variables do not co-vary) to 1 (the variables always vary together). Co-efficients may have negative values.

correlation matrix: a grid in which each column and each row represents a variable. The intersection of each column and row is a correlation co-efficient of the column and row variables.

criterion validity: the evaluation of validity by comparing results based on new measures of a concept with those using established measures.

cross sectional design: a study in which all observations are made at a single point of time. See also **longitudinal design**.

crosstabulation: a table consisting of rows and columns. The columns represent the categories of one variable while the rows represent the categories of another variable. The intersection of a column and a row produces a cell which represents cases having the attributes of *both* that column and that row.

deductive reasoning: the process whereby specific expectations or hypotheses are logically derived from more general principles.

dependent variable: the variable, frequently referred to as the Y variable, that is assumed to be the effect in a 'cause-effect' relationship.

descriptive statistic: statistics that summarise the characteristics of a sample as opposed to inferential statistics that are used to generalise to the population from which the sample is drawn.

dichotomous variables: a variable having only two categories.

double-barrelled question: a single question that effectively asks two questions at once.

dummy regression: a form of regression where nominal variables are able to be used by transforming them into a *set* of dichotomous (dummy) variables which are appropriate for regression analysis.

elaboration analysis: analysis which explores the influence of other variables on a bivariate relationship.

equal weight scales: a scale in which each item has the potential to contribute equally to scale scores. Each item will either have the same number of categories, coding scores and distributions or will be adjusted to achieve comparability between items.

factor analysis: analysis that detects the more general dimensions (factors) underlying responses to a set of questions. It helps detect the structure of attitudes, reduces data and assists in scale development.

factor based scales: scales in which the items are selected by factor analysing a set of items. The factor analysis identifies which items are suitable for the development of a unidimensional scale.

filter question: a question designed to divide respondents into those who need to answer a subsequent contingency question and those who should skip to a later question.

frequency distribution: the display of the number of sample elements that belong to each category of a variable.

hypothesis: a statement, logically derived from a theory, that states what one expects to find in the real world if the theory is correct.

independent variable: frequently referred to as the X variable, it is the assumed *cause* in a 'cause-effect' relationship.

indicator: specific measure of a more abstract concept.

indirect relationship: a causal relationship between two variables that is mediated via a third, intervening variable.

inductive reasoning: the process, used in theory construction, whereby one uses specific observations to draw general conclusions consistent with the particular observations.

inferential statistics: a class of statistics which enables one to estimate whether sample results are likely to hold in the population. They can only be used with probability samples—see **significance tests**.

intercept: the point at which the regression line crosses the Y axis. The value of the Y variable in regression analysis when X = 0.

interval level variable: a variable where the rank ordered categories are separated by numerically equal distances.

intervening variable: see **indirect relationship**

level of measurement: refers to the way that categories of variables relate to each other. The level of measurement is a function of whether categories of the variable can be ranked and whether there are numerically meaningful intervals between the categories. Level of measurement of variables is crucial when selecting statistics for the analysis of variables.

Likert scale: a composite scale developed by Renis Likert which typically uses attitude statements using the standardised strongly agree, agree, disagree and strongly disagree format. Before individual items are formed into a scale, the scale must meet statistical requirements of reliability and unidimensionality.

linear relationship: a relationship between two ordinal or interval variables in which a change in one variable is related to a change in the other variable in a consistent direction. As one variable increases, the other increases or decreases at a consistent rate.

longitudinal design: a study in which data are collected from the same cases at two or more points of time.

mean: an average for interval level data that is computed by adding the values for all cases and dividing by the number of cases.

measure of association: see **correlation co-efficient**

measure of dispersion: a class of statistic that indicates the extent to which cases in a sample differ from one another.

median: an average, appropriate for ordinal or interval data where the median is the value of the middle case in a ranked set of cases.

missing data: where an observation is missing for a case, that case is given a distinctive code indicating that they have not answered the question and should be excluded from the analysis of that question.

mode: an average, mainly used for nominal level variables, that reflects the most frequently observed value of a variable.

multiple dichotomy coding: where respondents can select more than one response to a question, one way of coding all their answers is to treat each possible response as a separate variable and to give each of these variables two codes: one to indicate that this response was not selected and the other to indicate that it was selected.

multiple regression: regression analysis in which there is one dependent variable and two or more independent variables.

multiple response coding: a method of coding questions where respondents can provide more than one answer. It involves determining the maximum number of responses given by any respondent and creating that many variables. Each variable will have identical categories and codes to cover the range of responses to the question. Each respondent's responses will be coded to these variables. If a respondent provides only one response then only one variable will be used (they will receive missing value codes on the others). If a person provides three responses then three of the new variables will be used to encapsulate these responses.

multiple response questions: a question to which a respondent may provide more than one answer.

multistage sampling: a sample involving a series of sequential samples. For example, a sample of school children might be obtained by first obtaining a sample of cities, then of schools within the selected cities and then of children within the selected schools. This is a useful method of sampling where a sampling frame of the final sample elements is unavailable.

multivariate analysis: analysis in which the simultaneous relationships of three or more variables are examined.

negative relationship: a relationship in which an increase in one variable tends to produce a decrease in the other variable.

nominal level variable: a variable in which the categories cannot be ranked or the intervals between categories quantified.

non-probability sample: a form of sampling in which cases are selected on a basis *other than* the random selection criteria required by probability theory.

null hypothesis: a hypothesis that states that there is *no* relationship between two variables in the population from which the sample is drawn. A null hypothesis is used in statistical inference where we begin with the assumption of no relationship and seek, via tests of statistical significance, to *reject* it. If we can reject the null hypothesis we assume a real relationship in the population.

open ended questions: a questionnaire item where, in the absence of set alternatives, the respondent is invited to formulate an answer.

operational definition: where a concept has been translated into a set of indicators, the indicators and the decisions about how to classify individuals provide the operational definition of the concept. For example, we might use education, occupation and income to operationalise social class and then specify the specific criteria to classify people into particular social classes.

operationalistion: the process of translating abstract concepts into operational definitions.

ordinal level variable: a variable in which the categories can be ranked but for which there is no meaningful numeric interval between categories.

partial correlation: the strength of a relationship between two variables in which the influence of at least one other variable has been removed (controlled).

path analysis: a form of multivariate analysis using multiple correlation and multiple regression which enables the analysis of direct and indirect relationships between the variables in the model. The relationships between the variables (paths) are represented diagramatically and the importance of each path is represented by path co-efficients (beta weights).

pilot testing: a test run of a set of questionnaire items to detect problems with the questions and questionnaire design.

population: a precisely defined set of elements from which a sample is drawn.

positive relationship: a relationship in which a change in one variable tends to produce a change in the other variable in the same direction.

probability sample: a form of sampling in which some form of random selection is used to select sample elements. Accordingly, every element in the population has a known probability of being included in the final sample.

purposive sample: a form of non-probability sample in which elements are selected for their presumed typicality.

quota sample: a form of non-probability sampling in which elements are selected to fill quotas of elements with particular characteristics. The quotas are established so as to reflect the population in relation to the quota characteristics.

recoding: altering the initial codes given to a variable. Changes are made to reorder categories of a variable and to combine a number of initial categories into a single, broader category.

regression co-efficient: a co-efficient used in regression analysis that estimates how much the dependent variable changes for each unit change of the independent variable.

regression: a method for describing the relationship between two or more interval level variables. It estimates the impact of one variable on another (i.e. how much does the dependent variable change for each unit change of the independent variable?), evaluates the relative impact of various independent variables (beta weights) and predicts the value of the dependent variable under various conditions.

reliability: a measure of the consistency with which people give the same response on different occasions assuming no change in the characteristic being measured. A consistent but false response is still reliable.

replication: a technical term used in elaboration analysis which is used to describe the pattern whereby the zero order relationship remains after control variables have been introduced. Also means duplicating a set of results by means of an identical study.

representative: the extent to which the characteristics of a sample match those of the population from which the sample is drawn. Representativeness is best achieved by probability sampling.

response rate: the percentage of a sample from which information is successfully obtained. Response rates are calculated differently depending on the method of questionnaire administration.

robust relationship: a zero order relationship that persists after controlling for various test variables—see **replication.**

sample: a subset of a population. The method of obtaining a sample affects the extent to which sample results can be extrapolated to the population.

sampling error: the extent, reflected by the standard error statistic, to which the sample differs from the population.

sampling fraction: the proportion of the population represented by the sample. If the sample is 5 per cent of the population, the sampling fraction is one in twenty. Except with small populations, the sampling fraction is unimportant.

sampling frame: the complete list of elements of the population from which a sample will be drawn.

scale: a composite measure where the individual measures are designed to tap the same underlying concept. The individual measures should be both logically and empirically related.

scattergram: a graphical representation of the relationship between two interval level variables in which each case is represented by point.

secondary analysis: the reanalysis of data often for a different purpose to that for which the data were originally collected.

significance tests: inferential statistics that indicate the likelihood that the relationship observed in the sample is due to sampling error or reflects a real relationship in the population. A low significance figure (e.g. 0.01) reflects that the observed sample results are unlikely to be due to sampling error while a high figure (e.g. 0.50) indicates that the observed relationship is very likely to be due to sampling error.

simple random sample: a form of probability sampling in which each population element is assigned a number and a set of numbers which are selected from a table of random numbers. Population elements matching the selected numbers constitute the sample.

skewness: the extent to which scores on an interval level variable are concentrated at either end of the distribution.

social desirability response set: the tendency of people to answer a set of questions in a socially approved manner rather than in a way that truly reflects their own views.

specification: see **conditional relationships**

spurious relationship: a relationship in which two variables co-vary and may therefore appear to be causally related but in fact co-vary because they are both consequences of a third, extraneous variable.

standard deviation: a measure of dispersion appropriate for interval level variables.

standardised scale: a scale in which each person's score on each variable is expressed in terms of the number of standard deviation units from the mean thereby adjusting for items with varying number of categories and different distributions.

standardised scores: see **z-scores**

stratified sample: a form of probability sampling in which the sample frame is ordered so that population elements with a particular characteristic in common (e.g. female) are listed together followed by the next grouping (e.g. male). The variables used to order the sampling frame are called stratifying variables. Once the elements have been ordered a systematic sample is drawn. This guarantees that the sample will be entirely representative in terms of the stratifying variable(s) used.

systematic sample: a form of probability sampling in which a sampling fraction is established (e.g. 1 in 20) and then every twentieth (or whatever) case is selected for the sample.

test variables: see **control variables**

testable proposition: a conceptual proposition in which the concepts have been operationalised.

theory construction/building: the process of developing explanations on the basis of data and observations—see **inductive reasoning**.

theory testing: deducing predictions from a theory and testing these against empirical observations. If the predictions hold, the theory is supported, but if they do not hold, the theory is revised or rejected.

theory: a set of interrelated conceptual causal propositions.

trichotomising: dividing a distribution into three groups each with a similar number of cases. The first group will be the third of cases with the lowest scores on the variable, the second group will be the middle third of cases while the final group will be the third of the sample with the highest scores.

unidimensional scale: a scale that taps one and only one concept.

unit of analysis: the element about which data are collected. In surveys the unit of analysis is frequently the individual respondent but it equally might be a whole family or household. In such cases we collect data that relates specifically to this different unit of analysis (e.g. household size, total household income, education of head of household).

univariate analysis: the analysis of a single variable.

validity: whether an indicator measures the concept that we say it does.

variable by case matrix: the form of structured data on which survey research is based. One dimension of the matrix (rows) will represent cases (e.g. individuals) while the other dimension (columns) will represent variables. The conjunction of any particular row and column will contain the value of a particular variable for a particular case.

variable: a characteristic that is not the same for all cases.

variance: a measure of dispersion appropriate for interval level variables.

variation ratio: a measure of dispersion appropriate for nominal level variables.

z-score: the difference between an individual's score and the mean score of a distribution expressed in standard deviation units.

zero order relationships: a relationship between two variables without controlling for the effects of additional variables.

Bibliography

Achen, C.H. (1982) 'Interpreting and Using Regression' Sage University Paper series on Quantitative Applications in the Social Sciences, 07-029, Beverly Hills: Sage

Alexander, C.S. and Becker, H.J. (1978) 'The use of vignettes in survey research' *Public Opinion Quarterly* 42: 93–104

Babbie, E. (1983) *The Practice of Social Research* 3rd edn, Belmont: Wadsworth

Baldamus, W. (1976) *The Structure of Sociological Inference* London: Martin Robertson

Barnes, J.A. (1979) *Who Should Know What? Social Science, Privacy and Ethics* Cambridge: Cambridge University Press

Barton, J.A. (1958) 'Asking the Embarrassing Question' *Public Opinion Quarterly* 22: 67–68

Bateson, N. (1984) *Data Construction in Social Surveys* London, George Allen & Unwin

Baumrind, D. (1964) 'Some thoughts on ethics in research: After Reading Milgram's "Behavioural study of Obedience" ' *American Psychologist* 19: 421–23

Beed, T. and Stimson, R. (eds) (1985) *Survey Interviewing: theory and techniques* London: Allen & Unwin

Bell, C. and Encel, S. (eds) (1978) *Inside the Whale* Sydney: Pergamon

Bell, C. and Newby, H. (1971) *Community Studies* London: George Allen & Unwin

—— (eds) (1977) *Doing Sociological Research* London: George Allen & Unwin

Belson, W.A. (1981) *The Design and Understanding of Survey Questions* Aldershot: Gower

Berger, P.L. (1963) *Invitation to Sociology* Ringwood: Penguin

—— (1974) 'Some second thoughts on substantive versus functional definitions of religion' *Journal for the Scientific Study of Religion* 13: 125–133

Berry, W.D. and Feldman, S. (1985) 'Multiple regression in practice' Sage University Paper series on Quantitative Applications in the Social Sciences, 07-050, Beverly Hills: Sage

Blalock, H.M. (1972) *Social Statistics* 2nd edn, New York: McGraw-Hill

Blumer, H. (1956) 'Sociological analysis and the variable' *American Sociological Review* 21: 683–90

Boruch, R.F. and Cecil, J.S. (1979) *Assuring the Confidentiality of Social Research Data* Philadelphia: University of Pennsylvania Press

Bradburn, N.M. and Sudman, S. (1979) *Improving Interview Method and Questionnaire Design* San Francisco: Jossey Bass

Burke, P. (ed.) (1973) *A New Kind of History: from the writings of Febvre* London: Routledge and Kegan Paul

Campbell, D.T. and Stanley, J.C. (1963) *Experimental and Quasi-Experimental Designs for Research* Chicago: Rand McNally

Carmines, E.G. and Zeller, R.A. (1979) 'Reliability and Validity Assessment', Sage University Paper series on Quantitative Applications in the Social Sciences, 07-017, Beverley Hills: Sage

Chavetz, J. (1978) *A Primer on the Construction and Testing of Theories in Sociology* Itasca, Illinois: Peacock

Clark, A.W. (1983) *Social Science: introduction to theory and method* Sydney: Prentice Hall Australia

Cohen, L. and Holliday, M. (1982) *Statistics for Social Scientists* London: Harper & Row

Converse, J.M. and Presser, S. (1986) 'Survey Questions: Handcrafting the Standardized Questionnaire', Sage University Paper series on Quantitative Applications in the Social Sciences, 07-063, Beverly Hills: Sage

Converse, P.E., Watson, J.D., Hoag, W.J. and McGee, W.H. III (eds) (1980) *American Social Attitudes Data Sourcebook 1947–1978* Cambridge: Harvard University Press

Cooper, H.M. (1989) *Integrating Research: A Guide for Literature Reviews* 2nd edn, Beverley Hills: Sage

Dale, A., Arber, S. and Proctor, M. (1988) *Doing Secondary Analysis* London: Unwin Hyman

Davis, J. (1968) 'Tabular presentation' in D.L. Sills (ed.) *International Encyclopaedia of the Social Sciences* 15, New York: Macmillan and Free Press

Davis, J.A. (1971) *Elementary Survey Analysis* Englewood Cliffs: Prentice Hall

—— (1985) 'The Logic of Causal Order' Sage University Paper series on Quantitative Applications in the Social Sciences, 07-055, Beverly Hills: Sage

Denzin, N.K. (1978) *The Research Act* 2nd edn, New York: McGraw Hill

de Vaus, D. (1980) The Process of Religious Change in Senior Adolescents, Unpublished PhD Thesis, La Trobe University

de Vaus, D. and McAllister, I. (1987) 'Gender differences in religion: a test of structural location theory' *American Sociological Review* 52: 472–81

Dillman, D.A. (1978) *Mail and Telephone Surveys: the total design method* New York: Wiley

Dubin, R. (1969) *Theory Building* New York: Free Press

Durkheim, E. (1970) *Suicide* Routledge and Kegan Paul

Edwards, A.L. (1957) *Techniques Attitude of Scale Construction* New York: Appleton-Century-Crofts

Ehrenberg, A.S.C. (1975) *Data Reduction: Analysing and Interpreting Statistical Data* London: Wiley

Fadden, R.R. and Beauchamp, T.L. (1986) *A History And Theory Of Informed Consent* New York: Oxford University Press

Finch, J. (1987) 'The vignette technique in survey research' *Sociology* 21: 105–14

Foddy, W.H. (1992) *Constructing Questions for Interviews and Questionnaires* Melbourne: Cambridge University Press

Fowler, F.J. (1988) *Survey Research Methods* rev. edn Beverly Hills: Sage

Freeman, L.C. (1965) *Elementary Applied Statistics* New York: Wiley

Freidheim, E. (1976) *Sociological Theory in Research Practice* Cambridge, Mass: Schenkman

Gallup, G.H. (1947) 'The Quintamensional Plan of Question Design' *Public Opinion Quarterly* 11, pp 385–393

Gallup, G. (1935–1971) *The Gallup Poll 1935–71*, 3 vols, New York: Random House

—— (1972–1981) *The Gallup Poll 1972–81*, 6 vols, Wilmington: Scholarly Resources

Glaser, B.G. and Strauss, A.L. (1967) *The Discovery of Grounded Theory* Chicago: Aldine

Glock, C.Y. and Stark, R. (1965) *Religion and Society in Tension* Chicago: Rand McNally

Gowers, E. (1962) *The Complete Plain Words* 2nd edn, Ringwood: Penguin

Green, B.F. (1954) 'Attitude Measurement' in G. Londzey (1984) (ed.) *Handbook of Social Psychology* Cambridge: Addison-Wesley

Groves, R.M. and Kahn, R.L. (1979) *Surveys by Telephone: a national comparison with personal interviews* New York: Academic Press

Guilford, J.P. (1965) *Fundamental Statistics in Psychology and Education* 4th edn, International student edition, New York: McGraw Hill

Hakim, C. (1982) *Secondary Analysis in Social Research* London: Allen & Unwin

—— (1987) *Research Design: Strategies and Choices in the Design of Social Research* London: Allen & Unwin

Hammond, Phillip E. (ed.) (1964) *Sociologists at Work* New York: Basic Books

Hardy, M.A. 'Regression with Dummy Variables' Sage University paper series on Quantitative Applications in the Social Sciences, 07-093, Beverly Hills: Sage

Hellevik, O. (1984) *Introduction to Causal Analysis* London: George Allen & Unwin

Henkel, R.E. (1976) 'Tests of Significance' Sage University Paper series on Quantitative Applications in the Social Sciences, 07-004, Beverly Hills: Sage

Hertel, B. (1976) 'Minimizing Error Variance Introduced by Missing Data Routines in Survey Analysis' *Sociological Methods and Research* 4: 459–74

Hilderbrand, D.K., Laing, J.D. and Rosenthal, H. (1977) 'Analysis of Ordinal Data' Sage University Paper series on Quantitative Applications in the Social Sciences, 07-008, Beverly Hills: Sage

Hillery, G.A. (1955) *Communal Organizations* Chicago: Chicago University Press

Hirschi, T. and Selvin, H. (1967) *Delinquency Research: An Appraisal of Analytic Methods*, New York: Free Press

Hoinville, G., Jowell, R. and associates (1977): *Survey Research Practice* London: Heinemann

Homans, G. (1967) *The Nature of Social Science* New York: Harcourt Brace Jovanovich

Huck, S.W. and Sandler, H.M. (1979) *Rival Hypotheses: Alternative Interpretations of Data Based Conclusions* New York: Harper & Row

Huff, D. (1954) *How to Lie With Statistics* London: Gollancz

Hyman, H. (1972) *Secondary Analysis of Sample Surveys* New York: Wiley

Johnson, A.G. (1977) *Social Statistics Without Tears* New York: McGraw Hill

Kadushin, C. (1968) 'Reason analysis' in D.L. Sills (ed.) *International Encyclopaedia of the Social Sciences* 13, New York: Macmillan and Free Press, pp 338–43

Kalton, G. (1983) 'Introduction to survey sampling' Sage University Paper series on Quantitative Applications in the Social Sciences, 07-035, Beverly Hills: Sage

Kelley, J., Cushing, R.G. and Heady, B. (1987) *Australian National Social Science Survey, 1984* Canberra: Social Science Data Archives, Australian National University

Kiecolt, K.J. and Nathan, L. (1985) 'Secondary analysis of survey data' Sage University Paper series on Quantitative Applications in the Social Sciences, 07-053, Beverly Hills: Sage

Kerlinger, F.N. and Pedhazur, E.J. (1973) *Multiple Regression in Behavioural Research* New York: Holt, Rinehart & Winston

Kerlinger, F.N. (1979) *Behavioural Research: A Conceptual Approach* Chapter 4, 11–13, New York: Holt, Rinehart & Winston

Kim, J. and Mueller, C.W. (1978a) 'Introduction to factor analysis: What it is and how to do it' Sage University Paper series on Quantitative Applications in the Social Sciences, 07-013, Beverly Hills: Sage

—— (1978b) 'Factory analysis: statistical methods and practical issues' Sage University Paper series on Quantitative Applications in the Social Sciences, 07-014, Beverly Hills: Sage

Kimmel, Allan J. (1988) *Ethics and Values in Applied Social Research* Applied Social Research Methods Series, Vol 12. Sage: Beverly Hills

Kish, L. (1949) 'A Procedure for Objective Respondent Selection Within a Household' *Journal of the American Statistical Association* 44: 380–387

—— (1965) *Survey Sampling* New York: Wiley

Kuhn, T. (1964) *The Structure of Scientific Revolutions* Chicago: University of Chicago

Labovitz, S. (1970) 'The Nonutility of Significance Tests: The Significance of Tests of Significance Reconsidered' *Pacific Sociological Review* 13: 141–148

Laslett, P. (ed.) (1972) *Household and Family in Past Time* London: Cambridge University Press

Lavrakas, Paul (1993) *Telephone Survey Methods: Sampling Selection and Supervision*, 2nd edn, Beverly Hills: Sage.

Lazarsfeld, P.F. and Rosenberg, M. (eds) (1955) *The Language of Social Research* Glencoe. Free Press

Lazarsfeld, P., Pasenella, A. and Rosenberg, M. (eds) (1972) *Continuities in the Language of Social Research* New York: Free Press

Lewis-Beck, M.S. (1980) 'Applied Regression: An Introduction' Sage University Paper series on Quantitative Applications in the Social Sciences, 07-022, Beverly Hills: Sage

Liebetrau, A.M. (1983) 'Measures of Association' Sage University Paper series on Quantitative Applications in the Social Sciences, 07-032, Beverly Hills: Sage

Loether, H.J. and McTavish, D.G. (1974a) *Descriptive Statistics for Sociologists* Boston: Allyn & Bacon

—— (1974b) *Inferential Statistics for Sociologists* Boston: Allyn and Bacon

McIver, J.P. and Carmines, E.G. (1981) 'Unidimensional Scaling' Sage University Paper series on Quantitative Applications in the Social Sciences, 07-024, Beverly Hills: Sage

Marsh, C. (1979) 'Opinion Polls—Social Science or Political Manouevre?' in J. Irvine, I. Miles and J. Evans (eds) 1979 *Demystifying Social Statistics* London: Pluto Press

—— (1982) *The Survey Method: the contribution of surveys to sociological explanation* London: George Allen & Unwin

—— (1988) *Exploring Data: An Introduction to Data Analysis for Social Sciences* Cambridge: Polity

Martin, E., McDuffee, D. and Presser, S. (1981) *Sourcebook of Harris National Surveys: Repeated Questions 1963–1976* Chapel Hill: Institute for Research in Social Science, University of North Carolina Press

Menard, S. (1991) 'Longitudinal Research' Sage University paper series on Quantitative Applications in the Social Sciences, 07-076, Beverly Hills: Sage

Merton, R.K. (1968) *Social Theory and Social Structure* 2nd edn, New York: Free Press

Milgram, S. (1964) 'Issues in the Study of Obedience: a reply to Baumrind' *American Psychologist* 19: 848-52.

Miller, D.E. (1970) *Handbook of Research Design and Social Measurement* New York: Mckay

Miller, W.E., Miller, A.H. and Schneider, E.J. (1980) *American National Election Studies Data Sourcebook 1951–1978* Cambridge: Harvard University Press

Mills, C.W. (1959) *The Sociological Imagination* New York: Harper & Row

Moser, C. and Kalton, G. (1971) *Survey Methods in Social Investigation* 2nd edn, London: Heinemann

Mueller, J.H., Schuessler, K.F. and Costner, H.L. (1977) *Statistical Reasoning in Sociology* 3rd edn, Boston: Hougton Mifflin

National Opinion Research Center (1990) *General Social Surveys 1972–1990: Cumulative Codebook* Chicago: NORC

Nie, N.H. et al. (1975) *SPSS; Statistical Package for the Social Sciences* 2nd edn, New York: McGraw-Hill

Norusis, M.J. (1983) *SPSSX: Introductory Statistics Guide* New York: McGraw-Hill

—— (1985) *SPSSX: Advanced Statistics Guide* New York: McGraw Hill

Oppenheim, A.N. (1968) *Questionnaire Design and Attitude Measurement* London: Heinemann

Parsons, T. (1949) 'The Social Structure of the Family' in R.N. Ashen (ed.) *The Family; its function and destiny* (1949) New York: Harper

Payne, S. (1951) *The Art of Asking Questions* Princeton: Princeton University Press

Reynolds, H.T. (1977) 'Analysis of Nominal Data' Sage University Paper series on Quantitative Applications in the Social Sciences, 07-007, Beverly Hills: Sage

Reynolds, P.D. (1979) *Ethical Dilemmas and Social Science Research* San Francisco: Jossey Bass

Ritzer, George (ed.) (1974) *Social Realities: Dynamic Perspectives* Boston: Allyn & Bacon

Robinson, J.P. et al. (1968a) *Measures of Political Attitudes* Ann Arbor: Institute for Social Research, University of Michigan

—— (1968b) *Measures of Social Psychological Attitudes* Ann Arbor, Institute for Social Research, University of Michigan

Rose, G. (1978) Deviant Case Analysis, unpublished paper presented to Sociology Department seminar, La Trobe University

—— (1982) *Deciphering Sociological Research* London: Macmillan

Rosenberg, M. (1968) *The Logic of Survey Analysis* New York: Basic Books

Runciman, W.G. (ed.) (1978) *Weber* Cambridge: Cambridge University Press

Schreiber, E.M. (1976) 'Dirty data in Britain and the USA: the reliability of "invariant" characteristics reported in surveys' *Public Opinion Quarterly* 4: 493–506

Schuman, H. and Presser, S. (1981) *Questions and Answers in Attitude Surveys* New York: Academic Press

Seiber, J.E. (ed.) (1982) *The Ethics of Social Research: Surveys and Experiments* New York: Springer-Verlag

Seiber, J.E. (1992) *Planning Ethically Responsible Research: A Guide for Students and Internal Review Boards* Beverly Hills: Sage

Selvin, H. (1957) 'A Critique of Tests of Significance in Survey Research' *American Sociological Review* 22: 519–527

Shaw, M.E. and Wright, J.M. (1967) *Scales for the Measurement of Attitudes* New York: McGraw-Hill

Shroeder, L.D., Sjoquist, D.L. and Stephan, P.E. (1986) 'Understanding regression analysis: an introductory guide' Sage University Paper series on Quantitative Applications in the Social Sciences, 07-057, Beverly Hills: Sage

Silvey, J. (1975) *Deciphering Data* Chapter 5, London: Longman

Singer, E. (1978) 'Informed consent: Consequences for response rate and response quality in social surveys' *American Sociological Review* 47: 416–27

Singer, E. and Frankel, M.R. (1982) 'Informed consent procedures in telephone interviews' *American Sociological Review* 47: 144–62

Singer, E. and Presser, S. (1989) *Survey Research Methods: A Reader* Chicago: University of Chicago Press

Smith, T.W. (1989) 'The Hidden 25 Percent: An Analysis of Nonresponse in the 1980 General Social Survey' in E. Singer and S. Presser (eds) (1989) *Survey Research Methods: A Reader* Chicago: University of Chicago Press

Sommer, R. and Sommer, B. (1980) *A Practical Guide to Behavioural Research* New York: Oxford University Press

Spector, P.E. (1981) 'Research Designs' Sage University paper series on Quantitative Applications in the Social Sciences, 07-023, Beverly Hills: Sage

Steeh, C.G. (1981) 'Trends in Non-response Rates 1952–1979' *Public Opinion Quarterly* 45: 40–57

Stinchcombe, A. (1968) *Constructing Social Theories* New York: Harcourt, Brace Jovanovich

Stouffer, S.A. (1950) 'Some observations on Study Design' *American Journal of Sociology* 55: 355–61

Strunk, W. Jr. and White, E.G. (1972) *The Elements of Style* 2nd edn, New York: Macmillan

Sudman, S. (1976) *Applied Sampling* New York: Academic Press

Sudman, S. and Bradburn, N.M. (1982) *Asking Questions: A Practical Guide to Questionnaire Design* San Francisco: Jossey Bass

Survey Research Center, University of Michigan (1969) *Interviewer's Manual* Ann Arbor: Institute for Social Research, University of Michigan

Tabachnick, B.G. and Fidell, L.S. (1983) *Using Multivariate Statistics* New York: Harper & Row

Turner, C.F. and Martin, E. (eds) (1984) *Surveying Subjective Phenomena*, 2 vols, New York: Russell Sage Foundation

Wallace, W.L. (1971) *The Logic of Science in Sociology* Aldine, Chicago

Warwick, D.P. and Lininger, C.A. (1975) *The Sample Survey: Theory and Practice* New York: McGraw-Hill

Willer, D. and Willer, J. (1974) *Systematic Empiricism: a Critique of Pseudoscience* Englewood Cliffs: Prentice-Hall

Zeller, R.A. and Carmines, E.G. (1980) *Measurement in the Social Sciences* Cambridge: Cambridge University Press

Index